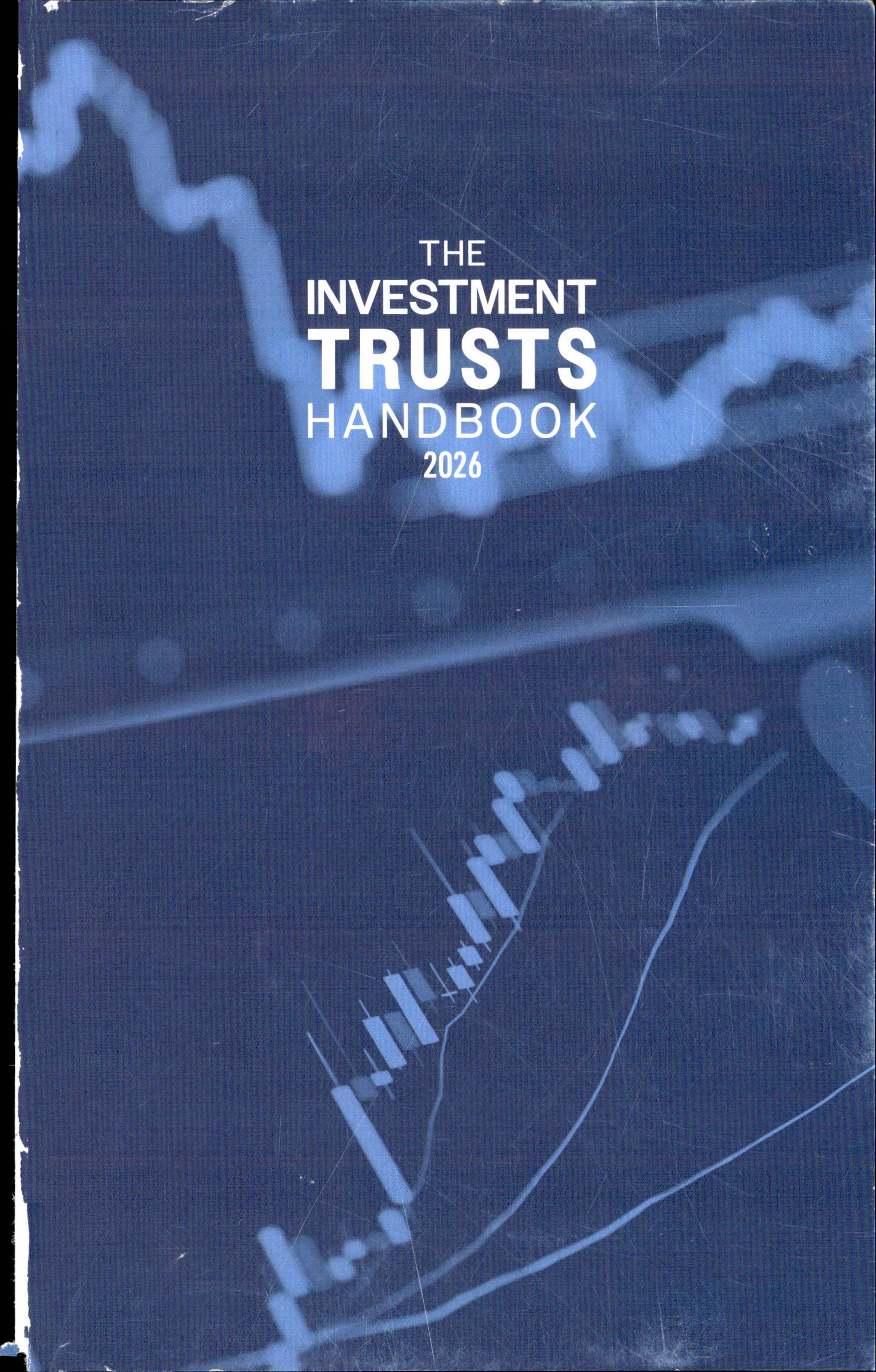

THE INVESTMENT TRUSTS HANDBOOK 2026

THE INVESTMENT TRUSTS HANDBOOK 2026

Investing essentials, expert insights, and powerful trends and data

edited by

JONATHAN DAVIS

Harriman House

www.ITHB.co.uk

HARRIMAN HOUSE LTD
3 Viceroy Court
Bedford Road
Petersfield
Hampshire
GU32 3LJ
GREAT BRITAIN
Tel: +44 (0)1730 233870

Email: enquiries@harriman-house.com
Website: harriman.house

First published in 2025 by Harriman House, an imprint of Pan Macmillan
EU Representative: Macmillan Publishers Ireland Ltd, 1st Floor, The Liffey Trust Centre, 117-126 Sheriff Street Upper, Dublin 1, D01 YC43
Associated companies throughout the world
www.panmacmillan.com

Hardback ISBN: 978-1-80409-435-8
eBook ISBN: 978-1-80409-436-5

British Library Cataloguing in Publication Data
A CIP catalogue record for this book can be obtained from the British Library.

01

Printed and bound by CPI Group (UK) Ltd.

Harriman House

www.ITHB.co.uk

CONTENTS

Editor's Introduction 1

YEAR IN REVIEW 17

Trust Performance Data 19

Month by Month News 23

Report Card: Yes, But… 41

By Ben Conway

Geopolitics and AI 45

By James Carthew

Popular No More 49

By Andrew McHattie

Investor Forum 55

Chairs Forum 71

VCTs: a New Era? 79

By Alex Davies

OUTLOOK 87

Adjusting to Stagflation 89

By John Baron

The Big Questions for 2026 95

By Hugh Gimber

The Year Ahead 101

By Paul Niven

A New World Order 109

By Alan Bartlett

Small is Beautiful 115

By Andrew Worne

Staying Active 119

By Mark Atkinson

THEMES 125

The Great Unwind 127

By Tom Treanor

Chasing the Retail Investor 133

By Joe Winkley

Are Active ETFs a Threat? 141

By Simon Elliott

My Ideal Portfolio 145

By Ben Williams

Trust Reflections 151

By Nick Greenwood

OPPORTUNITIES 155

UK Equities: Still Value 157

By Alex Wright

UK Equities Roundtable 161

By Jonathan Davis

The Case for Indian Equities 173

By Gaurav Narain

Coming Back 177

By Charlotte Morris

Schroders in Asia 183

By Abbas Barkhordar

Q&A on US Growth Trust 189

By Kirsty Gibson

DATA AND PERFORMANCE 197

Trust Basics 199

Useful Sources of Information 207

AI and You 209

By Daniel Summerland

The largest equity sectors 216

Specialist sectors 218

Property sectors 220

VCT sectors 224

Largest management groups 228

Vintage investment trusts 230

Long-serving managers 234

Investment trust style and size 238

Dividend heroes 240

Largest/most liquid trusts 244

Saba Capital 252

Best long-term performers 256

Issuance 264

Return of capital 266

Share buybacks and tenders 268

Discount movements 272

Discount control policies 278

Enhanced income trusts 282

Investment trusts vs open-ended funds 284

Skin in the game 286

Who owns investment trusts? 290
Fees 292
Fees charged on market cap 298
Fee changes 299
Platform costs 300
AIC website 302
Z-scores 306

SPONSORS 309

ACKNOWLEDGEMENTS 327

EDITOR'S INTRODUCTION

By Jonathan Davis

An uncertain world

IT HAS BEEN another fascinating and exciting year for anyone involved with investment trusts. Disruption and volatility have been a prevailing theme both for the sector and for the global markets in which trusts operate. Two names, Saba Capital and Donald Trump, have largely dominated the conversation, to the alarm of many, but the good news is that their impact has so far turned out to be more benign – and indeed more positive in some respects – than was initially feared.

Let's start, as always, with some numbers. Since the cutoff date for the last edition of *The Investments Trusts Handbook*, the financial markets have swooned at times, hence the noted volatility, but have still delivered above-average returns. The global equity market, still largely driven by an AI-led surge in the US stock market, has returned 15% (total return) and the UK stock market, to many people's surprise, has outperformed it by nearly 3% over the last 12 months.

Gilts, however, have remained becalmed, with the first cut in interest rates from the Bank of England over the summer helping to bring down some short-term gilt yields, but doing little to prevent a rise in the yields of longer-dated issues. The markets continue to fret about sticky inflation and the seemingly inexorable rise in government debt, although the latter is also a global problem that helps, among other things, to explain the stunning performance of gold, which recently hit a new all-time high of $4,300 an ounce.

Ten-year asset class performance

KEY	INSTRUMENT	1 YEAR	3 YEARS	5 YEARS	10 YEARS	START OF DATA
A	FTSE All Share	17.2%	14.4%	12.5%	7.6%	9.1%
B	FTSE All World ex UK	14.1%	14.9%	11.9%	12.9%	10.3%
D	UK Consumer Price Index	3.8%	4.0%	5.0%	3.3%	2.9%
C	FTSE Actuaries UK Conventional Gilts All Stocks	0.6%	3.7%	–5.6%	-0.4%	4.0%

Source: FE Trustnet.

Nevertheless, risk assets have, by and large, performed well, in spite of ongoing wars in Ukraine and Israel, and the election of a US President whose policy initiatives on tariffs, taxation and foreign policy have injected buckets of confusion and uncertainty into the minds of allies, enemies and observers alike. His decision to impose unilateral tariffs on all of America's trading partners has given them headaches and left investors scrambling to work out how this massive challenge to the postwar global trading system might unfold, and to whose ultimate benefit or loss.

The jury is still out on that, although my sense is that the tariff war, which has produced a number of new bilateral trade deals, including one with the UK, but at the time of writing has not yet bought China to heel, has failed to inflict as much damage as might have been expected. Companies are still working out how best to adapt to this new environment, and many of the details behind the headline deals have still to be worked out.

One clear outcome, however, has been a steady weakening of the value of the dollar, the lynchpin of the global financial system. Among the beneficiaries has been sterling, whose value has risen despite the dusty reaction of the markets to the incoming Labour government's first Budget, which did nothing for its stated ambition of going all-out for economic growth. A stronger pound has the effect of reducing returns from overseas investments and is normally a headwind for investment trusts, with their heavy focus on global rather than domestic markets.

Trusts repaying optimism

As for investment trusts, I concluded last year's notes by saying that despite my concerns about the impending Budget (fully borne out), high US equity valuations (which remain) and improving but still unhealthily wide discounts: "in my view there are good grounds for believing that the next 12 months will see further positive performance from the quality investment trusts that survive as we move into the next phase of the current cycle".

For reasons that have been cited often over the last four years, that cycle has involved a sustained period of widening discounts following the end of the 'never had it so good' boom that ran for most of the 2010s and had one last hurrah after the Covid-19 pandemic. The questions since then, with interest rates and inflation both rising, have been all about how successfully the investment trust world could take the necessary steps to rationalise itself and rebuild shareholder confidence in a much tougher environment.

That process of renewal began to be visible in the final quarter of 2023 and has gathered pace, slowly but not always steadily, since then. Having peaked at around 18% in the summer of 2023, the average discount across the trust sector came in to 14% a year ago but has struggled to move in more decisively since. At the time of writing, it stands at around 13%, having traded for most of the last 12 months in a range between 11% and 14%.

As in the previous year, while the average discounts on equity trusts have stabilised around the 10% mark, thanks to a lot of share buybacks and self-help initiatives by boards, for alternative assets trusts it has been a harder road to row. Discounts there have remained nearer 25% than 10% on average, and in many cases are materially worse than that.

Long-term discount history

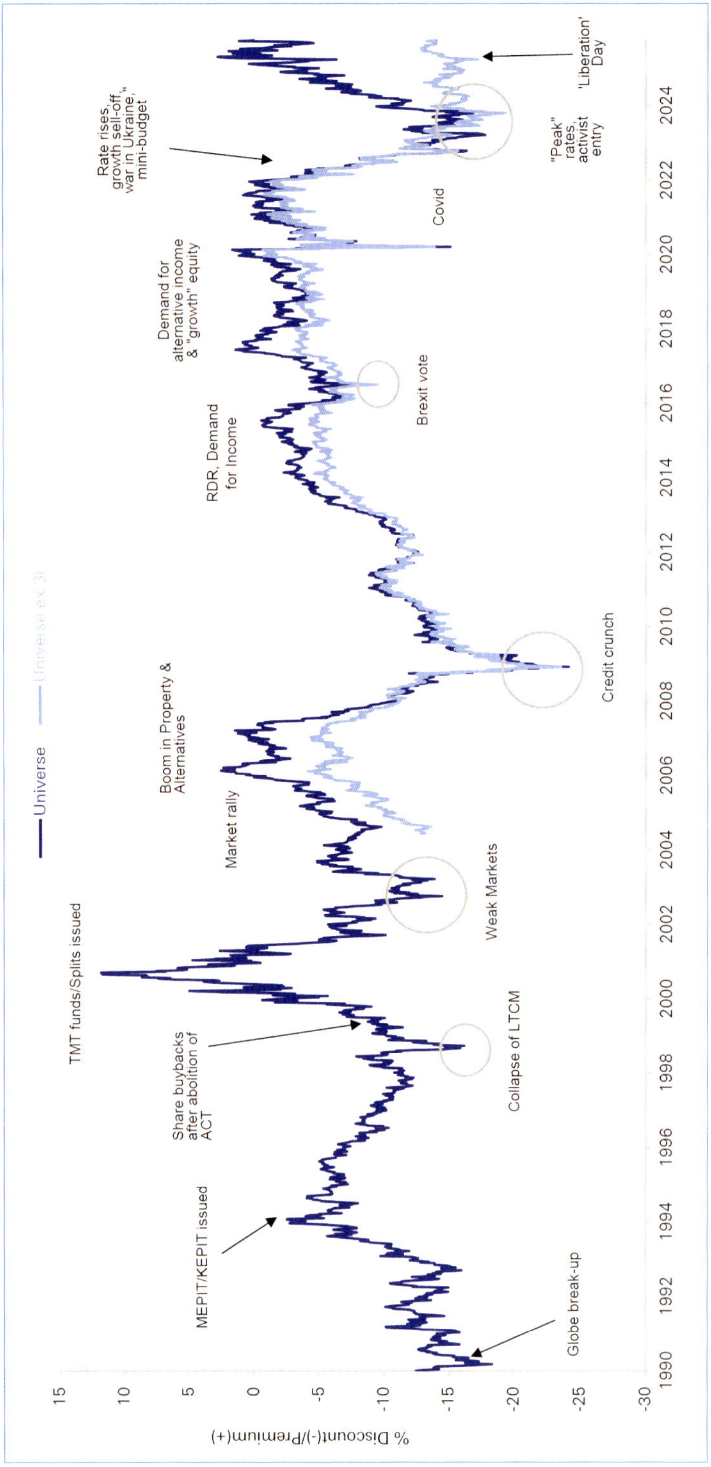

Source: Deutsche Numis. To 10 October 2025. Note how the inclusion of 3i distorts the overall figure for average trust discounts.

Nevertheless, the aggregate performance of the investment trust sector has been reasonable and positive. According to the Association of Investment Companies, the market-cap weighted average total return across the industry in the 12 months to the end of September this year, excluding Venture Capital Trusts, was 13.2% (the NAV total return) and 16.3% (share price total return). The 3% differential between the two reflects in part a mild improvement in discounts.

To put that in context, with consumer price inflation averaging nearly 4%, investment trusts have collectively rewarded shareholders with an average real (inflation-adjusted) share price return of 12%. That is broadly in line with the performance of the FTSE World and UK market indices, and comfortably ahead, as you would expect, of the performance of gilts (UK government bonds), which have failed to keep up with inflation and have suffered a dramatic loss of value since the start of 2022.

Shrinking but not dead

A cause for celebration then? Well, yes and no. The shakeout in the investment trust world has been marked, verging on dramatic. The number of investment trusts has fallen by around 20% over the last couple of years, depending on how you define the universe. Barely a week has passed without news of another merger, takeover or liquidation as the sector goes about the necessary Darwinian process of weeding out the weaker members. Few people in the business doubt that this process is set to continue for a while longer.

Assessing the performance of the industry on the basis of headline performance statistics can be a trifle misleading, because the numbers take no account of survivorship bias. For every four trusts that survive today, you have to remember the one that has now disappeared, and adjust for the fact that the reason it has disappeared was usually because its performance had been poor or disappointing.

It is true that in many cases the exit process for trusts that have merged, been bid for or taken private has offered shareholders a premium over the prevailing share price before the announcement of the decision. Yet it has rarely involved anything other than an exit at a discount to the last reported net asset value, meaning that shareholders who owned the departees may well still have experienced losses, depending on the date they first invested and the specific trust involved.

In the case of most of the newer trusts that came to the market in the latter stages of the pre-2022 boom, their share prices at the point of departure have been well below their issue price. In the most extreme cases, such as the horror show that is Home REIT, or Digital 9 Infrastructure, it may be pennies in the pound at most that are eventually recovered.

So while we can say good riddance to a number of the trusts that have disappeared, or are in the exit chamber, and admire the ruthlessness of the system that got rid of them, we need also to remember that there have been no IPOs of any size in the investment trust sector for nearly four years, and secondary issuance remains at subdued levels. Before we start to say that investment trusts are back in rude health, we need to see some evidence of replenishment, not just the pruning of the weak.

As it happens, in the last few weeks I have started to hear stories of brokers getting ready to try and bring new entities to the market. Mainly this has been a case of pitching private businesses, not investment trusts, to fund managers. It is no accident that the only significant trust IPO this year, a vehicle called Achilles, is an activist trust designed to take advantage of the wide discounts on offer in the alternative assets sector of the trust universe.

But that could change. A handful of trusts have bravely opted to start very small, raising whatever capital they could persuade investors to provide, and hope to acquire a reputation for good performance and grow from there. Two recent examples would be Ashoka Whiteoak Emerging Markets, up 48% since its launch two years ago, and Onward Opportunities, a UK equity trust, up 40% since its IPO in 2023. Both have made promising beginnings.

Ah yes, Saba

That brings us neatly to the topic of Saba Capital, whose name I mentioned at the outset of these notes. Saba is run by a New York arbitrageur called Boaz Weinstein, who came to prominence over here in December last year when he launched what can only be described as a 'smash and grab raid' on the assets of seven investment trusts. He announced, a few days before Christmas, that he had acquired large shareholdings in all seven of these trusts and was proposing to requisition extraordinary general meetings at which he would pitch for shareholder support to eject the incumbent boards and take over the management of the trusts himself.

It is not an exaggeration to say that these hardball tactics left many in the sector reeling from shock. The investment trust world, which likes to pride itself on its high standards and historical traditions, has never seen anything quite like it. There have always been a few examples of arbitrageurs, including American ones, coming over here and building stakes in investment trusts that are trading at larger-than-average discounts and seeking to force change on their boards.

Laxey Partners made a handsome profit from adopting just such an approach with the sleepy old Alliance Trust in 2011 and Elliott Management did much the same with Scottish Mortgage in 2023. No trust, however large and however steeped in history (as these two were), can afford to think of itself as untouchable (and rightly so).

At the same time there are a number of well-established UK fund management firms, such as City of London Investment Group, Asset Value Investors, and 1607 Investors, which have long looked to profit from using significant shareholdings to persuade boards to take action after periods of poor performance. In almost all these cases, however, any arm-twisting has taken place behind closed doors, and while activists have sometimes taken a seat on the board of one misfiring trust, nobody I know can remember an arbitrageur successfully pitching to take on the running of so many trusts simultaneously, or in such a brazen way.

The fact that Mr Weinstein accompanied his campaign with an extravagantly worded public dressing down of the boards of the trusts in his sights only added to the sense of outrage in their boardrooms. Claiming that his actions were motivated by concern for 'mom and pop' investors, rather than his own blatant self-interest, only inflamed matters more. It simply wasn't cricket.

In reality Saba had been building stakes in more than 20 trusts over a period of months, finding plenty of shares all too easily in those with wide discounts. The seven boards Weinstein publicly attempted to capture were just the biggest of his holdings. He was careful not to take his holdings above the 30% level at which he would be required under takeover rules to make a bid for all the shares at the same price, something that he clearly was not prepared to do.

That reticence reinforced the idea that his motives were tactical rather than strategic and gave the incumbent boards a chance to brand him as an opportunistic corporate raider, rather than the public-spirited crusader which he claimed to be, rescuing – in his words – private shareholders from the 'lazy and complacent' directors who had allowed the discounts to go so wide.

Into a showdown

He had a point of course, otherwise it would not have been so easy to build such large shareholdings. Many boards had been slow to realise that the market environment had changed and that without decisive action, wider discounts were here to stay. Muddling through was an easier option. Nevertheless, the shock of being so publicly exposed had a galvanising effect on the whole investment trust sector, not just the seven chief targets but the many others who knew or thought they might be next in line for the Saba treatment.

Boards and their advisers of the seven main targets scrambled over Christmas and the New Year to mount their defences for the general meetings that Saba had called (as it was fully entitled to do with such a substantial shareholding). The media went to town on the showdown between a sharp New York arb and the 'boring old investment trusts' he was aiming at, giving the sector a prominence in the news that had not been known for years.

In the event it turned out that the famed New York hedge fund guy had overplayed his hand. When it came to a vote, Saba gained hardly any support for its plans, failing to eject the existing directors or to win the mandate to manage their portfolios. Prodded into action by a sudden unwonted barrage of information from their boards, and a distaste for Weinstein's ungentlemanly behaviour, shareholders turned out in record numbers to see off the presumptuous raider.

But that of course is not the end of the story. By bringing the wide discounts into public focus, Saba's campaign has accelerated the process of rationalisation that could – and many think should – have started earlier. Of the seven trusts caught in the full glare of the headlights, three have since effectively given up their investment trust status, through liquidation, merger or rollover into discount-free open-ended alternatives.

The other four soldier on, with Saba hanging onto its chunky shareholding in three cases. While defeating Saba was a battle won, therefore, it is not the end of the fight. Some fund management houses, such as Blackrock, perhaps because they are American firms more familiar with the arbitrage game, have struck standstill agreements under which Saba agrees not to target them for a finite period, in return for some compensating actions on the other side of the Atlantic.

One or two have effectively paid Weinstein a ransom to go away by buying back his stake, shrinking their trust in the process. Most have tried to engage with Saba without much success, finding little clarity on what Weinstein ultimately wants, or perhaps how to give him the return he needs without alienating or giving favourable treatment to other shareholders.

In hindsight it is clear that Weinstein's campaign was badly thought out. His choice of targets was eccentric and appeared to be based on very little specific knowledge of their plans, their shareholder base or their history. He relied for advice on lawyers in the US, not on brokers with local knowledge over here. When I spoke to him for the Money Makers podcast, he was happy to thunder on for over an hour, but admitted that his choice of targets was driven primarily by those whose shares he could most readily buy, not on any real understanding of their history or popularity.

While some of his positions have generated a profit, others are still under water and we still do not know what his endgame is, or how he hopes to turn the kind of profit overall that investors in his own fund surely require. At the time of writing, reports suggest that he is trying to raise money for another fund, an active exchange-traded fund (ETF), designed to give him more firepower to continue his campaign in the investment trust sector. At the same time, having so far confined his stake building to listed equity trusts, where he can hedge his market exposure with derivatives, he has bought his first holdings in alternative assets trusts, where the discounts, as noted earlier, remain very elevated.

The reaction from the boards of the trusts in which he has built up significant shareholdings has been, to varying degrees, a compelling amalgam of fury and frustration. While pleased to have carried the day, those caught up in the initial campaign complain loudly about the cost, time and effort that was involved in seeing him off at the extraordinary meetings earlier this year. They remain tested, in many cases, by the difficulty of working out how to get Saba off their backs without giving him special treatment, and frustrated by the difficult choices that many of them now face.

Opinions about the impact that Saba has made remain divided. You can read a cross-section of opinion in the two forums on offer this year and in other articles elsewhere in the *Handbook*. For what it is worth, my view is that for all the rancour and trouble it has created, the arrival of Saba on so many share registers has been, net net, a positive for the sector. It has certainly been a wakeup call for any board which thought that it had plenty of time to react to the changing market dynamics with which investment trusts now have to contend.

Inconvenient truths

It has brought home a necessary but sometimes inconvenient truth, which is that while the ability to deploy 'patient capital' is one of the rightly vaunted attractions of the investment trust sector, the right to exist is not an absolute. It will always be conditional on performance. Any trust which moves to a wide discount, and stays there for more than a while, will become in time a legitimate target for complaint by shareholders of all kinds, not just opportunistic raiders such as Saba.

One of the ancillary benefits that has come out of the Saba campaign is that it has highlighted how difficult it can be to reach and motivate private investors. With one notable exception: the platforms which are now the dominant channel through which private investors own investment trusts have historically been reluctant to make it easy for clients to stay informed about trusts they own and to vote at meetings.

After a successful campaign by the AIC and other industry players this year, the government has now undertaken to make it mandatory for platforms to notify shareholders about important votes and make it less difficult for them to vote their shares. Saba can certainly take most of the credit for that welcome result.

How far in practice this overdue development leads to a higher turnout in routine votes remains to be seen. What cannot be denied is that investment trusts increasingly need more private investors for support if they are to survive. Nearly all trusts, according to research by the AIC, now have attracting retail investors as a priority, given a gradual decline in the involvement of wealth managers. As well as investing in digital communication, it also means improving disclosure and stepping up marketing activity. Three quarters of all trusts, for example, now pay for sponsored research and most are making efforts to improve their websites and annual reports.

If there is a single theme to this year's *Handbook*, it has to be what I like to call 'remaking the case for investment trusts'. The past three years have not been easy for the sector. The 'never had it so good', zero-interest-rate years have been replaced by a period of struggle, in which rising interest rates and widening discounts, while creating great opportunities for a minority of knowledgeable and discount-conscious investors, have combined to produce disappointment for many erstwhile fans of the sector. That needs to be redressed for the long-term health of the sector, and I am encouraged to think that it is now happening.

The buyback dilemma

One critical question that has dominated board discussions for the last three years, and has become even more pressing as the years go by, revolves around how best to address the issue of wider discounts. It is not as if boards lack the tools to tackle the issue.

Mergers, marketing, manager changes, share buybacks and tender offers are all in the mix; and in theory it is only once they have all been tried and failed that trusts should need to consider the ultimate solution of going out of business and giving shareholders back what remains of their money. Discounts will remain as long as the supply of shares exceeds demand and the obvious way to fix the problem is to reduce the former and increase the latter.

This is easier said than done. What has become clear is that there is no one solution that works for every trust. Share buybacks are the simplest way of restoring a balance between supply and demand, and trusts have turned to them in record numbers, as evidenced in the *Handbook*'s 'Trust Data and Analysis' section (page 197). Nearly 100 trusts have bought back shares equivalent to more than 10% of their market capitalisation in the last two years. An increasing number have outlined discount control policies that set levels at which they will automatically buy back shares.

Yet the results have been mixed. In some cases, discounts have come in, but in others there has been no real improvement, leading some boards, perhaps influenced by the reluctance of their fund managers to surrender management fees, to mutter that they just don't work. What is the point, they will say, of shrinking the size of our trust if discounts are simply going to remain so wide?

It sounds a plausible question, but rather misses the point. The answer is that buybacks will only fail to move a discount if the imbalance between supply and demand is unusually or persistently wide. That suggests that boards may be asking the wrong question, which is not about the efficacy of buybacks, but rather should they be staying in business at all? To have an impact in these cases, buybacks need to carry on until the imbalance is finally corrected.

The question also ignores the fact that what shareholders are often looking for is evidence that the board actually cares about the losses that discounts are imposing on shareholders. There is some evidence that the symbolic effect of taking action can itself in time be sufficient to convince others to come on board. It is a case of showing credibility and inspiring trust in the alignment of interest between board and investor.

It is particularly relevant when a trust has issued shares in the past, taking advantage of a period when the shares were trading at a premium. To issue shares in those conditions, but not to buy back when they move to a discount is rightly regarded as a breach of faith and evidence of double standards, well short of best practice. There are a fair few examples of trusts that have failed this simple test.

All that said, the evidence suggests that buybacks are not always the best answer. The numbers in the performance data shown on page 268 suggest other options may be worth investigating. Tender offers, whether automatic at given intervals or conditional on trust performance, are an alternative option that can enable a proportion of investors who want out to do so at close to NAV. They are becoming a more popular choice.

So too are continuation votes. The idea behind a continuation vote is that it allows the shareholders to vote periodically on whether they wish a trust to continue or not. If lost, the board is typically mandated to come up with a sensible solution. These types of votes are becoming more common and the intervals between votes more frequent. In practice the knowledge that a continuation vote is imminent and might be lost appears to have been a powerful factor in prompting boards to take remedial action in advance.

In the final analysis, the question for both boards and shareholders is whether a trust is doing enough to be kept in existence. How well does its performance compare to relevant benchmarks? Is the trust sufficiently differentiated to justify what it does, given the availability of low-cost passive alternatives? Is it taking full advantage of the investment trust structure?

The answers to these questions are a matter of judgement. A manager's style or regional focus may simply be out of favour. History gives us many examples of trusts that have jettisoned their manager at just the wrong moment. Boards need to balance the many conflicting pressures on them, but the most important thing is to demonstrate that they are on the case and genuinely trying to do the best for shareholders. Too often in recent years that has not been the case.

Highlights of the year

As always, many of the basic themes I have mentioned are well covered in the articles in this year's edition. If you are interested in AI, there is a helpful article from Daniel Summerland of Fidelity International about how it might help managing your own portfolio, while Kirsty Gibson of Baillie Gifford USA emphasises the transformational impact that AI holds out for business and society.

This seems a good moment to pick out some of my personal highlights from the last 12 months. Here are some of them:

The best performing trusts in 2025 year to date are listed in the upcoming table. At the top are trusts which have benefited from the extraordinary demand for gold this year, driven by a potent cocktail of central bank buying, geopolitical risks and inflation that refuses to lie down. It is a good example of how the trust universe typically offers some exposure to almost any market theme. (One of the resources trusts, CQS Natural Resources, was a target of Saba and used a tender offer to get them off the share register, since which the share price has risen another 50%.)

Also high up in the rankings are the two technology trusts run by Allianz and Polar Capital. This has been another year where it has been costly not to own the big tech stocks that have dominated the performance of the US stock market. Neither has managed to quite match the strength of the American index, but they have at least come close and offered decent exposure to the theme of artificial intelligence.

The biggest surprise in the rankings is probably the relatively strong showing of European trusts. As so often, an unfancied sector has confounded the sceptics by doing so well. With the war in Ukraine raging on, and Europe a primary target of President Trump's tariff measures, few picked out Europe as a potential strong performer at the start of the year.

Less of a surprise is the performance of the often-overlooked trusts that invest in debt. Rising interest rates work both ways, helpful for some, less good for others, and debt funds have been primary beneficiaries of a new environment in which most things with an impressive yield advantage over cash have tended to do well.

Debt trusts dominate the list of the small handful of trusts which have been able to issue shares in an otherwise barren year for issuance.

A final mention goes to trusts investing in biotechnology. Of the seven trusts to be found in the AIC's healthcare classification, three are specialist biotechnology trusts. The Biotech Growth Trust (BIOG), International Biotechnology (IBT) and RTW Biotech Opportunities have all suddenly sprung to life in the last six months after four years in the doldrums. The omens here seem good, for several reasons, including regulatory changes and more M&A activity as big pharma companies try to head off the looming expiry of patents on their most profitable mature drugs. I fancy the biotech trusts to continue their recovery unless interest rates suddenly start rising strongly once more. There are reasonable grounds for hoping that private equity and commercial property (what remains of a once large sector) should also show some improved performance, albeit with the same interest rate caveat.

Best- and worst-performing investment trusts

BEST PERFORMERS (SECTORS)	%	WORST PERFORMERS (SECTORS)	%
China / Greater China	44.8	India	-12.2
Latin America	39.6	North American Smaller Cos	-8.6
Commods & NatResources	36.7	Property - UK Residential	-0.2
European Smaller Coms	22.9	Property - RoW	0.1
Technology	21.2	Private Equity ex 3i	0.5
Global Emerging Markets	20.7	Property - UK Logistics	0.7
Infrastructure Securities	20.3	Debt - Direct Lending	0.9
Japan	19.7	Biotech & Healthcare	1.0
Asia Pacific Income	19.3	Growth Capital	1.4
UK Equity & Bond Income	17.4	Hedge Funds	1.7

BEST PERFORMERS (TRUSTS)	%	WORST PERFORMERS (TRUSTS)	%
Golden Prosp Prec Metal	120.9	British & American	-43.2
CQS Natural Resources G&I	61.9	abrdn New India	-14.4
Fidelity China Special Sits	44.7	India Capital Growth	-14.0
BlackRock World Mining	41.5	Bellevue Healthcare	-13.5
BlackRock Latin American	39.2	Tufton Assets	-13.0
Baillie Gifford China Growth	36.9	LMS Capital	-12.8
JPM China Growth & Inc	34.4	Ground Rents Income	-11.8
Fidelity Emerging Markets	31.7	JPMorgan Indian	-11.4
Marwyn Value Investors	31.2	Ceiba Investments	-11.4
JPM European Discovery	28.5	JPM US Smaller Cos	-11.3

At the other end of the spectrum, infrastructure trusts, particularly those with interests in renewable energy, also offer attractive yields, now around 10% in many cases, but they in contrast have signally failed to catch a bid. Discounts have remained wide – indeed have widened – and unlike the commercial property sector, there has been a notable absence so far of the corporate activity you would have expected to follow such a depressed rating.

Doubts about the future course of power prices, the withdrawal of subsidies for renewable projects in the US and questions about the validity of their marked to model NAVs have all contributed to the malaise. Infrastructure trusts have stubbornly continued to be priced off gilts, rather than their own projections of future cash flows. Will this turn in 2026? Many will hope so.

Other names that stood out for me this year include: Temple Bar (TMPL), a value-oriented UK equity income trust that under new management since 2020 has made an impressive recovery from the dark days of the pandemic; Seraphim Space (SSIT), a specialist recent newcomer that is profiting from soaring demand for defence uses of satellites and drones; Pantheon Infrastructure (PINT), an exception to the generally indifferent performance of its peers; and a long awaited broad revival of interest in emerging markets, traditional beneficiaries of a weaker dollar. China, the most important target in Trump's tariff war, has paradoxically been among the better-performing markets.

Among the poorest performers, alongside the renewables and infrastructure trusts, it is not a total surprise to find trusts investing in India, where valuations had reached unsustainable levels, bucking the general emerging markets trend, and many other smaller companies trusts, once again disappointing hopes of a long overdue revival. They remain very cheap on most criteria and the UK ones, having been clobbered by National Insurance and living wage hikes last year, will hope to have survived the latest Budget from Rachel Reeves, the chancellor, unscathed.

It is interesting to note the growing use of enhanced dividend policies (page 282) and the adoption by more trusts of management fees that are based, in part or in whole, on market capitalisation rather than net asset values (page 298). The trend in fees is already downward, and important given the competition from low-fee alternatives such as index trackers and active ETFs. Adopting a market-cap base for fees helps to align the interests of managers and shareholders more closely and is to be welcomed. Enhanced dividend policies, where a trust commits in advance to paying a known and fixed percentage of its value, regardless of the income it generates, is a more controversial issue, but one that appears to be popular with yield-seeking private investors in particular.

Some headwinds remain

The jury is out on the eventual outcome of the industry's campaign for improvements to the cost disclosure regime to which investment trusts and other types of fund are to be subjected. A year ago came welcome news that trusts were being given a reprieve from having to report double-counted costs in their reports to potential investors, pending the result of consultations about the new CCI arrangements that are intended to replace the old EU-inspired legacy regime.

A year on, however, as Ben Conway notes in his article (page 41), we still await definitive news of what that will look like, though he is optimistic that it will be positive. I merely add the comment that for a modern, supposedly sophisticated economy with a government that is committed to growth, it is frankly shameful that it should take so many years of bureaucratic dithering – nearly a decade in fact – to arrive at what is essentially a simple decision that could cease penalising one of the most effective providers of growth capital this country has.

The new chancellor has already put a dampener on the AIM market by reducing the tax advantages for businesses that list there and has talked the talk, but so far not walked the walk, about stimulating more pension fund investment in the UK stock market. There is next to zero chance of her abolishing stamp duty on share transactions, another notable deterrent to investment, despite our being the only major country to levy this type of tax on share transactions. These are all lingering headwinds that investment trusts are not alone in having to face.

It would be a brave observer who dared to suggest that the outlook for investment returns from here is unflinchingly positive. The performance of gold is a strong reminder that there is no shortage of risk in the world. It will take time for the uncertainty created by the new US administration's aggressive policies to be resolved. Nevertheless, I am encouraged by the way that investment trusts are getting their act together after a difficult period.

They are once again outperforming open-ended funds with similar mandates (see page 284). Standards of corporate governance are, in my view, improving. There are standout names in most sectors in which investors might wish to commit their money and still plenty of choice. That, combined with the persistent discounts of many surviving and well-managed trusts, continues to create good opportunities from which smart investors can profit. I very much hope that you will be among them.

JONATHAN DAVIS, Editor of *The Investment Trusts Handbook*
15 October 2025

I was delighted to be awarded the AIC Media award for Best Broadcast of the Year for the second year running this year. The Money Makers podcast, for which the award was given, has now completed more than 300 episodes and remains free to anyone interested in investment trusts. You can find out more and sign up to listen at www.money-makes.co, or on the Money Makers YouTube channel.

Important information

Please note that everything you read in these pages is independently edited and provided for information and research purposes. Without knowledge of your individual circumstances and tolerance for risk, it is impossible – and prohibited by the Financial Conduct Authority – to give individual investment advice. However, all the opinions expressed here are honestly held and believed to be accurate at the time of writing. Please remember also that past performance, while helpful, is not a reliable guide to future performance. The value of investments and the income from them can go down as well as up.

STAY INFORMED

For market commentary, performance data, in-depth trust profiles and weekly links to all the latest investment trust news, please check out the Money Makers Circle, our regular subscription newsletter (See www.money-makers.co for how to subscribe).

YEAR IN REVIEW

TRUST PERFORMANCE DATA

THE FOLLOWING CHARTS are drawn from the invaluable monthly and quarterly round-ups of investment trust news produced by research firm QuotedData. In addition to these regular charts, the round-ups also provide news and commentary on recent trends in the investment sector and are free for private investors who sign up at www.quoteddata.com.

2024 TOTAL

Figure 1: Best performing funds in price terms in 2024

	%
Livermore Investments	75.2
Alpha Real	73.3
Petershill Partners	68.9
Amedeo Air Four Plus	60.0
Seraphim Space	58.1
Baillie Gifford US Growth	56.0
Menhaden Resource Efficiency	52.2
Schiehallion	49.9
JPMorgan Emerg E, ME & Africa Sec	48.3
Baker Steel Resources	43.0

Figure 2: Best performing funds in NAV terms in 2024

	%
Doric Nimrod Air Three	59.2
Crystal Amber	56.8
Manchester & London	51.5
JPMorgan Emerg E, ME & Africa Sec	41.2
Allianz Technology	36.9
Doric Nimrod Air Two	36.5
Castelnau Group	35.0
Polar Capital Technology	34.9
Baillie Gifford US Growth	33.5
JPMorgan American	30.6

Source: Morningstar, QuotedData. Note: excludes trusts with market caps below £15m at 31/12/24.

Figure 3: Worst performing funds in price terms in 2024

	%
Regional REIT	−62.4
Gresham House Energy Storage	−57.9
HydrogenOne Capital Growth	−56.4
VPC Specialty Lending	−50.3
Ecofin US Renewables Infrastructure	−43.6
Gore Street Energy Storage	−40.4
Macau Property Opportunities	−38.4
Life Science REIT	−36.7
Digital 9 Infrastructure	−36.5
BlackRock Latin American	−34.1

Figure 4: Worst performing funds in NAV terms in 2024

	%
Regional REIT	−57.3
Digital 9 Infrastructure	−44.6
Phoenix Spree Deutschland	−38.6
BlackRock Latin American	−35.2
Riverstone Energy	−27.1
Premier Miton Glb Renewables	−25.8
Macau Property Opportunities	−25.0
ICG-Longbow Senior Sec. UK Prop Debt Inv	−25.0
Ground Rents Income	−23.3
VPC Specialty Lending	−22.6

Source: Morningstar, QuotedData. Note: excludes trusts with market caps below £15m at 31/12/24.

Figure 5: Money raised in 2024

	£m
JPMorgan Global Growth and Income	441.9
Regional REIT	110.5
Ashoka India Equity	105.9
Globalworth Real Estate	89.2
Invesco Bond Income Plus	36.9
TwentyFour Select Monthly Income	26.0
CQS New City High Yield	23.1
Odyssean	21.7
Rockwood Strategic	20.1
Law Debenture	12.3

Figure 6: Money returned in 2024

	£m
Scottish Mortgage	−1321.6
Smithson	−414.2
Finsbury Growth and Income	−384.7
Bellevue Healthcare	−312.2
European Opportunities	−294.7
Monks	−293.0
F&C	−280.9
Capital Gearing	−206.5
Worldwide Healthcare	−194.8
Personal Assets	−193.2

Source: Morningstar, QuotedData.

FIRST QUARTER 2025

Figure 7: Best performing sectors by total price return over Q1

	Median share price TR (%)	Median NAV TR (%)	Median discount 31/03/25 (%)	Median sector market cap 31/03/25 (£m)	No. of companies in the sector
China / Greater China	11.5	18.8	−9	210.9	3
UK Equity & Bond Income	4.8	3.8	−7.8	288.5	16
Infrastructure Securities	4.5	2.2	−14.3	110.4	2
European Smaller Companies	4	5.5	−7.7	417.3	4
Japanese Smaller Companies	3.2	−1.8	−7.7	295.80	3

Figure 8: Worst performing sectors by total price return over Q1

	Median share price TR (%)	Median NAV TR (%)	Median discount 31/03/25 (%)	Median sector market cap 31/03/25 (£m)	No. of companies in the sector
Technology & Technology Innovation	−16.9	−15	−11.3	2345.2	2
North American Smaller Companies	−13.4	−10.4	−9	192.7	2
Biotechnology & Healthcare	−11.8	−9.7	−7.5	313.8	7
India/Indian Subcontinent	−8.9	−9.8	−11.5	406.6	4
UK Smaller Companies	−8.4	−8.2	−11.2	101.4	20

Source: Morningstar, Marten & Co. Note: inclusive of sectors with at least two companies.
Note: Many alternative asset sector funds release NAV performance on a quarterly basis.

Figure 9: Best performing funds in NAV terms over Q1

	%
Golden Prospect Precious Metal	42
Baillie Giff China Growth Trust	15.6
Fidelity China Special	11.5
BlackRock Latin American	10.8
JPMorgan European Growth & Income	8.3
Chenavari Toro Income	8.3
JPMorgan China Growth & Income	8.2
City of London	7.3
Schroder Income Growth	6.8
CQS Natural Resources G&I	6.4

Figure 10: Best performing funds in price terms over Q1

	%
DP Aircraft I	83.3
Golden Prospect Precious Metal	40.8
Gresham House Energy Storage	39.4
Warehouse REIT	37.9
Livermore	34.9
Ground Rents Income	31
LMS Capital	28.5
Gore Street Energy Storage	23.2
JPMorgan Emerg EMEA Sec Plc	20.8
Baillie Giff China Growth	19.1

Source: Morningstar, Marten & Co.

Figure 11: Worst performing funds in NAV terms over Q1

	%
Geiger Counter	−34.4
Polar Capital Technology	−16.5
India Capital Growth	−16.1
Biotech Growth	−14.9
International Biotechnology	−13.9
Allianz Technology	−13.6
Edinburgh Worldwide	−12.9
Aberforth Geared Value & Income	−12.7
Onward Opportunities	−12.6
Mobius Investment	−12.5

Figure 12: Worst performing funds in price terms over Q1

	%
Digital 9 Infrastructure	−51.5
Geiger Counter	−25.5
US Solar	−23.5
Rights & Issues	−22.1
Baillie Giff US Growth	−21.6
Augmentum Fintech	−20.5
Herald	−19.6
Edinburgh Worldwide	−19.3
Syncona	−17.8
Polar Capital Technology	−17.5

Source: Morningstar, Marten & Co. Note: excludes trusts with market caps below £15m at 31/03/25.

Figure 13: Money raised over Q1

	£m
Invesco Asia Dragon	473.8
Scottish Oriental Smaller Cos	264.2
JPMorgan Global Growth & Income	26.9
M&G Credit Income	12.5
Ashoka India Equity	10.3

Figure 14: Money returned over Q1

	£m
Scottish Mortgage	−476.1
Pershing Square Holdings	−99.8
Smithson	−96.6
Monks	−87.6
Finsbury Growth & Income	−76.3

Source: Morningstar, Marten & Co. Note: evalue of shares issued/repurchased as at 31/03/25.

SECOND QUARTER 2025

Figure 15: Best performing sectors by total price return over Q2

	Median share price TR (%)	Median NAV TR (%)	Median discount 30/06/25 (%)	Median sector market cap 30/06/25 (£m)	No. of companies in the sector
Growth Capital	22.9	0.0	−35.7	387.0	6
Technology & Technology Innovation	20.9	20.4	−10.0	2898.8	2
Infrastructure Securities	17.7	14.2	−10.7	121.0	2
Renewable Energy Infrastructure	16.7	0.0	−25.7	410.5	18
European Smaller Companies	16.7	15.5	−7.4	408.0	4

Figure 16: Worst performing sectors by total price return over Q2

	Median share price TR (%)	Median NAV TR (%)	Median discount 30/06/25 (%)	Median sector market cap 30/06/25 (£m)	No. of companies in the sector
China / Greater China	−7.3	−5.6	−11.1	193.5	3
North American Smaller Companies	−1.6	−0.1	−9.5	185.0	2
Biotechnology & Healthcare	−0.2	−2.0	−8.2	291.2	7
Debt - Loans & Bonds	0.2	1.9	0.6	155.3	9
Private Equity	1.3	0.1	−31.9	457.7	16

Source: Morningstar, Marten & Co. Note: inclusive of sectors with at least two companies.
Note: Many alternative asset sector funds release NAV performance on a quarterly basis.

Figure 17: Best performing funds in NAV terms over Q2

	%
Geiger Counter	47.1
Manchester & London	25.3
Polar Capital Technology	23.2
Aberforth Geared Value & Income	20.2
Premier Miton Glb Renewables	19.4
Odyssean	19.0
Weiss Korea Opportunity	18.7
Strategic Equity Capital	18.1
Schroder UK Mid Cap	18.0
Allianz Technology	17.7

Figure 18: Best performing funds in price terms over Q2

	%
Seraphim Space	56.2
Manchester & London	34.2
VH Global Energy Infrastructure	31.5
Downing Renewables & Infrastructure	31.4
Geiger Counter	31.3
Schiehallion	26.0
Premier Miton Glb Renewables	25.7
Polar Capital Technology	24.4
HydrogenOne Capital Growth	23.6
Aquila Energy Efficiency	22.8

Source: Morningstar, Marten & Co.

Figure 19: Worst performing funds in NAV terms over Q2

	%
NB Distressed Debt Inv Extended Life	−8.4
VinaCapital Vietnam Opp Fund	−6.6
Baillie Giff China Growth	−5.9
JPMorgan China Growth & Income	−5.6
Bellevue Healthcare	−5.5
RM Infrastructure Income	−5.0
Worldwide Healthcare	−3.8
Vietnam Enterprise	−3.6
Polar Capital Glb Healthcare	−3.0
JPMorgan Global Core Real Assets	−2.6

Figure 20: Worst performing funds in price terms over Q2

	%
Ecofin US Renewables Infrastructure	−12.1
JPMorgan Global Core Real Assets	−10.8
NB Distressed Debt Inv Extended Life	−8.5
Globalworth Real Estate	−8.4
JPMorgan China Growth & Income	−8.3
Castelnau Group	−7.9
NB Private Equity Partners Class A	−7.4
Baillie Giff China Growth	−7.3
abrdn Diversified Income & Growth	−6.5
VietNam Holding	−6.5

Source: Morningstar, Marten & Co. Note: excludes trusts with market caps below £15m at 30/06/25.

Figure 21: Money raised over Q2

	£m
North Atlantic Smaller Cos	467.3
JPMorgan Global Growth & Income	350.3
TwentyFour Select Monthly Income	32.8
CVC Income & Growth GBP	24.2
Globalworth Real Estate	24.0

Figure 22: Money returned over Q2

	£m
The European Smaller Companies Trust PLC	−351.7
Scottish Mortgage	−325.6
Polar Capital Global Financials	−275.1
European Opportunities	−144.4
Smithson	−133.9

Source: Morningstar, Marten & Co. Note: evalue of shares issued/repurchased as at 30/06/25.

THIRD QUARTER 2025

Figure 23: Best performing sectors by total price return over Q3

	Median share price TR (%)	Median NAV TR (%)	Median discount 30/09/25 (%)	Median sector market cap 30/09/25 (£m)	No. of companies in the sector
China / Greater China	29.6	30	−8.2	254.10	3
Commodities & Natural Resources	28.9	30.1	−17	105.8	7
Technology & Technology Innovation	19.7	19.9	−9	3,415.30	2
Country Specialist	16.3	15.4	−12	674.6	4
Asia Pacific	15.4	13.7	−9.3	563.7	4

Figure 24: Worst performing sectors by total price return over Q3

	Median share price TR (%)	Median NAV TR (%)	Median discount 30/09/25 (%)	Median sector market cap 30/09/25 (£m)	No. of companies in the sector
India/Indian Subcontinent	−8.2	−4.7	−9.5	392.9	4
Renewable Energy Infrastructure	−7.9	0	−32.4	346	18
Property - Europe	−7.4	0	−45.3	142.6	4
Property - Rest of World	−6.2	0	−71	13.40	3
Financials & Financial Innovation	−3.6	2.5	−25.7	249.9	2

Source: Morningstar, Marten & Co. Note: inclusive of sectors with at least two companies.
Note: Many alternative asset sector funds release NAV performance on a quarterly basis.

Figure 25: Best performing funds in NAV terms over Q3

	%
Golden Prospect Precious Metal	54.1
Geiger Counter	45.5
CQS Natural Resources G&I	43.9
Biotech Growth	42.8
International Biotechnology	36.7
JPMorgan China Growth & Income	30.6
BlackRock World Mining Trust	30.1
Fidelity China Special	30
Baillie Gifford China Growth Trust	25.3
Vietnam Enterprise	24

Figure 26: Best performing funds in price terms over Q3

	%
CQS Natural Resources G&I	50.7
Golden Prospect Precious Metal	46.6
Biotech Growth	39.1
Petershill Partners	38.9
International Biotechnology	34
Geiger Counter	33.5
JPMorgan China Growth & Income	31.6
Baillie Gifford China Growth Trust	29.6
Fidelity China Special	29.2
BlackRock World Mining Trust	28.9

Source: Morningstar, Marten & Co. Note: excludes trusts with market caps below £15m at 30/09/25.

Figure 27: Worst performing funds in NAV terms over Q3

	%
NB Distressed Debt Inv Extended Life	−27.9
Finsbury Growth & Income	−6.1
India Capital Growth	4
abrdn New India Investment Trust	−5.1
Ashoka India Equity Investment	−4.2
Scottish Oriental Smaller Cos	−3.7
Premier Miton Glb Renewables Trust	−3.4
Montanaro European Smaller	−2.8
Montanaro UK Smaller Companies	−2.7
Lindsell Train	−2.6

Figure 28: Worst performing funds in price terms over Q3

	%
ICG−Longbow Senior Sec. UK Prop Debt Inv	−38.7
Aquila European Renewables Ord	−31.4
Macau Property Opportunities Ord	−25.5
Gore Street Energy Storage Fund Ord	−21.5
Life Science REIT Ord	−20.3
Seraphim Space Investment Trust Ord	−17.8
NB Distressed Debt Inv Extended Life	−15.6
Ground Rents Income Fund Ord	−14.7
Octopus Renewables Infrastructure Ord	−13.8
Bluefield Solar Income Fund	−13.6

Source: Morningstar, Marten & Co. Note: excludes trusts with market caps below £15m at 30/09/25.

Figure 29: Money raised over Q3

	£m
Caledonia Investments	1,788.30
Fidelity European Trust	432.2
TwentyFour Income	30.70
TwentyFour Select Monthly Income	30.3
M&G Credit Income Investment	28.8

Figure 30: Money returned over Q3

	£m
Scottish Mortgage	−395.8
Worldwide Healthcare	−194.7
Monks	−176
Pershing Square Holdings	−95.9
Finsbury Growth & Income	−83.4

Source: Morningstar, Marten & Co. Note: excludes trusts with market caps below £15m at 30/09/25.

MONTH BY MONTH NEWS

We summarise here some of the most important news announcements made by investment trusts over the past 12 months. These month-by-month summaries are extracted from the excellent monthly investment trust reports prepared by the Winterflood investment trust research team and are reproduced here with their kind permission.

October 2024

FUND	TICKER	SUMMARY
Conventional		
Gulf Investment Fund	GIF	Publishes circular in relation to liquidation; suspension of shares due 29 October
JPMorgan Global Growth & Income	JGGI	Publishes prospectus in relation to placing programme
Ashoka India Equity	AIE	Issues shares in relation to performance fee trigger
Alliance Witan	ALW	Quarterly dividend increased by +6% following merger
Gulf Investment Fund	GIF	Shareholders approve voluntary liquidation; shares delisted
UIL Limited	UTL	Announces redemption proceeds of 2024 ZDP shares
JPMorgan Emerging EMEA Securities	JEMA	Loses Russian court order but has 30 days to appeal
Hansa Investment Company	HAN	Portfolio company, Ocean Wilson Holdings, completes strategic review
JPMorgan Emerging EMEA Securities	JEMA	OFAC licenses expire, casting further doubt on realisation of Russian assets
Witan	WTAN	Shareholders approve proposed merger with ATST
Crystal Amber	CRS	Seeks approval for B share mechanism ahead of expected capital distribution
Alliance Witan	ALW	ATST and WTAN merger completed; name and ticker changed; Jennison appointed
JPMorgan Japanese	JFJ	Shareholders approve resolutions to merge with JSGI
Alliance Witan	ALW	Completes transition of assets from Witan; one underlying manager changed
Artemis Alpha	ATS	ATS and ARR publish merger documents; transaction due to complete on 29 November
JPMorgan Japanese	JFJ	JFJ and JSGI complete merger; cash option significantly oversubscribed
Asia Dragon	DGN	DGN proposes rollover into IAT
Weiss Korea Opportunity	WKOF	Announces strategic review, as manager deems prospects unattractive
Miton UK MicroCap	MINI	40% of shares elect for redemption; board to engage with shareholders
Bellevue Healthcare	BBH	Receives redemption requests for 36.4% of share capital
VietNam Holding	VNH	Sees 12.6% redemption take up

FUND	TICKER	SUMMARY
Alternatives		
Tufton Assets	SHIP	Shareholders approved continuation and name change to Tufton Assets Ltd
Doric Nimrod Air Two	DNA2	Received $61m sales proceeds for two aircraft
Doric Nimrod Air Two	DNA2	Received $31m sales proceeds for one aircraft
Private equity		
Literacy Capital	BOOK	Increases management fee and reduces donation allocation
Partners Group Private Equity	PEY	Portfolio company KinderCare completes IPO; +50% uplift to carrying value
Patria Private Equity	PPET	Agrees secondary sale of c.13% of portfolio
Infrastructure		
Riverstone Credit Opportunities Income	RCOI	NAV per share -7.9% over Q3 2024, as Harland & Wolff loan value declines further
Digital 9 Infrastructure	DGI9	Appoints InfraRed for managed wind-down process
Atrato Onsite Energy	ROOF	Shareholders approve policy changes to enable sale of portfolio
Aquila European Renewables	AERI	Appoints Rothschild & Co to oversee managed wind-down process
JPMorgan Global Core Real Assets	JARA	Proposes managed wind-down after failing continuation vote
Harmony Energy Income	HEIT	Asset sale process expected to conclude by end of 2024
Property		
Home REIT	HOME	Sale of 152 properties for £26.8m; proceeds to be used to fully repay Scottish Widows loan
Tritax EuroBox	EBOX	Agreement reached on cash acquisition by Brookfield; board recommends over SEGRO offer
Balanced Commercial Property	BCPT	Shareholders vote in favour of cash acquisition by Starwood Funds; transaction expected to complete around 15 November
Alternative Income REIT	AIRE	Proposed changes to investment policy; shareholder approval to be sought on 12 November
PRS REIT	PRSR	Christopher Mills and Robert Naylor appointed to board
Care REIT	CRT	Name changed from Impact Healthcare REIT (IHR) to align with updated SDR
Home REIT	HOME	Delayed FY22 results published; NAV per share -57.5%
Residential Secure Income	RESI	Board proposes managed wind-down following review of options
PRS REIT	PRSR	Strategic review initiated to explore all options, including potential sale of fund

November 2024

FUND	TICKER	SUMMARY
Conventional		
Aurora UK Alpha	ARR	Name changed from Aurora Investment Trust following merger with ATS
BlackRock American Income	BRAI	Name changed from BlackRock Sustainable American Income (BRSA) to comply with SDR
BlackRock Energy & Resources Inc	BERI	Fee changed to include ongoing charges cap of 1.15% p.a.

FUND	TICKER	SUMMARY
Montanaro UK Smaller Companies	MTU	Fee changed from 0.5% p.a. of gross assets to 0.5% p.a. of net assets
BlackRock American Income	BRAI	'Sustainable' removed from name, objective and policy; to become unlabelled ESG fund under SDP
Caledonia	CLDN	GM on 18 Dec to renew buyback authority and remove 49.9% cap on Cayzer family ownership
Montanaro UK Smaller Companies	MTU	Quarterly dividend rate increased from 1.0% to 1.5% of NAV
Pershing Square Holdings	PSH	$100m (5m shares) buyback programme announced
Syncona	SYNC	Autolus, co-founded by SYNC in 2014, receives FDA approval for blood cancer therapy drug
Artemis Alpha / Aurora	ATS / ARR	Merger completes; ARR acquires £100m net assets from ATS via issue of 38.4m shares
Bellevue Healthcare	BBH	Proposes replacing annual redemption facility with conditional tender offers and continuation vote, plus increase in number of holdings; GM convened for 19 December
Bellevue Healthcare	BBH	Proposals withdrawn and GM adjourned following additional shareholder consultation
Edinburgh Worldwide	EWI	Board proposes measures including commitment to a capital return opportunity in 2025
Finsbury Growth & Income	FGT	Continuation vote introduced, to be held in January 2026
Miton UK MicroCap	MINI	Wind-down proposed following high take-up of annual redemption; potential rollover option into open-ended fund
Weiss Korea Opportunity	WKOF	Announces strategic review, as manager deems prospects unattractive
Baillie Gifford China Growth	BGCG	Introduces 100% conditional tender offer if underperforms over four years to 30 November 2028
Baillie Gifford European Growth	BGEU	Introduces 100% conditional tender offer if underperforms over four years to 30 September 2028
Alternatives		
Blackstone Loan Financing	BGLF	EGM to seek approval for liquidation convened for 15 January; shares due to be cancelled on 16 January with redemption payments by 4 February
DP Aircraft I	DPA	Target $1m raised via issue of 16.67m shares at $0.06 per share
SLF Realisation – Ordinary / C Shares	SLFR / SLFX	Shareholders approve delisting of Ordinary (84% in favour) and C (99.9%); delisting due 27 December
Tufton Assets	SHIP	Name changed from 'Tufton Oceanic Assets' to 'Tufton Assets', effective 4 November
Doric Nimrod Air Two	DNA2	£30.7m sale proceeds received from final asset sale
GCP Asset Backed Income	GABI	50.4m shares (19% of share capital) redeemed at 89.34p per share
Private equity		
Dunedin Enterprise	DNE	GM convened for 17 December to approve liquidation; initial distribution of £19.3m expected week commencing 29 January 2025
HarbourVest Global Private Equity	HVPE	Metage issues letter to shareholders outlining concerns with capital allocation policy
Infrastructure		
JPMorgan Global Core Real Assets	JARA	Proposes managed wind-down after failing continuation vote
VH Global Energy Infrastructure	ENRG	Announces name and ticker change (to ENRG)

FUND	TICKER	SUMMARY
Property		
Ground Rents Income	GRIO	Disposal of largest asset for £7.9m, in line with 30 September valuation; proceeds required to be used to repay debt
Balanced Commercial Property	BCPT	Takeover by Starwood Funds completes; shareholders to receive 96p per share in cash
Tritax EuroBox	EBOX	Shareholders approve Brookfield takeover, with >90% of votes cast in favour; transaction due to complete on 10 December
Supermarket Income REIT	SUPR	Fee basis moved from NAV to market cap; outsourced functions transferred to Atrato
PRS REIT	PRSR	28% of votes cast against election of Christopher Mills due to over-boarding concerns
Home REIT	HOME	Shareholders do not approve receipt of FY22 accounts; only 45% of votes cast in favour
abrdn European Logistics Income	ASLI	Proposed adoption of B share scheme to return capital under managed wind-down
Ground Rents Income	GRIO	92% of shareholders vote in favour of continuation to proceed with orderly realisation
Residential Secure Income	RESI	GM convened for 6 December to approve wind-down; fee to be amended to ensure appropriate incentivisation
abrdn European Logistics Income	ASLI	Shareholders approve B share scheme
PRS REIT	PRSR	Board is in advanced discussions regarding potential sale of fund; continuing to explore all other options

December 2024

FUND	TICKER	SUMMARY
Conventional		
Invesco Perpetual UK Smaller Companies	IPU	Artemis appointed as new manager, with fee reduction and waiver
Montanaro UK Smaller Companies	MTU	Fee changed from 0.5% p.a. of gross assets to 0.5% p.a. of net assets
Caledonia	CLDN	Granted authority for share repurchases and waiver of takeover code
Crystal Amber	CRS	>30% of votes cast against re-election of directors
Edinburgh Worldwide	EWI	Shareholders approve investment policy changes
JPMorgan Asia Growth & Income	JAGI	Proposed increase to enhanced dividend rate
Montanaro UK Smaller Companies	MTU	Quarterly dividend rate increased from 1.0% to 1.5% of NAV
Pershing Square Holdings	PSH	Announces additional $100m buyback
AVI Global	AGT	Special dividend from largest holding; gross proceeds of €46.9m (3.4% of NAV)
JPMorgan Emerging EMEA Securities	JEMA	Fund warns that Russian assets may not be realisable

FUND	TICKER	SUMMARY
Multiple (USA/CYN/EWI/ ESCT/HOT/HRI/KPC)	USA / CYN / EWI / ESCT / HOT / HRI / KPC	Saba requisitions GMs for seven trusts
Keystone Positive Change & Baillie Gifford US Growth	KPC / USA	Boards urge shareholders to vote against Saba's resolutions at 3 February GMs
CQS Natural Resources Growth & Income	CYN	Board urges shareholders to vote against Saba's resolutions at 4 February GM
Keystone Positive Change / Edinburgh Worldwide	KPC / EWI	EWI notes that Saba submitted invalid requisition notice
European Smaller Companies	ESCT	Responds to Saba requisition; advises shareholders to vote against resolutions
ESCT & HOT	ESCT / HOT	Boards urge shareholders to vote against Saba's resolutions at February GMs
Herald	HRI	Board urges shareholders to vote against Saba's resolutions at 22 January GM
Saba vs HRI	HRI	Saba to support HRI 100% cash exit in a year's time
Bellevue Healthcare	BBH	Proposes replacing annual redemption facility with conditional tender offers and continuation vote, plus increase in number of holdings; GM convened for 19 December
Bellevue Healthcare	BBH	Proposals withdrawn and GM adjourned following additional shareholder consultation
Finsbury Growth & Income	FGT	Continuation vote introduced, to be held in January 2026
Jupiter Green	JGC	Wind-down proposed with option to roll into open-ended fund
Keystone Positive Change	KPC	GMs convened for 27 January and 7 February to approve wind-down; cash payments expected by 17 February
Menhaden Resource Efficiency	MHN	Proposes a managed wind-down, following shareholder feedback
Alternatives		
Taylor Maritime Investments	TMI	Circular published proposing to transfer share listing away from closed-ended funds
Blackstone Loan Financing	BGLF	Fund to return €260m (98% of share capital) at NAV by 4 February
Private equity		
Dunedin Enterprise	DNE	Shareholders approve liquidation
Oakley Capital	OCI	OCI converts $107m of preferred equity position in North Sails
Infrastructure		
VH Global Energy Infrastructure	ENRG	Announces name and ticker change (to ENRG)
JPMorgan Global Core Real Assets	JARA	Publishes circular in connection with proposed managed wind-down
Greencoat UK Wind	UKW	Management fee to be charged on lower of NAV and market cap
HydrogenOne Capital Growth	HGEN	Investment adviser, HydrogenOne Capital, acquired by Cordiant Capital
Atrato Onsite Energy	ROOF	Shareholders approve voluntary liquidation
JPMorgan Global Core Real Assets	JARA	Shareholders approve managed wind-down

FUND	TICKER	SUMMARY
International Public Partnerships	INPP	Provides portfolio update; dividend frequency to change from semi-annual to quarterly
Ecofin US Renewables Infrastructure ($)	RNEW	Proposes disposal of 63.7MW solar assets at c.26% discount
Pantheon Infrastructure	PINT	First sale since IPO executed, Calpine, with +2.6% NAV uplift expected
Property		
Home REIT	HOME	Southey Capital proposes tender offer for HOME at 4p per share, valuing fund at c.£32m
Tritax EuroBox	EBOX	Shares suspended; shareholders to receive 69p per share in cash by 24 December
Social Housing REIT	SOHO	Atrato formerly appointed manager; fee reduced and based on market cap
Home REIT	HOME	Shareholders do not approve receipt of FY22 accounts; only 45% of votes cast in favour
Social Housing REIT	SOHO	Name changed from 'Triple Point Social Housing REIT' following manager change
Phoenix Spree Deutschland	PSDL	Board is in advanced discussions regarding potential sale of fund; continuing to explore all other options
Residential Secure Income	RESI	Shareholders approve wind-down, with 99.7% of votes cast in favour
abrdn Property Income	API	Shareholders approve capital return; total of 55p per share to be returned by 10 January

January 2025

FUND	TICKER	SUMMARY
Conventional		
Henderson European	HET	Co-managers resign; board announces strategic review and discount target
abrdn Asian Income	AAIF	Introduces enhanced dividend (6.25% of NAV p.a.) and three-yearly continuation vote
Baillie Gifford UK Growth	BGUK	To use buybacks to maintain discount in single digits
Downing Strategic Micro-Cap	DSM	Proposes liquidation following managed wind-down
Miton UK MicroCap	MINI	Arranges rollover option into open-ended equivalent
Multiple (USA/CYN/EWI/ESCT/HOT/HRI/KPC)	USA / CYN / EWI / ESCT / HOT / HRI / KPC	CYN, ESCT, KPC and USA note proxy adviser recommendations against Saba
CQS Natural Resources Growth & Income / Henderson Opportunities	CYN / HOT	CYN and HOT announce Saba resolutions defeated
European Smaller Companies	ESCT	Announces Saba resolutions defeated
Henderson Opportunities	HOT	Publishes circular on proposed wind-down; notes Saba could block it

FUND	TICKER	SUMMARY
Herald	HRI	Announces Saba resolutions defeated
BlackRock Funds (BRAI, BERI, BRSC, BRWM)	BRAI / BERI / BRSC / BRWM	Saba reaches standstill agreement with BlackRock, impacting multiple funds
Invesco Asia	IAT	Shareholders approve DGN merger; 20% of votes cast against tender offer changes
Alternatives		
Taylor Maritime	TMI	Shareholders approve transfer of listing away from closed-ended funds
Amedeo Air Four Plus	AA4	Notes clawback of performance fee
Amedeo Air Four Plus	AA4	Completes £28m redemption
Blackstone Loan Financing	BGLF	Fund to return €260m (98% of share capital) at NAV by 4 February
Doric Nimrod Air Two	DNA2	Completes compulsory redemption and cancels listing
Private equity		
Dunedin Enterprise	DNE	Shareholders approve liquidation
HarbourVest Global Private Equity	HVPE	Outlines buyback increase, structure simplification and continuation vote
Infrastructure		
Digital 9 Infrastructure	DGI9	NAV per share -25% over H2 2024 as asset valuations further reduced
HydrogenOne Capital Growth	HGEN	NAV per share -12.2% over Q4 2024; 12-month revenue growth rate slows
Ecofin US Renewables Infrastructure	RNEW	Shareholders approve managed wind-down
Gresham House Energy Storage	GRID	Management fee to be charged on equal weighting of NAV and market cap
Digital 9 Infrastructure	DGI9	Agrees to sell Aqua Comms at -28% discount to carrying value
Property		
abrdn European Logistics Income	ASLI	Disposal of three assets for €45.4m, in line with or above latest valuations
Ground Rents Income	GRIO	Victoria Property makes improved offer at 37.5p per share; board think it still undervalues the fund
Home REIT	HOME	Delayed FY23 results: NAV per share -37%; portfolio valued at 40% of acquisition cost

February 2025

FUND	TICKER	SUMMARY
Conventional		
Bankers	BNKR	Jamie Ross, regional portfolio manager, resigns from Janus Henderson
BlackRock American Income	BRAI	Announces changes to investment process and tender offers
Brown Advisory US Smaller Companies	BASC	Moves fee basis to lower of NAV and market cap and introduces conditional tender
Henderson European	HET	Co-managers resign; board announces strategic review and discount target

FUND	TICKER	SUMMARY
Invesco Perpetual UK Smaller Companies	IPU	Name & ticker change to Artemis UK Future Leaders (AFL)
Ruffer	RICA	Co-manager Duncan MacInnes leaves Ruffer with immediate effect
Smithson	SSON	Board proposes broadening of market cap range; manager amends process
BlackRock Energy & Resources Income	BERI	Introduces one-off continuation vote in 2026 following shareholder feedback
Downing Strategic Micro Cap	DSM	Shareholders approved liquidation proposals; delisted week of 3 March
Henderson Opportunities	HOT	Shareholders approved managed wind-down proposals; second GM on 14 March
Montanaro UK Smaller Companies	MTU	Formalises discount control policy, targeting single-digit discount
Weiss Korea Opportunity	WKOF	Proposes managed wind-down following strategic review
Multiple (USA/CYN/EWI/ESCT/HOT/HRI/KPC/MCT/SCP)	USA / CYN / EWI / ESCT / HOT / HRI / KPC / MCT / SCP	CYN and HOT announce Saba resolutions defeated
Middlefield Canadian Income	MCT	Saba withdraws requisition for 60 days following constructive discussions
Achilles	AIC	New fund launch: Achilles Investment Company
Asia Dragon / Invesco Asia	DGN / IAT	DGN sees 69% of shareholders elect for cash, scaled back to 25%
Asia Dragon / Invesco Asia	IAT	IAT-DGN merger completed; IAT ticker changed to IAD
Henderson International Income / JPMorgan Global Growth & Income	HINT / JGGI	HINT agrees rollover into JGGI
Vietnam Enterprise	VEIL	Introduces 100% conditional tender for 2030
Private equity		
NB Private Equity	NBPE	Commits $120m to buybacks over next three years
Partners Group Private Equity	PEY	Amends investment management agreement, reduces fees
Schroders Capital Global	INOV	Shareholders approve managed wind-down
Infrastructure		
BBGI Global Infrastructure	BBGI	Agrees takeover offer at +3.4% premium to NAV
JPMorgan Global Core Real Assets	JARA	To return £33.7m via compulsory partial redemption of 17% of shares
Triple Point Energy Transition	TENT	Shareholders approve liquidation
Aquila Energy Efficiency	AEET	Disposes of certain assets, generating returns ahead of initial expectations
Greencoat UK Wind	UKW	Net cash generation -31% over 2024; 1.3x dividend cover
Greencoat Renewables	GRP	Net cash generation -24.5% over 2024; management fee amended

FUND	TICKER	SUMMARY
Property		
Ground Rents Income	GRIO	Victoria Property makes fifth offer at 40.0p per GRIO share; board believes it still undervalues the fund; offer deadline extended to 25 February
PRS REIT	PRSR	Fund receives several non-binding offers at premium to share price but discount to latest NAV; board continues to explore all options
Victoria Property	GRIO	Announces it does not intend to make a firm offer
Warehouse REIT	WHR	Board rejects cash offer from Blackstone and Sixth Street at 110.5p per share
Value & Indexed Property Income	VIP	GM convened for 20 March to seek shareholder approval to enter UK REIT regime

March 2025

FUND	TICKER	SUMMARY
Conventional		
CT Global Managed Portfolio – Growth / Income	CMPG/ CMPI	Peter Hewitt, manager since inception, to retire in October; Adam Norris and Paul Green to take over management
Fidelity Japan	FJV	Manager Nicholas Price to retire, to be replaced by assistant manager Ying Lu
Henderson Smaller Companies	HSL	Manager Neil Hermon to retire in September; co-manager Indriatti van Hien to continue
Impax Environmental Markets	IEM	Bruce Jenkyn-Jones to retire as co-manager in 2026; Jon Forster and Fotis Chatzimichalakis to continue as co-managers
Montanaro European Smaller Companies	MTE	Management fee reduced
Achilles	AIC	Shareholders representing 8.8% of SHED intend to requisition EGM to replace three directors
AVI Japan Opportunity Trust / Fidelity Japan	AJOT / FJV	AJOT proposes merger with FJV with 25% cash exit option
Bellevue Healthcare	BBH	Board discussing increased number of holdings and enhanced sell discipline
Henderson Opportunities	HOT	Shareholders approve liquidation; 43% to roll over into open-ended fund
Jupiter Green	JGC	Shareholders approve wind-up; 56% to roll into open-ended fund
Keystone Positive Change	KPC	Shareholders approve liquidation at GM; 30% elect to roll into open-ended fund
Menhaden Resource Efficiency	MHN	Shareholders approve liquidation; sale of unlisted investments under review
Fidelity Japan	FJV	Board proposes 100% unconditional tender offer in 2028
Montanaro European Smaller Companies	MTE	Introduces semi-annual 5% tender at 5% discount
Private equity		
LMS Capital	LMS	Board proposes managed realisation following strategic review
Oakley Capital	OCI	Announces >£20m p.a. buyback programme
Schroder British Opportunities	SBO	Proposes policy change to focus entirely on private equity; advances continuation vote

FUND	TICKER	SUMMARY
Infrastructure		
Harmony Energy Income	HEIT	Receives takeover bid from Foresight at +29% premium to previous close
Harmony Energy Income	HEIT	Receives cash takeover bid from Drax at 88.0p per share
Harmony Energy Income	HEIT	Irrevocable undertaking to vote for Foresight's possible cash offer lapses
Octopus Renewables Infrastructure	ORIT	Extends buyback programme, targets asset sales and reviews fees
Warehouse REIT	WHR	Board rejects cash offer from Blackstone and Sixth Street at 110.5p per share
Care REIT	CRT	Agreed terms for all-cash takeover by CareTrust at 108p
Warehouse REIT	WHR	Board 'minded to recommend' Blackstone's final offer
Supermarket Income REIT	SUPR	Proposed internalisation of management arrangements and transfer of listing category
Urban Logistics REIT	SHED	Proposed internalisation of management arrangements and transfer of listing category
Phoenix Spree Deutschland	PSDL	Shareholders approve realisation strategy; number of units marketed for sale as condominiums significantly increased
Value & Indexed Property Income	VIP	Shareholders approve admission to REIT regime, with 95.8% of votes cast in favour
Supermarket Income REIT	SUPR	Internalisation completes; Rob Abraham and Mike Perkins appointed CEO and CFO
Urban Logistics REIT	SHED	Board recommends shareholders vote against requisitioned board changes and notes that it has received suggestions from shareholders regarding changes to internalisation; Achilles responds further
Life Science REIT	LABS	Board initiates strategic review, including potential sale of fund

April 2025

FUND	TICKER	SUMMARY
Conventional		
abrdn UK Smaller Companies Growth	AUSC	Management fee reduced and tiers amended
Franklin Global	FRGT	Name changed from Martin Currie Global Portfolio Trust (MNP)
Impax Environmental Markets	IEM	Bruce Jenkyn-Jones announces retirement effective July 2026
Pershing Square Holdings	PSH	$900m investment in Howard Hughes results in management fee reduction
abrdn Diversified Income & Growth	ADIG	Board rejects sale offer for all remaining portfolio assets
AVI Japan Opportunity / Fidelity Japan	AJOT / FJV	AJOT proposes merger with FJV offering 25% cash exit option
Bellevue Healthcare	BBH	Introduces zero discount policy, replacing annual redemption facility
BlackRock American Income	BRAI	Shareholders approve new investment strategy focused on systematic active approach
Middlefield Canadian Income	MCT	Proposes wind-up with option to roll over into actively managed ETF
Miton UK MicroCap	MINI	Reconstruction and wind-up approved at GM

FUND	TICKER	SUMMARY
Weiss Korea Opportunity	WKOF	Wind-down approved by shareholders at EGM
JPMorgan Global Emerging Markets Income	JEMI	Introduces five-year conditional tender for 25% of NAV at 2% discount
Pacific Horizon	PHI	Announces 25% conditional tender offer linked to performance
Alternatives		
LMS Capital	LMS	Publishes circular outlining managed realisation proposals
Harmony Energy Income	HEIT	Irrevocable undertaking to vote for Foresight's possible cash offer has lapsed
BBGI Global Infrastructure	BBGI	Shareholders approve takeover offer
HydrogenOne Capital Growth	HGEN	Investment adviser no longer proceeding with acquisition by Cordiant
Harmony Energy Income	HEIT	Receives improved 92.4p bid from Foresight
Tritax Big Box REIT	BBOX	50% of UKCM portfolio has now been sold
Care REIT	CRT	Offer documents published; Court meeting and GM convened for 29 April
Urban Logistics REIT	SHED	Revised proposal, under which SHED shareholders would receive 0.5612 new LondonMetric shares and 42.8p in cash for each SHED share held; board minded to recommend offer
Value & Indexed Property Income	VIP	Confirmation of change of tax status to REIT status
Home REIT	HOME	Publication of delayed interim results for 6m to 28 February 2023
Urban Logistics REIT	SHED	Achilles withdraws GM requisition in light of takeover offer

May 2025

FUND	TICKER	SUMMARY
Conventional		
CQS Natural Resources Growth & Income	CYN	Management fee reduced from 1.2% NAV scale to flat 1%
Schroder AsiaPacific	SDP	Management fee reduced and tiered structure amended
CQS Natural Resources Growth & Income	CYN	Proposes 100% tender offer, enhanced dividend, and delayed continuation votes
Fidelity Japan	FJV	Seeks shareholder approval to amend articles following failed continuation vote
JPMorgan Indian	JII	Announces new tender policy, dividend enhancement and fee reduction following review
Miton UK MicroCap	MINI	Shareholders approve placing fund into liquidation at second GM
Riverstone Energy	RSE	Investment manager agrees to managed wind-down of remaining portfolio
Schroder Income Growth	SCF	Board announces new discount control and performance initiatives
Third Point Investors	TPOU	Announces reverse takeover of Malibu Life Reinsurance; will transition to reinsurance company
European Smaller Companies	ESCT	Completes tender offer; 42.2% of shares tendered and repurchased under 'in specie' consideration

FUND	TICKER	SUMMARY
Alternatives		
VPC Specialty Lending	VSL	Executes second £43m capital return via B share redemption
Chrysalis	CHRY	Commits to no new investments until 2026 AGM
LMS Capital	LMS	Shareholders approve managed realisation
Schiehallion Fund	MNTN	Begins process to attain UK tax residency and move to Main Market
BBGI Global Infrastructure	BBGI	Offer declared unconditional with 94% acceptances; shares to de-list on 18 June
Harmony Energy Income	HEIT	Acquisition by Foresight receives shareholder approval; last dealings expected 12 June
Ecofin US Renewable Infrastructure	RNEW	Moves to register as FCA self-managed
Greencoat Renewables	GRP	Shareholders reject discontinuation vote with 82.5% of votes cast against
VH Global Energy Infrastructure	ENRG	Proposes realisation strategy, initially targeting realisations <15% of Reference NAV
Digital 9 Infrastructure	DGI9	NAV per share -56.7% over 2024, driven by divestment consideration adjustments
Property		
Care REIT	CRT	Takeover becomes effective; CRT shareholders to receive 108p per share in cash
Urban Logistics REIT	SHED	Agreement reached on acquisition of SHED by LondonMetric for 42.8p in cash and 0.5612 new LondonMetric shares per SHED share
Warehouse REIT	WHR	Offer price reduced to 110.6p (incl. 1.6p dividend); takeover deadline extended to 6 June
Home REIT	HOME	Sale of full remaining portfolio and publication of outstanding results expected in Q3 2025

June 2025

FUND	TICKER	SUMMARY
Conventional		
abrdn New India	ANII	Tiered fees introduced: 0.8% on first £300m, 0.6% thereafter
JPMorgan European Discovery	JEDT	Management fee reduced to 0.70% up to £300m, 0.65% thereafter
Majedie	MAJE	Manager in advanced discussions to join Brown Advisory
MIGO Opportunities	MIGO	Nick Greenwood steps back as co-manager; Tom Treanor joins Charlotte Cuthbertson; new fee structure adopted
Caledonia	CLDN	Proposes 10:1 share split at AGM on 16 July
Lindsell Train	LTI	Proposes 100:1 share split at AGM scheduled for 11 September
European Opportunities	EOT	River Global agrees to acquire Devon Equity Management, EOT's manager
European Assets / European Smaller Companies	EAT / ESCT	Boards agree to merge with 15% cash exit option for EAT shareholders
Fidelity European / Henderson European	FEV / HET	Boards agree combination; HET to wind up and roll over into FEV with 33% cash option

FUND	TICKER	SUMMARY
Hansa	HAN / HANA	Reaches preliminary agreement to acquire Ocean Wilsons Holdings, creating >£900m vehicle
MIGO Opportunities	MIGO	Adopts higher-conviction strategy focusing on 10–15 holdings; new fee and capital return policy
CQS Natural Resources Growth & Income	CYN	100% tender offer open to shareholders on 29 May; 45.7% of issued shares tendered
European Opportunities	EOT	25% tender offer completed at 953.6p (98% of NAV)
European Smaller Companies	ESCT	Cash exit pool fully realised; repurchased 50.7m shares at 213.8p
JPMorgan Indian	JII	Replaces 25% performance tender with 30% one-off tender and triannual continuation vote
Polar Capital Global Financials	PCFT	100% tender offer completed; 43.8% of capital tendered at 209.43p
Alternatives		
BioPharma Credit ($)	BPCR	Shareholders approve continuation of fund
NB Distressed Debt ($)	NBDD	Proposal to re-elect Chairman narrowly passes with 50.1% of votes
Private equity		
3i Group	III	Sells MPM to Partners Group for £400m (+17% uplift to carrying value)
Infrastructure		
Harmony Energy Income	HEIT	Acquisition of HEIT by Foresight completed
Downing Renewables & Infrastructure	DORE	Proposed cash acquisition of DORE by Bagnall Energy at +24% premium to share price
Foresight Environmental Infrastructure	FGEN	Announces results from strategic review
Downing Renewables & Infrastructure	DORE	Five yearly continuation vote passes with 88.9% support
Gore Street Energy Storage	GSF	Dividend policy changed from fixed distribution target to operational cashflow
NextEnergy Solar	NESF	Fee calculation will have a 50% NAV, 50% market cap weighting
Ecofin US Renewables Infrastructure	RNEW	Approval to become self-managed alternative investment fund granted
Property		
Custodian Property Income REIT	CREI	Acquisition of £22.1m portfolio via all-share acquisition of Merlin Properties, to be satisfied via issue of shares on NAV-for-NAV basis
Tritax Big Box REIT / Warehouse REIT	BBOX / WHR	WHR agrees takeover by Blackstone at 109.0p per share, representing -14% discount to 31 March 2025 EPRA NTA per share
PRS REIT	PRSR	Confirms receipt of non-binding takeover offer from Long Harbour at 115p per share, representing -18% discount to 31 December 2024 NAV per share
Urban Logistics REIT	SHED	Shareholders approve takeover by LondonMetric, with 99% of votes cast in favour
Tritax Big Box REIT / Warehouse REIT	BBOX / WHR	BBOX and WHR agree terms of acquisition, with WHR shareholders to receive 0.4236 new BBOX shares and 47.2p in cash, representing +4.8% premium to Blackstone offer
Supermarket Income REIT	SUPR	Shareholders approve listing transfer, with 99.9% of votes cast in favour

FUND	TICKER	SUMMARY
Residential Secure Income	RESI	Ben Fry to step down as lead manager on completion of secondment on 31 July
PRS REIT	PRSR	Board continues to explore all options under strategic review; further update expected by end of July following consultation with shareholders

July 2025

FUND	TICKER	SUMMARY
Conventional		
CT Global Managed Portfolio	CMPG/ CMPI	Fee reduced from 0.65% of total assets to 0.60% of NAV from 1 September
BlackRock Energy & Resources Income	BERI	Introduces new dividend policy: higher of prior year or 4% of NAV, from 1 December 2025
Biotech Growth	BIOG	AGM continuation vote passes with 76.7% shareholder support
Geiger Counter	GCL	Reaches standstill agreement with Saba until 2028 AGM
Golden Prospect	GPM	Signs standstill agreement with Saba until 2028 AGM
Worldwide Healthcare	WWH	At AGM, 30–32% vote against reappointing two board members
Hansa Investment Company / Ocean Wilsons Holdings	HAN / HANA	Boards agree all-share merger to create £900m investment vehicle
Schroder BSC Social Impact	SBSI	Initiates strategic review with managed wind-down among options
Third Point Investors	TPOU	Revises redemption offer to $136m (25% of NAV) after shareholder feedback
Third Point Investors	TPOU	Investor opposition group TPIL gains support, now representing 24% of shares
CQS Natural Resources Growth & Income	CYN	45.7% tender offer result announced; payment due 30 September
JPMorgan Indian	JII	30% tender oversubscribed at 38.7%; 19.7m shares to be repurchased
River UK Micro Cap	RMMC	Launches £2m buyback at 10% discount; proposes wind-down vote in 2028 if no capital returned
Private equity		
Apax Global Alpha	APAX	Recommended cash takeover by Apax/Ares at €1.90 per share (-17% discount to NAV)
Augmentum Fintech	AUGM	Shareholders approve GM proposals to reverse internalised management
Schroders Capital Global Innovation	INOV	Tender oversubscribed; 21.4% of shares repurchased
Literacy Capital	BOOK	Sells and reinvests in Velociti at +52% uplift; plans >£6m return via B shares
Infrastructure		
Gore Street Energy Storage	GSF	Announces strategic review and notice of GM
Hydrogen Capital Growth	HGEN	Proposes managed wind-down and delays publication of 30 June NAV
International Public Partnerships	INPP	£250m investment for c.3% equity stake in Sizewell C nuclear project

FUND	TICKER	SUMMARY
Property		
Tritax Big Box REIT / Warehouse REIT	BBOX / WHR	WHR publishes response document and recommends increased Blackstone offer
Value & Indexed Property Income	VIP	Proposed 30% tender offer, fixed life to 2033 and 10% discount target

August 2025

FUND	TICKER	SUMMARY
Conventional		
Diverse Income	DIVI	Annual redemption sees 72.8m shares submitted (30.8% of share capital)
River UK Micro Cap	RMMC	£2m share buyback at ≥10% discount; full cash exit if no redemptions by 30 June 2028
Pacific Assets	PAC	David Gait resigns as co-PM; Jack Nelson appointed co-PM at Stewart Investors
Pershing Square Holdings	PSH	Fee reduction following $900m HHH investment
BlackRock Energy & Resources Income	BERI	New dividend policy from 1 December 2025: target higher of prior year or 4% of year-end NAV
Murray International	MYI	Benchmark to change to MSCI ACWI High Dividend Yield Index from 1 July 2025
AVI Japan Opportunity / Fidelity Japan	AJOT / FJV	FJV completes review; board enters non-binding terms to merge with AJOT
Bellevue Healthcare	BBH	Board announces strategic review due to underperformance and fund size
Oryx International Growth	OIG	Discontinuation vote not passed; 96.7% of votes cast in favour of continuation
Riverstone Energy	RSE	Enters managed wind-down after all resolutions passed at 22 August EGM
Third Point Investors	TPOU	Merger resolutions passed at 14 August EGM; over 30% of votes cast against
Alternatives		
TwentyFour Income	TFIF	Board announces three-yearly realisation opportunity at 2% discount to NAV; election deadline 17 October
Doric Nimrod Air Three	DNA3	Completes £32.7m A380 sale to Emirates; three aircraft remain on lease
Private equity		
Apax Global Alpha	APAX	Shareholders approved proposed take-private, effective 17 September
HarbourVest Global Private Equity	HVPE	Committed $125m to new SMA structure (80% Primary / 20% Co-investments)
Oakley Capital	OCI	24% of votes cast against Dubens re-election due to independence concerns
Infrastructure		
International Public Partnerships	INPP	Appoints Jamie Hossain as lead portfolio manager effective 1 September
Gore Street Energy Storage	GSF	Resolutions to replace directors receive 30% support at requisitioned EGM

FUND	TICKER	SUMMARY
Octopus Renewables Infrastructure	ORIT	Amends management fee basis to average of NAV and market cap
Property		
Tritax Big Box REIT / Warehouse REIT	BBOX / WHR	BBOX confirms that it will not increase its offer for WHR
Tritax Big Box REIT / Warehouse REIT	BBOX / WHR	Blackstone announces ownership of >30% of WHR shares, resulting in mandatory cash offer
Tritax Big Box REIT / Warehouse REIT	BBOX / WHR	BBOX confirms withdrawal from takeover process for WHR
Value & Indexed Property Income	VIP	Proposed 30% tender offer, fixed life to 2033 and 10% discount target

September 2025

FUND	TICKER	SUMMARY
Conventional		
Alliance Witan	ALW	WTW appoints Brown Advisory and Artisan Partners, replacing SGA (11%) and ARGA (9%)
Majedie	MAJE	Manager Marylebone joins Brown Advisory; MAJE to receive cash for 7.5% stake; fee cut
Monks	MNKS	Spencer Adair to retire March 2026; Michael Taylor to join management team
Pacific Assets	PAC	Introduces tiered fees to address discount
Polar Capital Global Healthcare	PCGH	Board proposes removal of performance fee; adopts tiered fee structure
Lindsell Train	LTI	Executes 1:100 share split effective 24 September
Caledonia	CLDN	Sells Stonehage Fleming stake (7.5% NAV) for £288m (+30% to book value)
Barings Emerging EMEA Opportunities	BEMO	Cancels 25% tender; continuation vote and new conditional tender introduced
Fidelity European / Henderson European	FEV / HET	HET shareholders approve wind-up and merger into FEV; 71% rollover, 29% cash exit; merger completed
JPMorgan Emerging Markets	JMG	Adopts new dividend policy: annual payout of 4% of NAV effective 7 November
JPMorgan India Growth & Income	JIGI	Sets dividend equal to ≥4% of prior year NAV, paid in four equal interims
Third Point Investors	TPOU	$136m redemption completed at 4.8% NAV discount; merger with Malibu Life completed
Alternatives		
CVC Income & Growth	CVCG	Launches placing and WRAP offer; new shares issued at 0.65% premium
Fair Oaks Income	FAIR	Proposes converting Master Fund to evergreen structure with four-year liquidity cycle
TwentyFour Income	TFIF	Launches placing at 2% NAV premium; expands investable universe to US and Australia
Private equity		
Apax Global Alpha	APAX	Shareholders approve take-private by Apax/Ares; fund delisted
Pantheon International	PIN	Announces enhanced capital allocation policy, linking buybacks to distributions

FUND	TICKER	SUMMARY
3i Group	III	Exits MAIT for £143m (+30% uplift to March valuation)
Chrysalis	CHRY	Klarna IPO at $15bn valuation (1.6x MOIC); retains stake post-listing
Infrastructure		
Foresight Environmental Infrastructure	FGEN	Just 6% of votes in favour of discontinuation; continuation vote approved
Gore Street Energy Storage	GSF	RM Funds calls for greater transparency and board accountability
Gore Street Energy Storage	GSF	Two special dividends declared; board refresh announced
Hydrogen Capital Growth	HGEN	Shares suspended due to delays in results publication; material deterioration expected from last NAV
Octopus Renewables Infrastructure	ORIT	2030 strategy announced; increased allocation to construction assets
Premier Miton Global Renewables	PMGR	Proposes wind-down with 100% cash exit and open-ended rollover option
Property		
PRS REIT	PRSR	Agrees sale of assets to Waypoint Asset Management at 115.3p per share
Warehouse REIT	WHR	Takeover by Blackstone declared unconditional; de-listing on 9 October
Starwood European Real Estate Finance	SWEF	H1 2025 results: NAV per share -3.1%; final loan due Q3 2026

LISTEN IN

Join Jonathan Davis every week on the award-winning Money Makers podcast as he discusses all the latest news from the investment sector with a wide range of professional experts – directors, fund managers, analysts and media commentators. The podcast, now in its sixth year and with more than 300 episodes behind it, remains free and is available on You Tube and all leading podcast channels.

REPORT CARD: YES, BUT...

Fund manager BEN CONWAY *reports on the progress being made in the sector since his firm Hawksmoor Investment Management set out its manifesto for reform two years ago.*

Cost disclosure

THE FCA CONSULTATION on the new Consumer Composite Investments (CCI) regime closed in January. As a reminder, this is the regulatory framework that will replace the old EU-derived PRIIPs regime in the UK. Investment trusts are to be labelled as CCIs, as are funds that own them. Since January the FCA have been digesting the huge response to the consultation that the industry campaign group helped galvanise.

Many of those who responded worried that the hard-won cost disclosure victory we wrote about in last year's *Handbook* article had been lost. Language within the consultation paper suggested that any funds holding investment trusts would still have to treat their costs in the same way as open-ended funds treat theirs.

This is despite the fact that costs incurred by investment trusts are deducted from published net asset values (NAVs) and already reflected in their share prices. Aggregating these costs into overall fund cost figures on the same basis would continue to penalise investment trusts.

As this edition goes to print, we are awaiting the outcome of the consultation on the whole CCI regime. Pleasingly, progress has been made in the intervening months, and we are confident that an effective regulatory framework will be created that does not unfairly treat investment trusts. This will end the current uncertainty and (we hope) enable retail platforms to develop the necessary systems to report investment trust costs correctly.

This is something that without clarification of the new regime they have so far been reluctant to do. In addition, the new framework should give larger investors, such as wealth managers and multi-asset funds, the confidence to invest in the sector without fear of their portfolios that hold investment trusts being made to look optically too 'expensive'.

Trust discounts

The IPO market remains shut, with discounts remaining wide. At the end of September, excluding 3i, the sector was trading on a 13.2% discount (data courtesy of Winterflood Securities). This is only a smidge narrower than at the start of the year (14.9%), although narrower than the 18.6% discount seen in the wake of President Trump's tariffs announcement in April.

Trusts that invest in alternative assets and private equity remain on the widest discounts. One bugbear of ours is the way that the renewable energy trusts, of which there are many, all use different assumptions in formulating their NAVs. For example, they all need to make an assumption about the path of future power prices, as well as apply a discount rate to the cash flows their assets are expected to generate.

The power price curves they adopt are obtained from various consultants, who can (and often do) disagree wildly. Discount rates can also be quite different, even for assets that are relatively similar. We think that the lack of uniformity in assumptions adds to the uncertainty and cynicism around the validity of NAVs.

On a more positive note, this year has seen a sea change in the way that investment managers are paid, with fee calculations increasingly being based, at least partly, on market capitalisation as opposed to being wholly based on NAV. This is something we had been calling for and will create a better alignment of interest with shareholders.

Despite an improvement in capital allocation discipline, private equity trust discounts remain stubbornly wide. We think the sector offers tremendous value, especially when compared with the newly introduced alternative of long-term asset funds (LTAFs), discussed in the next section.

In the main, demand for investment trust shares remains lacklustre. The sector is still struggling to attract new buyers to replace those that have left in the past few years, driven away by confusion over cost disclosure and the continued consolidation of the wealth management industry.

LTAFs: shining a light

The FCA has giving its blessing to the introduction of LTAFs, which are a new variant of open-ended fund, designed to give investors access to less-liquid asset classes, such as private equity and infrastructure. A key advantage of LTAFs is that investors can deploy a lot of capital quickly and benefit from a vehicle whose investment value, unlike an investment trust, will always match the NAV. On the other hand, being open-ended and investing in illiquid assets, redemptions are restricted to just a few times a year, and potentially with limits on how much investors can take out.

We like to say that had LTAFs come to the market first, investment trusts would have had to be invented to overcome the drawbacks of the new fund type. To cope with being open-ended, LTAFs will have to hold around 15% of the portfolio in cash or near-cash to meet potential redemption requests. As a result, an investor's initial £1 investment will only buy about 85p worth of exposure to less-liquid assets.

Contrast this with investment trusts. Being closed-ended, the portfolios can be fully invested. The managers can deploy gearing while the investment management fees are often lower. With share prices being well below NAV, the value proposition compared to LTAFs owning very similar assets is stark. A £1 initial investment will buy far more than £1 of assets.

We think the advent of the LTAF, far from being a threat to the investment trust sector, is quite the opposite. Even without the added boost from wide discounts, an investment trust trading around par will give a much bigger bang for the investor's buck. It is possible that LTAFs will be able to use investment trusts for liquidity, which would be a new source of demand for the sector.

Corporate governance

It has been noticeable how boards have become far more amenable to our entreaties for more efficient capital allocation. A cynic might suggest that this is simply a function of necessity. Discounts have remained wide for too long and the retreat from the sector of traditional buyers continues.

Nonetheless, I detect that there is a growing realisation from boards that they cannot stand by and allow discounts to persist. The presence of high-profile activists such as Boaz Weinstein and the successful launch of the activist trust Achilles has helped to inject a sense of much-needed urgency within boardrooms.

2024 was a bumper year for buybacks, tenders and realisations, and 2025 has seen this trend continue. For example, in August 2025 buyback volumes were up 40% year over year and a record 130 investment trusts bought back stock in February 2025. The flipside is that the sector is shrinking, as it has to do in the absence of growing demand.

Examples of poor corporate governance do still plague the sector. We are particularly concerned by instances in which boards are clearly not providing sufficient oversight of the investment manager. Such oversight is crucial for specialist asset classes.

We have also been disappointed to hear that some boards have rejected consolidation approaches without exploring their options fully. We are still keen on greater professionalisation of non-executive boards, with higher pay for directors to attract specialist talented individuals with relevant expertise and experience.

Outlook

We believe in a halcyon upland in which the sector in aggregate trades much closer to NAV, or even at a premium. The arrival of LTAFs should not be feared. It highlights the value opportunity that the sector currently offers. Meanwhile a priority must be for new sources of demand to be unearthed.

It is a shame that policymakers have not given more support to a sector that not only channels private sector capital into productive areas of the economy but also democratises access to diversifying and higher-return assets, especially in private markets. Our lobbying efforts continue, and we are fortunate that some determined individuals and organisations continue to push the case for this wonderful 150-year-old sector.

BEN CONWAY *is chief investment officer at Hawksmoor Investment Management and one of the primary movers behind the campaign for reform of the cost disclosure rules.*

GEOPOLITICS AND AI

JAMES CARTHEW, *a director of research firm QuotedData, reviews an extraordinary 12 months of the Trump administration and other global political developments.*

Two global themes, Trump and AI, have dominated markets for the past year. Many commentators, myself included, thought that the impact of a new Trump presidency would be reasonably predictable, a case of extrapolating from the last one, perhaps. However, the period since the US election has become increasingly chaotic.

The American president is aiming to reduce the US trade deficit in goods and bring manufacturing jobs back to US soil, using tariffs as his main policy tool. Having hit the ground running with the imposition of levies on imports from Canada and Mexico, the main event was the so-called 'Liberation Day' on 2 April 2025, when Trump unveiled tariffs on almost all imports. Markets dived and discounts widened: the median discount across the whole London-listed closed-end fund sector spiked to 15.5%. Over the past 15 years, it has only been wider than that in November 2023 and in the panic around Covid in March 2020.

However, Trump blinked after just a few days, the proposed tariff regime was paused and a temporary 10% rate applied instead, helping to create the TACO (Trump Always Chickens Out) meme and a sharp recovery in markets.

There has been a limited impact on inflation so far, but the fear of that is cited as one reason why the US Federal Reserve has been dragging its heels on interest rate cuts. The White House is calling for a change of leadership at the Fed, which has unnerved some investors. That has been compounded by the passing of the One Big Beautiful Bill (OBBB), an amalgam of deregulation and tax cuts, which looks set to lead to rising fiscal deficits. The global bond market is looking queasy, although debt funds have been one of the few parts of the investment companies sector that has been able to grow by issuing new shares this year.

Nervous investors are looking for safer homes for their money. One beneficiary of this has been gold, which has been hitting new highs recently. Unsurprisingly, Golden Prospect Precious Metals (GPM) has been a beneficiary of this and, at the time of writing, is one of the year's best-performing investment companies.

Investors also seem to be wondering whether to diversify away from US markets. The combined market caps of Nvidia, Microsoft, Apple, and Amazon are bigger than the whole of the MSCI Europe index (including the UK). It would not take a lot of switching out of the US leaders to drive a big rally in other stock markets.

We have seen signs of this at work already, with stronger returns from European-focused trusts. Notably, European small-cap stocks have been outperforming large caps, to the benefit of trusts such as JPMorgan European Discovery (JEDT) and The European Smaller Companies Trust (ESCT). Trump's desire for the US to shrink its overseas defence commitments was an important factor in Germany's plan for significantly increased defence and infrastructure spending, which has contributed to an improvement in sentiment towards Europe. However, France is doing its best to undermine this currently with what seems to be a rolling series of political crises, driven by the failure of any parliamentary combination to agree on needed spending cuts.

Trump also hopes to weaken the US dollar, and this is working well, with the US trade-weighted dollar index falling since the start of the year. As tends to be the case, we are already seeing signs of a rally in emerging markets as the dollar falls. In China, lacklustre growth is still a problem, but markets are climbing. In fact, Fidelity China Special Situations is amongst the year's best-performing investment companies. However, India has been going the other way as investors look nervously at valuations. Normally high-flying Ashoka India Equity is languishing at the bottom end of its peer group.

A bump in the AI road

AI mania and the rise of the Magnificent Seven were big stories last year. On 27 January 2025, confidence in this theme took a heavy knock as China's DeepSeek announced a new large language model (LLM) that it claimed had been developed for a fraction of the price of equivalent US models. This triggered a sharp selloff.

However, when investors worked out that the true cost of the DeepSeek model was much higher than indicated and noted that the big tech firms were doubling down on their capital expenditure programmes, confidence began to recover. Manchester & London, which has gone all-in on the AI theme and is operating with a very concentrated portfolio, leads the pack of technology-focused trusts.

Investors in the US have also realised that AI creates huge demand for power. Some of the best-performing US stocks have actually been in the power generation sector, to the benefit of trusts such as Ecofin Global Utilities and Infrastructure. However, in stark contrast, the renewable energy companies have been hit by cuts to long-term forecast power prices, which are weighing on their NAVs. In addition, renewables funds with US exposure have been hit by the unwinding of the hefty incentives that President Biden had put in place for the sector and the Trump administration has now cancelled.

While technology is flying high, the same cannot be said for the healthcare sector. Trump's choice of Robert F. Kennedy Jr to head up the US health department caused consternation, which has proved well-founded as research budgets have been slashed, key agencies gutted, vaccine research halted, and medical studies that disagree with the new orthodoxy suppressed. One of the worst-hit trusts has been Bellevue Healthcare, which has underperformed in a weak sector. The board introduced a zero-discount-control mechanism, but this has only served to shrink the size of the trust dramatically and called into question its ability to survive as an independent entity. In recent months we have seen something of a rally in biotech as cash-rich pharma companies hoover up companies with promising drug pipelines.

Japan's corporate governance revolution has continued to gather pace, to the benefit of the two small-cap trusts (AJOT and NAVF) focused on this area, but the country is also having to adjust to a world of inflation and positive interest rates, as well as renewed political uncertainty.

In the UK, there is disappointment about the way that Labour squandered the upbeat mood in the wake of the election by talking down the economy, publishing a budget that penalised job creation, and coupled this with a removal of tax reliefs on AIM stocks, which hit some small-cap trusts. UK investors are on tenterhooks as 2025's Budget comes around, I think it is still within the government's grasp to rekindle some enthusiasm for UK equities, but I am not overly confident that it will do so.

Generally, the small-cap revival that we have seen in Europe has not been echoed in the UK, although some trusts have done well for stock-specific reasons (often takeover-related). Here, the star performer is Temple Bar, as its value-driven style has paid off for another year, driving it to the top of the performance table. Remarkably, its managers feel that the stocks it holds still look cheap, relative to the rest of the UK market and to equivalents in other markets.

For the investment trust sector, there was more bad news, with the FCA kicking the can down the road on cost disclosure reform, Chancellor Rachel Reeves declining to shake up ISA rules to encourage investment in the UK, and the government failing to promote a greater role for pension funds in the listed private equity sector.

One win we have achieved came in the wake of the Saba attacks on trusts and a realisation that it had singled out trusts with a high proportion of retail investors who tended not to vote at AGMs. Now, after an effective industry campaign, platforms will be compelled to pass on material from companies and to allow investors to vote at meetings.

Saba Capital garnered a lot of headlines, and although its attacks were clumsy, it has scored some successes. Discounts are narrowing as boards have become more proactive. That process has gone further in equity-focused trusts than in alternatives. However, there are still bargains to be had, and it is interesting that the one successful new issue of recent times has been Achilles, an activist trust targeting the alternatives sectors. The main backers of Achilles have already had a fair bit of success in the property sectors. Now we are watching to see if the bids for infrastructure and renewables trusts that we have seen will continue.

Looking forward

The current market landscape does feel a bit like a re-run of the inflation of the last tech bubble in the late 1990s and 2000. However, we may be some way off the peak yet, and I remember well as a fund manager how miserable it felt missing out on the rise.

The managers of the tech-focused trusts believe we are some way off the peak of the AI story. Nevertheless, even they are cautioning that there will be losers as well as winners and that some of the US mega-caps that have been making the running in markets might end up on the losing side of AI.

Regardless of that, my feeling is that with Trump actively destabilising the Fed and the dollar, we may well have seen peak-USA in markets. The ripples of his actions, both domestically and overseas, will continue to be felt in markets and the investment trust sector for months and years to come.

JAMES CARTHEW, *a former fund manager, has been a director of QuotedData since it was founded in 2013. He is a regular contributor to the* Money Makers *podcast.*

POPULAR NO MORE

ANDREW MCHATTIE *explains why alternative asset trusts are down and still facing an uncertain future.*

How quickly things change. Wind the clock back just a few years and alternative asset trusts were all the rage. Money was pouring into new sectors such as infrastructure, renewable energy, specialist property, growth capital, and debt financing. The pace of expansion was blistering, and these novel offerings frequently traded on premium ratings.

Two complementary forces conspired to fuel this rapid growth. On the supply side, investment trusts stepped in to provide finance, filling in the gaps left by a cautious and regulatory-constrained banking sector in the aftermath of the Global Financial Crisis of 2008–09. Just as investment trusts had once funded the railways, industrialisation, post-war reconstruction and new emerging markets overseas, so they were again at the forefront when the energy transition came knocking. At the same time, investors were desperate for yield and searching for higher returns during the prolonged period of near-zero interest rates, completing a virtuous circle of growth.

The first renewable infrastructure trusts arrived in 2013, when four IPOs raised £840m, and growth accelerated rapidly thereafter. By 2019 the stockbroker Winterflood estimated that 37% of all new capital raised by the whole sector was directed into infrastructure, and only one of eight IPOs was traditional in nature. That was the backdrop then.

The changing landscape

Today, the picture could hardly be more different, with money flowing out almost as quickly as it once rushed in. Over the last year the news has been dominated by mergers, takeovers and winding-up petitions, collectively dressed up under the euphemism of 'consolidation'. Put more bluntly, this cyclical contraction has laid waste to the alternative assets sector, with many trusts already delisted and a long list of others now heading the same way.

A 'normalisation' of interest rates lies at the heart of the issue. The Bank of England pulled the plug on the near-zero rate environment at the end of 2021, and both demand and supply dried up rapidly. Five interlinked factors go a long way to explain why we have reached today's messy state. First, most alternative asset trusts investing in infrastructure, property and private equity rely on debt as a key component of the proposition. Without leverage the returns don't really stack up, and with today's higher borrowing costs the numbers look very different. Rising interest expenses have placed considerable strain on many trust structures and covenants, forcing managers to reduce debt by selling assets into weak markets.

Second, the era of easy money encouraged over-issuance, leaving the market oversaturated with too many similar products. Third, in the rush to launch, the quality of assets and management slipped, and some later entrants quickly ran into operational problems. Fourth, rising yields elsewhere – particularly on gilts – prompted investors to reassess whether the risks of alternative assets were justified.

Many concluded they were not, and this fall in demand crucially tipped the ratings of alternative asset investment trusts from premium ratings to sizeable discounts. This is the fifth factor – those wide discounts shut the door on secondary capital issuance, thwarting expansion plans that might otherwise have added greater diversification and scale to fledgling portfolios.

Lack of scale, lack of quality, and lack of diversification are amongst the problems that have dogged the investment trusts sector over the last couple of years, compounded by investor frustration over persistently wide discounts. To understand the extent of the damage, let's take a look at developments in the various sub-sectors.

Sector breakdowns

Starting with infrastructure, BBGI Infrastructure agreed an all-cash takeover in March that valued the trust at just over a billion pounds. Scale was not the issue here, but the depressed market rating was sufficiently attractive for British Columbia Investment Management to offer a 21% uplift to the prior share price. For completely different reasons, DGI9 Infrastructure is in the process of winding up and says it plans to return more capital to shareholders in early 2026, though it seems in no rush to sell its stake in the UK broadcasting infrastructure group Arqiva, whose value seems highly uncertain.

Amongst the renewables there has been a considerable thinning-out. Atrato Onsite Energy, Downing Renewables & Infrastructure, Harmony Energy Income Trust, and Triple Point Energy Transition have all exited. Aquila European Renewables looked to be approaching the end of its asset disposal programme, only to pause when several deals fell through. Unsurprisingly, it is difficult to achieve fair value when the entire market knows you are a forced seller. More shutdowns are in the pipeline, with Aquila Energy Efficiency Trust, Ecofin US Renewables, Hydrogen Capital Growth, and Premier Miton Global Renewables all heading towards the exit.

There has been even more upheaval in real estate, arguably the most sensitive of all parts of the economy to changes in interest rates. Here, trusts have been disappearing at such a pace that it raises serious questions about what will be left standing. A wave of predatory takeovers has seen opportunistic buyers sniffing value in the wide discounts and realising they do not need to pay full asset value to secure a deal.

Amongst the casualties are Balanced Commercial Property Trust, Care REIT, Empiric Student Property, PRS REIT, Tritax EuroBox, Urban Logistics REIT, and Warehouse REIT. That has not been the only route out of town though, and some trusts have opted for managed wind-downs as the best way to realise shareholder value, selling assets on a piecemeal basis. While slower, this approach can make sense for specialist portfolios that are complex or unattractive to a single buyer. Abrdn European Logistics Income, Ground Rents Income Fund, JPMorgan Global Core Real Assets (a mixed portfolio, but heavily weighted to US real estate), Life Science REIT, and Phoenix Spree Deutschland are all heading down this path, at varying speeds.

There is a third escape route for REITs as well, which is to shed the investment company structure, sometimes seen now as more of a burden than a benefit. Supermarket REIT chose to internalise its management and convert into an operating property company, betting this would improve its market rating and restore access to fresh capital. This is a sad indictment of the sector in its present state. The regulatory impasse over trust cost disclosure rules may have played a part in this case.

Something similar happened with the hedge fund Third Point Investors, which left the sector in the late summer to become an operational reinsurance company. It used a change in the listing rules to force through the proposals against the wishes of many shareholders, who were unable to exit at a full or satisfactory price.

Moving on to private equity and growth capital, the calls for change have generally been more subdued. Apax Global Alpha agreed a recommended takeover in June, and Dunedin Enterprise finally closed its doors after a managed wind-down that took more than eight years – a salutary reminder of how protracted the process can be. Crystal Amber Fund has also been in run-off for an extended period, having not made any new investments since 2018. It has one remaining large position in an unquoted medical devices business called Morphic Medical, which it aims to develop further before disposal in line with its policy of maximising value for shareholders. Riverstone Energy is also winding down and has realised most of its assets.

Elsewhere in the growth capital sector, one case strikes a particular note of melancholy. Schroders Capital Global Innovation Trust is the husk of what was once Woodford Patient Capital Trust. In February the shareholders voted for a managed wind-down, finally drawing a line under a vehicle launched in 2015 with huge fanfare and a record £800m raised at IPO.

Finally, there is the debt sector, where there is a plus and a minus for trusts deciding to wind down. On the positive side, most loans are agreed with fixed maturities, creating a natural and predictable run-off of assets and return of capital. The downside, however, is that some maturities stretch many years into the future. Blackstone Loan Financing, which eventually decided to sell the bulk of its remaining assets to a related party at a discount, had previously warned that its wind-down could take several years.

Alpha Real Trust has also delisted, along with Marble Point Loan Financing, while a number of others remain deep into the process. In practice this often means shareholders receive chunks of capital back in several tranches, over time. GCP Asset Backed Income, ICG-Longbow Senior Secured UK Property Debt Investments (in wind-down since early 2021), Riverstone Credit Opportunities Income, RM Infrastructure Income, Starwood European Real Estate Finance (which has already made eight distributions to shareholders), and VPC Specialty Lending Investments are all progressing through their capital realisation programmes.

It is not easy to keep track of all the names, nor to be sure that any list is fully comprehensive, but what is certain is that the shrinkage continues. We are not at the end of the process. While the contraction of these sectors may not feel too draconian at present, they will be considerably smaller once the current round of wind-downs has run its course. Further M&A and corporate activity also seems likely, with many trusts still emphasising the need for greater scale, and with arbitrageur Saba Capital now entering the fray, having taken stakes in SDCL Efficiency Income and Life Science REIT.

Survival of the fittest?

Optimists will argue this has been a necessary spring-clean, leaving the best and strongest trusts to form a core of higher-quality exposure going forward: Darwinism in action. There is some truth in this view, although it is equally clear that not all of the casualties were weak; several high-quality trusts have been swept away as well. Survival to date is no guarantee of superiority, though it does suggest some resilience. Some sub-sectors have also been wiped out completely – think of music royalties, student property, supermarkets, ground rents, European warehouses, hydrogen – and competition has been thinned out in those that remain. The net result is a sharp reduction in choice, and that is rarely a good outcome for investors.

Another feature of periods like this is the rise of certain fallacies, one of the most persistent being that trusts must have at least £500m of assets in order to appeal to wealth managers and to build a sustainable future. In reality there are many smaller trusts that are good performers, on reasonable market ratings, and with a good strategic rationale. AEW UK REIT is a prime example: with less than £170m of assets it has consistently ranked among the top-performing real estate trusts for several years, maintaining a tight discount to net asset value at the same time. It deliberately targets smaller lot sizes, where it can apply its asset management skills to unlock value.

And has this great unwinding of the excesses of alternative asset trusts left behind a core of finely tuned winners trading on strong market ratings? In a word, no – or at least, not yet. At the time of writing, discounts remain wide across most alternative sectors, signalling that more work lies ahead (and perhaps more opportunity). What the contraction has achieved, however, is to focus minds and strip boards of any lingering complacency.

Many trusts have sharpened their strategies, improved shareholder communication, reduced fees, launched buybacks, and sought to broaden their appeal to new investors. Lower interest rates may also provide some relief. But if discounts fail to narrow of their own accord over the next couple of years, there is as yet little reason to expect the current selling pressure to ease.

In sum, the past decade's exuberant expansion of alternative asset trusts has given way to a sobering retrenchment. The 'great unwind' has swept away whole sub-sectors, pared back investor choice, and left even the survivors trading on wide discounts. Yet it has also forced boards and managers to sharpen their focus, improve governance, and re-engage with shareholders. Whether this process ultimately produces a smaller but healthier core of vehicles will depend on execution, investor confidence, and the interest rate environment.

For now, the sector is still in transition – leaner, chastened, and with much to prove before it can win back the premium ratings of the past. And maybe that is too negative a note on which to conclude – it is equally fair to celebrate some excellent alternative asset trusts that have delivered strong returns for shareholders over the last five years. Trusts such as Oakley Capital Investments, CT Private Equity Trust, HgCapital Trust, Fair Oaks Income Fund, Volta Finance, 3i Infrastructure, and AEW UK REIT have kept their end of the bargain, showing that well-managed vehicles with clear strategies can still thrive even in tougher conditions.

ANDREW MCHATTIE *is the editor of the* Investment Trust Newsletter, *available by subscription at www.tipsheets.co.uk or at www.trustlibrary.co.uk.*

INVESTOR FORUM

We asked some of the most experienced professional investment trust investors we know to give their answers to some topical questions.

Who's who?

Alan Brierley is the director of investment company research at Investec and has covered the sector since the early 1990s.

Richard Curling is an investment director at Jupiter Fund Management and manages the Jupiter Fund of Investment Trusts.

Nick Greenwood is a former fund manager of MIGO Opportunities Trust, WS AVI Worldwide Opportunities Fund and Miton Global Opportunities (MGO).

Peter Hewitt is a non-executive director of both the Odyssean Investment Trust and the Association of Investment Companies (AIC).

Alastair Laing is CEO of Capital Gearing Asset Management and a co-manager of Capital Gearing Trust since 2011.

Anthony Leatham has been head of investment trust research at broking firm Peel Hunt since 2015.

Have boards been slow to tackle the issue of persistent discounts?

Alan Brierley: An extended golden age undoubtedly bred complacency by all parties, and the industry was flat-footed as tailwinds brutally reversed, with too many hiding behind the 'buybacks don't work' mantra. Although in mitigation, the macro excesses of the everything bubble, pandemic, and horrors in the Ukraine, along with the transition to a new regime of higher inflation and interest rates created the most brutal of perfect storms. More recently, we have seen much greater proactivity – corporate actions, mergers, buybacks, tender offers – and this is a welcome development.

Richard Curling: Yes – especially in the alternatives sector. Saba's activity has certainly acted as a wake-up call for equity investment companies and seems to have been a catalyst for a much more shareholder value approach.

Nick Greenwood: I think many in the sector have taken the view that investment trusts always trade at a discount and therefore were slow to see the threat to a number of trusts.

Peter Hewitt: Yes. Many investment companies have and are buying back shares which is a positive, but to really influence a discount the quantum needs to be much higher. Each trust is in a different situation, and a close analysis of the share register is needed to ascertain what is the optimal approach. Sometimes it could be that a tender or some other mechanism is best, however, generally share buybacks need to be much greater to have an influence.

Alastair Laing: Yes. However, activity has picked up recently, and the issue is being taken more seriously. Saba's intervention in the market was certainly a driver of that, adding a level of fear in the boardroom on top of the pre-existing general concern.

Anthony Leatham: Looking at the last few years, we have seen record buyback activity, and we believe that boards have generally been on the front foot when it comes to discount control. When we think about discounts, there are several factors to consider. Shareholders can often point to buybacks as the default option for discount control, but sometimes the decision is not as clear cut for a board. Factors that we look at when considering the most effective discount control mechanism include: the peer group average discount and the mean reversion capacity; a trust's shareholder register; the size and liquidity of a trust; the competition for capital and the investment rationale for buybacks; the gearing position; and whether there are other forms of capital allocation that could help to narrow a discount. We have also seen a number of mechanisms introduced which include a performance trigger or a continuation vote component.

Did Saba Capital deserve the criticism they got?

Alan Brierley: Saba's initial salvo was an egregious, ham-fisted and opportunistic attack which seemingly galvanised the entire industry against it. Although we were highly critical of the initial attack, their actions also sent a powerful wake-up call which has been a catalyst for an acceleration in corporate actions, and the industry should emerge stronger as a result. We believe that activist investors have an important role to play in the evolution of the industry.

Richard Curling: I think Saba's approach was surprising in many ways and certainly could have been pursued in a more sensitive way, which I suspect would have yielded more favourable results for them, but their activity has also had a positive impact for all shareholders because discounts have narrowed.

Nick Greenwood: There is nothing wrong with building a big position in a trust languishing at a wide discount and using this stake to force a return of capital much closer to NAV. It was irritating to hear Saba claiming that their actions were altruistic, and trying to become managers of the trusts they were targeting was poorly thought out given these had very different mandates compared to what was proposed. They also seemed to know surprisingly little about the trusts that they were attacking.

Peter Hewitt: Yes, most definitely. Their proposals were self-serving and principally were to benefit Saba.

Alastair Laing: Saba was the wrong answer to the right question. They were right to highlight the issue of persistent discounts; however, the solutions they proposed were too self-serving.

Were boards to blame for allowing Saba to build its stakes?

Alan Brierley: Initially yes, as Saba was able to start building meaningful positions on relatively wide discounts. The market was well aware this was happening given RNS announcements and register moves.

Richard Curling: I think many boards were slow to realise what was happening and their lack of focus on discount management gave Saba the opportunity to build their stakes.

Peter Hewitt: Yes, they should take the responsibility for Saba taking the stakes they did. To be fair, no one really realised their intentions until it was too late. However, it is a key role for the board, in conjunction with the manager, to manage the discount.

Alastair Laing: Each company had its own specific circumstances, and some had limited options to control their discounts. However, for many targets, the company could have been buying back its own shares rather than allowing Saba to build its stake.

What in your experience are the best methods to tackle discounts?

Alan Brierley: Discounts are a feature of the closed-end structure but more needs to be done to maintain them on a relatively low level and to dampen volatility. Ultimately performance is key, but tools include active buyback programs and conditional tender offers. We have now entered a new era for discount management and moving forward we believe that boards should review buyback parameters, both in terms of quantum and levels.

Richard Curling: Ultimately investment performance is the best way to reduce discounts, but beyond that clearly stated DCM policies followed through by boards (which too often in the past has not happened) is probably the best approach.

Nick Greenwood: Keeping an eye on the state of the market in a trust's shares.

Often a discount can be triggered by a relatively small number of shares that overhang the market. If these are bought in then the balance of supply and demand is brought back into equilibrium, and the shares can trade closer to net asset value. Should oversupply be persistent then the board should continue to buy back. Whilst this will shrink the trust, trading close to par gives hope that the trust can, in the future, issue again when its mandate comes back into favour. Buyback policies are not a solution in isolation. Plenty of shoe leather needs to be spent promoting the trust to create buyers.

Peter Hewitt: To really influence a discount a significant and consistent buyback is often needed to tighten the discount. That, however, is only part of the answer. Seeking to stimulate demand for the shares is key, and that requires a carefully thought-out marketing and communications strategy. Not enough trusts do both.

Alastair Laing: For companies with liquid underlying portfolios, we believe active discount- and premium-control policies should be widely adopted. These involve vigorous share buybacks or issuances if the share price moves 1–2% either side of NAV. For companies with illiquid underlying holdings, there should either be fixed-life vehicles or periodic tenders, with the expectation that structures will move into a managed wind-down if a large portion of shareholders vote to tender.

Anthony Leatham: A consistent and transparent approach. We have analysed buybacks and note that those trusts that were in the market buying back their own shares most frequently had a better chance of reducing discount volatility. The most robust mechanisms can include an annual redemption facility or a fixed life. We also note that some of the more recent discount triggered, or performance triggered, tender offers have been effective – providing the tender offer is generous enough and the timeframe or measurement period reasonable. A continuation vote is a clear line in the sand, but is not always a catalyst for discount narrowing. A manufactured or enhanced dividend can help to drive incremental buying demand, but this has had mixed results.

Has the trend of declining fees reached its limit?

Alan Brierley: Although significant progress has been made in reducing fees in recent years, given the growth in passive funds and now active-ETFs, we expect pressure to remain on fees. Some companies are still behind the curve in reducing fees.

Richard Curling: No – fees are continuing to fall across the investment industry and investment companies must remain competitive and relevant. Boards have a duty to drive down costs wherever possible.

Nick Greenwood: Expense ratios will continue to be a point of obsession for the market. Very big funds needed by the massive wealth management chains are too large to add much from a management point of view, so one way that they can stand out from the crowd is costs. Many investment trusts have little choice but to bend to this pressure.

Peter Hewitt: Certainly, I hope so with regard to funds investing in mainly listed equities. With alternatives you have to look on a case-by-case basis. Private equity is the sector where overall fees could be lower.

Alastair Laing: No, although the rate of fee decline is likely to slow. Investment companies are relatively expensive structures with certain minimum costs – such as governance, listing, and administration fees – that can only be reduced with scale. However, ETFs remain formidable competitors to investment trusts and will continue to exert downward pressure on costs. Investment managers will resist reductions until pushed very hard, but over time the direction of travel is clear for all but the most differentiated products.

Anthony Leatham: The fee debate can be an unhelpful distraction, and it has cast a shadow over the trust universe and caused buyers of trusts to hesitate. Investors have benefitted from strong NAV and share price total returns from trusts, net of fees, and we see plenty of scope for this to continue. We also need to ensure that the best managers in the industry continue to want to manage investment trusts and if the fees fall too low, the incentive might disappear with it. If we sort the trusts on our datasheet by ongoing charges figure (OCF) and take the top 20 cheapest trusts, the average OCF is 0.46%.

What is the biggest threat to the sector's survival?

Alan Brierley: An unsuccessful resolution of a flawed cost disclosure regime and the seemingly inexorable rise of passive investments.

Richard Curling: The biggest threat to the sector is that we do not remain relevant and competitive with our investment propositions. The rise of Active ETFs and LTAFs amongst others mean the sector must remain on its toes.

Nick Greenwood: Regulation – the drive is for standardisation, and investment trusts are a purely British phenomenon that don't fit global distribution models. They are not understood by many at the FCA, and the regulator's actions might herald extinction for a structure which has survived two world wars. Closed-end funds in investment terms are superior vehicles given they protect their managers from inflows and outflows, allowing them to make longer-term decisions and invest in less-liquid stocks. Neither have helped in recent years, where performance has been driven by a few big stocks, but a new phase will show investment trusts in the best possible light.

Peter Hewitt: Persistently wide discounts are a major threat. Retreat of major private wealth is another – they have become legacy holders at best.

Alastair Laing: In my opinion, there is no real threat to the sector's survival. Investment companies have been around for 150 years and will almost certainly be around for another 150. The sector has a long history of adapting and innovating, which has allowed it to thrive.

Anthony Leatham: We have seen a shift in buying demand for trusts, with a number of typical market participants reaching a level of AUM that requires large trusts with robust liquidity. Other trust buyers such as multi-asset funds have been experiencing redemption pressures. Some firms have been changing their approach to asset allocation and portfolio construction, which can impact the use of trusts. In some cases, this increases the reliance of trusts on the retail component of a shareholder register, and we have seen the retail platforms become an increasingly important source of demand. The challenge is going to be ensuring that investment trusts are handed down from one generation of investors to another and that the benefits of the closed-ended structure are not overlooked.

What are you thoughts on enhanced dividend policy?

Nick Greenwood: I'm not a fan – it's often handing shareholders their capital back as taxable income.

Peter Hewitt: Yes, it can work and highlights the flexibility of the investment company structure. However, you can also go too high, so the capital of the trust is eroded. Somewhere in the 4–6% range is sensible. There is clearly a demand from retail shareholders on the platforms, and it can bring some trusts who invest in low-yielding areas a new audience. It is not a panacea and can not make up for poor performance.

Alastair Laing: I struggle to see the purpose of creating income out of capital. Each shareholder can sell whatever portion of their capital they need to convert into 'income' at any time. That said, I cannot deny that certain shareholders value the certainty of income, and if the shares are held within a tax-sheltered account (such as a pension or ISA), then there is no tax downside.

Anthony Leatham: This is still a marmite decision – some investors love enhanced dividends, others hate them, and tax considerations can often play an important role in this. As we see more examples of enhanced dividend policies, there is a growing recognition that a more noticeable yield can lead to a larger addressable market of buyers. In certain cases, we have seen enhanced dividends offer portfolio managers more flexibility in their stock selection and portfolio construction. Examples include Asian equities, where a pure income investor could be constrained to certain markets or sectors for dividend income, or in healthcare the opportunity set can be much greater for a manager, if they are not wedded to the highest yielding stocks in the sector.

What is the future of alternatives as a group?

Alan Brierley: There is a clear supply/demand imbalance in the alternatives sector, with this problem most prevalent in the renewables sub-sector where there are too many sub-scale companies trading at wide discounts. In the absence of bids, we think mergers represent a way forward as larger, combined portfolios would provide greater flexibility to dispose of assets and return capital to shareholders over time and/or help position the company for future growth. Further, benefits of scale often lead to lower fees and reduced ongoing charges, which has become a key consideration for shareholders. However, boards need to drive these transactions and be prepared to accept the need for holistic change.

Richard Curling: I think alternatives have a bright future within the investment company sector, although they have been out of favour in the past few years since interest rates started rising. Investment companies are the ideal vehicle to provide ordinary investors access to illiquid assets.

Nick Greenwood: Probably quite bright once a period of consolidation, removing some of the weaker players, is out of the way. There is money to be made during this process.

Peter Hewitt: They do have a future although they will shrink quite a bit due to persistently wide discounts, which eventually leads to corporate activity. Renewables have been especially disappointing. Long term, private equity trusts have been good investments, though very wide discounts may lead to corporate activity here also.

Alastair Laing: As a group, the future must be bright. There is strong demand for certain classes of illiquid alternative assets, and well-governed investment trusts are an excellent structure to facilitate this. That said, many existing alternative funds are unlikely to survive in their current form.

Anthony Leatham: 'Alternatives' captures so many asset classes that it is hard to generalise, but we think they continue to play an important role for investors. We see very attractive long-term IRRs available for core, core-plus and renewable infrastructure trusts, particularly at these wide discount levels. In addition, when we look at the yields on offer, we see a significant yield premium over gilts, and we see this as attractive particularly as many of the portfolios benefit from inflation-linkage and fully covered dividends.

What are the longer-term implications of wealth manager consolidation?

Richard Curling: Wealth manager consolidation has led to bigger firms who want bigger, more liquid trusts; but at the same time, it has also led to the rise of several smaller spin-off firms who may like smaller, more nimble trusts.

Nick Greenwood: I think that the longer-term implications have already arrived. The larger chains cannot buy most trusts as the tickets they need to write to move the needle are just so large. A lot of shares will need to find new homes to avoid discounts widening again.

Peter Hewitt: As I said earlier, the larger groups are quasi-institutions and for them liquidity is a key issue. Cost disclosure does not help either. They are no longer the marginal new buyer. Having said that, they will not all rush for the door and will remain a key audience for a long time.

Alastair Laing: As wealth managers have consolidated, they have increasingly focused on the most liquid fund structures rather than investment trusts. This trend is likely to continue. However, investment trusts still appeal to self-directed retail investors, who are becoming a larger share of the market.

Anthony Leatham: The consolidation of wealth managers and the growth in assets under management at these firms, is likely to impact how they invest and what fund structures they utilise. Therefore, scale matters and liquidity is an important consideration. We also note that wealth manager consolidation has also give rise to smaller, more nimble wealth businesses building up their headcount and their client base. This may be a welcome development for the investment trust sector as these smaller firms can have a less constrained approach to investing and potentially offer greater discretion over investment selection and deployment.

Do trusts use enough gearing (one of the advantages of the trust structure) in practice?

Alan Brierley: Far too many companies have been too conservative in terms of their use of gearing, a key competitive advantage, and this is disappointing. As we have consistently said for more than a decade, if you act like an open-ended fund, then why not become one?

Richard Curling: Gearing works both ways, and boards need to be cautious about too much gearing. Having said that, there was a wonderful opportunity when interest rates were very low to lock in long-term cheap debt (which several trusts took advantage of).

Nick Greenwood: I don't think you can generalise on this one, but the ability to borrow is one of the reasons why trusts are superior investment vehicles.

Peter Hewitt: Yes. Quite a number took out long-term, low-cost debt during the era of very low-cost interest rates and will benefit accordingly over the years in terms of performance. Some have too much debt, e.g., certain alternatives.

Alastair Laing: Almost certainly. One of the main attractions of gearing is that interest payments are tax deductible, providing a tax shield. However, most investment trusts do not pay corporation tax, so gearing simply introduces greater volatility without that benefit. We believe trusts would be better served by focusing on more rigorous discount controls rather than introducing gearing, which can often make discount management more complicated at exactly the time it is most needed.

Anthony Leatham: Gearing is an important feature of the investment trust structure and can be used in a variety of ways, ranging from a revolving credit facility that acts like an overdraft, or longer-term debt that provides structural gearing. Some strategies involve debt finance as a matter of course; others deploy it more tactically. The cost of debt is an important consideration, particularly around strategic capital allocation decisions, so too the contribution to risk and beta of the portfolio. Across the conventional equity trusts, the average level of net gearing is 6%. As investment trust managers and boards are challenged by shareholders on maximising their use of the closed-end structure, the topic of gearing is a common feature in these conversations.

Has the FCA got a problem with investment trusts? If so how can we improve the relationship?

Richard Curling: All investment trusts want is a level playing field – so that they are treated fairly compared with other investment vehicles.

Nick Greenwood: I have touched on this already. I don't think the FCA realises there is a problem. Given the enormous staff turnover at the regulator, I have little confidence that the organisation can attract employees of the quality to recognise the attractions of closed-end funds.

Peter Hewitt: I don't think the FCA is anti investment trusts, but I am not convinced they understand them and where they fit in the retail shareholder landscape. It feels like they operate in a silo, unsure if trusts are investment products or listed companies. Of course, they are both, which may be why they appear to have such difficulty with them. The AIC is doing its best to improve the relationship and improve their understanding of investment trusts.

Alastair Laing: The FCA has a very complicated job. However, there does seem to be a lack of understanding about the fundamental differences between operating and investment companies.

What do boards need to do to keep the sector from shrinking?

Alan Brierley: In an increasingly competitive world, boards must ensure investment companies are differentiated, fit-for-purpose and relevant. This includes using all the tools in the toolkit, most notably gearing.

Richard Curling: Shrinking is not necessarily bad if the quality of the investment proposition is improving.

Nick Greenwood: The sector faces a perfect storm. Cost disclosure, activism, oversupply from the 2021 new issue boom and wealth manager consolidation combined means that shrinkage is inevitable and to some extent healthy.

Peter Hewitt: Keep governance standards high and discounts narrow. Marketing and communication via a variety of different routes needs to be at a higher level. The goal being to improve understanding of trusts and to stimulate demand from retail shareholders.

Alastair Laing: It is not a board's job to worry about the sector shrinking, or even their own company shrinking, if that reflects the wishes of their shareholders. Their sole focus should be on delivering the best outcomes for stakeholders, which in the case of an investment company essentially means the shareholders. Sector growth should not be an objective, but it will be the natural outcome of effective investment management and good governance.

Anthony Leatham: Boards need to ensure that their companies continue to offer relevance and value-add to the shareholders. Whilst outperformance will do a lot of the heavy lifting, we think the promotion of investment trusts is an ongoing process, whereby trusts need to find innovative and engaging ways to promote themselves and expand their shareholder base. In addition, justifying the use of the closed-end structure will also help to increase longevity. In addition, boards do need to keep an open mind when it comes to future-proofing their strategies, and this can sometimes mean engaging with the concept of mergers and other corporate actions.

What do boards need to do to improve retail participation?

Alan Brierley: Product, performance and promotion.

Richard Curling: This is a difficult challenge, but I suspect better communication, PR and use of influencers amongst others will be important.

Nick Greenwood: It will be hard, but speaking at retail-focussed conferences such as Mello, coverage in platforms' literature such as that produced by AJ Bell and fostering a good relationship with the magazines that are read by self-directed investors such as MoneyWeek would be a start. Reducing discount volatility would also be helpful as retail investors do not respond well to sudden and erratic moves in share prices.

Peter Hewitt: It's all about communication and marketing – particularly via new avenues: digital, internet, etc.

Alastair Laing: It is not clear to me that boards are the central players in improving retail participation. Ultimately, retail platforms provide investment access, and investment managers are typically responsible for marketing the funds. Boards should maintain an open dialogue with these parties; however, governance is an independent function from market development.

Anthony Leatham: This is clearly an agenda item for a lot of investment trust boards. Understanding the end retail investor can help to hone the messaging and the promotional material that goes with a trust. Capturing the investor's attention and positioning a strategy as an investment solution that can add value or solve a financial need is critical. We would also point to market intelligence as being helpful in this targeting – knowing the buyer profile, working with retail platforms to make the investment journey seamless and efficient spend of marketing budget through the most effective channels.

Which trusts have impressed you most this year?

Alan Brierley: HVPE – having been critical of a lacklustre approach to capital allocation, we were impressed by more decisive action taken at the start of the year, including increasing the allocation to the distribution pool from 15% to 30% of gross distributions.

Richard Curling: It is nice to see the growth capital sector doing better this year with discount narrowing and better news on valuations.

Nick Greenwood: Georgia Capital. They reacted to a political crisis which triggered a substantial widening of their discount by aggressively buying back and shrinking the trust materially. Their hands-on management of their assets has been highly successful.

Peter Hewitt: Over the last year (to 9 September) the two big technology specialists have once again performed the best – PCT +46 and ATT +45 NAV total return respectively. However, I would credit Scottish Mortgage with +42 as having done well and recovered strongly from the depths of 2022–23 when there were worries over gearing and the private company exposure. Having said that, I think the best in terms of outperforming its benchmark due to stock selection may well be Temple Bar at +28 NAV and share price +38. Not bad given what it invests in.

Alastair Laing: Temple Bar Investment Trust plc – two deeply out-of-fashion areas are the UK stock market and value investing. Temple Bar stuck to its knitting by remaining focused on these areas and has been richly rewarded over the past year. Also Polar Capital Financials Trust plc – there are very few fixed-life investment trusts remaining, but this is a great example of a sector-focused vehicle that delivered very strong performance over the past year. This allowed it both to return capital to those who wanted it and to continue the vehicle for another five years. A clear case of strong investment management combined with strong governance.

Anthony Leatham: We have been particularly impressed with the resilience of private equity strategies – most notably HarbourVest Global Private Equity (HVPE) which has not only delivered robust performance through a difficult and volatile period but also shown thought leadership through its capital allocation policy. In the multi-asset/flexible sector, we have been impressed by Caledonia Investments (CLDN) which has delivered the best performance in the sector (13% five-year annualised NAV TR) and has had some eye-catching and accretive exits from the private capital pool. We have been impressed by the outperformance generated by some unconstrained equity income strategies such as Law Debenture (LWDB) and CC Japan Income & Growth (CCJI). Country specialists have also stood out to us, most notably the differentiated investment approach from Ashoka India Equity (AIE) and the performance of Vietnam Enterprise Investments (VEIL). In alternatives, we have been impressed by Cordiant Digital Infrastructure (CORD) and the recovery from Gresham House Energy Storage (GRID).

Which have disappointed you most?

Richard Curling: Third Point Investors' board would have done a better job on governance performance if they had offered investors a full exit when their mandate changed. The renewable infrastructure companies have disappointed and seem to have failed to find support despite their high yields amidst an array of potential investor worries.

Nick Greenwood: I won't name and shame, but it has become clear that a number of infrastructure and renewable trusts launched during the boom were actually managed by financial people rather than sector specialists, which meant they were ill-equipped to face the inevitable challenges when they arrived.

Peter Hewitt: Definitely the renewables, where NAVs are down by single digits and share prices by 15–20%. There is continual underperformance in that area. Also, healthcare trusts have performed poorly, all recording NAV falls.

Alastair Laing: European Opportunities Trust plc – a series of missteps has caused this vehicle to dramatically lag the market for years. It famously invested heavily in Wirecard AG, a high-profile fraud. It also held a very large position in Novo Nordisk A/S, which has suffered a sharp derating over the past year. High conviction investing always carries the risk that a manager falls in love with their stocks; in this case, it has happened too often, raising real concerns about exit discipline. It may be time for this vehicle to return capital to investors. Also NextEnergy Solar Fund Limited – this trust, which holds solar power generation projects, has struggled with poor performance, wide discounts, and a very complex capital structure. Its attempts to sell assets have been limited, and recent discussions around a potential combination with Foresight Solar Fund ended in failure. Shortly thereafter, the chair resigned, with limited explanation provided.

Anthony Leatham: Sectors such as healthcare have had a tough time and the most notable within that peer group has been Bellevue Healthcare Trust (BBH). Some of the smaller, regionally focussed renewables trusts have been disappointing, including names such as Ecofin US Renewables Infrastructure (RNEW), Aquila European Renewables (AERI) and US Solar Fund (USF).

Positives and negatives about the outlook for the trust sector?

Richard Curling: The Darwinian process of weeding out weaker trusts is undoubtedly good as is the increased focus on shareholder value. The sector needs to focus on ensuring that investment propositions are relevant, focused and good value with costs remaining an important issue.

Nick Greenwood: I have already discussed many of the negatives – the positive is that investment trusts have always evolved to adapt to the environment they have found themselves in. The betting money must be on this happening again despite the current challenges.

Peter Hewitt: Discounts offer great value. If mid and small caps relatively outperform then so will trust managers. Further consolidation is no bad thing, and neither are boards changing managers if performance is poor. On the downside is the question of where the new buyers are if large private wealth is reducing exposure to the sector. Further activism is not necessarily a negative, but I would be loath to see Saba succeed. Finally, I fear the whole issue of cost disclosure is some way from being resolved.

Alastair Laing: The investment trust sector has faced a challenging few years due to widening discounts and a structural underweight to large US technology stocks. However, we believe these headwinds will turn into tailwinds over the next decade. Consolidation and the natural rebalancing of share registers should help discounts to narrow. After many years of relative underperformance, we believe the UK, Europe and small-cap stocks are well positioned to outperform. Markets always swing back and forth, and when the trust sector has its moment in the sun, many of the other issues it faces will fall down the list of investor concerns in the face of strong relative performance.

Anthony Leatham: It may have gone largely unnoticed, given how bearish some of the commentary has been around the UK political, economic and market backdrop, but the investment trust sector has had a strong 12-months period. If we look at the conventional equity trusts, the 12-month average share price total return has been 16% across the c.170 names on our datasheet. This has outperformed the FTSE All-Share TR of 14% over the same period. Discounts across the conventional equity trusts have also narrowed noticeably. In terms of income, the yields have been competitive, and the dividend track records have been extended such that we now have 20 trusts that have delivered 20 years or more of consecutive annual dividend increases. We are also encouraged by trusts seeking to maximise the use of the structure through active use of gearing, revenue reserves, small caps and access to private companies. On the negative side, the volatility in gilts and the macro uncertainty has taken its toll on alternatives – particularly infrastructure – but as rates fall, we could see a recovery here too.

Any ideas on what styles/sector/markets might do well over the next three to five years?

Alan Brierley: A generation of investors have only experienced US exceptionalism, and material underperformance by the UK, Europe, Japan and emerging markets. One day this will change, and these headwinds may reverse or at least subside, and there is undoubted value here for the contrarian investor.

Richard Curling: I am a believer in mean reversion, and so those sectors that have been out of favour may be due a run (e.g., healthcare and biotech). I think the US market is very expensive, and history would suggest future returns from this level may be better elsewhere – particularly if the US dollar remains weak. Japan, emerging markets and even the perennially cheap UK (especially small caps) should perform relatively well.

Nick Greenwood: The dominance of a handful of US tech stocks must break down at some point, which will trigger turmoil as investors stampede once they realise how exposed they are with closet tracking portfolios. Old school active managers will have their moment in the sun. For now, momentum is the name of the game and bubbles always get bigger than you would believe before they burst. Nevertheless, it is wise to place bets now on stock pickers such as Lowland and Diverse Income. Seraphim Space, which is a play on defence spending, should (sadly) do well given the geopolitical environment.

Peter Hewitt: Secular growth trusts: PCT, ATT and SMT. Any portfolio should have these as core positions. Private equity – wide discounts and NAV growth potential: Oakley Capital and HG Capital. UK equity trusts run by proven stock-pickers: Fidelity Special Values, Temple Bar, JPMorgan UK Smaller Growth & Income, and Odyssean Investment Trust.

Anthony Leatham: We are seeing value and recovery potential in the private equity sectors, across fund of funds, direct and growth capital, driven by a pickup in transaction activity, broader market support for private equity both in the UK and the US and improved transparency around capital allocation policies. Here we would highlight HarbourVest Global Private Equity (HVPE), Oakley Capital Investments (OCI), Augmentum Fintech (AUGM) and Chrysalis Investments (CHRY). In listed equities, we have a positive outlook on Japan and Emerging Markets – here we would highlight CC Japan Income & Growth (CCJI), Nippon Active Value Fund (NAVF), and BlackRock Frontiers (BRFI). We also like the recovery story in the UK market and prefer a small- and mid-cap bias – here we would combine Fidelity Special Values (FSV), Mercantile (MRC) and Aberforth Smaller Companies (ASL). In alternatives, everything looks cheap but we see a recovery playing out across renewable infrastructure funds Octopus Renewables Infrastructure Trust (ORIT) and Gresham House Energy Storage (GRID), and in core-plus infrastructure we are positive on the outlook for Cordiant Digital Infrastructure (CORD).

STAY INFORMED

For market commentary, performance data, in-depth trust profiles and weekly links to all the latest investment trust news, please check out the Money Makers Circle, our regular subscription newsletter (See www.money-makers.co for how to subscribe).

CHAIRS FORUM

We also asked four highly experienced investment trust chairs to give their answers to the same topical questions.

Who's who?

Michael Balfour is chairman of Smithson (SSON) and Fidelity China Special Situations (FCSS).

Rachel Beagles is chairwoman of Mercantile (MRC) and a non-executive director of Alliance Witan (ALW).

Arthur Copple is chairman of Montanaro UK Smaller Companies (MUT) and a former chairman of Temple Bar (TMPL).

Neil Rogan is chairman of Invesco Asia Dragon (IAD) and Baillie Gifford UK Growth (BGUK).

Have boards been slow to tackle the issue of persistent discounts?

Michael Balfour: Probably. It's a cyclical thing. Discounts were artificially low while interest rates were artificially low, they then became artificially high as markets adjusted. Having said that, there is probably no one silver bullet that can reduce discounts for individual trusts quickly.

Rachel Beagles: Managing discounts is an art, not a science. But it's fair to say that Saba's attack on the sector late last year has changed boards' mindsets on what an acceptable level of discount is. Also there should not, in normal market conditions, be a significant disconnect between NAV performance and share price performance.

Arthur Copple: Boards' reactions to persistently wide discounts have varied across the sector; some have been very proactive in addressing the issue, others less so. I don't think you can generalise. Each trust's situation is different.

Neil Rogan: Some boards have been slower than others, but even the slow ones have now acted where they can.

Did Saba Capital deserve the criticism they got?

Michael Balfour: Their actions are healthy for the sector in the medium term. Their tactics the first time around weren't particularly smart, but they seem to be more subtle the second time around. I suspect they are keener to do things behind the scenes than they were.

Rachel Beagles: Shareholders may have supported a more traditional activist attempt to close discounts and improve performance at some of the companies that were targeted. But by trying to remove the independent boards, installing their own representatives on those boards and floating the idea of taking over the management contracts themselves, Saba looked to be putting its own interests above those of other shareholders. It lost the moral high ground and the ear of other shareholders at that point. In the aftermath, I think all boards are keeping much closer eyes on their share registers, their discounts, and ensuring that they are in tune with the views of their shareholders as a whole.

Arthur Copple: Saba was acting in the interests of its investors. That is what the managers are paid to do. They could perhaps have gone about it in a more politic way.

Neil Rogan: In some cases yes, for example they didn't seem to appreciate that UK investment trusts have fully independent boards. But for tackling persistently wide discounts, I think if they hadn't done it somebody else would have.

Were boards to blame for allowing Saba to build its stakes?

Michael Balfour: Easier said than done. We are quoted companies – anyone can buy or sell!

Rachel Beagles: Boards can't stop any organisation or individual buying shares should they want to. But the lessons learned are that if boards allow shares to trade at excessive discounts they may attract opportunistic investors who may have different time horizons and objectives to others. Balancing those objectives after the event may not be easy without shrinking the company and reducing liquidity for remaining shareholders.

Arthur Copple: It is difficult for boards to influence who buys or sells their company's shares. Possibly some could have been more proactive in narrowing the discount through buybacks.

Neil Rogan: Blame the high discounts rather than the boards.

What in your experience are the best methods to tackle discounts?

Michael Balfour: Combine good governance with good performance. You should consistently apply buyback policies in good times and bad and then the market can have confidence that you'll always be there. Having good performance in a market that is in favour also helps! A year ago, China was seen as uninvestable. Fidelity China bought back a ton of stock over a prolonged period of time. Now it trades happily around 7% with a very occasional buyback.

Rachel Beagles: It depends on the investment trust, the liquidity profile of its investments, the shape of its shareholder register and their time horizons. Assuming that the investment proposition is compelling, and performance is good, consistent buybacks over time can assist in closing the discount. But that can take a long time, and quite a bit of share capital. Some trusts don't have that luxury. A well-resourced marketing program and sales activities can help support demand too.

Arthur Copple: Make every effort to ensure the shares of your investment trust are in the hands of investors who want to retain that exposure for the long term.

Neil Rogan: In my mind there are two aspects to an investment trust. One is the investment case, the proposition and the people, process and performance that the manager displays. The second is the corporate proposition which is the sum of all the levers that a board can pull to make their trust more attractive to investors. It would include discount policy, dividend policy, gearing, marketing etc. To retain an attractive rating an investment trust has to strive to have a strong investment case and a strong corporate proposition at the same time.

Has the trend of declining fees reached its limit?

Michael Balfour: I don't think so. There are fewer trusts around, but those that have grown should charge less (relative to the value of assets). Also AI should reduce costs at investment managers which should be passed on.

Rachel Beagles: In recent years, active management overall has provided disappointing returns relative to cheaper passive peers. Until this changes, it's likely that fee pressure will continue. Managers who have proven long-term track records should be able to buck this trend to some extent, but fees are certainly not going up!

Arthur Copple: I suspect the downward pressure on fees still has some way to go.

Neil Rogan: No, I don't think so. I think the trend of gradually declining charges will continue. A speed of one basis point per year is entirely reasonable to expect.

What is the biggest threat to the sector's survival?

Michael Balfour: Performance and relevance. Active managers must outperform over the longer term. If they don't, there are plenty of alternatives, some of which are a lot cheaper. Does the mandate address a longer-term need? If no one wants to be invested in China, commercial property or global small- or mid-cap stocks, then give shareholders their money back.

Rachel Beagles: Focusing on my own trust rather than the sector as a whole, the concept of US exceptionalism has, for a number of years, marginalised other markets, including the UK. Should this continue, eventually investment choice becomes constrained due to de-equitisation. However, recent developments in the US look to be causing global investors to pause for thought on this, and the investment opportunities within the UK market are currently stronger for exceedingly low starting valuations.

Arthur Copple: Continuing negativity about the asset class and the management style.

Neil Rogan: Ultimately it's performance and the discount.

What are you thoughts on enhanced dividend policy?

Michael Balfour: Smoke and mirrors – but it seems to work, sometimes!

Arthur Copple: My trust operates an enhanced dividend policy, which I strongly believe has contributed to a growing participation in the shares from self-directed individual investors. These are the natural buyers of investment trust shares.

Rachel Beagles: These made sense when interest rates were very low. However, with many gilt yields in excess of 4%, income is a more competitive space and enhanced yields have to be very high to attract attention. This limits real capital returns to shareholders over time. Also, those companies which have agreed to pay out a fixed and high percentage NAV are likely, in a market downturn, to announce cut dividends which in difficult market conditions may put pressure on their ratings.

Neil Rogan: In my experience, it's controversial before you do it, but shareholders have been universally positive afterwards. I think it does showcase a key benefit of the investment trust structure: you can provide a good income from a portfolio while the fund managers retain their flexibility to invest in a lower-income strategy such as Asia or growth. It's popular with retail shareholders for the income uplift and it's popular with many of the corporate investors because it's effectively a return of capital at NAV.

What is the best size/composition for a board?

Michael Balfour: Depends on size but typically five members with a mix of skills, experiences, and age.

Rachel Beagles: What's important is that boards have the right range of skills and experience represented for the company, its business strategy and the complexity of its asset class or business model. From my experience, somewhere between five and seven is ideal – but you really have to look at it on a company-specific basis.

Arthur Copple: It very much depends upon the size and complexity of the trust.

A very simple listed equity trust could be effective with a board of three directors, especially if it is of modest size. A large trust with a complicated investment strategy might need five or even six directors. It's hard to envisage a situation where a trust would need more than that.

Neil Rogan: Four to six members. Below four is too few for the responsibilities of the board. Above six on a permanent basis makes it harder to be effective. One or two investment people, an accountant, a lawyer, an investment trust expert and a wildcard would be my recommended formation, plus a diversity of thought and background.

What are the longer-term implications of wealth manager consolidation?

Michael Balfour: Not great for their clients!

Rachel Beagles: It's likely to continue to drive sector consolidation, given the focus on costs and liquidity of this shareholder cohort. The relative winners in the sector will be those which have scale, competitive OCRs and a strong investment proposition, which stands up to competition from other more liquid investment collectives such as OEICs and ETFs. In addition, boards will rightly look to direct retail investors as a source of incremental demand.

Arthur Copple: I think it's almost inevitable that UK wealth managers will continue to reduce their participation in the sector. Very few trusts can offer the liquidity now required by them. In addition, they have massively increased their in-house fund management capabilities, which negates their need for outside management.

Neil Rogan: With their centralised buy lists, the bigger trusts will benefit if they have good enough people, process and performance to win a place on those lists. It's as simple as that.

Do trusts use enough gearing (one of the advantages of the trust structure) in practice?

Michael Balfour: No. If you do the arithmetic, having gearing of 4–5% makes very little difference to NAV total return. If you've got 15–20% it can really have an impact. You've got to have strategic commitment to having a high level of gearing. Don't try and time the market. If you can get debt at a reasonable price the equity risk premium should bring long-term rewards.

Rachel Beagles: This is a huge benefit of the structure and over the cycle should augment returns. Heightened levels of volatility, and increased cost of short-term gearing has perhaps put boards off from using it more recently. A number of trusts, including The Mercantile, issued fixed-rate debt at low rates in the aftermath of the global financial crisis. This gives them a competitive advantage now rates are higher.

Arthur Copple: Again, it depends on the individual trust, the beta on the portfolio and the liquidity of the underlying asset class. There is no 'one size fits all'.

Neil Rogan: Most sectors seem to have some trusts that gear permanently, some that use it flexibly and some that rarely if ever gear. In my experience those that gear permanently are most influenced by their boards and those that rarely gear are most influenced by their fund manager.

Has the FCA got a problem with investment trusts? If so how can we improve the relationship?

Michael Balfour: I'm not sure, but there is enough regulation around without them getting more involved.

Rachel Beagles: The problem the industry has is that investment companies look like funds but, as listed companies, they are not regulated under the FCA's fund regulations. Also, the sector is tiny in size in comparison with the funds industry. So investment trusts are often overlooked when it comes to regulation. We need to continue, as an industry, to make the case for the important role that investment companies can play in democratising access to attractive and often less liquid asset classes, in an appropriate and advantageous structure. And to try to drive the regulatory debate from cost to return.

Arthur Copple: I don't think the FCA has any underlying problem with investment trusts, but constant communication between the AIC and the FCA is essential to making sure the FCA understands the sector's needs.

Neil Rogan: I suppose the FCA is just doing its job in bringing forward ever more regulation. The problem is that much of it is irrelevant or has minimal effect and just adds complexity and costs to investment trusts. The investment trust sector has over 150 years of history of helping finance infrastructure projects and emerging industries. It has a clear record of investing in and enabling growth. At a time when the government is desperate for growth you would think they would turn to us for help.

What do boards need to do to keep the sector from shrinking?

Michael Balfour: Keeping the sector thriving is not the role of individual boards. If each board acts appropriately on behalf of shareholders, then the sector will bounce back. The investment trust is a great product, but supply and demand hasn't been balanced for a while. The sector might have to shrink further until the right balance is achieved.

Rachel Beagles: Boards need to adapt to ensure trusts are fit for purpose in today's world: that means offering a compelling investment proposition, attractively priced against other collectives, with suitable levels of scale and liquidity so that it can meet its shareholders' needs. If trusts don't offer this, the market is likely to continue to recycle capital to those who do – forcing more mergers to retain or build scale; or wind-ups for those who can't achieve this. We also need to give investors confidence that boards will act if discounts widen excessively. I can't see merger activity abating for some time.

Arthur Copple: Make every effort to communicate the attractions of their trust to individual, self-directed investors. They are the future for the industry.

Neil Rogan: Individual boards can only focus on what is best for their own shareholders. If that means merging with another trust then so be it, it does bring down costs and it means one fewer investment trust each time but doesn't necessarily mean a shrinkage in assets.

What do boards need to do to improve retail participation?

Michael Balfour: There are huge flows into individuals auto-enrolled DC pension funds. It all goes into open-ended funds. Someone needs to figure out a way of getting some of that invested in investment trusts.

Rachel Beagles: Firstly, ensure that the company's investment proposition is compelling and attractive to a retail market. It's a non-starter if they don't. Secondly, make sure there is the expertise on the board and the resources to embark on a well-designed retail marketing strategy which is going to establish a retail presence and attract new shareholders. Boards shouldn't be under any illusions how expensive this can be, however. Attracting direct retail investors is more affordable to those with scale.

Arthur Copple: Make sure their website is as easy to navigate as possible; make every effort to publicise their trust through all media, including social media. I also think enhanced dividends help increase retail participation.

Neil Rogan: As measured by the participation of execution-only platforms on our registers, retail participation is increasing. It's just that we'd all like it to accelerate. A strong investment case and corporate proposition is essential here and needs to be marketed well, clearly and persistently.

Positives and negatives about the outlook for the trust sector?

Michael Balfour: Positives: it's a perfect place to get exposure to illiquid and semi-illiquid investments. Trusts are getting bigger and more liquid. Discounts will narrow until activist shareholders are no longer interested, enhancing shareholder returns. Revenue reserves allowing steadily appreciating dividends are great for pensions. Negatives: the potential for increased regulation.

Rachel Beagles: Much of this interview has focussed on the negatives, so I am going to focus on two positives! Investment trusts offer access to permanent capital and an investment return augmented by gearing – this should continue to provide a competitive advantage over other collectives if used well. Finally, boards are taking proactive and often radical action against the challenges presented to the sector, including full strategic reviews, a much greater focus on discount control, fee negotiations and merger activity. The sector will emerge fitter for this.

Arthur Copple: Positives: On the whole, over the long term, investment trusts outperform other types of pooled investment vehicle. I think that is becoming increasingly recognised. Negatives: I think we will see continued net selling of investment trust shares from the larger wealth managers.

Neil Rogan: Investment trusts still tend to perform better than their open-ended counterparts and they are cheaper and offer the flexibility for enhanced income. There are lots of strong ones out there. There are some weak ones too; those are the duty of their individual boards to tackle.

What are the emerging issues for the sector?

Neil Rogan: I'd flag board remuneration. Historically, investment trust directors' salaries have been low by comparison with other non-executive directors. This could be explained by an abundant supply of candidates and a perception that the risks of being a director were relatively low. Risk and reward were in balance. Now, however, with the growing influence of activists and an increased number of mergers, the risks have multiplied while the pool of able candidates seems to have started to shrink. Existing and potential directors are being deterred by the risks of increased workload and responsibilities plus the higher likelihood of what were previously perceived as black swan liabilities. I think the only way for boards to retain their collective expertise is for rewards to rise in tandem with the increased risks.

VCTs: A NEW ERA?

ALEX DAVIES, *founder and CEO of specialist broker The Wealth Club, offers his regular annual review of how venture capital trusts have fared in the last 12 months.*

REMEMBER 2021? As the fear and uncertainty that gripped hearts at the beginning of the pandemic faded, tech companies, startups in particular, emerged as the heroes of Covid lockdowns. Money started to flow freely into new and emerging companies, with investors doubling down on the sector, buoyed by low interest rates and relatively low inflation. Company valuations skyrocketed.

Global venture investment in 2021 was more than ten times higher than a decade earlier. Early-stage funding showed the greatest increase, growing 100% year on year. In the UK, VCT fundraising broke the £1bn barrier for the first time. So-called 'unicorns', private companies valued at $1bn-plus, were minted at an unprecedented pace, more than ten a week on average globally.

2021 was a miracle year. But as harsh realities set in, the miracle turned sour. Higher inflation and a tighter monetary environment triggered a downturn in mid-2022 as interest rates started to rise. Fundraising cooled, returning to pre-pandemic levels. Valuations dropped sharply across the board and have moved little, if at all, since.

Now, after three years in the doldrums, are things finally looking up? There is cause for measured confidence. After valuations fell in 2022, companies initially held off raising funds for as long as possible. Subsequently the businesses that needed cash have either found it, often at lower valuations, or fallen by the wayside.

A quick glance at VCTs' net asset values (NAV) and their movement over the last three years suggests that asset values may have now normalised, with most of the bad news priced in. The question at the top of every investor's mind will be: where might NAVs go from here? Here are some reasons to be positive about the outlook.

Revenue growth

Not all VCTs have been impacted to the same extent by the valuation drops of the last few years. Some, mainly VCTs with an investment bias towards later-stage opportunities, have been comparatively steady. Octopus Apollo VCT and Puma VCT 13 are examples. Meanwhile, newer VCTs, such as Fuel Ventures VCT,

Guinness VCT and Praetura Growth VCT, have largely bypassed the troubles, as they started to build their portfolio after the exuberance of 2021 had begun to cool.

Moreover, looking at both new and established VCTs, across all investment strategies, revenue growth of the underlying portfolio companies remains encouraging across the board, according to our research.

We looked at the portfolio of 36 VCTs, together accounting for around 94.3% of the assets of all active VCTs, and divided them into three categories: trusts experiencing revenue decline; trusts experiencing modest growth of 0–25%; and those with high growth (revenue growth of 25%+).

We have then applied the same categorisation to the constituents of the FTSE All Share index, excluding investment trusts and insurance companies. You can see how the two markets compare in the following chart. It shows that VCT-backed companies continue to deliver higher revenue growth than the listed market.

Figure 1: exposure to growth – VCTS vs UK main market

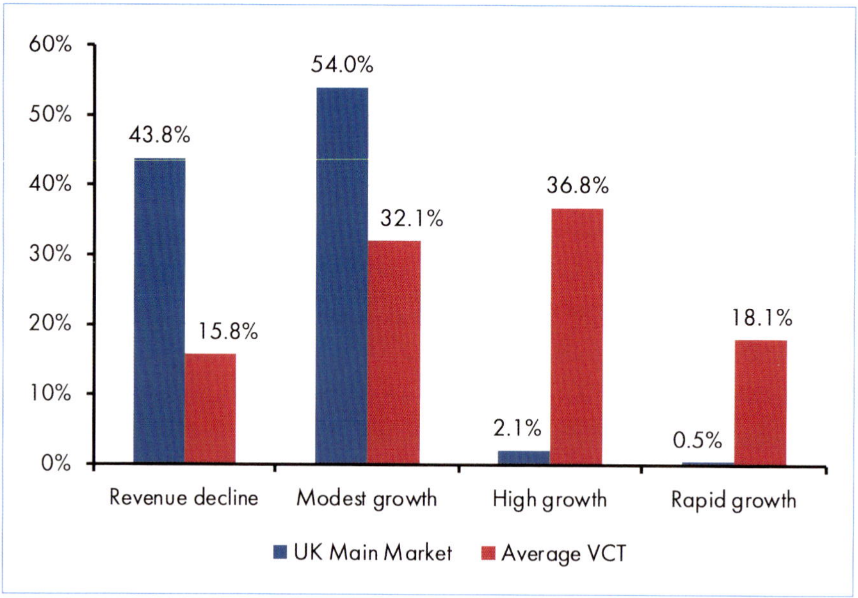

Over a third (36.8%) of VCT portfolios in our sample had investments in businesses that have grown revenues by more than 25% year on year. By contrast, only a tiny minority (2.1%) of the FTSE All-Share constituents, excluding investment trusts and insurance companies, have achieved that.

If we were to look at a fourth category, rapid-growth companies, VCTs fare even better. 18.1% of their portfolios are invested in companies growing revenues at more than 50%, compared with just 0.5% (by market capitalisation) for the main market. If this revenue growth continues, there is scope for this to translate into increased valuations and potentially exits.

Outstanding successes

These revenue growth figures are averages. While useful for tracking the progress of the market, they don't do justice to some of the most exciting growth stories. As in the past, VCTs continue to generate some truly notable individual success stories.

One is Albion VCT's largest investment, Quantexa. The big-data analytics firm uses artificial intelligence to uncover hidden relationships and emerging risks, helping financial institutions spot and prevent fraud. Its clients span blue-chip banks (including HSBC, Standard Chartered Bank, and Danske Bank), insurers and government organisations.

It was established in 2016 and in 2024 achieved 'centaur' status, surpassing $100m in annual recurring revenue (ARR) and joining an elite group of SaaS companies. In March 2025, Quantexa raised $175m in a Series F investment round which valued it at $2.6bn.

Another example, from a completely different sector, is Pembroke VCT's largest investment, LYMA Life, which applies cutting-edge technology to wellness products. Founded in 2018, it started with the launch of the LYMA Supplement and later introduced the LYMA Laser, which was named one of *TIME* Magazine's best inventions of 2023. LYMA featured in the *Sunday Times* Fastest Growing UK Businesses and the *Financial Times* 1000 Fastest Growing European Companies.

Unusually for a VCT-backed company, LYMA has only ever received £2m in investment. It has grown every year and most recently reported £32m revenue and £3.6m of EBITDA (earnings before interest, taxation, depreciation and amortisation). Pembroke's stake is currently valued at £33.8m (as at March 2025), against a cost of just £2m.

Another very different example is MPB, backed by the ProVen VCTs. MPB started life with its founder selling photographic gear on eBay as a student. It launched formally in 2011 and is now active in ten countries. It has become the largest global platform to buy, sell and trade used photo and video gear.

In its latest accounts, the company reported record revenue of £137m, and a growth rate of 40%, with more than 65% of revenue now generated outside the

UK. The ProVen VCTs' stake in the company is currently valued at £18.2m (as at February 2025), against a cost of £2.9m.

All three companies have consistently grown, year in, year out, bucking the general post-Covid downward trend in valuations. It's worth noting that private companies tend to track the valuation multiples of their main-market counterparts, though usually with a delay. Stock markets have rallied over the past year, but valuations of private companies are yet to catch up. If that general market trend continues, one might reasonably assume they will do so at some point soon, although it's not guaranteed.

Performance holds up

Overall, returns seem to be holding up. Investors have continued to receive regular tax-free dividends – a very tangible and immediate benefit of VCT investing.

But dividends are only one aspect of a VCT's return. A more rounded view of how well a VCT has done is the NAV total return figure. This takes into consideration both a VCT's NAV (broadly speaking, the value of its invested portfolio and cash) and any dividends paid. And here the picture is more nuanced.

The strong NAV total returns of the pre-2021 period are still evident in the five- and ten-year numbers, but returns over three years have been weaker.

The weakest performance has come from AIM VCTs and generalist VCTs with high exposure to businesses reliant on accessing additional capital. The most high-profile example is Octopus Titan VCT. It has cut its net asset value several times and has now confirmed, after a long-awaited strategic review by the board, that it will raise no new money, make no new investments and may not be able to sustain dividend payments in the short-to-medium term.

Drivers of demand

Nevertheless, in spite of short-term declines in share prices and NAVs, demand for VCTs remains very resilient. When we ask Wealth Club clients what prompted them to invest in VCTs, nearly all believe investing in VCTs helps back the next generation of UK entrepreneurs. The exposure to high-growth-potential investments, the diversification VCTs can add to one's portfolio and the opportunity to support UK entrepreneurship are also mentioned.

But tax inevitably plays a key role. When you invest in a VCT, you can currently receive up to 30% income tax relief. That's a saving of up to £60,000 on your income tax bill (if you use the whole VCT allowance of £200,000 per year), which should be welcome to anyone facing a higher bill.

Moreover, any growth is tax free and so are any dividends VCTs pay. So, if a VCT pays a 5% dividend, that means you get 5p for every £1. To match that, assuming the dividend allowance has already been used, a higher-rate taxpayer would have to receive a taxable dividend of 7.55% (8.24% for a top-rate taxpayer).

As tax-efficiency is a key driver behind investor appetite for VCTs, we might be in for a bumper year for the sector again this year. HMRC's income tax takings have been on a sharp upward trajectory since 2020/21 when thresholds were frozen and fast-rising inflation thereafter has pushed many more people into higher tax bands.

Although we do not know at the time of writing what will be in the budget at the end of November 2025, nobody doubts that the chancellor will need to raise the overall tax take to fill an estimated £50bn hole in the public finances.

Where is that money going to come from? Higher and top-rate taxpayers may well be in the crosshairs again. Three quarters of all income tax payments this year are expected to come from the top 25% of taxpayers. That's not the ultra-rich. If you earn more than £47,400, you'll likely be in that top 25%.

If you earn £71,600, you'll be in the top 10%, who pay nearly 60% of all income tax. That's before considering the impact of dividend tax, where the tax-free allowance has been reduced to a measly £500 per annum, and capital gains tax, which is also reported to be in the Treasury's crosshairs.

As they have been from the outset, VCT investments are a way to mitigate the impact of tax on your wealth. And this is one of the reasons why VCT fundraising has held up so well, even at times, like the past few years, when performance and investor sentiment has been poor.

Historic VCT fundraising (£m)

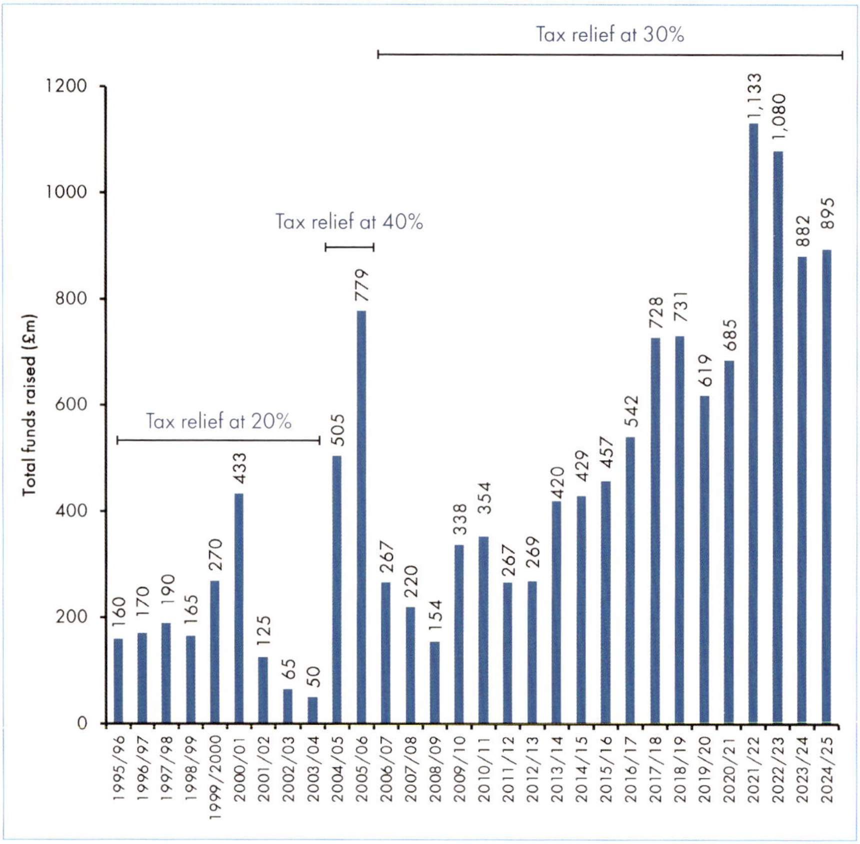

So, who invests in VCTs?

Contrary to what many may think, there is no such thing as a typical VCT investor.

The average age of our clients who invest in VCTs is just over 60. The youngest who invested in the year is 20, the eldest 96. The fastest-growing group of investors is those in the 30–40 age bracket. Around 80% are male, 20% female. In the 2024/25 tax year, they invested £38,739 on average across a number of VCTs per tax year. The average amount invested in each VCT was £18,890.

We don't record occupation, but many we speak to who invest are professionals, such as doctors, lawyers, higher earners in the City, business owners, but also the likes of head teachers and senior civil servants. They tend to have investments elsewhere (e.g., ISAs, pensions, property) to which VCTs add diversification, and they tend to have been affected by tax rises and pension restrictions.

If you have sufficient assets elsewhere and a certain level of financial sophistication, VCTs may well be a worthwhile option for you to consider, after using your pension and ISA allowances. As a rule of thumb, VCTs should account for no more than 10% of your total portfolio.

When you invest in a VCT, your money would typically be spread over 30 to 100 companies, which provides an important degree of underlying diversification. In addition, it may be prudent to spread your annual investment over several VCTs, preferably with different investment styles, to further diversify your risk. Don't forget you also have a 30% cushion in the form of tax relief should things go wrong.

Clearly, for someone who doesn't have sufficient assets or earnings, and doesn't fully understand the risks, VCTs are unlikely to be a suitable investment. Young, small companies are more likely to fail than older and larger ones. If something goes badly wrong for a small company, it is much harder for it to recover than it is for a large and well-established company. Small companies are also a lot more illiquid, as are VCTs themselves, meaning it may be difficult to buy and sell the shares.

Fundraising outlook

The VCT season has only just started this year. Taxes are still at a record high and quite likely to get higher. Pensions, whilst slightly improved, remain non-viable for many. If you are after future growth, and understand the risks, the case for VCT investment remains compelling. We don't know if the total funds raised will surpass last year's total. The most popular offers tend to sell out quickly, however, a reminder to investors that if they spot a VCT they like, they should act promptly whilst there is still capacity.

ALEX DAVIES *is the founder and CEO of Wealth Club, the largest broker of VCTs and tax-efficient investments for experienced investors.*

Ethereum (USD)
2 Jahre
1 Tag
Voreinstellungen
Mittel
Forum
Favoriten
Zeitraum
224.182,31 €
command

OUTLOOK

5.690
5.350
0.410
0.000
2.750
2.440
1.830
1.600
2.310
2.300
3.100
0.000

ADJUSTING TO STAGFLATION

Having been positive about equities in recent years, investment trust expert JOHN BARON *explains why he has now adopted a more cautious diversified approach within the ten live trust portfolios he manages for the website www.johnbaronportfolios.co.uk.*

I FIRST OUTLINED WHY future asset allocation needed to reflect a changing investment landscape in my *Investors Chronicle* column 'Preparing for inflation' (13 March 2021). Portfolio construction up to that point, indeed ever since my first monthly column in 2009, had been influenced by the view that interest rates were going to stay low for much longer than the consensus believed. The portfolios benefitted as a result. My columns since have highlighted the importance of recognising that higher and more volatile inflation, together with low growth, is gradually changing the investment dynamic and reinforces the need for investors to adjust asset allocation accordingly, especially when seeking diversification.

An inflection point

Four years ago investors had witnessed an extraordinary period during which governments, for various reasons, had kept interest rates artificially low. Perhaps the best example was the Bank of England's policy, given its remit to keep inflation at 2%. While the invasion of Ukraine is often cited by the bank as an external shock nobody could rightly foresee, it ignores the fact that the month before the invasion interest rates were still only 0.5% while inflation was already 5.5% and rising. In the *Alice in Wonderland* world of quantitative easing (QE), economic reality, policy responses and asset prices across the risk spectrum became distorted and growth stocks inflated. Equity markets tended to perform well.

While accepting that humility is an essential component of good portfolio management, I suggest we have now reached a different juncture. Talk of slow economic growth has been contributing to the view that a series of interest rate cuts are on the cards. Investors should be wary about the extent. Stagflation is upon us. This sluggish growth is being fostered in part by high debt levels, the tendency of governments to overspend, growing statism and the marginalising of the wealth-creating private sector. There are also a range of factors fostering inflationary pressures and higher-than-expected inflation, which bode ill for certain equities. This combination is unwelcome and has investment implications.

Having benefitted from their equity growth bias since 2009, in recent years our portfolios have gradually shifted away from growth in favour of value. They are now also underweighting equities relative to standard benchmarks, in part because history suggests stagflation tends to be a headwind for equities. The other part of the equation going forward involves securing effective diversification which is more necessary than ever, given usual norms can no longer be relied upon. A rethink is required as to the mix of assets. The good news is that the right combination can not only help to protect past gains but be profitable as well.

Achieving diversification

By way of explanation, actions speak louder than words. The ten live investment trust portfolios managed in real time on the website www.johnbaronportfolios.co.uk pursue a range of investment remits and income strategies. Five portfolios are part of a risk-adjusted investment journey which sees exposure increasingly diversify away from equities into more defensive assets as progress toward financial goals is achieved, to help reduce risk and so protect past gains. The website's diversification table (Table 1) highlights this journey in percentages as one proceeds through the LISA, Spring, Summer, Autumn and Winter portfolios – each column totalling 100% once the portfolios' equity exposure is added.

History suggests that higher inflation and interest rates tend to result in a more positive correlation between the various alternative asset classes, thus making diversification more challenging. All boats catch a rising tide. The reverse tends to be true in periods of lower inflation. The period of low inflation and rates lasting some decades prior to 2022 favoured more traditional diversification proxies, especially government bonds. Since then, the current economic environment questions those key assumptions and requires fresh thinking about the possibilities on offer and the potential (or otherwise) they hold.

A good example is bonds, particularly government issues. Historically, a 60/40 split between equities and mostly government bonds was thought to provide sufficient diversification. Recent research shows such a split resulted in average annual volatility of c.8% in the decade leading up to 2022. Decades of low inflation and rates embedded the concept. Yet in the years since 2022, the figure has risen to c.13%, which is far less effective. Higher inflation rightly brings into doubt the credibility of bonds as an asset class when it comes to reducing risk.

Table 1: Other asset classes – a diversification journey in numbers

	PERCENTAGE OF TOTAL PORTFOLIO				
	LISA	SPRING	SUMMER	AUTUMN	WINTER
Bonds	Nil	Nil	4.5	10.5	18.5
Infrastructure	Nil	4.0	4.0	5.5	7.5
Specialist lending	Nil	Nil	2.5	4.0	7.5
Environmental	Nil	Nil	2.0	3.5	5.0
Capital preservation	Nil	5.5	6.5	10.0	12.5
Gold/silver	Nil	6.0	10.0	11.5	13.5
Commodities	Nil	10.0	12.0	12.0	12.0
Real estate	Nil	Nil	2.5	3.5	5.0
Cash	1.0	1.0	1.5	3.0	2.0
Total	**1.0**	**26.5**	**45.5**	**63.5**	**83.5**

Source: www.johnbaronportfolios.co.uk. Data to 30 September 2025.

Within the fixed income asset class, we favour corporate bonds and private debt over gilts, given the scale of government debt and politicians' lack of will to rein in spending. Portfolio holdings include CQS New City High Yield (NCYF), Invesco Bond Income Plus (BIPS), CVC Income & Growth (CVCG) and M&G Credit Income Investment Trust (MGCI). Both types of debt, particularly higher-yielding corporate debt, should cope better with higher inflation. However, in general, the portfolios are very underweight this asset class as the table shows. Benchmark bond weightings are 7.5%, 32.5% and 47.5% for the Summer, Autumn and Winter portfolios.

Adding alternatives

Given the underweighting of both equities and bonds, Table 1 illustrates the extent to which alternative assets are employed by the portfolios to achieve their respective objectives and risk profiles. The aim is to increase exposure to a broad spectrum of asset classes which to varying degrees are 'uncorrelated', meaning assets that tend not to move in the same direction as equities over a given period. Some are more sensitive than others. A further consideration is the objective of increasing the income level of the portfolios as the investment journey unfolds, with the Winter portfolio yielding 5.4%. Capital preservation trusts, cash, and physical gold and silver are the exceptions in this regard.

The infrastructure and renewable energy sectors are certainly out of favour, as evidenced by their wise discounts. Portfolio holdings include HICL Infrastructure Company (HICL), International Public Partnerships (INPP), The Renewables Infrastructure Group (TRIG) and Foresight Environmental Infrastructure (FGEN). Such discounts have not escaped notice, with M&A activity picking up. While accepting that sentiment is poor, the quality of the businesses and management in these trusts bodes well. Meanwhile, these holdings are high yielding, with most if not all increasing their dividends. The extent to which their revenues benefit from inflation is sometimes underappreciated by markets.

Other asset classes which offer attractive and sustainable levels of income include specialist lenders and commercial property. Holdings here include BioPharma Credit Investments (BPCR), Sequoia Economic Infrastructure (SEQI) and Schroder Real Estate Investment Trust (SREI). Attractive businesses together with company discounts, combined with experienced management teams with good track records and handsome yields, suggest optimism going forward. Revenues in some cases will again benefit from higher inflation. The difference in their businesses assists with the search for diversification, with BPCR often securing additional revenues from their investments if certain success rates are achieved.

However, the key change in recent years has been the meaningful increase in exposure to precious metals and miners, which complements our existing exposure to commodities. This has been influenced by such assets usually performing well during sustained periods of higher inflation and slow growth. Holdings include physical gold, silver and precious metal exchange-traded funds (ETFs), where there is no investment trust alternative, CQS Natural Resources Growth & Income (CYN), which recently introduced an 8% of NAV dividend policy, Golden Prospect Precious Metals (GPM), which focuses on smaller companies, and BlackRock World Mining Trust (BRWM) which favours larger companies.

Recent events suggest that precious metals continue to look attractive despite their strong run. The increasing unpredictability of the US administration, further straws in the wind regarding higher-than-expected inflation, growing evidence of sluggish economic growth globally, and interesting commentary from central banks, all reinforce their lustre. As for gold, whereas central bank buying largely accounted for the rise in the price over recent years, recent ETF data suggests investors (institutional and retail) have now also become net buyers for the first time since 2020, the larger US technology companies having perhaps distracted investors' attention in the meantime. This may help provide a second wind.

A final word on diversification. It is worth noting that while it is rightly seen as a defensive posture to protect past gains during market setbacks, it can also produce good returns. Challenging times present both risks and opportunities. It is perhaps no coincidence that the more defensively positioned Winter portfolio has so far this year kept pace with the Summer portfolio during a period of rising (if volatile) equity markets. While there is no reason to believe the long-term case for correctly positioned equities is still not valid, diversification reflecting the current investment landscape should continue to reap rewards – and perhaps become increasingly valued.

Equity positioning

As referred to earlier, the portfolios are underweight equities relative to their benchmarks. Periods of high inflation, particularly when allied to sluggish or no economic growth, have usually not been kind to equities. For example, the Summer portfolio has a 55% exposure to equities compared to 77.5% for the MSCI PIMFA Growth index. The figures for the Autumn portfolio are 37% compared to 47.5% for the MSCI PIMFA Income index, and 17% for the Winter portfolio compared to 30% for the MSCI PIMFA Conservative index. There is a modicum of additional equity exposure within each of the portfolios' capital preservation holdings.

Within their equity weighting, the portfolios are underweight the US in part because history has often questioned the extent of market concentration as that now represented by the larger technology companies. Few are disputing these are good companies, but valuations still matter, especially as cashflows are increasingly committed to artificial intelligence (AI), where the extent of profitably is still uncertain. Investors' patience and enthusiasm will come to wilt. It is interesting to note that in recent years US corporate earnings outside the top technology stocks have been flatlining. A sluggish economy will not come to their rescue. Neither will higher than expected inflation, which will continue to ebb away at confidence.

Outside the US, the portfolios are overweight markets such as the UK and Europe more generally, which appear to offer better risk-adjusted returns while proffering reasonable levels of income. Given these markets were approaching historically low ratings not so long ago despite their sound fundamentals, it is not surprising they have been rewarding investors of late. This looks set to continue with money flows now beginning to suggest institutional investors are becoming more positive. Their case is being reinforced by M&A activity, mostly in the UK. Meanwhile, cheaply rated emerging markets are the giant waiting to stir.

Within the portfolios' equity exposure, there has been a gradual increase in recent years in exposure to value stocks. Key examples include Temple Bar Investment Trust (TMPL), Fidelity Special Values (FSV) and Murray International Trust (MYI). Periods of low interest and discount rates have usually favoured fast-growing growth stocks which promise potential – think the large US technology stocks

– because lower discount rates increase the value of future cash flows given the value of money decreases with time. By contrast, periods of high inflation usually favour value stocks as higher discount rates question the valuation of growth stocks' future cash flow.

In such an environment, the more reliable near-term cashflows and cheaper ratings of value stocks become more attractive. Just as reality prevailed, and value regained its crown after the internet and dot-com bubble of the 1990s, I suggest value is again about to emerge from the shadows. If correct that inflation does indeed continue to be stickier and more volatile in the coming years than the consensus currently believes, regardless of sluggish economic growth, growth stocks will face a strong headwind which perhaps will be felt first and most by the US technology stocks. Such a shift in investment style will also help income objectives.

JOHN BARON *is one of the UK's leading experts on investment trusts, a regular columnist and speaker at investment seminars, and author of* The Financial Times *Guide to Investment Trusts. Since 2009, he has reported on two real portfolios in his popular monthly column in* The Investors Chronicle.

His website www.johnbaronportfolios.co.uk reports in real time on the progress of ten live investment trust portfolios which achieve a range of risk-adjusted strategies and income objectives and possess good track records relative to benchmark. He also chairs the Investment Committee of Baron & Grant, a discretionary fund management company (www.baronandgrant.com).

John has used investment trusts in a private and professional capacity for over 35 years. After travel, university and the Army, he ran a broad range of investment portfolios as a director of both Henderson Private Clients and then Rothschild Asset Management. Since leaving the City, he has also helped charities monitor their fund managers.

THE BIG QUESTIONS FOR 2026

HUGH GIMBER, *global market strategist at J.P. Morgan Asset Management, looks forward to the year ahead.*

How do you assess the economic impact of the Trump administration so far?

THE TRUMP ADMINISTRATION has certainly kept investors on their toes. We've seen the biggest shakeup in US trade policy in more than 100 years, and yet the economy has so far proven resilient. Activity levels are holding up, and inflation has been surprisingly well behaved, with the passthrough from tariffs yet to fully materialise.

While this year's tax cuts are likely to support growth into 2026, inflation is a bigger watch item. There is little evidence that tariffs are being paid for by foreign exporters, which means that the bulk of these costs are going to fall on the shoulders of US corporates and consumers. Provided this burden is shared as I expect, inflation should be manageable. Yet if companies feel bold enough to pass on the vast majority of these cost increases to consumers, we will be facing a sharper pickup in US inflation ahead.

What do you think about the behaviour of the Fed and its future independence?

Jerome Powell is unlikely to be on the president's Christmas card list but, in truth, central bank independence is yet to face the real test. Rate cuts in 2025 have been justified by the slowdown in job growth, given that the Fed's remit not only covers inflation but also the health of the labour market.

If inflation reaccelerates and growth stabilises, US policymakers are going to be presented with a much more difficult conundrum next year. Longer-dated bonds are unlikely to respond well to rate cuts that are clearly motivated by political pressure, rather than the economic data.

Will the AI theme continue to power ahead in 2026?

The capex commitments from the AI 'hyperscalers' have shown few signs of slowdown, and it's been reassuring to see that the majority of this year's gains for the US tech giants have been driven by earnings growth, not increasing valuations. There are parts of this story that bear watching, however.

Investors are becoming increasingly alert to the somewhat circular nature of AI investment. Perhaps most notably, some companies are starting to turn to debt markets to fund future growth as free cash flow is exhausted. Ultimately, we remain some way away from being able to answer the most important question – are businesses going to find genuine revenues and cost savings from this technology, which in turn will create the demand required for the tech giants to deliver a healthy return on their investment? The answer to this question will determine whether current valuations are justified over time.

Capital spending from the five major US AI hyperscalers

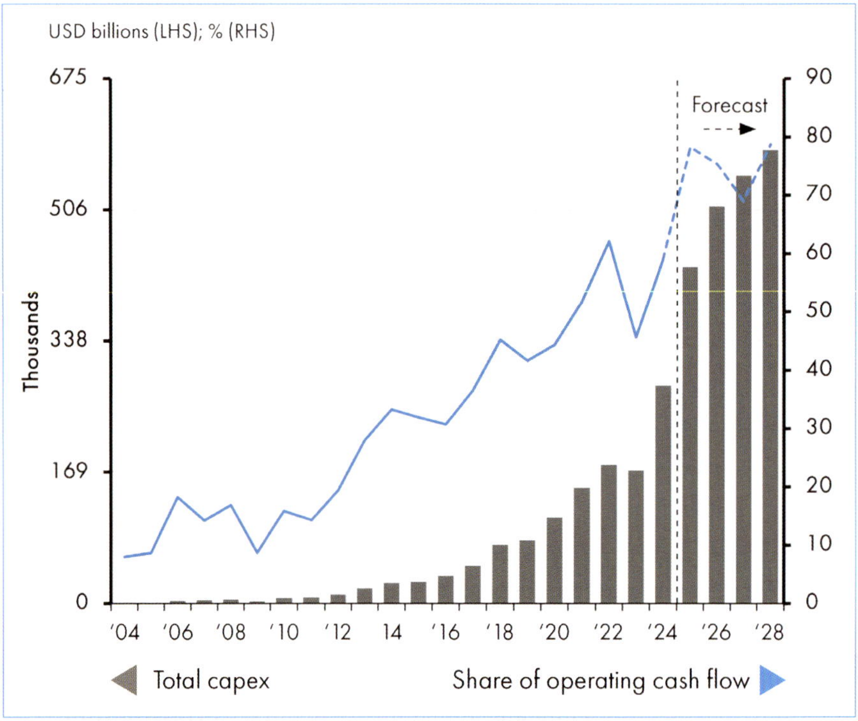

Source: Bloomberg, J.P. Morgan Asset Management. The chart shows the total company capex for Alphabet, Meta, Microsoft and Oracle, as well as an estimate of Amazon's AWS spend. Operating cash flow represents cash flow before capital expenditures. Guide to the Markets – UK. Data as at 21 October 2025.

For investors looking to diversify their US equity exposure, where should they look first?

In my view, many investors are underestimating the prospects for European stocks heading into 2026. Earnings growth in the region has again disappointed this year relative to the US, but much of this can be explained by the strength of the euro rather than fundamental weakness in the underlying companies.

Looking forward, Germany's 'fiscal pivot' is about to kick into gear, and it's hard to overstate what a shift this represents relative to the last 15 years. With policymakers in Europe's largest economy not just easing off the brake, but finally hitting the accelerator, we expect stronger levels of government investment to help to narrow the growth gap between the US and Europe.

French politics may be one factor keeping international investors wary. A path to fiscal sustainability remains elusive, but I see this as a can that will be kicked down the road until we reach the 2027 presidential elections.

Germany real government investment

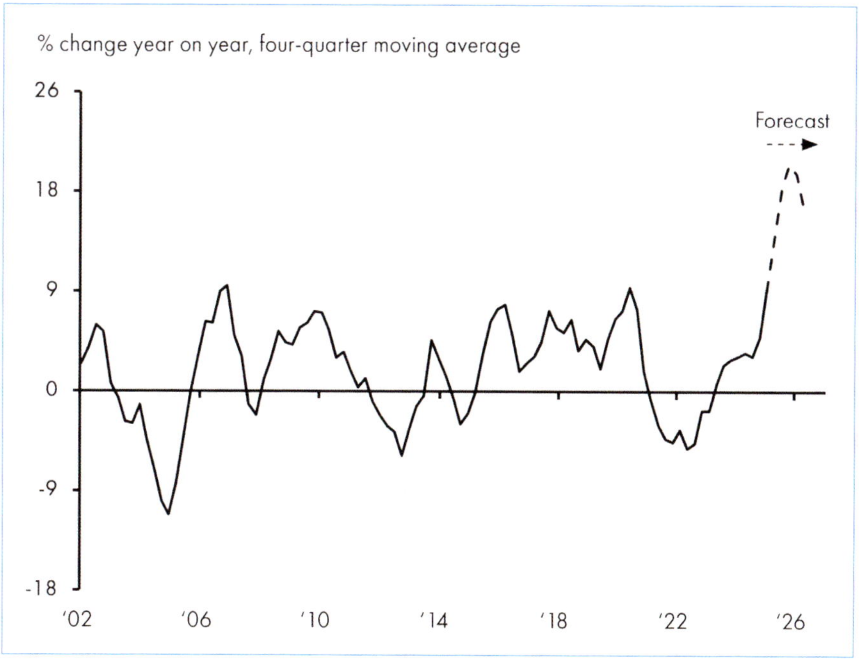

Source: LSEG Datastream, OECD, J.P. Morgan Asset Management. Forecasts are from the OECD. Guide to the Markets – UK. Data as at 21 October 2025.

Do you view the UK equity market in a similarly positive light?

An investor that was solely focused on UK politics may well have been tempted to steer clear of the FTSE 100 in 2025. Had they done so, they would have missed out on what has been, at the time of writing, one of the UK market's best years in the last decade.

Due to the well-reported constraints on our government's finances, the economy is missing out on the fiscal bonanza that others are enjoying, but UK stocks should remain well supported by other factors next year. Share buybacks and M&A activity are putting a floor under valuations, and while the FTSE's lack of technology has been the market's Achilles heel for a decade, it now appears increasingly attractive for investors who have seen their overall technology exposure dragged higher and higher by global market moves.

Will next year see a further slide in the US dollar?

Currencies are a topic that is back on investors' radars, and rightly so, given how heavily they are influencing stock market returns. I do think that the US dollar can weaken further, but would distinguish between two main scenarios.

An orderly scenario would be driven by fundamentals, with US growth looking less impressive and US interest rates moving lower relative to the rest of the world. This is my base case, which would likely result in a slower pace of dollar depreciation compared to 2025.

There are disorderly scenarios that should also be considered, however. For example, if the institutional framework that supports the independence of the Federal Reserve was more seriously challenged, this would drive a sharper reallocation of capital, and in turn a much bigger move in the greenback.

How does this view on the US dollar influence your outlook for emerging markets?

A weaker US dollar is typically positive for the emerging markets, and I see no reason why this should be different in 2026. Of course, given its 30% weight in emerging market benchmarks, the outlook for China will be another critical factor. China's domestic backdrop remains sluggish, with consumer confidence still muted and the real estate sector at best showing signs of stabilisation.

More interestingly though, policy support for the technology sector appears to have turned a corner. Access to world-class technology infrastructure is increasingly viewed as a matter of national security, and when Chinese policymakers throw their weight behind a sector, they tend to be highly effective.

Should we be looking to the bond market, rather than the stock market, for the big surprise next year? What is the risk of a sovereign crisis given surging debt levels?

Faced with increasingly angry electorates, governments around the world are determined to spend, spend, spend. With debt levels already high and populations ageing rapidly, these spending commitments do appear increasingly unsustainable. How bond markets react to this situation is dictated by where this conversation started. It is all about inflation.

Provided that I'm right in my assumption that inflation will remain at tolerable levels, central bank rate cuts should help to keep bond markets well behaved next year. If, however, there are signs that inflation pressures are starting to become entrenched, bond investors will be quick to signal their unease, pushing bond yields higher and in turn threatening equity valuations.

Roll on 2026. If one thing's for certain, it's not going to be dull!

HUGH GIMBER *is responsible for generating research-driven analysis of the global economy and markets, and communicating this to J.P. Morgan's clients and the media across the UK and Europe.*

THE YEAR AHEAD

PAUL NIVEN, *manager of the F&C Investment Trust, gives his views on the outlook for the year ahead.*

How do you assess the market impact of the Trump administration?

THE FIRST NINE months of President Trump 2.0 have been marked by controversy and uncertainty. Despite this turbulence, global equities have surpassed pre-Liberation Day levels and are up at all-time highs, with the US up by around 30% from the lows and the S&P 500 rising from below 5000 to above 6500. This is despite downgrades to economic growth expectations.

Historical context shows that US tariff rates have not been this high since the era of US Protectionism before the Second World War. The Tariff Act of 1930 serves as a cautionary tale, having contributed to a devastating two-thirds collapse in world trade within five years, worsening the Great Depression. Following this period, we witnessed a gradual decline in average tariff rates, entering an extended era of free trade agreements after the Second World War.

While President Trump's first-term tariffs were maintained under Biden's administration, Liberation Day proposals threatened a dramatic shift, potentially raising average US tariff rates from a few percentage points to approximately 25%. Although some moderation has since occurred, current projections indicate that the world will end with an average tariff rate of 17.5% if all the tariffs are implemented.

Even in an optimistic scenario, US tariffs will likely settle at around 10%, substantially above the previous 2.3–2.6% level. The average actual effective rate in July was 10% and the impact of this in economic terms is analogous to that of a major tax hike. There will be a rise in custom duties to the equivalent of 1.5% of GDP in the US.

So, the overall impact of new tariffs is, in effect, an additional, continuous layer of taxation, plus a one-off adjustment in the shape of higher inflation. While Trump appears now to have halted trade war escalation, significant two-sided policy risk persists. The ultimate outcome depends on the economic impact though. Our base case, centred around current tariff levels, remains a slowdown (but not recession) in the US.

How has the trust adapted to the significant volatility?

Markets have been volatile in recent months, with several issues to contend with, not just the Liberation Day tariff announcements and subsequent negotiations, but also the downgrade of the US government's bond rating by Moody's, concerns over the fiscal position in the UK and elsewhere which is pressuring government bond markets, and concern about a possible AI-related bubble in stocks.

The reaction to the tariff announcements was a sharp downward movement, with the S&P dropping to around 5000 before a subsequent 30% rally, although the so-called Magnificent Seven, the big tech stocks that have dominated the market's performance, have gained more, now up over 50% from lows earlier this year.

We have retained a balanced exposure across our portfolio through all this, having reduced US and dollar exposure at the margin, upped our weighting in emerging market assets, and reduced our position in Japanese equities.

How do you assess the market outlook from here?

Fundamentals are reasonable in terms of the overall growth backdrop and, critically, we expect that recession will be avoided in the US. While inflation remains sticky in some places, we do expect rate cuts in the US alongside ongoing growth in earnings after a reporting season which produced very strong results versus expectations. Valuations are full but not excessive, in our view, and should not prevent progress in equity markets.

The outlook for emerging markets is more interesting than in the recent past, as valuations are attractive and this group should benefit from declining US rates, a weaker dollar, and reasonable growth prospects, alongside greater fiscal flexibility than is available in many developed markets.

What are your thoughts on US exceptionalism?

The US economy and stock market has been exceptional for a number of years, although equity market performance relative to other regions has been less exceptional over the past 12 months for sterling investors, in part due to dollar weakness.

The US maintains several structural advantages at the macro and corporate level. Broad energy independence and lower energy costs contrast sharply with other regions, particularly Europe. At the corporate level, the US corporate sector produces superior earnings delivery and profitability, with mega-cap tech stocks maintaining effective oligopolies across new technology areas, including AI.

The US equity market has delivered strong excess returns, and the dollar has typically acted as a safe haven during periods of crisis. Since 2012, the US dollar and US equities have outperformed globally, driven by superior earnings growth. The US has delivered a 4% higher EPS compounded annual growth rate versus the rest of the world over the past decade.

Our view is that the US economy and market remains in a strong place in relative terms, but that performance in equity markets should broaden both geographically and within the US. On any criterion other than valuation there are few signs of exceptional positive geographic opportunities elsewhere. More is required than this to deliver excess returns. That said, the outlook is brighter for emerging markets and in the longer-term Japanese corporate reform may also yield positive results for shareholders.

How are you playing the AI revolution? How will it play out?

AI is a significant theme in the market and the wider economy, and we expect it will have a profound change across and within industries. It should boost overall economic productivity which would be good for the corporate sector and for owners of capital.

We have exposure to many of the leading players in AI, including Nvidia, which is our largest holding, Microsoft, and others. It is interesting, however, that we have also benefited from the AI involvement of positions outside of these well-known names. A good example of this is Vertiv, owned by our US value manager, Barrow Hanley.

Vertiv is an industrial company which, amongst other activities, provides cooling solutions for data centres, where demand has increased significantly as a function of AI. It was the best performing stock in our portfolio in 2023 – better than Nvidia that year – and delivered almost 140% in USD terms in 2024. Barrow Hanley sold out of that stock late 2024, but bought it back after the share price fell in the wake of the DeepSeek announcement early in 2025.

As a collective, the Magnificent Seven are trading on a prospective P/E of around 28x, which is rich, but needs to be considered in the context of strong (but variable) growth prospects. This group delivered year-on-year earnings growth of around 26% in their second quarter – well ahead of both consensus expectations and the wider market. They will, however, need to maintain that superior growth outcome to justify their current valuations.

How do you compete against passive alternatives? Is your portfolio active enough?

We strongly believe that diversification is an important principle that investors should adopt. Hence we seek to deliver an appropriately diversified portfolio of growth assets – both listed equity and private equity – for investors looking for a one-stop solution for their needs.

Diversification in equity exposure is important even though it has been shown that the 'skew' in equity market returns mean that only around 4% of US companies drive all the market's investment returns. Indeed, most stocks lose money or do worse than short-term bills (cash returns). Of course, if we could identify that small number of winning stocks in advance, then we could forget the 96% of companies that do not add value. But these companies are the proverbial needles in the haystack.

It is tempting to form simplistic and extreme conclusions to this observation: either a) run highly concentrated portfolios which try to only include the winners (find the needles); or b) simply buy the haystack (the whole market), as by definition it then guarantees inclusion of all the winners, as well as all the losers.

The unfortunate reality is that if you hold a highly concentrated portfolio, you are more likely to miss the really important winners. Portfolio concentration, in our view, is not the solution, but we do need to be active to have any chance of delivering excess returns versus the general market.

That is why we employ specialist managers to run focused portfolios for us. We think if they do their job, it means that we are more likely to capture winners and avoid losers. We also diversify across styles that have a positive payoff through time, such as quality, value, and growth/momentum.

We have a strong proof statement which supports our approach. At the end of 2024, our NAV had beaten our benchmark over one, three, five, ten and 20 years, and NAV and shareholder returns were ahead of average peer returns over all these time periods. This consistent return profile and delivery of performance was unique amongst our peers.

Discrete annual performance as at 30 September 2025 (%)

	2020/21	2021/22	2022/23	2023/24	2024/25
NAV	25.7	−1.6	7.2	18.6	16.7
Share price	27.8	6.3	−0.4	18.5	18.5
Benchmark	22.7	−3.6	11.1	20.2	17.4

Source: Lipper and Columbia Threadneedle Investments. Benchmark: FTSE All-World TR Index. Basis: percentage growth, total return, net income reinvested. This discrete annual performance table refers to 12-month periods, ending 30 September 2025.

Have you made any style/fund adjustments in the past 12–24 months?

We have modestly reduced exposure to US equities and the US dollar as well as Japanese equities over the past year, while increasing our exposure to emerging market equities. We also changed our emerging markets equity mandate to Invesco from an in-house managed strategy previously run by Columbia Threadneedle

Investments, our parent company. We have not made any significant stylistic adjustments on the portfolio.

When will your private asset exposure yield results? Is it worth the trouble?

We have invested in private equity for many years and have, over the long run, typically generated results above those available from listed equity markets. We have continued to make selective investments in this area with a focus on mid-market buyouts through both fund investments and co-investments, sourced by our team within Columbia Threadneedle Investments. We also have exposure to hard-to-access venture capital and growth managers through a bespoke programme managed for the trust by Pantheon.

Our portfolio weight in private equity is currently around 11%. In contrast to the longer-term picture, recent periods have seen our private equity exposure lag returns from listed equities. In H1 2025 the value of our PE holdings declined by –3.8% vs a 2.3% return from global equities and in 2024 our holdings gained by 10% vs a 17.6% return from listed equities.

Notwithstanding these numbers, we retain confidence that our private equity exposure provides us with diversifying and differentiating investment opportunities with strong return prospects. In 2024 we received positive net distributions from our private equity portfolio, receiving more back than we paid in. There were several successful realisations including Jollyes, a pet supply retailer, which returned 3.7 times our initial investment.

What lessons do you draw from Saba and the widening discounts phenomenon?

Discounts in the investment trust sector have widened since 2020 for a combination of reasons. The primary ones were a) the rise of bond yields which gave investors an alternative to equity investment after years of low interest rates; b) the PRIIPs cost disclosure framework which put the 'perceived' cost of owning some investment companies in a less favourable light; and c) the merger of some of the wealth managers which constrained demand and skewed investment away from some of the smaller investment companies.

A fourth factor, that is relevant for trusts with US or global mandates, is that the performance of the Magnificent Seven has skewed returns, resulting in many funds beginning to underperform their benchmarks. The ensuing discounts encouraged market arbitrageurs and new 'fast-money' hedge funds into an area of the market to which they rarely venture. Saba Capital's pursuit of UK investment trusts is the most visible of several names.

Whether one agrees or not with the approach which Saba Capital took, the experience brought to light some inefficiencies in a sector that may have relied upon low interest rates and high demand for too long. This has resulted in a number of improvements.

One of them is that investment trust boards, and indeed the fund managers themselves, must remain closer to shareholders and encourage more regular two-way communication. The shareholder should never be taken for granted. Information flow and regular updates are key for corporate messaging and shareholder confidence. F&C has an active presence through traditional marketing channels, as well as adopting new paths recently to connect with the younger investor by way of social media platforms such as TikTok.

As well as low management fees, we retain a resolute focus on delivery of strong investment performance for shareholders, to make sure that our investment proposition represents value for money and that we have a robust governance structure, allowing our independent board to challenge the manager and ensure that the trust is delivering outcomes in line with shareholder objectives and expectations.

Is a sovereign debt crisis likely – and if so how would you manage it?

Rising inflation and declining growth creates a dilemma for central bankers. The ECB has cut rates four times this year; the Bank of England three times. The Fed remains on hold awaiting the impact of tariffs, but markets expect rate cuts over the remainder of the year. Growth risks have increased, which is likely to command central banks' primary attention over any short-term inflation rise.

Yield curves have been steepening, particularly in longer-dated government bonds. For example, we have had five rate cuts by the Bank of England so far this cycle, but longer-dated interest rates are moving higher. The UK ten-year yield is up by around 0.8% over the past year.

Inflation progress continues as slowing rent inflation shows through in the US this year and the latest CPI print came in below expectations. Without tariffs, we would expect core inflation below 2.5% in 2025 and near target in 2026. However, core inflation remains notably above 2%.

On the fiscal position, government debt trajectories appear unsustainable in some countries, and this is leading to fears over the market's ability to absorb government supply – though there are no obvious signs of significant concern. Current US debt stands at $36 trillion, representing 122% of GDP, with an annual budget deficit exceeding 7%. French debt to GDP is around 115% and, in the UK, levels are 95–100%.

Partly driven by the US administration's stance, significant changes are occurring elsewhere. Greece has already heavily reined in spending. In Europe as a whole, the recent agreement for the removal of a fiscal debt brake coincides with plans for substantial military and infrastructure spending increases, led by Germany. German plans include €100bn in extra defence spending over four years.

We expect that governments will muddle through in the near term, though we are concerned that another French PM has resigned, driven by their inability to pass an 'austerity' budget. There are also questions in the UK about the appetite for and ability to reduce government expenditure, following the government's well-aired backdown on welfare reform.

We face a significant budget here in the UK towards the end of November. There is no doubt that a sovereign debt crisis would present a real challenge for risk assets and for equity markets, but we do not envisage that risk materialising in the near term.

What is your UK weighting and how does that compare to the average in the past?

The trust made a strategic decision more than ten years ago to cut the benchmark weight in UK equities from 40% to a global market cap weighting. At the time the weighting was 8%; now it is around 3.5%. This was a well-timed decision as global equities have delivered a cumulative return of more than twice that of UK equities since that decision was made (around 330% vs 155%, or 12.2% per annum vs 7.7% per annum). The weight of UK equities within the listed component of our portfolio is currently around 5.5%. We have no immediate plans to increase this allocation.

PAUL NIVEN *has been the manager of F&C since 2014. The trust is second only to Scottish Mortgage in the global trust sector, measured by market capitalisation.*

A NEW WORLD ORDER

ALAN BARTLETT *of Goodhart Partners, sub-managers of the multi-asset Global Opportunities Trust, explains why the world's changing investment landscape calls for radically different strategies.*

THE KEY FORCES that have shaped the global investment landscape for many years have passed tipping points which will have profound implications for society and how to invest successfully over the coming decades. In simple terms we believe that investment strategies must evolve to become more agile and flexible in order to navigate the shorter economic, industry and market cycles now evident around us. This also means that investors must be more willing to step away from benchmark indices and focus on specific investment opportunities. This is in contrast to the relatively inflexible broad index-oriented strategies and asset allocation frameworks that have served investors well for many years now. The change required is a significant one.

The era of globalisation

'Globalisation' has been the dominant investment theme of the last three decades. It resulted from the benign alignment of four key forces.

Demographics

The industrialisation of emerging markets increased the amount of labour available to the global economic system, as did a step-shift in the proportion of women entering the workforce.

Technology

The Japanese taught the world how to manufacture goods more efficiently in the 1980s with the advent of 'just in time' supply chain manufacturing. Then in the 1990s advances in technology made it logistically easier for companies to operate with extended global supply chains, able to manufacture goods in low-cost locations and take full advantage of what economists call 'comparative advantage'.

Security

When the Berlin Wall fell and the true weakness of the Russian economy became apparent, western democracies saw an opportunity. They reasoned that the Western approach to capitalism and democracy was now so obviously superior that all they had to do was remove the barriers and countries such as Russia and China would naturally evolve into capitalist democracies.

Buoyed by the additional benefits of the so-called 'peace dividend' from the end of the Cold War, globalisation became a geopolitical objective, not just an economic one. The taps were turned on to export physical and intellectual capital to encourage and accelerate economic development in these traditional adversary countries.

Environment

For much of the 30 years preceding Covid, people were still arguing over whether global warming was actually man-made, and environmental issues were largely seen as local, not global. Society operated as if the world's resources were unlimited and maximising short-term consumption for the lowest direct cost possible was more important than concepts like 'sustainability'.

The forces that drove globalisation have been strongly deflationary. They meant developed market governments (and the US in particular) were able to suppress interest rates, which in turn created a strong period for asset price inflation. Companies took advantage of globalisation to 'optimise' their tax positions, moving operations to wherever taxes were lower, which increased profits.

In the background, however, many issues were brewing. Over the 30 years to Covid, global GDP growth averaged around 2.7% in real terms, which is a healthy number by long-term standards, albeit lower than that seen during the 1950s and 1960s. Policymakers around the world wanted higher economic growth and tried to stimulate consumption as the 'engine' to drive investment and increased supply. Whilst this didn't really work, it did inflate asset prices (equities, bonds, property etc.) without causing a problem for consumer inflation.

The future looks different

Three of the four forces that shape the world we live in have now passed tipping points that mean they have changed from being tailwinds for global economic growth to headwinds. Outside Africa the world's population is ageing quickly. Humanity has no choice but to recognise that it lives on a planet with finite resources and an ecosystem that we can destroy if we are not careful. Covid highlighted the risks of globally extended supply chains and the importance of security of supply in an uncertain world.

As these new powerful forces act to constrain 'supply', geopolitical tensions are inevitable. When nations cannot enrich themselves through co-operation, history tells us they will seek to do it through force. Money spent on upgrading military capabilities is money not available for healthcare or to subsidise investment in green energy. The lone remaining source of optimism is technology. While we are hugely positive on the potential for artificial intelligence (AI) to drive improvements in productivity over the long term, we believe that realism about what can be achieved in the shorter term is important.

People in the US and Europe that are in their 50s and 60s have been huge beneficiaries of asset price inflation. Many benefit from incredibly generous defined benefit pension schemes and live in houses that are worth ten or even 20 times the most they have ever earned in a year. But taxes on their children must rise to pay for the healthcare needs of older people, while they are saddled with debt from university, despite their parents receiving a free education. Unwinding the inequities of society will be difficult, but the status quo is not viable.

Covid brought forward the earnings of large tech companies that empowered the 'work from home' phenomenon. But it also accelerated the wider issues facing society as the tailwinds of the 1990–2012 period fade away. Governments are creaking under huge debt loads that are becoming increasingly expensive to service as inflation and interest rates prove stubbornly higher than we have been used to in recent years.

Viewed from the perspective of the four forces, it is clear these issues are not going away, and will only get worse. Such analysis provides a useful prism through which to view much of what is happening around the world. Witness President Trump wanting to 'acquire' Greenland, secure the Panama Canal and cut the fiscal deficit through tariffs. It helps explain the political opportunity that the Reform party sees in the UK and other new parties are capitalising on across Europe.

If economic growth cannot be fast enough to pay down debt and rebalance fiscal deficits, taxes must rise and public spending must be cut. That isn't going to be a popular political message, and so we are set for a long period of deeper and shorter cycles, as governments battle economically and potentially militarily with each other and the new realities.

Implications for investors

Over the decades leading to Covid, investors were perfectly rational when they dramatically increased focus on index returns and passive investing. Given the benign global environment, it was also rational to lock capital away for long periods in private equity and use leverage to increase returns. But on a forward-looking basis things now appear rather different.

We expect economic, industry and market cycles to be shorter and probably deeper. Overall market returns will be lower and volatility higher. Against this background agility is going to be key. A willingness to navigate the cycles and step away from indices and focus on specific opportunities rather than broad market returns is required.

The shift required by the asset management industry is huge. The median open-ended global equity fund[1] has had a correlation to the MSCI World index over three years of +0.89.[2] Perhaps more shockingly, the median multi-asset fund[3] over the same period had only a slightly lower correlation of +0.83. Investors would be forgiven for thinking that a high correlation with broad market indices is inevitable if you invest in a diversified portfolio, but it just isn't true.

The median correlation of all possible equally weighted 30-stock global equity portfolios[4] to the MSCI World over the three years to 31 May, 2025 was much lower at +0.78. Global equity and multi-asset strategies deliberately 'track' benchmark indices because historically stepping away from them has been risky. But the forces that underpinned this have now changed, and it is time for the investment industry to change as well.

This will only happen if clients demand it – that is, if they start to value the ability to produce attractive returns that are not driven by market index returns. An investment trust is an ideal vehicle for agile investment strategies, benefitting from more stable capital and greater investment flexibility than typical open-ended

1 Median global equity fund within the combined Morningstar fund sectors of global large-cap growth equity, global large-cap value equity, global large-cap blend equity and global equity Income.

2 Correlation of monthly total returns of funds to MSCI World GBP monthly total returns (net of dividend withholding tax) from 31/05/2022 to 31/05/2025.

3 Median Multi-Asset Funds with the combined Morningstar Fund Sectors of GBP Allocation 60-80% Equity, GBP Allocation 40-60% Equity and GBP Flexible Allocation.

4 Based on 10,000 simulations of equally-weighted 30-stock portfolios with randomised stock selection from a universe of 7,119 North American and European equities (as included in UBS Holt dataset).

cousins. The opportunities to differentiate positively over the coming years will be enormous.

The way that the portfolio of Global Opportunities Trust is managed is designed to prosper in this new world. Since the investment policy was amended in late 2021 its net asset value has had essentially zero correlation to global equity indices, whilst still generating a real return for investors.

It does not benchmark itself against any index. When opportunities are abundant the trust is tolerant of market risk and volatility in search of higher returns. But during periods of elevated valuations in which genuinely attractive opportunities are scarce (as in recent years) it is more focused on capital preservation. We call the approach 'agile investing'.

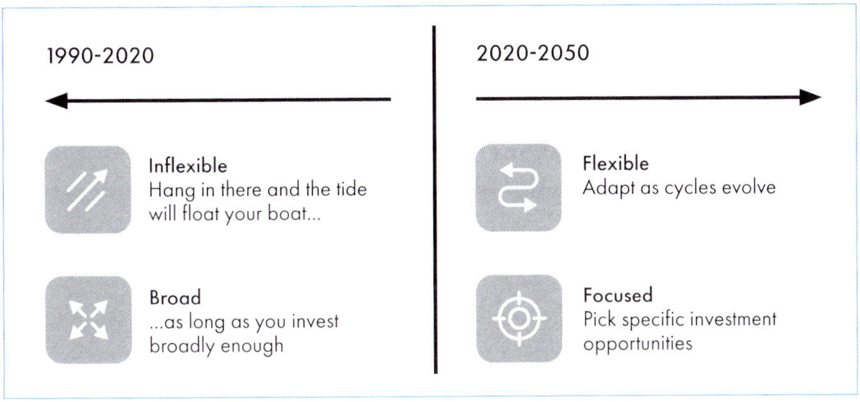

Source: Goodhart Partners.

Global Opportunities Trust, (GOT), a multi-asset trust managed by Sandy Nairn and Goodhart Partners, revised its mandate three years ago to adopt a more flexible strategy based around the analysis presented above. Alan Bartlett was appointed the CEO of Goodhart Partners in 2009.

SMALL IS BEAUTIFUL

ANDREW WORNE, *head of investment trust corporate broking at the broker Cavendish, takes issue with the argument that only the biggest investment trusts can survive in a period of consolidation.*

When asked whether one would prefer a larger fund with lower costs over a smaller one with higher fees, most investors instinctively lean toward the former. Yet, as the Canadian pop star Shania Twain told us back in 1998, "That don't impress me much". Consider this: will making a trust a few hundred million pounds larger and a few basis points cheaper suddenly convince investors who have long overlooked it to change their minds?

The race for scale is driven almost entirely by the desire to remain relevant to increasingly consolidated wealth management groups. But the investment trust 'wrapper', as we are so often reminded, has endured world wars, pandemics, and decades of change. Over Shania's lifetime alone, we have seen the rise of unit trusts, OEICs, ETFs, and now the emergence of the 'active ETF' and LTAFs.

So the trust structure has stood the test of time. However, today's technology provides investors with low-cost, large-scale access without discount volatility, conveniences that were unimaginable only a few decades ago.

For a handful of trusts the pursuit of scale is entirely laudable, but probably at a size approaching FTSE 100 membership. For the majority, however, the future lies in serving the informed, self-directed investor, the kind of person you might meet at an AGM, who then shares their conviction with friends and peers. They may not be TikTok influencers, but they have children, grandchildren, neighbours, and even a respected voice at the local book club. In their own way, they are the traditional influencers who matter most.

The conventional wisdom that small trusts are 'too small' and therefore irrelevant is misguided. What, after all, is wrong with a well-governed company of modest size delivering strong, differentiated performance for a loyal and growing retail audience? The case for smaller trusts is compelling and needs no lengthy explainer.

In short: they can invest with conviction, exploit niches, bring influence and engagement, and act with agility. Above all, they can add genuine value.

Conviction

Smaller trusts can concentrate capital in their best ideas. Conviction investing carries risk, but when managers have an informational edge through deep, focused research, the benefits can be substantial. The closed-ended trust structure is designed precisely for this.

Specialism

Niche and frontier markets are largely absent from mainstream ETFs and large-cap funds. Smaller trusts give investors access to less-researched areas where inefficiencies – and opportunities – abound. Here, investors may discover companies with pricing power, strong margins, and significant growth potential before they are recognised by the wider market.

Influence and engagement

Cost-cutting alone cannot replicate what might be called the 'influence premium'. This comes from skill, active ownership, and a willingness to devote time and capital to ideas that managers truly believe in. Of course, large shareholders actively talk to large companies. But a more precise partnership approach to active engagement can directly improve company outcomes, unlocking shareholder value through discipline and focus.

Agility

Smaller pools of capital can respond quickly. Whether it's a mispriced micro-cap, an under-researched equity, or a niche theme, small trusts can take meaningful positions without moving the market. This flexibility allows managers to seize emerging opportunities early, while also reducing risk exposure swiftly when necessary.

The investment trust sector already provides shining examples of companies delivering shareholder value without scale. Take Rockwood Strategic (RKW), where the top ten holdings represent more than 60% of assets. This concentrated approach reflects a philosophy centred on structural opportunities and active engagement, consistently delivering excellent outcomes for shareholders.

For specialism, Manulife/CQS offers Golden Prospect Precious Metals (GPM) and Geiger Counter (GCL). These trusts are not 'all-weather' portfolios, but for investors seeking expert access to junior gold miners or exposure to uranium exploration and development, they can provide targeted, specialist diversification.

Even the largest managers see the value in focus. BlackRock Frontiers (BRFI), for instance, specialises in companies from the economies of tomorrow, offering both diversification and potential rewards less correlated with developed markets.

Managing discounts

No discussion on investment trusts would be complete without a reflection on discounts. It is hard to escape the conclusion that the smaller the trust, the more volatile the discount is likely to be. Distinctive management styles can drift out of favour from time to time leaving a board struggling, without the firepower of larger trusts, to defend the discount with consistent buybacks. It is therefore essential that boards reassure shareholders that 'form is temporary, but class is permanent', and communicate this with clarity and conviction.

The stock market, at its core, exists to raise equity capital. Yet the IPO market, particularly for investment trusts specifically is almost entirely dormant. Still, from small acorns do great oak trees grow. Two recent examples, Ashoka Whiteoak Emerging (AWEM) and Onward Opportunities (ONWD), come to mind where trusts have come to market at a modest scale, with a tight group of founding shareholders. Both trusts came to market in 2023 and have rewarded shareholders with returns between 30% and 40%, at the time of writing. They are premium rated, which indicates that discounts aren't inevitable, and provide compelling 'small is beautiful' role models in the toughest IPO environment in memory.

Summary

Investment trusts of modest size are not handicapped by their dimensions; rather, they are often liberated by them. Smaller structures allow managers to invest with conviction, to access overlooked niches, to influence outcomes through meaningful engagement, and to move with genuine agility. For investors, this translates into differentiated opportunities and the potential for strong long-term returns that larger, more index-aware vehicles may struggle to deliver. They might even impress Shania Twain.

ANDREW WORNE *has been a stockbroker for more than 25 years and head of investment trust corporate broking at Cavendish, formerly Cenkos, since 2023.*

STAYING ACTIVE

MARK ATKINSON, *of Willis Towers Watson, manager of Alliance Witan, makes the case for including actively managed trusts in your portfolio.*

Reasons for concern

"IN THE LONG run we are all dead," said the economist and philosopher John Maynard Keynes. Writing in 1923, the great man was criticising complacency among classical economists who believed that, if you waited long enough, output and employment would always right themselves during an economic crisis.

It took the Great Depression for governments to wake up and intervene. Today, investors in active equity funds could be forgiven for feeling just as frustrated as Keynes was then. "How long do we have to wait until active managers justify their fees by delivering on their implicit promise to outperform industry benchmarks? Never mind the long run, how about in my lifetime?"

There is little doubt that many active managers are testing investors' patience. AJ Bell's 'Manager versus Machine' report revealed that only about one third of active equity managers outperformed their passive counterparts in 2024. The same is true over a ten-year horizon. The proportion outperforming in the global sector was even lower at only 17–18% in 2024. No wonder so many investors are abandoning active products and flocking instead to cheaper passive rivals.

UK retail investors have withdrawn over £100 billion in the last three years, according to AJ Bell, in favour of trackers, exchange-traded funds (ETFs), bitcoin, mortgages and cash. There's no clear evidence of a recovery in demand for active funds among retail investors. Interactive Investor's Top 50 Fund Index for the second quarter of 2025, which ranks the most-popular funds, investment trusts and ETFs, based on the number of purchases made by ii customers, included a majority of 30 tracker products. Morningstar predicts that European passive assets will surpass active equity funds within the next five years.[1]

The main drag on the performance of active managers in the North American and global sectors has been the concentration of returns in US mega-cap technology

1 'Manager vs Machine', AJ Bell, Dec 2024.

stocks, which form a large part of the indices. As at 31 July, the ten largest stocks by market capitalisation in the S&P 500 index accounted for 38% of its value and 24% of the MSCI All Country World Index.[2] Most recently, these stocks have benefitted from the explosive growth of (and investor enthusiasm for) artificial intelligence (AI).[3]

This has massively increased their market capitalisations, which now dwarf the whole stock markets of many countries. Before that, many of them benefitted from Covid lockdowns and remote working. The sheer size of these mega-cap stocks has made life very difficult for active managers who now need extremely large, high-risk positions just to keep pace with the index, let alone to outperform it.

The ten-year performance of Alliance Witan

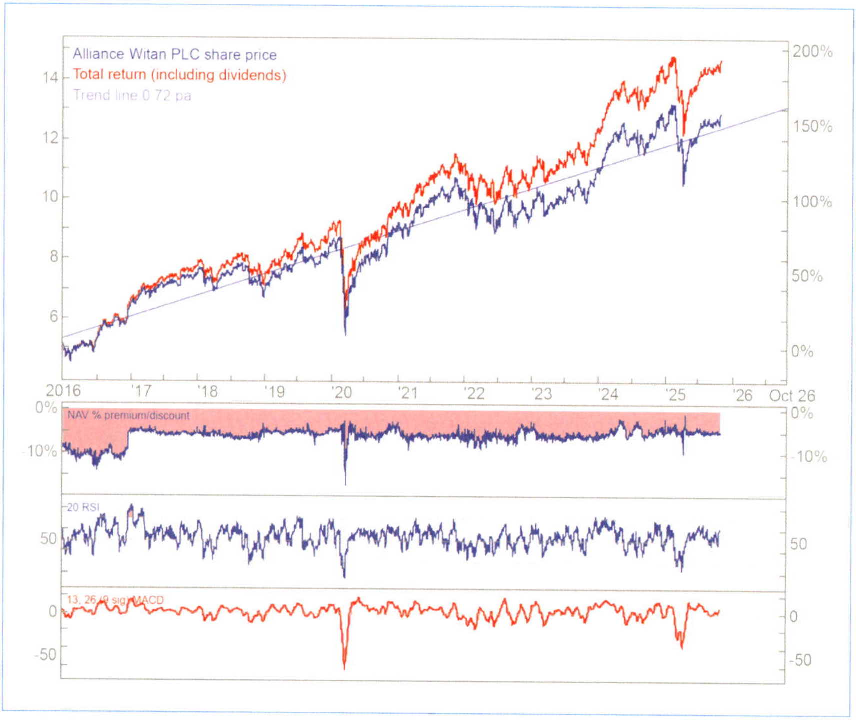

Source: ShareScope, as at 30 September 2025. Past performance does not predict future returns.

2 These ten stocks are: Nvidia, Microsoft, Apple, Amazon, Meta, Broadcom, Alphabet A, Alphabet C, Berkshire Hathaway, and Tesla.

3 Interactive Investor's Top 50 Fund Index, second quarter, 2025.

History suggests caution

Given the expectation that AI will increasingly become embedded in almost every industry, it is tempting to conclude these tech giants can go on outperforming forever. Yet, while it is unwise to place blind faith in mean reversion, history suggests that such narrowness rarely persists. With some exceptions, the biggest companies by market capitalisation at the end of one decade are not usually the same as the next.

Furthermore, periods of transition away from concentrated markets have historically created more favourable conditions for active managers. Take the 1996–2000 period, another time of narrow leadership in equity markets. Active managers struggled. But when the dot-com bubble burst, the tables turned. Over the next decade, the median global active manager delivered cumulative outperformance of 28%.[4]

The need for managing market concentration risk and the likelihood of a more positive future environment provide greater credence to the case for active management. However, just switching more of your money into actively managed funds is not enough. It is important for investors to think carefully about how to build robust diversified portfolios to maximise their chance of success.

Alliance Witan's approach

We see significant merit in carefully blending different investment styles. The Alliance Witan approach, which is unique in the investment trust world, involves choosing 11 highly skilled and specialist active managers to pick stocks for our portfolio. Each manager contributes up to a maximum of 20 of their best ideas from their specialist universe, looking for high potential returns, but balanced between different styles to ensure diversification of risks.

It's certainly been a challenging period for active managers since the strategy was launched in 2017, one in which share prices have been driven more by macroeconomic and geopolitical news flow – Covid, wars in Europe and the Middle East, Trump and on-off tariffs – than corporate fundamentals. But there are reassuring signs that we may be entering a better environment for active managers. With artificially low interest rates no longer propping up weak companies and markets becoming more fragmented as we move towards a new regime of 'de-globalisation', investors are being more discriminating about what they buy and sell.

Recent trends show that equal-weighted benchmarks of US stocks have started to outperform market-cap weighted benchmarks, indicating that more stocks than just

4 WTW, August 2025.

the tech giants are beating the index. And as doubts about US stability grow, stocks outside the US have also started to shine. From 01 January 2025, through to the end of July, MSCI China and MSCI UK were the strongest performing markets, measured in sterling, and mid cap outperformed large cap, while growth and value styles delivered similar returns.[5]

This broader participation by companies across different geographies with less demanding valuations increases the opportunity for active managers to outperform. Additionally, correlations between stocks have fallen and price dispersion – the differences in stock returns between best and worst performers – has been rising after a period of low dispersion. Both lower correlation and higher dispersion enhance the potential for active managers to generate differentiated returns from the index from stock selection.

After such a long period in the doldrums, the comeback by active managers is still in its early stages. But there does seem to be a tailwind developing. AJ Bell's 'Man versus Machine' report for the first half of 2025 showed that a record 51% of actively managed funds in the Investment Association (IA) global sector outperformed a passive alternative in the first half of 2025. It was the first time since the report was launched in 2021 that global active funds had approached anywhere near a 50%-win rate versus their passive peers over any time period.

It's worth highlighting that active and passive strategies are not mutually exclusive. Indeed, it's quite sensible to deploy both, depending on the asset class, sector and region that you are investing in, and at different times, as history shows active and passive styles both have their own performance cycles. Passive strategies may have worked much better than active ones in recent years, but the trillions flowing into market-cap-weighted products have increased the co-movement of stocks within an index, which reduces diversification. It also undermines so-called price discovery, the process by which buyers and sellers interact in the marketplace to determine the current price of a stock.

The choices today

With prices divorced from fundamentals in some cases and driven by non-economic flows, reality will eventually bite. Ultimately, it is earnings that determine share prices, not sentiment and flows. Active strategies, like that of Alliance Witan, which steadfastly focus on healthy corporate fundamentals should do well in rational markets.

Alliance Witan has the added advantage of the investment trust structure, which

5 MSCI, August 2025.

enables us to gear the portfolio up or down depending on the market environment to enhance or protect returns. It means the board can also use the company's extensive distributable reserves to keep increasing the annual dividend if portfolio income is insufficient, a track record that now stretches to a joint industry-leading 58 consecutive years. And, being a global multi-manager portfolio, Alliance Witan has the flexibility to rebalance exposures between managers depending on market conditions or performance. This is all for a competitive fee of less than 0.6% (60 basis points) per annum.

As a pioneering investor himself, Keynes saw that equity markets can be driven by speculative manias for long periods of time, with each participant second-guessing the next one about what prices should be rather than using research to uncover reasonable estimates of true value. In such a "beauty contest", he warned "markets can remain irrational longer than you can remain solvent".

Keynes stayed solvent by buying undervalued companies with solid intrinsic values and holding them for the long term. His fundamental-based investment philosophy and process served him well. Born into an academic family, he died in 1946 with a net estimated worth of between $22m and $30m in today's money.[6]

MARK ATKINSON *is a Senior Director at Willis Towers Watson, which manages the Alliance Witan investment trust.*

6 *The Financial Times*, 7 May 2021

1.00
1.4508
SL/TP

THEMES

THE GREAT UNWIND

TOM TREANOR *of Asset Value Investors explains why wide discounts can – and should – be tackled by purposeful boards.*

ANYONE INVOLVED IN the investment trust, also known as closed-end fund, sector will spend a lot of their time talking about discounts. At AVI, as the manager of three investment trusts, all of whose strategy involves investing in assets trading at discounts, we certainly do.

The discount challenge

Discounts exist due to demand being lower than supply, an axiom about as insightful and interesting as being told 'there are more buyers than sellers' when asking why a stock is going up. There is a plethora of academic research on the subject, perhaps reflecting what to many must seem at first glance like the proverbial dollar bill lying untouched on the pavement. In theory a closed-end fund with a portfolio of listed liquid equities trading at a 10% discount to the market value of that portfolio could liquidate and provide an immediate 11% gain to anyone who had bought shares in the fund.

On the face of it, this is a very simple form of arbitrage that seemingly shouldn't exist, and it's perhaps unsurprising that many of the world's most famous value investors began their investment careers in this area: Benjamin Graham, Warren Buffett, Edward Thorp, Seth Klarman, to name but a few.

However, in the timeless words of Yogi Berra "in theory there is no difference between theory and practice. In practice, there is". Discounts have proved persistent in closed-end funds all over the world, so you don't need academic theory to tell us that this must mean there are limits to this kind of arbitrage, caused by real-world frictions.

In the example quoted above, to force through a liquidation one would have to be able and willing to acquire a sufficiently large stake in the fund and then garner sufficient support from other shareholders. In situations where the underlying portfolio is a lot less liquid (say in micro-cap equities), the market impact of selling such securities is likely to erode at least some of the potential gains. And this is before we start thinking about funds holding private assets, where there may be no easily accessible market into which to sell.

Aside from the portfolio liquidity issue, a non-exhaustive list of why discounts exist would also include: valuation (NAV) uncertainty, large or controlling management stakes, unusual voting structures, high fees, large potential termination payments to the manager, a poorly regarded manager and/or board, and/or simply a lack of interest in the trust's strategy.

Aside from closed-end funds, AVI also invests in holding companies, conglomerates, and Japanese operating companies with large amounts of surplus financial assets. While the unifying theme is the fact that they trade at discounts to NAV, the nature of the assets and the way that we think about discounts have different nuances across these different types of companies.

With closed-end funds, engagement and activism play a key role in our investment approach. Given our years of experience and knowledge of the sector, as an engaged and constructive shareholder we aim to add value by helping boards find ways to tackle discounts. Capital allocation is arguably the most important strategic decision taken by boards, and we firmly believe that all funds should have a clear and rational policy that demonstrates that they understand the superior returns that can usually be achieved when trading on a wide discount by preferring share repurchases over new investments.

A 5% buyback at a 30% discount to NAV, for example, provides a return on investment of 45%. Given this return is risk-free and compounds with the forward return on the existing portfolio, heroic assumptions are required for a new investment to better this.

Alternatives in the frame

The vast majority of our closed-end fund holdings are invested in alternative assets (real estate, infrastructure, renewables etc.) which, unlike equity-focused vehicles, don't have the 'easy option' of eliminating their discounts by swiftly liquidating their portfolios and returning the proceeds to shareholders. The quid pro quo for investors in the current environment, however, is that on average alternative asset funds trade at significantly wider discounts.

Alternatives offer attractive rewards for those willing to do the work to help ascertain the validity of the reported NAVs and establish in the process whether these discounts are real or illusory. The next step then is to form a thesis about how these discounts might be narrowed or eradicated and persuade the boards of the companies to take the necessary remedial action.

So, what does the playbook look like for alternative asset funds at this point?

Alternative fund discounts over ten years

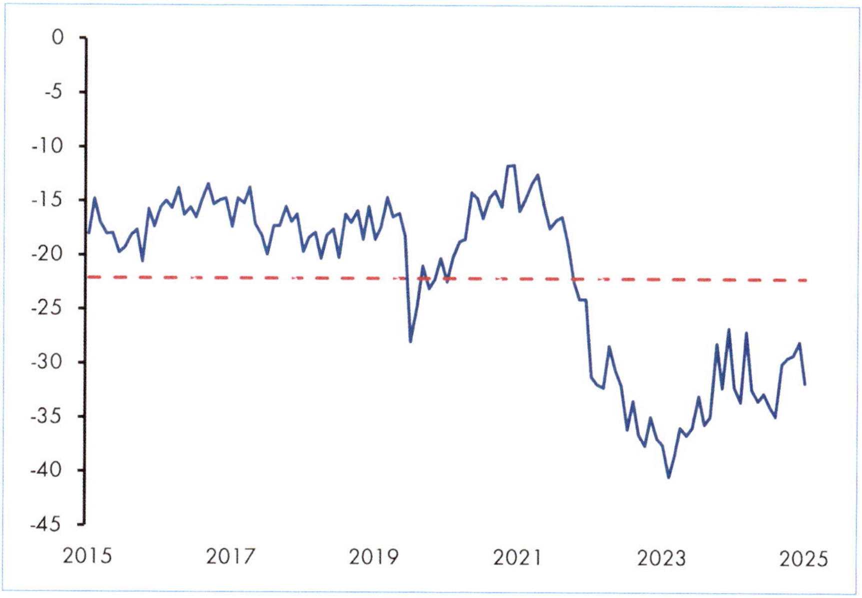

Source: Morningstar.

Equity fund discounts over ten years

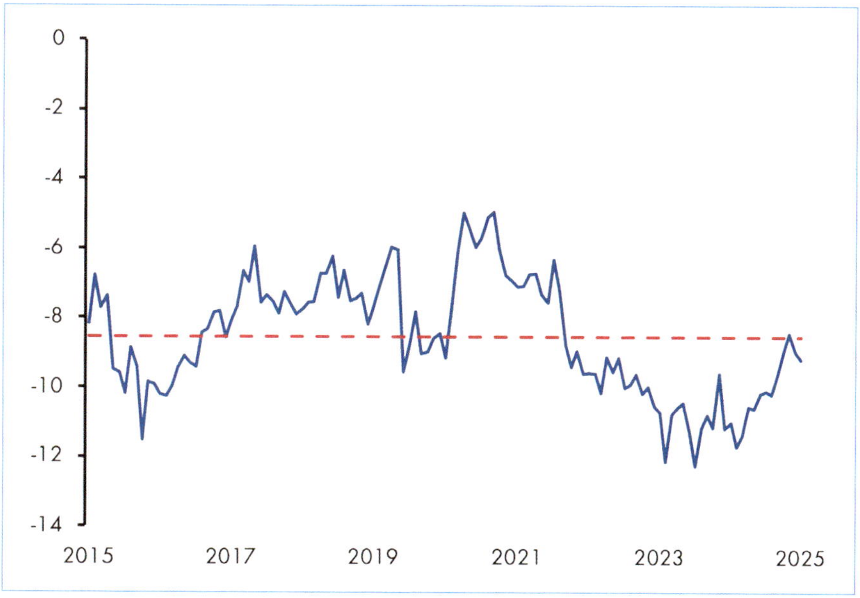

Source: Morningstar.

First, some context. The nailing of interest rates to the floor in the wake of the global financial crisis heralded a 15-year boom in issuance of alternative income funds. Various shades of infrastructure, renewable energy, and sub-sector specialist real estate plays came to the London market in quick succession, followed by even more esoteric asset classes such as shipping and music rights. What these vehicles all had in common were tempting dividend yields of more than 4%, designed to appeal to investors starved of yield in the new low (and briefly zero) interest environment.

We are now in the 'Great Unwind' phase of this boom. Rising interest rates, wealth manager consolidation, and flawed and misleading cost disclosure rules have led to a slump in demand, producing sharply wider discounts for these funds. The industry needs to work hard to find new sources of demand, but while there are clearly secular or idiosyncratic factors at work, a large component of the malaise is cyclical. To put it bluntly, there are too many investment trust shares around and the sector needs to shrink.

Only then, once equilibrium is restored, are we likely to see new issuance and a thriving trust market. In the case of equity trusts, Saba Capital have parked their tanks on the lawn of a large swathe of the market. While many will question the tactical astuteness of their approach when they broke cover late last year, in many instances, the complacency of boards about discounts allowed them to build their positions at wide discounts in the first place.

The fundamental and existential question that Saba, with its vast pot of capital, poses for the boards of equity trusts is that if you're going to operate like an open-ended fund, then why not become one? The answer must surely mean making full use of the closed-end structure: using gearing, investing in less-liquid parts of the market, buying back when on a discount to enhance returns, and so on. Otherwise, it is difficult to argue against eliminating the discount by becoming an open-ended fund, or active ETF.

Scale is also an important factor, and there are many equity trust mergers that would make sense if egos and self-interest could be set aside. To their credit, many boards of alternatives funds have woken up to the new paradigm. There has been an increasing recognition, belated in some cases but welcome nonetheless, that the hurdle rate for new investments is at historically elevated levels, given the returns available from buying one's existing assets cheaply via share repurchases.

The playbook adopted across the infrastructure and renewable funds, in particular, has been to try to sell assets close to, at, or above NAV, to prove the carrying values and provide cash that can be used to pay down expensive debt or buy back shares. Some have been more successful in doing so than others. We accept the difficulties in selling assets into a market where everyone has the same idea! This disciplined approach to capital allocation is necessary, but not sufficient, for a rerating and we think it is incumbent on boards to think radically beyond this.

Consolidation should certainly be one of the options on the table. We remain to be convinced that the sector needs three UK solar funds, for example. Boards must accept, if they haven't already done so, that there may be potential private owners of these assets who are willing to put a higher valuation on them than public markets ever will over a realistic timeframe. While we don't want to see boards roll over at the first approach, we do want them to recognise that reported NAVs for private assets are not seen as gospel and that shareholders will often be open to entertaining bids even if they are below the latest reported NAV.

As such, we applaud the pro-activeness of the board of Apax Global Alpha in finding a solution to the persistently wide discount at which the shares traded. By running a process to establish secondary interest and a private market clearing price for the shares, shareholders who chose not to roll their investment were able to exit at a share price level unlikely to be achieved as a public company for some considerable time. In doing so, they have also provided a template for other boards grappling with entrenched discounts in the listed private equity sector to consider.

The vast majority of our engagement/activist activities are conducted wholly in private and remain so, but we were involved in an unusually high-profile campaign at Hipgnosis Songs Fund in the recent past. In our view, this episode confirmed the difference that can be made with the right directors in place, with the new appointees that we helped bring onto the board overseeing a sale of the company, a successful outcome few would have thought possible just months earlier.

Towards the future

How does this all end? We foresee, in time, a healthy bifurcated market consisting of fewer, larger, liquid funds at one end of the market and smaller specialist funds making full use of the closed-end structure to generate above-market returns in less efficient market areas. The journey to get there, the Great Unwind, offers the most compelling opportunity that we can recall seeing in the London-listed closed-end fund market. And it has only just begun to run its course.

TOM TREANOR *is a portfolio manager and head of research at Asset Value Investors. He has specialised in closed-end funds for 20 years, and was appointed a director of Asset Value Investors in 2017 and co-manager of MIGO Opportunities in June this year.*

CHASING THE RETAIL INVESTOR

JOE WINKLEY, *head of investment trusts at Winterflood Securities, explains why private investors are being actively pursued by investment trust boards and managers.*

THE OWNERSHIP OF the investment trust sector has undergone a number of fundamental changes over the last 20 years. In 2005 wealth managers represented the single largest shareholder group and there was also significant institutional and pension fund ownership across the sector. The overall quantum of retail ownership was hard to estimate in 2005, with a number of manager-administered savings schemes in place and a large contingent of direct holders.

Execution-only platforms – percentage ownership of investment trust sector (2005–2024)

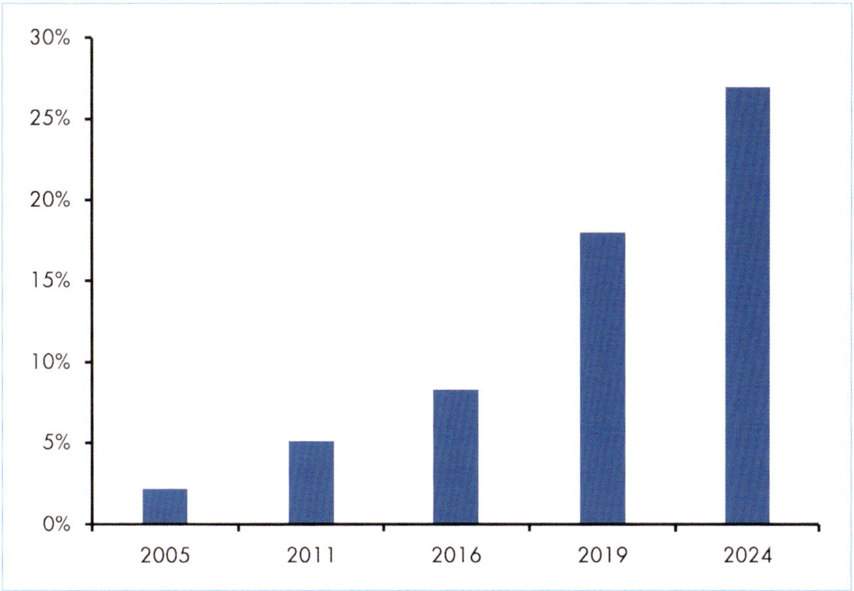

Source: RDIR/AIC/Warhorse Partners.

Based on historic shareholder analysis, we estimate that retail holders constituted approximately 15% of the sector at that time and it is notable that only 2.2% of the sector was owned by execution-only platforms such as Hargreaves Lansdown, AJ Bell and interactive investor.

Since 2005 we have seen a number of fundamental shifts in ownership, with institutional and wealth manager holdings declining in many areas of the investment trust universe. This has been accompanied by an ongoing increase in retail ownership, signified by the amount of the sector held by the execution-only platforms. By the end of 2019 this stood at 18% of the sector and the most recent estimates, at the end of 2024, put execution-only ownership at 27% with total retail ownership (including savings plans and direct retail) potentially as high as 36% of the sector. Bearing in mind that the sector itself had grown in market capitalisation from £73.6bn in 2005 to over £200bn by 2025, this marks a very significant increase in retail ownership both in absolute and percentage terms.

What has fuelled the growth in retail ownership?

Retail Distribution Review

The Retail Distribution Review (RDR) was implemented in the UK in 2012 with the aim of raising standards in financial advice through, among other measures, banning commission payments from product providers. This change served to address a long-standing bias toward open-ended funds, which had traditionally paid commissions, and created a more level playing field for investment trusts, which did not offer such incentives. It is no coincidence that the level of retail ownership across the investment trust sector has accelerated in the post-RDR environment.

Growth of retail platforms

At the time of the Retail Distribution Review in 2012 there was approximately £94bn of assets held by execution-only and other direct-to-consumer retail platforms. By 2025 this had grown to over £471bn across 12 million customer accounts (source: Market Monitor). In many ways the growth in retail ownership of investment trusts has mirrored the rapid expansion in the assets held on these platforms. The drivers behind this growth include the use of technology that makes DIY investing easier and more attractive, alongside a number of regulatory and tax incentives, such as ISAs and SIPPs, that have encouraged self-directed investing.

Income

Low interest rates for many years post the financial crisis in 2008 made cash savings less attractive and acted to push investors towards seeking alternative sources of income. This desire for sustainable income investments played to the strength of the investment trust sector, which has structural advantages over open-ended funds in allowing companies to use revenue reserves to smooth dividends or even to pay uncovered dividends out of capital.

The popularity of the AIC's 'dividend heroes' among retail investors is a testament to the attraction of reliable and growing dividends in a low-interest-rate environment. This dynamic also helped to fuel the growth in alternative investment trusts, providing exposure to income-generating real assets such as renewables, infrastructure, credit and real estate.

Shareholder engagement

The rise of retail ownership over the last few years is in many ways a positive for the investment trust sector. Retail investors in investment trusts tend to be long-term, supportive shareholders, who also provide valuable secondary market liquidity. However, with increasing numbers of retail holders on investment trusts' share registers, this ownership shift has also served to shine a spotlight on a key aspect of corporate governance. This is the voting (or rather lack of voting) by retail shareholders.

The vast majority of retail shares in investment trusts are held through investment platforms and, under existing Companies Act legislation, these intermediary firms have no legal obligation to provide voting information and voting rights to their customers. In practice a number of platforms do provide information and facilitate voting for their customers, but this is by no means a universal position. An individual investor's ability to receive notifications about upcoming general meetings and vote their shares is determined on a case-by-case basis. This has led to a position where historic voter turnout from the retail shareholder base has been very low in the investment trust sector, with voting levels of less than 10% (and often significantly less) being commonplace.

The issue of voter turnout was very much in the spotlight during Saba Capital's recent attack on seven investment trusts. It was notable that the widespread publicity around Saba's requisitions led to a material increase in retail voter participation. As an example, AJ Bell released some analysis of its customers' voting on the seven trusts, which showed that a minimum of 60% of shares voted on each trust, and up to 76% in the case of European Smaller Companies Trust and 78% for Keystone Investment Trust.

It is clear therefore that when voting is needed, retail investors can respond, but the challenge is to ensure that retail voting and engagement remains high on an ongoing basis. In April 2025 the AIC launched its 'My Share My Vote' petition, with the aim of amending the Companies Act 2006 to ensure that investment platforms and other nominees are required to pass on company information and voting rights to customers. This campaign was withdrawn in July 2025 when the UK government committed to implement the recommendations of its Digitisation Taskforce. These include establishing a 'Bill of Shareholder Rights' requiring platforms and other intermediaries to provide customers with company information, enable them to vote their shares and to take part in general meetings.

Regulatory developments

The importance of retail investors to both the investment trust sector and to the UK's wider equity markets has not gone unnoticed by the Treasury and the Financial Conduct Authority (FCA). The UK's new prospectus rules, which come into force in January 2026, significantly benefit investment trusts, with closed-ended funds able to issue up to 100% of their existing share capital without the need to publish a prospectus, reducing the cost and administrative burden for follow-on offerings.

Availability of research

The 2023 Investment Research Review, led by Rachel Kent, examined the decline of investment research in the UK, and while the focus was much wider than the investment trust sector, one of the key recommendations was the need to improve access to research for retail investors and support issuer-sponsored research with suitable safeguards. The government accepted all of the proposals from the Kent review although, as yet, no significant changes have been implemented.

In the investment trust sector, research suitable for retail investors is not uncommon and there are a number of longstanding issuer-sponsored research providers. The banking and broking community has been slower to embrace the retail investor community, although Winterflood has launched its pioneering Fund Insight product, which provides in-depth research for private investors and sits alongside its institutional research offering.

Looking ahead

Looking forward, the shift toward increased retail ownership of UK investment trusts is likely to continue. The combination of low-cost trading platforms, persistent demand for high-quality investment products, and retail engagement through digital tools suggests that the retail investor audience will continue to play a critical role in shaping the future of the sector.

At the same time, investment trust boards and managers need to remain vigilant. The strength of the competition for investor capital cannot be underestimated, and the investment trust sector needs to capture investor attention in an environment where open-ended funds, ETFs and, more recently, active ETFs and long-term asset funds (LTAFs) will all be competing to gain market share.

Against this backdrop and given the currently wide levels of discounts across the sector, it is perhaps not surprising that investment trusts have struggled to attract additional retail investors over the last year or so. Looking at the 12 months to the end of August 2025 there was net selling of investment trusts by the execution-only platforms of over £400m. Considering that retail investors have historically been net buyers of the sector, this decline in investor demand from a critical part of the shareholder base helps to explain some of the problems the sector has faced in terms of wide discounts and ongoing share buybacks.

Investment trusts net demand by month from execution-only platforms (£m)

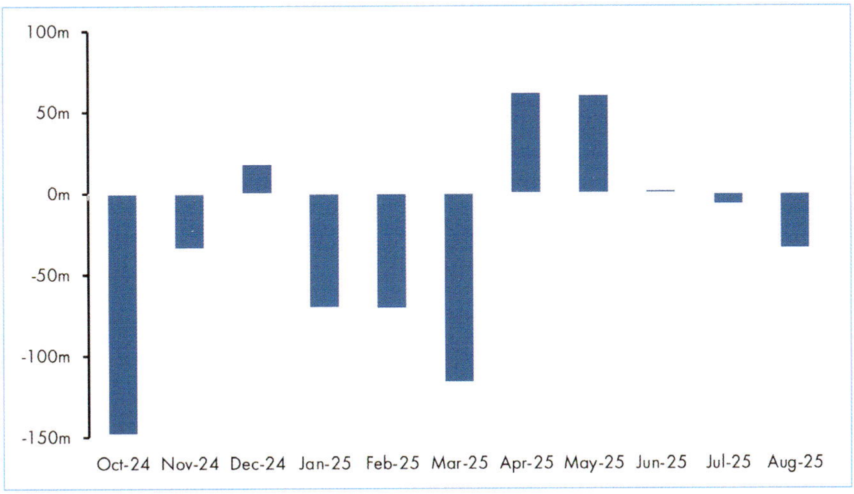

Source: Winterflood Retail Intelligence.

The more positive takeaway is that there are embryonic signs that retail investor sentiment is turning and the last few months have seen overall net inflows into the sector, somewhat reducing the pressure on company buybacks. However, it is notable that this trend is not uniform and, while some sectors are seeing net retail buying, a number of sectors still remain out of favour.

In an environment where ongoing retail buying has yet to become entrenched and where a number of sectors continue to see net selling, it is likely that consolidation will continue across the sector over the short to medium term, as underperforming or sub-scale trusts are merged or liquidated. Those that remain will need to focus on continuing to attract retail demand through performance, differentiation and investor engagement.

Execution-only platform net demand 12 months to end August 2025 (£m) – top 5 AIC sectors for inflows and outflows

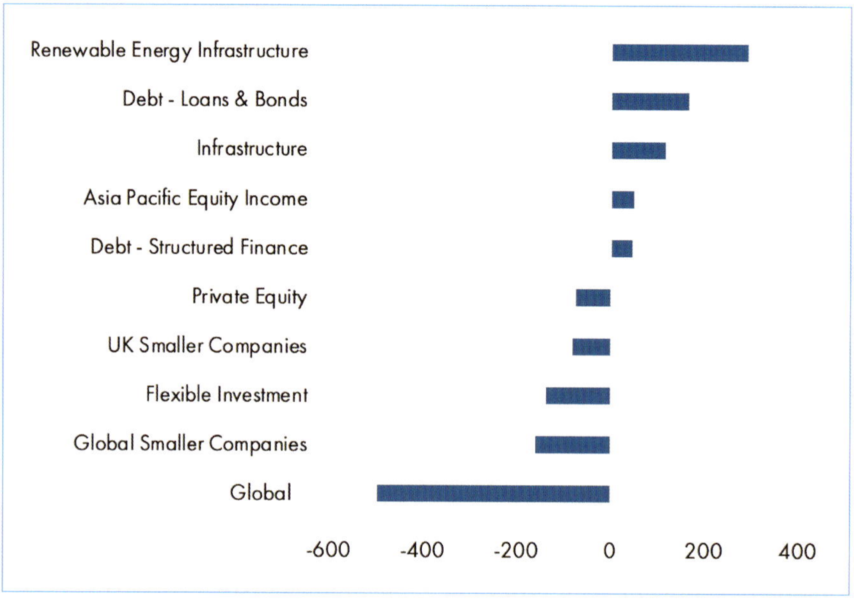

Source: Winterflood Retail Intelligence.

Conclusion

The ownership of UK investment trusts is constantly evolving. While institutions and wealth managers continue to play a significant role in the sector, retail investors are becoming ever-more important. The expanding retail demand over the last few years has reshaped the ownership of many investment trusts and it is likely that this trend will continue.

This means that investment trust boards and management groups are focusing more on retail investor engagement, marketing, transparency and competitive fee structures. This all costs money, but digital engagement is helping to target a range of investor demographics with the increasing use of podcasts, videos, online presentations and social media.

JOE WINKLEY *is head of investment trusts at Winterflood Securities.*

ARE ACTIVE ETFs A THREAT?

SIMON ELLIOTT *of J.P. Morgan Asset Management discusses whether active ETFs are likely to take demand away from investment trusts.*

The rise of ETFs

THE PAST YEAR has been especially eventful for the investment companies sector, marked by a flurry of corporate activity: takeover bids, mergers, managed wind-downs and strategic reviews. Yet, perhaps one of the most interesting developments has been the recommendation by the board of Middlefield Canadian Income to convert their investment company into an active exchange-traded fund (ETF). This is a first for the sector, but a number of commentators have suggested that it is unlikely to be the last. Indeed, some have gone further, speculating that the rise in active ETFs presents an existential threat to the future of the industry.

ETFs are not a new phenomenon. The first ones were launched in the early 1990s, but it was only after the turn of the millennium that they began to gain serious traction. Their appeal lies in their scalability, cost efficiency, and ease of access, while they also offer attractive tax advantages for US-based investors. The numbers are striking: in 2014, global ETF assets under management (AUM) stood at approximately $2trn. By the end of July 2025, this figure had soared to $16trn, representing a compound annual growth rate of 20%. The vast majority of these assets are in passive ETFs, which track a wide variety of indices and tend to offer exposure to broad markets at minimal cost.

While passive ETFs have historically dominated the market, the last decade has seen a surge in active ETFs—funds that employ active investment management strategies. In 2014, active ETFs accounted for only a small fraction of the market, with AUM of just a few billion dollars. Fast forward to July 2025, and active ETF AUM had reached $1.4trn, reflecting a compound annual growth rate of 46%. In the first seven months of 2025 alone, active ETFs attracted $1trn in global flows, accounting for more than a quarter of total ETF inflows. Today, 38% of ETFs by name are classified as active, making this the fastest-growing segment of the ETF universe.

Many would argue that active ETFs combine the best of both worlds: the flexibility and transparency of ETFs, with the potential for outperformance offered by active management. They provide daily transparency, intraday liquidity, and typically lower fees than traditional active funds. Investors can buy and sell active ETFs throughout the trading day, unlike open-ended funds, which only transact at the end-of-day net asset value. This liquidity and transparency are particularly attractive to institutional and professional investors.

Moreover, the cost structure of ETFs, both passive and active, is highly competitive. Passive ETFs charge fees well below those of traditional funds, and active ETFs, while more expensive than their passive counterparts, still tend to be priced lower than more traditional vehicles such as open-ended active funds. However, it is important to note that the requirement to be able to scale up (or down) means that an ETF structure is unsuitable for less-liquid asset classes.

Investment trusts compared

In considering the threat that ETFs present, it is first necessary to consider the structural advantages that investment trusts enjoy. Their closed-ended structure allows managers to take a long-term view, invest in less-liquid assets, and avoid forced selling during market downturns. Investment trusts can also employ gearing (leverage) to enhance returns, a feature not typically available in ETFs.

In addition, many investment trusts have a compelling track record in providing greater dividend certainty than is the case for an equivalent open-ended fund, or indeed an ETF. This is best reflected by the Association of Investment Companies' (AIC) 'dividend heroes', 20 investment trusts that have increased their dividends by 20 consecutive years or more, of which half can boast 50 years or more.

Another advantage that investment companies have over ETFs, or indeed open-ended funds, is the role of independent boards of non-executive directors. Boards have become increasingly active in recent years as market conditions have become more challenging and many investment companies have been derated. By representing the interests of shareholders, boards have put pressure on investment managers to improve performance, reduce fees, take measures to narrow discounts or consider changes in their approach. Their ultimate sanction is to appoint an alternative manager or, with shareholder support, look to wind-up and return capital.

While the advantages are numerous, the main disadvantage of investment companies is the disparity between NAV and share price performance. This can work both ways, either adding to or detracting from performance, but overall it adds to greater volatility in returns. In contrast, ETFs are designed to trade close to NAV due to the creation/redemption mechanism.

In terms of fees, active ETFs would appear to have a clear advantage. According to the AIC, the average OCF for an investment company at present, excluding venture capital trusts, is 1.01%, which will be substantially higher than for most ETFs. However, this figure reflects the diversity of the sector: over 40% of the investment companies universe provide exposure to alternative assets, which tend to have higher fees and are impossible to replicate in an ETF given their illiquid nature.

For more comparable long-only equity strategies, we suspect the gap is much closer, reflecting the repricing of investment companies as a result of the efforts of independent boards and innovations such as tiered management fees. For instance, there are two investment trusts in the JPMorgan stable, JPMorgan American (29bps) and JPMorgan Global Growth & Income (38bps), which currently offer a blended investment management fee lower than 40 basis points. The overall blended investment fee for the JPM stable is 49bps at present.

A challenge or a threat?

While it's easy to frame active ETFs as a direct threat, the reality looks more nuanced. The advantages and disadvantages of the investment company structure are well known (and well rehearsed). The better question perhaps is whether the advantages are being used sufficiently and are they sufficient to negate the advantages that ETFs possess?

According to the AIC the average level of gearing across the sector at present is 9%. However, as at 30 September, 70 of the 169 investment companies in the AIC equity sectors were not using any leverage. While some investment companies pursue strategies that are not easily compatible with gearing, this would appear too high.

Similarly, the average yield of investment companies is just over 3% at present, and, according to data from Winterflood Securities, around 60 investment companies currently offer no yield at all. Exposure to less-liquid asset classes or companies is slightly more difficult to gauge. However, around 40% of the sector's assets are invested in alternative asset classes, such as infrastructure and private equity, which cannot be accessed by an ETF due to their inherent illiquidity.

For these investment trusts, the question is: if you do not deploy gearing, or seek to provide greater dividend certainty, or invest in less-liquid investments, why bother using the investment company structure? Assuming the asset class is scalable, it is a reasonable assumption than an ETF could provide the same exposure for a lower cost and without the risk of discount volatility.

Summary

Rather than an existential threat, active ETFs represent evolutionary pressure. They are undoubtedly capturing market share and attracting flows that might previously have gone to passive ETFs or open-ended funds. Their advantages in liquidity, transparency and cost are a positive development for investors seeking actively managed portfolios. However, investment trusts retain unique strengths. Their closed-ended nature allows for investment in illiquid assets and the use of gearing, while they can also offer greater dividend certainty. The challenge is to fully make use of these advantages.

A small number of investment trusts may consider converting to ETF structures, but for the time being, particularly while active ETFs remain anchored to indices, it seems unlikely to be a significant trend. That said, boards cannot afford to be complacent and must be clear why their respective trusts continue to be relevant. Investment trusts operate in a highly competitive world and do not have a natural right to exist. Meanwhile, the emergence of active ETFs is encouraging all fund types to sharpen their proposition. For investors, that's no bad thing.

SIMON ELLIOTT *is a client director at J.P. Morgan Asset Management and was previously head of investment trust research at Winterflood Securities.*

MY IDEAL PORTFOLIO

BEN WILLIAMS, *who spent 15 years at wealth management firm Saunderson House, explains why he has most of his personal pension in investment trusts and sees good opportunities in the sector this year.*

As head of fund research at a leading UK wealth manager, our 'buy list' consisted mainly of open-ended funds, but we made extensive use of investment trusts in certain areas, notably:

- As alternatives to similar open-ended funds, for example, preferring Fidelity Special Values to Fidelity Special Situations. In cases where clients were unable to hold an open-ended equivalent fund for compliance reasons, we would often access the closed-end trust to obtain similar exposure.
- For tactical reasons. We also used investment trusts strategically if a trust was trading at an attractive discount to NAV, or was lagging in performance. While in some cases the difference in performance might be due to a structurally higher weighting towards smaller UK companies, long-term performance has been far stronger for the closed-ended version (see Figure 1).
- For access to less-liquid asset classes and sectors. We made extensive use of trusts in UK commercial property, infrastructure, private equity and UK smaller companies, when the underlying assets are more illiquid and difficult to trade. The investment trust 'wrapper' provides an easy way of accessing the asset class.

Since 'semi retiring' from the industry I have transferred my defined contribution pension to a SIPP and now manage that almost exclusively through investment trusts, with the exception of a basket of nominal and index-linked UK government bonds. Despite now being an experienced retail investor and no longer a professional, I can still get fantastic access to investment trust managers and boards. Investment trusts are, in my experience, much better than their open-ended counterparts in providing information and answering questions. Sources such as Money Makers, Kepler, QuotedData, Edison and the AIC provide invaluable research data and access to the latest thoughts of managers.

Figure 1: Fidelity Special Values against FTSE All-Share

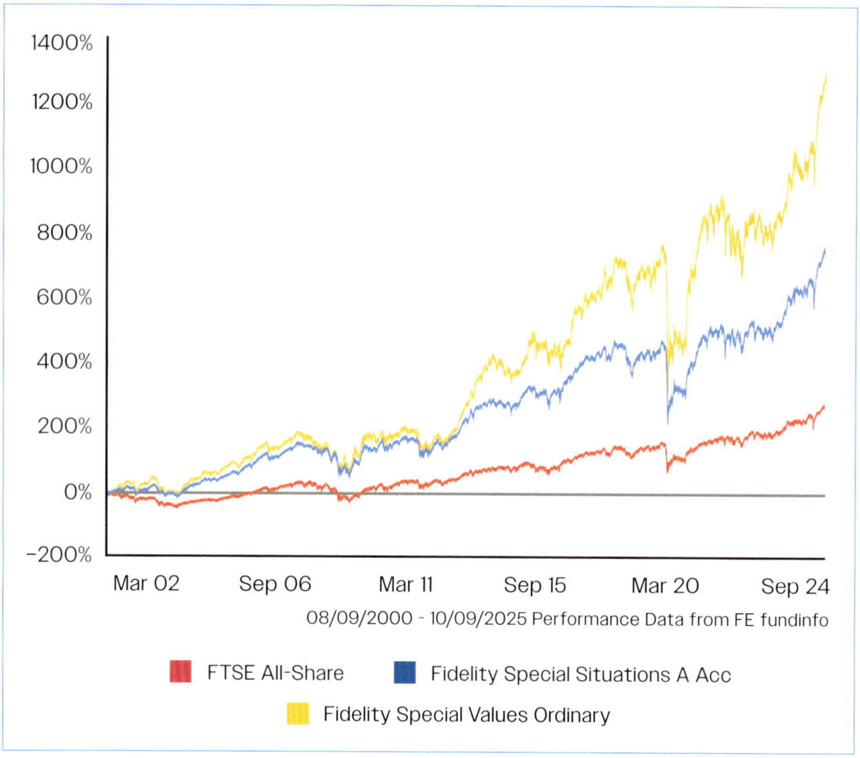

Source: Trustnet.

Lessons from the last five years

The reasons for investing in investment trusts – the ability to use gearing, independent boards, superior performance, freedom from fund flows and so on – are well documented. The last few years have been tough for the investment trust world, however, with a number of significant headwinds:

- Alternative income-focused trusts launched at a time of historically low interest rates have seen their share prices and discounts to NAV collapse (from premia in many cases) as bond yields have risen and investors have rotated into 'safer' fixed-income assets or cash.
- Higher rates have also had an impact on debt levels in the case of property and renewable infrastructure and on discounted cash flow valuations for private equity and growth capital trusts.

- Cost disclosure rules that came in following MIFID have forced wealth managers to present an unwarranted further layer of charges for many trusts to clients, meaning demand has fallen significantly and discounts have slipped further.
- Mergers and takeovers between big wealth managers mean that much of the investment trust universe is now a no-go area, since the consolidated wealth managers' weightings in several trusts are at a level that no further investment can be made.
- A continuing move towards model portfolios and a greater focus on compliance prevents many wealth managers from buying smaller investment trusts and open-ended funds. For institutional investors, trusts need to be far larger than five to ten years ago to make it into portfolios.

Despite these negatives, many of these issues are receding in importance and the outlook for a number of investment trust sectors is improving.

- Interest rates are still coming back down. Weaker employment data and evidence of slowing economy and dovish messaging from the MPC should see rates continue to fall into 2026. As cash rates drop, this should see investors relocate deposits and money market funds that have served them well into higher-yielding trusts.
- Cost disclosure rules have been updated, if not yet finally resolved. A temporary exemption for investment trusts has given shareholders a much better picture of their cost structure and may prompt investors who were put off by the previous double-counting structure to start putting money back into the investment trust universe. Sectors such as private equity, property and infrastructure that have looked optically expensive should benefit from renewed demand.
- Consistent buybacks from many trusts, while maybe not having an immediate and consistent daily impact, will have a highly accretive effect on a trust's NAV per share over time.
- 2025 has been a very active year for trust mergers and acquisitions. Activist investors and wealth managers' requirements for larger, more liquid trusts should see a further continuation in merger and M&A activity, given there are still too many sub-scale trusts that have no real need to exist.
- Liquidations have also increased across a wide range of sectors including UK smaller companies, global equities, renewable energy and property. For the last two sectors in particular, wide discounts have prevented trusts raising funds to invest in new assets so liquidation or asset sales are the only way forward.

A good time for trusts

What has all this meant for my personal SIPP portfolio? My view is that this is a fantastic time to be investing in investment trusts, with attractive opportunities across a number of sectors.

I'm a contrarian, valuation-driven investor by heart, so I'm attracted to trusts that may have performed well in the past, but which have lagged more recently.

Wide discounts to NAV are an obvious buying opportunity, although it is important to understand how they have arisen. A large discount alone is not enough to justify a purchase. Z-scores (see page 306) are probably more useful indicators of value in the shorter term. Discounts and premia are typically driven by performance. Commentators can always find reasons why a trust may be in or out of favour. However, in my experience it is usually simply down to investor behaviour.

One benefit of now being a private investor is that I'm not beholden to clients or investment committees to justify what I'm buying. That means I'm more willing to invest in trusts which may make me look a bit foolish for a while. While I'm not an income investor, I appreciate an above-average dividend yield, ideally a genuine one, not a synthetically generated one. Given that I am often buying on share price weakness, a healthy dividend at least 'pays me to wait'.

Charges and performance fees are also important, as is evidence that boards are actively buying back shares on weakness. I'm happy to buy something small and illiquid and wait for performance to come through rather than sit in a bigger, more comfortably sized trust.

My ideal trust therefore is one that has underperformed materially, has traded at a premium in the past but is now on a chunky discount, and whose board is looking to make a material corporate change. Fortunately, I see plenty of such opportunities presenting themselves at the moment.

At the time of writing, they include:

- China trusts (FCSS, BGCG). I have taken some profits after share prices have rallied more than 50% since the country was deemed uninvestable 12 months ago. China trusts still look undervalued and out of favour to me.
- UK smaller company trusts (SEC, RIII, THRG, INV, OIT) are unloved and undervalued relative to large-cap UK stocks and other markets, but the positives include: some early evidence of money flowing into the asset class from US and international investors, potential government intervention to boost sentiment and increased M&A activity. The trust sector has a wealth of experienced managers in this area.

- Healthcare and biotech (WWH, SYNC, PCGH). Political and macro concerns have hit these sectors hard over the past 18 months. But it seems likely to me that we have passed 'peak fear'. There has been a pickup in activist and corporate activity.
- Renewable infrastructure (GSF, BSIF, FGEN, SEIT, UKW, SEQI, HGEN). These trusts should benefit from rates continuing to fall, sector consolidation and activists building stakes. Saba's recent 5% stake in SDCL shows that the Boaz Weinstein's activist fund has moved on from pure arbitrage. Given the illiquid nature of the underlying assets, it will have to rely on discount narrowing and improved share price performance and/or pushing management to wind up or return capital.
- Non-US equities, with a tilt towards small cap quality growth (PHI, BGS, IEM, LTI). Growth has struggled over the past five years as a style outside the US market, but now looks much more attractively valued, with tailwinds of corporate activity and activism. I don't really suffer from FOMO (fear of missing out), so having minimal allocations to the US, where many investors are currently heavily invested, is fine with me. Valuations point to meagre returns over the next ten years, so I'm happy to have more exposure in other regions.
- Private equity (APAX (now de-listed), GROW). These trusts continue to trade on large discounts despite long-term strong performance and, as the recent APAX deal has shown, there is the potential for corporate activity and consolidation to pick up.
- UK commercial property (AIRE, RGL, SUPR). These trusts offer dividend yields of 7%+, combined with the potential for some capital growth as sentiment continues to improve and we see further consolidation and M&A.
- Defensive multi-asset trusts (PNL, RICA, RCP, CGT, BHMG). With equity indices hitting record highs, meme stocks flying but macroeconomic conditions looking less positive, a large chunk of my portfolio is dedicated to these trusts. They have a track record of performing well during periods of market weakness and are trading at multi-year lows relative to UK indices. Sentiment towards them has been poor, largely due to some lacklustre recent performance, but I expect this to be a time that these trusts prove their worth.

BEN WILLIAMS *was head of fund research at wealth manager Saunderson House. Prior to that he worked as a UK and European portfolio manager for one of the UK's largest in-house pension funds. Now he is an active SIPP investor who runs a boutique cycling B&B in South Wales.*

TRUST REFLECTIONS

NICK GREENWOOD, *who stepped down this year as manager of MIGO Global Opportunities, looks back at his 40 years of professional involvement in the investment trust sector.*

NOW THAT I have finally hung up my investment trust anorak and am now officially a former fund manager, I can look back at well over four decades of investing, the vast majority of which were focussed purely on the world of investment trusts.

I stumbled into this civilised corner of financial markets quite by chance. Trusts had quite a successful run during the early 1990s and the powers that be at the shop I worked for decided that what the world needed was a fund of investment trusts. They were hoping to exploit the sector's newfound popularity and just needed a manager. They decided that my background in private client stockbroking meant that I must know all things knowable about investment trusts and elected to appoint me, whether I thought it was a good idea or not.

It turned out that my location in Exeter proved a boon as the presence of two major institutions in the regional capital meant that a steady flow of the great and the good from the sector were happy to put a third meeting in their diaries whilst they were in Devon. I learnt quickly.

I soon discovered that pricing of trusts was highly inefficient and you did not need to be a rocket scientist to spot a situation which had become mispriced. This was a much easier way of making a living than competing with the hundreds of talented investors who were striving to work out the right price for the likes of Midland Bank or Boots.

Buying shares in perfectly good trusts which had become completely unloved and were waiting for their turn in the sun proved lucrative. Fantastic rides came from the likes of Gartmore Irish, Radiotrust and SR European (all long gone but certainly not forgotten!). These all demonstrated how powerful the combination of a rising net asset value and a narrowing discount could be.

This was a time when the fund management industry believed that tracking error was the key metric. Perfectly sensible managers would happily tell you that they were bearish about the prospects for Vodafone despite it being their largest holding. This was because the stock dominated the UK indices, and an underweight position still required a material investment. I took the then radical stance that I would only take positions in trusts where I believed positive absolute returns could be achieved.

That decision laid the foundations for some long periods of decent performance. Looking back, another good call was to dedicate significant time visiting potential and existing investors to ensure they understood the rationale behind the positions taken. I enjoyed literally travelling the length and breadth of the country, from Aberdeen to Mousehole in Cornwall, updating an incredibly supportive share register.

This strategy, combined with corporate moves – initially to London then Bournemouth, Reading and back to London, meant spending an unhealthy amount of time in budget hotels as my family stayed rooted in Exeter. This was a 15-year period which I termed 'IBIS life'. One year I clocked up 150 nights in Accor hotels, which made my loyalty card my most valuable asset. It was difficult to know whether to laugh or cry at the receipt of a Christmas card signed by everyone who had ever worked at the Reading Central IBIS hotel.

Probably my happiest memory was a 'research trip' I organised for a group of journalists to study the business models of the largest holdings within Taverners Trust. This was a fund of bars and restaurants managed by Aberdeen and was friendless as the world only wanted tech stocks at the time. The manager, Billy Whitbread (a scion of the brewing dynasty), agreed to accompany us.

Virtually all the journalists made it through all 12 locations, and many still talked about the event years later. Brewing shares were very cheap. The floatation of lastminute.com marked the peak of the tech-media-telecom (TMT) bubble. At that time, it was said that lastminute's entire revenues came to less than those of Greene King's smallest pub. Sanity was soon restored and Taverners proved to be a spectacularly good investment.

Changing times

Sadly, recent years have been hostile for investors in investment trusts. Headwinds have included chronic oversupply, consolidation of the wealth management industry and poorly drafted cost disclosure rules. This toxic mix has led to widespread discounts. They drifted to historically wide levels, then simply got wider again.

It would be easy to write investment trusts off, but history shows that they have always evolved and adapted to the environment. When I started my career, trusts were heavily owned by institutions. Private client stockbrokers then became the natural owners. Over the years these have been consolidated into a handful of mega-chains of wealth managers. These are now too large to trade trusts. Rathbones' merger with Investec has created a £100bn monster.

The trend across the industry is for standardisation of portfolios. Should Investec/Rathbones want to commit 1% of their pot to a single trust, then they would have to write a ticket for a billion pounds. That would be challenging even in Scottish Mortgage, the largest trust (excluding 3i). This consolidation means a lot of trust shares now need to find new homes and, in all likelihood, means that discounts will remain wide until demand and supply return to equilibrium.

This is creating a wide array of profitable opportunities for those employing an activist approach. There is money to be made whilst we wait to see what shape the sector takes. The investment world seems to be full of 30-somethings with a command of the Greek alphabet. Hopefully one or two will stumble by chance into a civilised corner of the stock market where they find returns easier to come by away from the crowds.

NICK GREENWOOD *was manager of MIGO Global Opportunities from 2004 until his retirement this summer.*

Busi

OPPORTUNITIES

UK EQUITIES: STILL VALUE

ALEX WRIGHT, *the manager of Fidelity Special Values (FSV), says that UK equities look relatively attractive despite some gloomy headlines.*

UK EQUITIES HAVE performed exceptionally well this year, with the FTSE 100 hitting new all-time highs. While the market's optimism and rise in valuations should warrant caution, this marks a significant milestone in what has been a genuine revival in UK equities. It comes against a backdrop of the market consensus at the end of 2024 overwhelmingly expecting US dominance to persist.

However, US trade policy announcements and concerns surrounding the US exceptionalism narrative have led to the dollar weakening and thus the US underperforming other major indices. This turnaround highlights the benefits of a contrarian investment approach, going against prevailing market trends, and the importance of exercising caution in areas with excessive optimism and heightened valuations.

More broadly, we are starting to see buying interest returning to the UK market, particularly from international investors. While the valuation gap has narrowed slightly between UK and global markets, the UK continues to trade at a meaningful discount to other regions, both on an absolute basis and when adjusting for sectoral differences in markets.

We maintain a structural bias towards mid- and small-cap companies, as these businesses are typically less well known to investors and often poorly covered by the sell side. This allows us to gain an analytical edge, supported by Fidelity's extensive analyst network, helping us to explore unloved areas of the market and uncover hidden investment gems.

Since Fidelity Special Values launched in 1994, it has consistently followed a contrarian-style investment approach. We look for unloved companies with the potential for positive change that the market has not yet recognised. We follow a disciplined investment process that focuses first on evaluating downside risk and then on identifying positive change and potential upside. The focus is first and foremost on downside protection.

Our philosophy is to primarily base investment decisions on company fundamentals rather than top-down or macro-economic factors. This contrarian approach is research intensive. The insight and expertise of our large team of analysts have been central to the long-term success of our approach. As at the end of September 2025, the trust has generated a NAV total return of c.18% per annum over five years and 10% over ten years, significantly outperforming its benchmark, the FTSE All-Share index.

Compelling opportunities

The UK's unpopularity in recent years has prompted frequent questions around what catalyst is needed to improve domestic performance and close the valuation gap. My response continues to be that nothing needs to change. We don't require a re-rating to deliver attractive returns. Forecasts for company earnings across our holdings remain strong and we work closely with Fidelity's analyst team to assess the likelihood of these earnings being delivered.

Overall, we remain happy with the performance environment and it remains a fertile hunting ground for contrarian stockpickers. Within the UK, value is being found further down the market-cap spectrum. Large-cap companies are trading close to their long-term average price/earnings ratios, whereas mid- and small-cap companies present a more pronounced valuation opportunity.

12-month forward price/earnings ratio

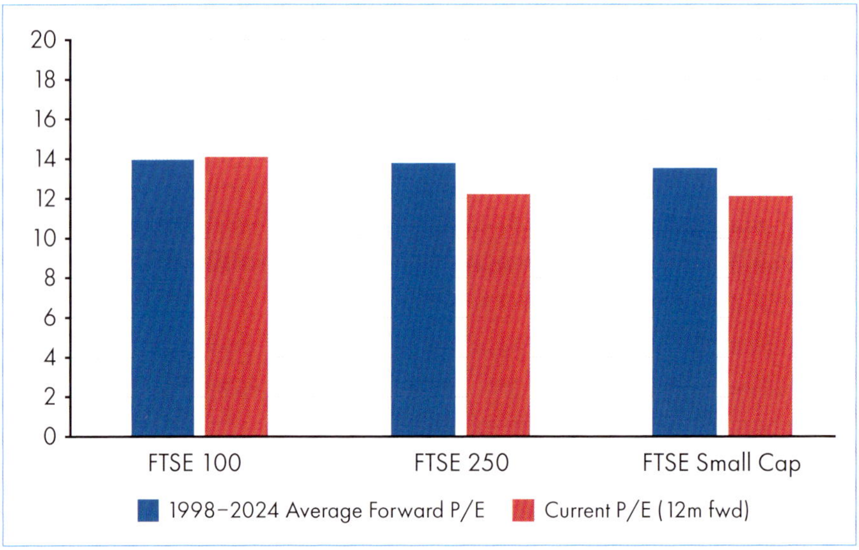

Source: Fidelity International, LSEG Workspace / IBES estimates, 27 August 2025. Data for FTSE 250 and FTSE Small Cap not available pre-1998.

We believe that the current market conditions continue to favour our contrarian-value investment style. While it's still a developing trend, it's encouraging to see other market participants showing increasing interest in UK equities.

Despite turbulent markets and sharp currency moves, there has been no pause in takeover activity this year. Mergers and acquisitions (M&A) have largely accelerated in the UK compared to the rest of the world. The value of deals in the UK rose by 120% in 2024, outpacing the European average growth of 16%.[1] The increase in M&A activity for the UK market began in 2021 and has continued since.

We have also seen consolidation within the investment trust sector, with vehicles of all sizes subject to a higher level of corporate activity, including mergers and wind-ups. There are economies of scale to be made by larger trusts, resulting in lower charges, an improvement in liquidity and a route to unlocking shareholder value for trusts with high persistent discounts. Given its brand, scale and size, Fidelity Special Values is well placed to be a beneficiary in this environment.

M&A activity has been underpinned by companies, private equity firms and other corporates taking a longer-term perspective, seeking to capitalise on value through share buybacks, asset purchases or outright takeovers. Domestic investors are often too close to appreciate the hidden value in their own market, wile overseas investors can see it more clearly, helping to close the valuation gap.

The UK remains a preferred destination for US investors, given the highly international nature of UK companies. They can see that many domestic companies trade at substantial valuation discounts to US and global peers. The valuation gap means that takeovers, particularly by private equity companies, can anchor on US valuations, offering shareholders a significant premium.

UK market's future

Takeover activity and shareholder activism have long been important features of the UK equity market, helping to unlock shareholder value. However, the number of bids, a slowdown in UK initial public offerings (IPOs) and some companies opting for US listings have raised fears among some market participants that the UK equity market is set to shrink.

We feel these concerns are overdone. It wasn't long ago, in 2020 and 2021, that the UK enjoyed a strong wave of IPOs. While some high-profile companies have switched exchanges, they are relatively few in number. We would have to experience

1 Data from Refinitiv and analysis by BCG as at 8 January 2025. For more details visit 'M&A Outlook 2025: Expectations Are High', BCG.

several consecutive years of high takeover activity, combined with few new listings, to create legitimate concerns. There have been three recent IPOs that highlight a renewed interest in companies choosing to list in the UK.

In any event, these issues are not unique to the UK. Equity markets outside of the US face similar challenges, largely because US stocks have been trading at substantial premiums when compared to the rest of the world, and there are clear signs that IPO activity is starting to rise globally. For us, the UK offers an attractive and deep investable universe, offering plenty of choice and investment opportunities.

Over the past year, UK equities have staged a resurgence, but they have actually performed well for several years. The return of overseas investors is an encouraging trend, as they capitalise on the relative value available in the UK market. Given that the UK represents only a small share of global indices, less than 4%, even a modest pickup in allocations from abroad can have a meaningful positive impact.

Encouragingly, despite subdued domestic economic data and political uncertainty, UK market performance has remained positive. This highlights that attractive returns are available in an uncertain environment, which can in fact act as a driver of investment opportunities. We remain excited in the prospects of our holdings and in the UK market's ability to generate long-term performance.

Performance for 12-month periods in GBP (%)

	2020/21	2021/22	2022/23	2023/24	2024/25
NAV	55.7	−9.5	16.5	18.6	19.9
Share price	70.7	−15.8	17.0	19.5	29.0
Benchmark	27.9	−4.0	13.8	13.4	16.2

Source: Morningstar as at 30 September 2025, bid-bid, net income reinvested. Benchmark: FTSE All-Share Index.

ALEX WRIGHT *has been manager of Fidelity Special Values since 2012. The trust is the largest and best performing trust in the UK All Companies sector.*

UK EQUITIES ROUNDTABLE

With Alex Wright having set the scene, JONATHAN DAVIS *spoke to four other managers of UK equities for this roundup of the challenges and opportunities they see in the UK equity market.*

Simon Gergel – chief investment officer, UK equities, Allianz Global Investors

The UK equity income sector is one of the strongest and most competitive of all those in the investment universes. Three of the trusts in the sector changed either their mandate or their manager in 2020 and it looks likely that another, Murray Income, may be doing the same shortly. The board there has announced a strategic review the outcome of which is likely to be known around the time that the *Handbook* is published.

It is a period therefore when every manager, however long their experience and track record, has to be on their mettle. Simon Gergel, manager of the Merchants Trust (MRCH), has more years under his belt than many others, having been in post since 2006. While his long-term performance record is above average, it is not the first time that he has to had to face a period of shorter-term underperformance.

One way of tracking that is to look at the dividend yield that the trust is able to pay. At the start of October, it was running at 5.2%, which is comfortably towards the higher end of its historic range, and the second highest amongst his directly comparable larger peer group. The yield has been pushed up by the near 8% discount at which the shares have been trading. Nevertheless, the trust's total return has been ahead of its benchmark, the FTSE All-Share index, over five years and is about 1% behind, but still top quartile, over ten years.

As a value investor, Gergel has no difficulty explaining why his trust has been lagging recent months. He points to the divergence in performance between large-cap stocks on the one hand, and small- and mid-cap stocks on the other. His portfolio has been tilted more than many of his peers towards the latter, because that is where he sees the greater value, but the market has not yet come round to sharing his view.

"We're trying to be true to what we stand for, which is trying to buy good companies with a high yield, and grow the dividends over time. The income story has continued to be very robust in Merchants. We've got a yield of over 5%, we've grown that dividend in 43 consecutive years, and the dividends are paid out of income, not out of capital, which is different from some of the peers".

The current composition of his portfolio reflects a tilt toward mid-caps, where Gergel sees particularly favourable valuations: "For the first time in 20 years, the mid-cap index is yielding significantly more than the FTSE 100. That's highly unusual. The 250 index has fallen a long way behind in terms of share prices, and that's pushed the yields up. But that's where we're finding a lot of opportunities".

The shift has led to what is for Merchants an unusually high rate of portfolio turnover: "In the first six months of this financial year, we introduced eight new companies, which is normally what we do in a whole year, and we sold nine out of a portfolio of 50-odd stocks. That's a high level of turnover compared to normal, and it really reflects this polarisation". It is a measure of how extreme the divergence between the two segments of the UK market (7% in performance over the first nine months of the year) has become.

"On the new company side, we've bought companies like Serco, the outsourcing company, where 50% of its profits now come from defence; Sirius Real Estate, an industrial property company; B&M European Value, which is obviously a value discount retailer; the insolvency specialist Begbies Traynor and RS Group, which is a component distributor, so there is quite a broad spread". The trust has sold out of companies that have reached his estimate of fair value, such as Tesco and Next.

The market, Gergel continues, has been largely tracking earnings momentum, while the UK economy has not been strong enough to reward most cyclical areas where the value has been appearing. Such periods of transition are part and parcel of any committed value investor's life. "These periods are actually what makes value investing work. There's got to be periods where buying companies that are cheap is hard work. If it was easy, everyone would do it. It's got to be painful. If cheap companies always got rewarded, everyone would do it all the time".

What about the political background? The incoming Labour Government has not so far been able to deliver on its objective of higher growth, and Gergel says "It's hard to avoid the conclusion that this government so far has been unhelpful, shall we say, to UK-based businesses". However, he stresses the need for perspective, recalling the greater turmoil of the potential Corbyn era and Brexit uncertainty. "We've got a government that has had some problems, but they do have a large majority, which is very different to the last government. We have a more stable environment than many other countries. I mean, just look what's happening in France. Look what's happening in America". He thinks media pessimism is exaggerated, and "the economy is growing a bit faster than people think".

He accepts that the UK Equity income sector is under scrutiny again, as it was in 2020. Boards are keeping a closer eye on discounts and performance. Despite the UK market's recent stronger performance, risks to his more positive view clearly remain. "If I think about what's gone wrong in the last few years, nobody saw the pandemic coming. Things that hit us tend to be extraneous factors that we weren't really thinking about". That said, he highlights the evidence of global bond markets demanding higher yields and warns of possible reversals in speculative or momentum-driven sectors.

He reiterates his message about the need for discipline in chasing yield. "We pay our dividend out of income generated by the portfolio. We don't have a barbell. We don't pay dividends out of capital. I think that's potentially dangerous if you do it over a sustained period of time. I think we are true to what an equity income fund should be".

Whatever the market may be doing, Gergel is adamant that he is not going to change the value investment style that he has followed over his multi-decade career: "When I look at the portfolio, I feel optimistic that we've bought a collection of businesses that can generate high income and growth. They're cheap and well diversified".

Nevertheless, it could continue to be an uncomfortable period until the current polarisation of returns unwinds. About a quarter of stocks in the FTSE All-Share index are on price/earnings multiples of more than 18, whereas the comparable figure in the Merchants portfolio is just 1%, so the value is certainly there to be realised in time.

Thomas Moore – senior investment director, Aberdeen

Another experienced manager in the UK equity income sector has a quite different investment style and finds himself in a rather different place. Thomas Moore has been involved in managing UK equity funds since 1998. For the last 14 years, he has been responsible for managing the £183m market capitalisation Aberdeen Equity Income investment trust from Edinburgh, where he moved 20 years ago after an early graduate job with Schroders in London.

While he also is happy to describe himself as a value investor, his approach is not to look just at a company's fundamentals, but to try and anticipate where there are potential catalysts for a change in its fortunes. "We call the style 'focus on change', asking if there is going to be change that will drive a re-rating in the valuation of that company or a corresponding increase in earnings".

Unlike so-called quality investors who might "sit there from one cycle to the next, just owning the same stocks", his emphasis is on market dynamics, looking for companies that are undergoing fundamental shifts that the market hasn't yet fully appreciated. "Maybe a company doesn't look particularly high-quality now, because something's gone wrong, or there's been a regulatory change, but maybe things are improving, and the share price still assumes that things are going to stay tough. Those are the ideas that we are looking for".

A key part of his approach is being index-agnostic. Rather than starting with the index weightings and modifying from there, as many equity managers do, the trust builds its portfolio from the bottom up. "Its weightings reflect our conviction levels on those companies. If we don't like Shell, we will own 0% of Shell. There are big sectors where at the moment we own zero, for example pharmaceuticals".

As a result, the trust often deviates significantly from benchmark weights. "We're very keen to emphasise that we are a genuinely active portfolio. Our belief is that, more often than not, it will be good news for our shareholders that we are active". The trust's active share, a statistical measure for how different a portfolio is to the market portfolio, is 74%.

Moore remains proudly value-oriented at a time when "it's actually quite unusual for people to use the word value, because it's gained quite a chequered reputation. A lot of people, when you say you're buying something with a yield of 6%, 7% or even 10%, will have a sharp intake of breath and say 'Oh, you really are taking some risks there, aren't you?'. The reason is that paying up for higher than market yield often produces capital losses.

Moore thinks that is too simplistic: "The way I like to think about valuation is by taking the yield of a company and inverting it. That gets you to the number of years that a company is expected to generate profits. If you look at a free cash flow yield, and we've had companies in our portfolio with free cash flow yields of 20%, you will have made back your market cap within five years. These are not necessarily companies that are heavily indebted. There's an awful lot of bad news priced into a company's share price, if it's got a free cash yield of 20%".

After several years, he sees encouraging signs that the value style may be coming back into vogue. "At its core our philosophy is that we can achieve our investment objective, not by going for companies with the fastest top-line growth or the highest-quality characteristics. If high-yield companies are still growing their dividends, we can get capital growth as well as our desired income. It's not because they are high yield, it is because we've spotted an opportunity which has been mispriced, and the yield can compress or the P/E can expand".

He cites Imperial Brands, the tobacco company that has diversified beyond cigarettes, as a case study: "There is a very clear strategy by the management team to return about £2.5bn of cash every year, which is equivalent to about 10% of the market cap. We get a dividend yield of a bit over 5% and a bit over 5% in buybacks too. It becomes this flywheel, because you've got fewer and fewer shares in issue, which means your earnings per share goes up, which means your dividend per share, logically, goes up as well". The fund management house M&G is another example of a high-yielding stock that has delivered capital gains on top of the income.

In finding stocks, the Aberdeen team have access to a proprietary in-house model called the Matrix, which some readers may remember from an interview in the *Handbook* with the firm's distinguished small companies manager Harry Nimmo some years back. It generates a lot of helpful analysis, particularly on trends in earnings estimates, and provides an objective check on the manager's own judgments. In the event, the performance of the trust has flourished recently as the market has taken to Moore's style.

Going into October this year, Aberdeen Equity Income was one of the best-performing UK equity income trusts on the basis of NAV total returns, despite having a headline dividend yield that is the highest of all its peers, at over 6%. That historically has been a rare sight, given that the UK equity market typically trades on a yield between 3% and 5%. The strength of sterling against a weakening dollar has helped domestic-facing companies to do better relative to the more international FTSE 100 index.

Moore points to the valuation metrics of the stocks he owns to justify his claim to be a value investor. The median price/earnings ratio of the portfolio at the end of September was 10.0×, compared to the FTSE All-Share (ex ITs) index's 12.1×, the free cash flow yield was 9.7%, 4.4% above the index while dividends were growing at 3.8%, marginally lower than the index's. Although the trust's dividend was paid out of reserves for two years after Covid, it is once again covered by earnings, according to Aberdeen's figures.

It is fair to say that the bounce back in Aberdeen Equity Income's performance follows other periods of poor relative performance. Over five years the trust ranks 6th out of 19 peers in the sector for share price performance, pretty much in line with Merchants, but over ten years is near the bottom, a period over which Merchants shows close to the top.

The volatility in performance displayed by Aberdeen Equity Income has been influenced not just by its style, but also by its use of gearing, the highest of any equity income trust apart from its sister trust Shires Income. It also, like Merchants, has a relatively concentrated portfolio with 50 stocks, unlike say the much larger City of London, which has 76 holdings.

That only underlines how important it is to look behind the headline numbers to drill into what is driving a trust's performance. In a world where scale matters, Aberdeen Equity Income has no choice but to pursue a differentiated strategy if it is to tap what Moore also expects will be a continued revival in the UK equity market.

David Moss – senior portfolio manager and head of European equities research strategy, Columbia Threadneedle

Although having 30 years of fund management experience at a number of different companies (thanks mainly to mergers), David Moss only started managing the CT UK High Income investment trust in July 2023. He was brought in to revive the trust's fortunes after a period of indifferent performance, with a mandate to rebuild the company's dividend capacity and end its habit of paying uncovered dividends out of reserves.

Moss is a rare example these days of a fund manager who left school without going to university, something he rectified later by acquiring banking qualifications and a degree in economics from Loughborough University. His first job was at Barclays, the high street bank, putting bank statements into envelopes, before retraining and moving into fund management. He spent a number of years managing European equities, originally for Friends Provident and subsequently for the many successive owners of that fund management business up to and including Columbia Threadneedle today. His experience in running European equity funds, he says, may give him a broader perspective on the UK market than others who have never run anything else.

Columbia Threadneedle UK High Income Trust was originally an Ivory & Sime trust which was merged with another trust and relaunched under its new name in March 2007, an inauspicious beginning on the eve of the global financial crisis. The performance was good for a while, but faltered after Covid sufficiently for the board to decide on a change. While it sits in the UK equity income sector, a clue to its objective lies in the 'High Income' part of its name.

While a target yield is not explicitly mentioned, the trust clearly aims to offer a higher-than-average dividend yield while holding out the hope of capital appreciation as well. To achieve the higher yield, the trust has two share classes, one that distributes dividends in the normal way and another B share that makes an identical payment, but out of a special capital reserve instead. This allows the ordinary shares to receive a somewhat higher dividend than the 4.3% running yield of the portfolio. Boosted also by net gearing of 9%, the yield on the ordinary shares is currently 6.1%, according to the AIC, ranking it third in the UK equity income sector on that measure.

The trust remains quite small, with a combined (ordinary and B share) market capitalisation of around £120m. Columbia Threadneedle manages a second larger investment trust in the same sector, Columbia Threadneedle UK Capital and Income, with a market capitalisation of £350m, and it might seem a sensible step to combine the two at some stage, given that their performance has been very similar. Moss cannot comment on that, but says it is obvious that the trust, while it has a largely retail investor share register, needs to grow to be viable in the longer term.

When he took it on, Moss says he and the board were clear that the absolute first priority was to restore the dividend cover. "When I started the trust was following a sort of barbell strategy, with a handful of very-high-yielding stocks topped up with smaller growth stocks. That faltered when smaller companies started to underperform. The higher-than-average yield is clearly the key attraction of the trust for many shareholders. It has a high level of income that has grown, though not very fast, for the past 14 years and we have to ensure that the dividend is securely underpinned by earnings".

The most important change that Moss has made to achieve that in the portfolio was to diversify its sources of income, increasing the size of the portfolio from around 35 stocks to 55 today. The medicine seems to be working. The trust had a scheduled three-year continuation vote in March 2025, but with the NAV back ahead of its benchmark at that point, the vote was not triggered. The next continuation vote, again dependent on performance, is in March 2028.

The gearing on the trust is provided by a £15m borrowing facility, equivalent to around 9% of assets after recent performance. While there is flexibility to reduce the debt on tactical grounds, as happened last year around the time of the US election, Moss says he and the board agree that equity trusts should normally make use of structural gearing, one of the key advantages that the investment trust structure allows. That has worked well so far in 2025, with the trust's shares up by more than 25%, second only to Temple Bar in its sector, helped by the narrowing and virtual elimination of the discount.

Like many other UK equity managers, Moss and his European colleagues had been hoping for a better performance from companies exposed to the UK domestic economy in the last year. "Frankly, that's not come through very well because of politics and confidence. For example, we own two housebuilders and one brickmaker. It's clear there's a structural shortage of houses in the UK and the government's very keen to do something about it. What's been less clear is *how* they can do something about it. In some ways they seem to have made things worse rather than better in the last 12 months. Every company that we saw in the summer of last year was reasonably positive. Every business told us Labour really wanted to go for growth.

"Unfortunately, their ideas of how you drive growth include a huge pickup in government spending and National Insurance rises, and that's not really had the effect they would have hoped for. So, I think at the moment confidence is pretty low. Real wages are just about growing. There are still Covid-era savings that haven't been spent, so the consumer balance sheet is in pretty good shape. Interest rates have come down a bit and mortgage rates have come down a bit more".

So the backdrop, Moss says, has remained broadly supportive, but sentiment is "just dire". "You will have seen that we hardly built a single house in London in the last few months. Until we get through the Budget in November, I'm not sure we'll see much positive noise from many businesses".

By the time you read this, the Budget will have been and gone and there will at least be a clearer picture, however palatable, of what lies ahead.

The clear positive looking ahead, Moss says, is that short-term interest rates appear set to come down, which is positive for higher-yielding alternatives, even if the yields on cash still look reasonably competitive when compared to the 6% headline yield on his trust. That is one reason why the shares of CT UK High Income have this year been trading intermittently around par, enabling it to issue some x million new shares.

For a shareholder base that clearly wants yield, the trust can claim to be doing its job in delivering both a sector-beating dividend and a strong capital performance as its discount has come right in. There is genuine growth potential, Moss reckons, in some of the higher yielding stocks in the portfolio. He thinks that both tobacco and insurance companies, for example, are poorly understood and mispriced at the moment.

While the UK market offers "a plethora of yield opportunities", he also sees potential to use his mandate to invest up to 10% in European stocks to add some more capital growth. Most importantly, like all the other managers I talked to, he knows that the market is cheap in historical terms, even after performing much better over the last two years. "If we just focus all the negativity surrounding the UK, you wouldn't think that it is one of the better performers of all markets this year.

"Despite that, it remains attractive value, particularly the domestic businesses. Most of the councils, for example, are trading below book value. The last time they did that was after the financial crisis, but that's because they had huge amounts of debt. This time around, balance sheets are in really good shape and some even have net cash. So there's a huge amount, I think, of pent-up value. We do need action in some way, shape or form from government and most of us perhaps don't have a lot of confidence that they can do that, but fingers crossed". So far, so good, in other words.

George Ensor – partner and portfolio manager, River Global

If there is a clear message from recent performance of UK equity investment trusts, it is that a manager's style (growth or value, small cap or large cap, and so on) has been a powerful differentiating factor in the returns achieved. Spare a thought therefore for George Ensor, the manager whose trust has the highest exposure to the smallest of small-cap listed UK stocks.

His trust, River UK Micro Cap, as its name suggests, invests only in stocks with a free float market capitalisation of under £100m at the point of investment. That is by design of course, because there are good reasons for thinking there should be bargains in this space, where many companies are not followed by analysts and liquidity is often poor. On paper the investment trust structure is ideally suited to capitalise on these opportunities.

Yet it has been a bruising period for this style of investment. Ensor's only rival in this space, Miton UK Microcap, has opted to wind up after several years of disappointing performance. Smaller companies generally have lagged those of larger UK counterparts, which in turn have underperformed the US and other international markets. The micro-cap market has felt the full force of the diminishing enthusiasm for UK equities.

The share price total return of the trust over five years has, ostensibly at least, been dismal. Its 5% per annum annualised rate of return over five years is fully 20% per annum worse than that of Alex Wright at Fidelity, currently the best long-term performer of all UK equity managers. It has been, Ensor notes, "the second worst UK small cap cycle since 1990" and sentiment towards small caps remains very negative.

But there have been some signs of light emerging. "Valuations are extremely cheap and we are starting to see that come through. I think the UK market was put on the Brexit naughty step for a while, but there are signs of renewed interest from non-UK investors. What I'm surprised by is that they're coming right down to the £100m-market-cap range. There was a week where I think we got a message in about five or six of our holdings, asking if we would be willing to let some stock go. We haven't seen that consistently for a long time".

It is also the case that the 5% per annum return figure is misleading, as it takes no account of the redemption policy that the trust has operated since its launch. Under this policy, whenever the trust's own market capitalisation rises above a certain threshold, the board commits to allow shareholders to take some profits and return the trust to its original target sub-£100m size. That way the trust is able to avoid being constrained by outgrowing its target investable universe.

There were redemptions in January and May 2021 at a price of 253p and 302p respectively, against a recent share price of 200p. "If you look at what we have delivered since inception, if you do it money-weighted to adjust for when we've returned capital, the compound annualised return is about 12.5% percent. The reported NAV annualised return is lower than that, because obviously it doesn't adjust for the capital returns that we've made at those earlier cyclical peaks".

Nevertheless, in the light of the persistent small-cap underperformance, the trust has spent the last two years in an extensive consultation period with its shareholders, contacting more than 50% of the largest names on the register, attempting to address concerns that UK small caps might be facing "structural decline" and reviewing the capital return policy.

The upshot is that the shareholders have opted to keep the trust going in return for it adopting a new forward-looking performance hurdle, the effect of which is that the trust must deliver a compound return of at least 11.5% per annum between now and June 2028 to ensure its continued survival at that point. The new target date strikes a balance, says Ensor, between being "far enough away to allow for a cyclical improvement, but sufficiently ambitious to demonstrate management discipline and justify the illiquidity risk shareholders take on by investing in the micro-cap space".

He thinks it is a fair bargain. "For the liquidity risk that our shareholders are taking, we do need to show a premium return, and I don't think it really matters whether we call it 12% or 15% per annum". The market cycle will clearly continue to be big factor. "If we've got a supportive market, we should do that very easily. If we've got a market that's similar to the last three years, it will be difficult, but not impossible. And if the structural decline camp are right, then it will probably be game over.

"But to be honest, if that's the case, we won't have returned any capital since 2021, so that would be seven years. If that happens, I think we'd say we've given it a good go at that point, and everyone's got better things to do with their time". His optimism about the target is based on the fact that valuations are still so low and if the market shows any sign of reversing direction "we're well placed to benefit from that".

Ensor has no illusions about the challenges that remain. "Sentiment is still extremely depressed. There's been this tax narrative again over the summer ahead of the Budget. Is it to scare the Labour backbenches or is it to prepare the market for higher taxes?" Surveys of business sentiment have been close to record lows. "Yet the same surveys asked people how they thought about their own business prospects and they were much better. It is almost like the UK is talking itself into lower growth by being so pessimistic".

The micro-cap portfolio looks good value, however. The free cash flow yield is about 7%, and earnings growth for the portfolio over the last three years has been more than 10%. The great majority of portfolio companies have net cash on their balance sheets. "When you add in our discount to NAV (about 17%, we have an 8% cash flow yield, which is pretty attractive".

A critical missing factor for recovery is the return of inflows into UK small-cap funds. "We have not seen a single month, let alone a quarter or a year, where we've got inflows into open-ended small-cap funds. That is the missing piece that we need for the next cycle to properly start". Ensor acknowledges that "the simple argument that small cap is cheap on its own doesn't really work". He sees it fundamentally as a momentum and sentiment issue, driven by the persistent derating of small caps versus large caps.

The third quarter of 2025 has been encouraging as far as triggering a small-cap revival is concerned. Going into the fourth quarter, the trust's share price was up 17% year to date, some 10% ahead of both the FTSE All-Share and Small-Cap indices. "It's not going to be a miraculous change overnight. But what we really want to see is a couple of really good quarters, with fully blown inflows coming back into UK small caps". The sector's sole surviving microcap trust will be a geared play on that outcome if and when it happens.

THE CASE FOR INDIAN EQUITIES

GAURAV NARAIN, *the principal adviser of India Capital Growth (IGC), revisits the case for Indian equities after a volatile and challenging year, in conversation with* JONATHAN DAVIS.

A volatile market

THE PAST YEAR, we all know, has been marked by market volatility, trade wars and geopolitical uncertainty. All of those have impacted the Indian economy and its stock market, one of the best performers anywhere in recent years, more than most. This tough year culminated in Donald Trump slapping 25% tariffs on a wide range of Indian exports in July 2025 and upping the rate to a punitive 50% soon after, the highest of any country.

The president appeared to have been motivated in part by a spat with India's prime minister Narendra Modi over its foreign policy and continued imports of Russian oil. At the time of writing, no new trade agreement between the United States and India has been reached. It has not been the easiest period, therefore, for the four trusts in the Indian equity sector.

In the 12 months to the start of October, their shares were all down, by between 1% and 14%. India Capital Growth, as the smallest of the four, and one that specialises in more volatile small- and mid-cap shares, has been hurt the most, although for much the same reason its five- and ten-year returns remain the best of the quartet.

Tariff troubles

After a nervous first quarter, as the companies awaited 'Liberation Day', India's real GDP growth for the April–June 2025 quarter came in at 7.8%, well above market expectations. It reflected robust domestic demand, with the services sector growing 9.3%, and healthy contributions coming from manufacturing and construction. That is a pointer, Gaurav Narain suggests, to what may happen if and when there is a resolution of the ongoing trade dispute.

Narain admits that India appears to have been caught off guard by the sudden imposition of 50% tariffs, the highest of any country without a trade agreement with the US. "It was widely anticipated" he says "that India would actually be one of the biggest gainers out of the Trump tariffs because relations between Trump and Modi were very strong and many thought we would be one of the first countries to sign a free trade agreement. Instead, we now have the highest tariff of them all".

The sectors which are worst hit by the tariffs, such as textiles and agriculture, are all very labour-intensive sectors, critical for employment, so there is pressure on the government to sort something out sooner rather than later. In response to the first Trump tariffs in April, the government reduced income tax rates to boost consumption, stepped up its infrastructure spending and the central bank cut interest rates. More recently the government has rationalised indirect taxes, which has led to price reduction across many consumption categories like automobiles and air conditioners, for example. All these measures attempt to accelerate domestic growth.

Even before the tariffs, Narain points out, a modest slowdown in India's impressive rate of economic growth had been pencilled in for the run up to the last general election in May 2024, which saw Mr Modi surprisingly losing his overall majority in parliament, but remaining in power as head of a coalition government.

Nevertheless, the macro-factors which have fuelled India's strong recent growth remain strong and supportive. "India is likely to remain one of the fastest-growing economies in the world over the next decade. GDP growth forecasts range from 6 to 7% per annum, stretching out for over a decade ahead. The government has a clear roadmap for continued growth, and with GDP per capita still low relative to global peers, there is a lengthy runway for sustained future gains".

The strategic case for India, as is well known, is rooted in its positive demographics, reformist government and rapidly growing labour force and middle class. "India is the largest populated country in the world with 1.4bn people, but what really stands out is that it's a very young population. The median age is about 29 years, with almost 60% of the population below 25 years". India could easily add almost 100m people to the workforce over the next decade, with the numbers of middle class and rich reaching 500m in five years.

Infrastructure spending by the government has almost trebled in recent years and is helping to modernise the country's once-sclerotic economy, with digital innovation integrating poor rural communities with better-off urban centres. At the same time the government's fiscal deficit has been steadily coming down since Covid, inflation is at all-time lows and foreign exchange reserves of $700bn provide around 11 months of import cover.

These positive influences have helped drive the Indian stock market to exceptional levels of performance, with the main market BSE Index having doubled over the past five years. Over ten years the annualised rate of return from the Indian market has been 11.5%. That has not been quite enough to match the runaway US equity market, but still impressive in comparison with other global markets.

With its small- and mid-cap bias, shares in IGC have veered between over- and under-performing the main indices, depending on your choice of measurement period. In its last full financial year, to the end of May, the trust did well in absolute terms with an NAV return in sterling of 16.0%. This was however comfortably behind its benchmark, the BSE Midcap total return index (GBP), which rose 25.6%.

Valuation concerns

The biggest challenge for any fund manager looking to outperform has been the rich valuations at which Indian companies have come to trade. "Navigating the market" says Narain "demands patience and selectivity". International investors have become wary of the high price/earnings ratio of listed Indian stocks and what appears to be a declining trend in company earnings growth.

He points out, however, that the decline in foreign investment into India has been more than matched by the continued rise in domestic investor demand. "It has been domestic demand that has been driving the market in recent months, not overseas demand. In the process it is becoming a much more liquid market".

"Since 2021 foreign investment flows have been negative to the tune of $8bn. They've pulled out almost $15bn this year alone. In contrast, however, domestic funds have seen inflows of almost $200bn in these four and a half years, including $60bn of net inflows from domestic investors this year. The ownership of foreign investors in the Indian equity markets is at record lows, at just 16%".

"So it's become a very vibrant market driven by domestic demand. A third of all IPOs globally are happening in India and all this capital raising is absorbing a lot of surplus liquidity. The companies which are listing range from digital companies to auto companies to hospital chains. They are definitely deepening the breadth of the market".

Earnings outlook

The biggest reason behind the indifferent recent performance of the market, according to Narain, has been a drop in earnings growth. "If I go back to December last year, India was the best-performing emerging market on a three-year perspective. This last year it has actually been the worst performer. It means our markets have consolidated after three strong years".

"We had expected 2025 to be a weaker year. One of the big reasons was valuations. India is amongst the most expensive markets in terms of valuations, and we'd hoped a weaker year would allow the earnings to catch up. But what we've actually seen are earnings downgrades. I would say that over the last year earnings estimates have been cut by 10% to 12% while valuations have remained high. Whereas the Indian market used to trade at a premium of 60% against other emerging markets, that has now normalised, but they remain high in absolute terms".

The investment approach IGC adopts is based on a simple premise: if you can find companies that are compounding earnings 15% per annum, the share price will eventually do the rest, compensating for the high initial valuations you may have to pay. The average stock in the portfolio is trading at a prospective 2027 price/earnings ratio of 21, some 2% higher than the main market index.

Narain's style is to look for fast-growing companies with capable managements and positive cash flow. He favours a concentrated portfolio for maximum impact. Two thirds of the 38-stock portfolio, which is concentrated by comparison with its peers, is currently invested in higher-risk smaller companies. Turnover remains low, consistent with a long-term mindset.

The growth strategy has worked well over the past decade, at least until this year's hiccup. Clearly much will depend on whether companies can turn around the faltering earnings growth momentum and, as he says, catch up with the expectations built into current share prices. The shares have been trading at a discount of high single digits, protected by a regular redemption policy that allows up to 100% of shareholders to exit at NAV minus 3% every two years. 15% did so at the last opportunity in December 2023, leaving a share register that is heavily dominated by retail investors. With a market capitalisation of little more than £140m, unlike the larger trusts in the sector, the trust is too small for institutional investors. It sees its future as a differentiated offering with greater exposure to fast-growing small- and mid-cap stocks than its peer group.

Scale or niche player? That has become the issue for many investment trusts in the post low-interest-rate world. India Capital Growth is one of those on the frontline in this evolving market and the fallout from India's battle with Trump is among the factors that will determine how it fares over the coming years.

GAURAV NARAIN *has been the principal adviser of India Growth Capital since 2011. He and his team of six, based in Mumbai, have been part of the River Global fund management company since 2023.*

COMING BACK

CHARLOTTE MORRIS of Pantheon International sees light at the end of the tunnel for listed private equity, after four challenging years, she tells JONATHAN DAVIS

IT IS THREE years since the board of Pantheon International, one of the stalwarts of the listed private equity market, set out on an initiative to overcome a wall of scepticism and faltering demand that had resulted in discounts across its sector widening to levels not seen since the global financial crisis.

Under John Singer, an industry veteran who stepped up to become chairman in 2022, the trust announced a three-part strategy to revive interest in the asset class and demonstrate that boards were actively putting the interests of shareholders first, something that many analysts and market observers had begun to question as discounts widened so dramatically.

The strategy began with a hefty £200m share buyback and was followed in 2024 by the announcement of a new capital allocation policy, a first for the sector, setting out how the board would aim to allocate cash proceeds from its portfolio between share buybacks and new investments. Stage three, which has been a primary focus in 2025, involves going out to create new sources of demand for the trust with a beefed-up marketing programme.

Alarmed and similarly under pressure from shareholders after discounts widened to 40–50% in several cases, the boards of other listed private equity trusts began to follow suit with their own remedial measures, including introducing capital allocation policies. Along with other professional trust watchers, I have been carefully tracking Pantheon's progress since, as both a potential investment and a proxy for the industry generally. The issues raised by its experience have become a hot topic and part of a wider industry debate about the future of listed private equity.

What is the best way to assess where we have reached? I think it is fair to say that there is now a general recognition that private equity, after a decade of exceptional returns in a low-interest-rate environment, has been going through one of its periodic down-cycles. Fundraising has become harder, the ability for managers to realise returns from existing holdings has declined and cash flow has been squeezed. The discount in investment trust share prices in part reflects this industrywide experience, a period of both weaker NAV growth and weaker investor demand.

Those pressures are reflected in the performance of Pantheon's share price, which peaked at 350p in December 2021, fell to a low of 225p in mid-2022 and has been recovering since, albeit with a sudden but brief downturn after President Trump gave us his tariff bonanza Liberation Day at the start of April this year. At the end of September, the shares had climbed back to just a fraction below their last peak.

As a result of the buyback programme, which has served to reduce the share count by 17%, the market capitalisation of the trust is now £1.5bn, down from its 2021 level. The discount has however come in from a peak of 45% to 32%, which is solid progress, albeit still wider than its average for the previous 15 years. Those who were smart enough to buy at the bottom have since seen a 50% gain, but longer-term investors will be grateful just to see the shares back where they once were.

The overall picture therefore is one of a recovery, but one that is not yet complete. Charlotte Morris, who took over as the lead partner managing the trust this year, after the retirement of Helen Steers, is positive about the outlook, but argues that investors need to show patience before a recovery in the industry cycle materialises and the trust's remedial measures take a firmer hold.

In its latest 12-month results, to the end of May 2025, Pantheon reported an NAV gain of just 1.2%, with adverse currency movements, principally the weakness of the dollar, offsetting the portfolio's valuation gain of 8.3%. 2024–25 was the trust's third successive year of single-digit NAV returns. With the discount widening out again in the immediate aftermath of Liberation Day, the share price total return for the financial year was a negative 9.2% (although the currency impact has subsequently reversed and the shares, as noted earlier, have recovered further).

Over one, three and five years, the results showed Pantheon's NAV total return lagging its two preferred benchmarks, the FTSE All-Share and MSCI World indices, but still ahead on both a share price and NAV total return basis over ten years. With the market for private equity assets gummed up, the average holding period has edged up to 5.6 years.

More encouragingly, the trust experienced a welcome £130m in net cash flow, higher than in the previous two years; its gearing remains modest at 9%; the roughly 250 companies it was able to realise were at an average price of 25% above their carrying value; and undrawn commitments remain well covered.

Comparisons with other listed private equity trusts are not easy to make, since the companies in its sector have such different strategies and business models. Having originally been established as one of a handful of trusts that only invested in other managers' private equity funds, since 2013 Pantheon has been steadily reducing its exposure to funds in favour of more direct investments into specific companies, whether as co-investors or so-called manager-led secondaries.

Direct investments now account for 54% of its portfolio by value. The managers say they have been putting a lot of energy into 'portfolio optimisation', in an effort to smooth out the impact of industry cyclicality, and increasing the use of secondary sales is an important element in that. More secondaries, transactions between fund managers that don't require new fundraising, give the managers greater flexibility in managing cash flows and tweaking the asset mix of the portfolio. Secondaries have been growing in number across the industry and are now at record levels globally.

As a large, well-diversified trust offering core exposure to a range of leading global private equity managers, Pantheon's history has been one of consistent long-term returns of 10–12% per annum. The current run of three successive annual single-digit NAV returns is anomalous from that perspective, but the history does include a favourable environment of zero interest rates following the global financial crisis that is unlikely to be repeated any time soon.

So it is too early to be sure that this pattern of lower returns is over. Investors, some of whom remain dubious about the validity of the reported NAVs, have been looking for signs of the industry cycle picking up for some time, but while deal flow increased in 2024 the evidence is not yet conclusive. The macro environment, not helped by President Trump's tariff policies, remains uncertain.

In Pantheon's favour is that its board has clearly demonstrated its commitment to managing the discount more effectively than in the past. The buybacks and pre-announced capital allocation plans, the latter recently tweaked in response to shareholder feedback, have produced an improvement in the discount, but the next big challenge is to attract new investors.

Pantheon has promised greater transparency and more intensive engagement with shareholders. That will cost money, take time and won't be simple to pull off, but more activity on that front, including a new website, is promised for this autumn and beyond. The annual report has already been expanded and includes significantly more detailed information than before.

Where next?

So where does Charlotte Morris think we go from here? According to her, the outlook for her industry is improving, but a return to a period of more normal higher returns may take time. "I personally think that we are in a multi-year transition in the private equity market. There is a shift happening. When you look at fundraising statistics, for example, the landscape is clearly shifting".

In hindsight, she says, the decade up to 2021 was "a really benign period with very cheap debt and the ability for pretty much anybody to generate good returns. That has changed dramatically and I think is altering the landscape going forward. Not everybody that was able to generate good returns in the past will be around and able to do so going forward."

Managers who relied heavily on financial engineering or multiple expansion alone for outperformance, she argues, will struggle in this tougher environment, meaning that it will be increasingly important to have money invested with the best managers in the private equity world, something for which Pantheon, with its long history and seasoned industry relationships, has good credentials.

"Where we want to focus our investment and support is with the managers that have genuinely transformed their businesses and where their returns have been primarily from operating company performance, growing the top revenue line, helping them grow market share, genuinely growing the company and increasing its performance." The underlying performance of portfolio companies continues to be positive, with average revenue gains in the last financial year, based on a sample of buyout holdings, more positive than previous years at 11%, albeit below the prior average.

In other words, while she hopes that private equity "will be able to continue to generate strong returns and outperform public markets, I think the groups that are doing that and the composition of the manager landscape will change". With its decades of experience in finding and working with the best managers, Pantheon hopes to remain a go-to destination for investors looking for broad private equity exposure in a portfolio actively overseen by an experienced board, to which three new non-executive directors with private equity experience have now been appointed, in line with chairman John Singer's expressed target three years ago.

As for the issue of persistently wide discounts, Morris says: "There are different things that have affected it and made it so persistent. The biggest one is the perceived disconnect between public and private market valuations. I think there still is some scepticism in the market about private valuations, and it's difficult to dispel that, especially while exit activity has been quite muted."

She stresses the importance of finding new sources of demand for private equity, including private investors and pension funds, by increasing transparency through webinars, speaking at conferences and other educational initiatives, and "explaining better what's in the portfolio, what's doing well, what's not and how to think about the composition of the portfolio".

There is no doubt that the discount experience of the last four years has somewhat soured sentiment towards listed private equity. There has been criticism that boards of trusts were slow to react to discount widening. Acknowledging the need for patience, Morris says she remains optimistic: "We're at a point where we're coming out of what's been a challenging few years. Periods of volatility like this create interesting opportunity too. We're still really excited about the growth in the years to come in private equity more widely".

The sector's future will likely be shaped by a renewed focus on manager selection and operational value creation, underscored by improved communications with investors. The 32% discount at which Pantheon was recently trading still leaves room for further narrowing if the combination of a wider market recovery and its continued active self-help bears fruit.

CHARLOTTE MORRIS *took over as lead partner for Pantheon International in 2025, having been co-manager with Helen Steers since June 2024.*

SCHRODERS IN ASIA

ABBAS BARKHORDAR, *co-manager of Schroder AsiaPacific (SDP) revisits the case for Asian equities as the trust celebrates its 30th anniversary.*

"THE COMPANY WILL aim to achieve capital growth from a portfolio principally comprising equities of companies located in the continent of Asia (excluding the Middle East and Japan), together with Far Eastern countries bordering the Pacific Ocean (excluding Australasia). The directors believe that the equity markets of these relatively fast-growing economies should provide returns superior to those of the industrialised countries… the manager will utilise its extensive local research resources to identify companies which are believed to have a competitive advantage and whose growth potential is undervalued by investors."

These words encapsulate some of the reasons investors should consider allocating part of their portfolio towards an actively-managed Asian equities fund. As it happens, these words are taken directly from the original prospectus that accompanied the launch of Schroder AsiaPacific Fund in October 1995. The 30th anniversary is a good moment to look back at how events have unfolded in Asia and how the opportunity set has evolved.

Relatively fast-growing economies

In 1995 Asia was widely viewed as a region of great economic promise. The so-called 'tiger' economies, Hong Kong, Singapore, South Korea and Taiwan, were already industrialising rapidly, largely through export-led manufacturing, and their success had inspired other countries across the region to follow suit.

China, meanwhile, galvanised by the industrial success of its neighbours, was on the cusp of a transformation that would fundamentally reshape the global economy. Following sweeping economic reforms in the 1980s, momentum was building towards full integration with the world trading system, culminating in its accession to the World Trade Organisation (WTO) in 2001. India had also embarked on a programme of liberalisation but remained a relatively closed and bureaucratic economy – full of potential, but yet to earn the confidence of international investors.

Collectively, however, the region was increasingly seen as the world's next growth engine, albeit one with underdeveloped capital markets, uneven governance standards and limited financial infrastructure. The opportunity was clear, but not without risks.

From the perspective of economic growth, that opportunity has indeed proved substantial. Data from the International Monetary Fund (IMF) demonstrates that Asia delivered annualised GDP growth of 6.5% between 1995 and 2024, compared with 1.7% per annum from the G7 group of developed economies. The "relatively fast" growth targeted by Schroder AsiaPacific at launch has, in that sense, been more than delivered.

Annualised GDP growth from 1995 to 2024

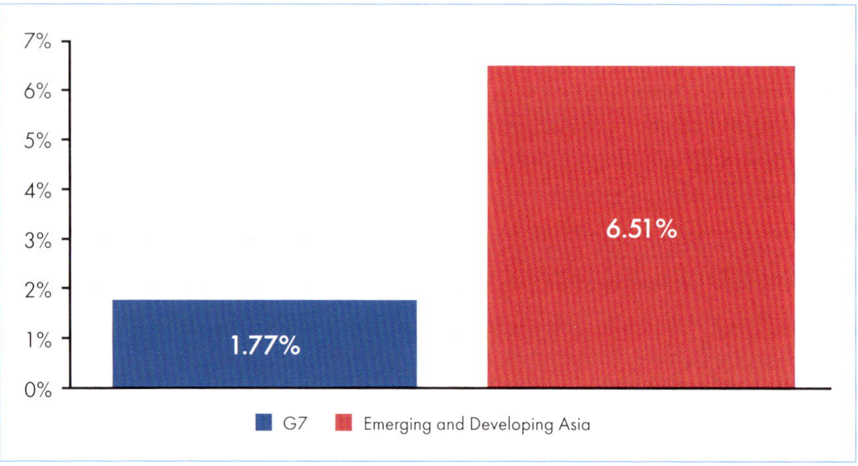

Source: IMF using annual GDP data from 1995 to 2024.

Bumps in the road

It has, however, been far from a smooth journey. Just two years after the trust's launch, the region was hit by the 1997 Asian Financial Crisis, a severe and destabilising event that exposed underlying fragilities in many economies. The crisis began in Thailand, where a fixed exchange rate, rising current account deficit and overheating property market led to a sudden loss of investor confidence, prompting speculative capital outflows. The Thai baht was forced to devalue, triggering a broader collapse in regional currencies and stock markets.

What followed was a painful reckoning. Weak banking systems, excessive foreign borrowing and limited policy coordination across the region contributed to a protracted downturn. For many economies, the scars of the crisis, from lost growth to political upheaval, would take years to heal.

Over the decade following the Asian financial crisis, the region underwent profound economic reform. Central banks accumulated foreign exchange reserves, current account balances moved into surplus and corporate debt levels fell significantly. Some currencies were allowed to float more freely, financial systems were strengthened and regional institutions, such as the Chiang Mai Initiative, a multi-billion-dollar currency swap pact between ASEAN, China, Japan and South Korea, were introduced to guard against future shocks.

These steps materially improved Asia's resilience and stood it in good stead for what came next. When the Global Financial Crisis (GFC) hit in 2008, its roots lay far from Asia, but the effects were felt around the world, with no region escaping unscathed. Even so, Asia, having learnt some important lessons from its own crisis, weathered the storm better than most. The region's stronger external balances and lower dependence on short-term overseas borrowing reduced its vulnerability, as did the health of its banking systems.

China's large-scale financial stimulus in 2008–09 also played a pivotal role in the crisis recovery. Infrastructure spending surged, credit growth was strong and commodity-intensive sectors boomed, offering a vital counterweight to the collapsing demand in the West. It marked a turning point in the global economic order, signalling that Asia was no longer just a passenger in the global cycle, but increasingly a driver of it.

Equity market performance

While Asia's economic progress over the last 30 years has been notable, the relationship between GDP growth and stock market performance isn't always straightforward. Fast-growing economies can be home to lacklustre or volatile equity markets, just as those in more mature, slower-growing economies can generate decent returns. Nevertheless, the superior economic growth delivered by Asia over the last 30 years has provided a solid foundation for its equity markets, as the next chart illustrates.

Many other factors also influence equity market performance, not least starting valuations. If equity prices are already high, even strong fundamental growth can be insufficient to drive future long-term returns. Meanwhile, low starting valuations can set the stage for stock market gains even when underlying economic growth is moribund.

Beyond that, changes in return on equity, governance standards, policy, regulation and swings in investment sentiment also play important roles. This has proved to be particularly marked in emerging markets, where political shifts and capital flow dynamics can have outsized effects. In Asia's case, the economic story has been directionally supportive of its equity market's returns, even if short-term correlations have often been weak.

Schroder AsiaPacific Fund at 30

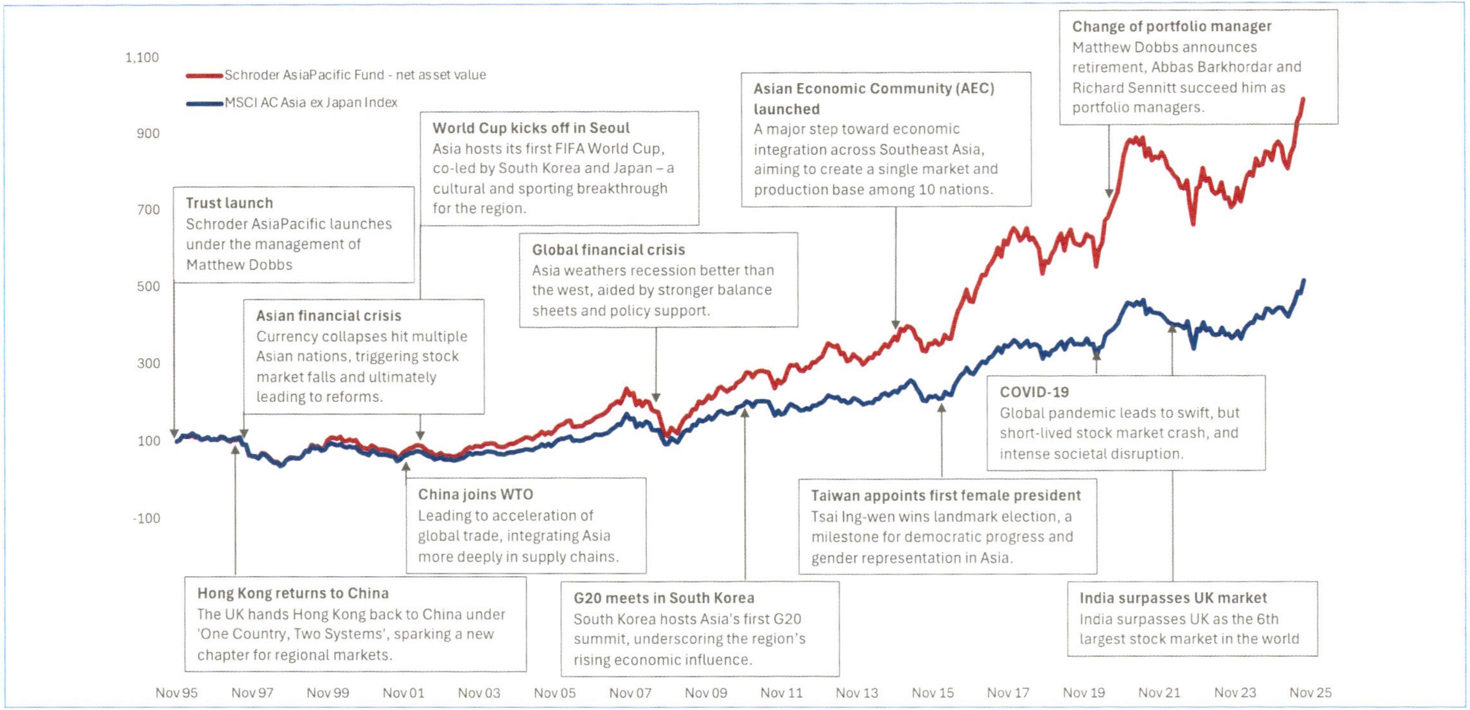

Source: Morningstar, Schroders on a total return, net of fees basis in UK sterling to 31 July 2025. 100 = 20 November 1995, Schroder AsiaPacific Fund's launch date. Prior to 31 January 2011, the trust's benchmark was the MSCI AC Far East ex-Japan Index. The index returns shown above are chain-linked, illustrating the former index to January 2011, and the current index thereafter. The regions and countries shown are for illustrative purposes only and should not be viewed as a recommendation to buy or sell.

The financial crises of 1997 and 2008 now appear as temporary setbacks on the chart, visible but transient, ultimately overwhelmed by the positive long-term impact of compounding returns. Asia's equity markets have rarely moved in a straight line, but the broader trajectory has been one of growth and resilience.

Extensive local research resources

At the time of the trust's launch, Schroders was already recognised as a leading investor in Asian equities, with significant experience, a strong regional presence and a reputation for deep fundamental research. The company's ability to deploy these strengths for the benefit of UK shareholders was a key part of the original investment case for Schroder AsiaPacific and remains so today.

As managers we are supported by a team of over 40 analysts, based across six countries in the Asia-Pacific region. Over the years, Schroders has invested heavily in maintaining an on-the-ground presence, with local offices providing direct access to companies and their leadership, enabling the investment team to build a more nuanced understanding of the key drivers of corporate performance.

Our belief is that high-quality company research is the key to long-term outperformance. The investment process focuses on understanding the structural dynamics, competitive advantages and governance of individual businesses, and identifying those whose future potential is not yet fully reflected in their valuations.

In a region where research coverage remains inconsistent and capital markets are often less efficient, this bottom-up focus has historically served shareholders well. It has helped the trust back a number of long-term winners across the region, including early and long-standing holdings in some of Asia's most prominent corporate success stories, such as TSMC and Samsung Electronics.

Looking ahead

While Asia's growth story has matured since 1995, many of the characteristics that inspired the launch of Schroder AsiaPacific – relatively positive demographics, an expansion of choice and superior long-term growth potential – remain firmly in place today.

The region still benefits from relatively favourable population dynamics in many countries. Asia's economies are home to the majority of the world's working-age population, and while the demographics in some countries now look more challenging, most notably for China, other parts of the region continue to enjoy population growth and rising incomes. This demographic breadth supports domestic consumption, builds resilience and underpins long-term demand for goods, services and infrastructure.

Choice has expanded too. Since 1995, many of the region's capital markets have grown significantly in size and sophistication, with improved governance and better access for international investors. What was once a relatively narrow opportunity set is now vast and diverse – encompassing everything from global technology leaders to early-stage innovators, from large, export-driven manufacturers to fast-growing consumer franchises.

Many of Asia's economies may still be export-reliant, but they now also enjoy powerful internal growth engines of their own. Importantly they have become much more resilient. With deeper capital markets, stronger institutions and a more balanced mix of growth drivers, Asia is arguably better placed to weather the uncertainties of global trade than at any point in its modern history.

On valuations, the region remains reasonably priced by historical standards, particularly when compared to other regions (by consensus the AsiaPacific ex-Japan forward price-earnings ratio is lower than the average P/E of developed markets). Investor attention has been dominated recently by the US equity market, particularly its large-cap technology sector. With concerns rising around concentration risk, stretched valuations and the sustainability of 'US exceptionalism', professional investor flows are beginning to shift towards other markets.

Asia offers an appealing alternative: stronger long-term growth prospects and a more diversified set of opportunities, and all crucially at more reasonable valuations. That sets a favourable stage for selective stock picking in a region where market inefficiencies and valuation anomalies remain plentiful.

Over the past three decades, the Schroders team has demonstrated that it is able to capture such opportunities, backing some of the region's most successful long-term growth stories from an early stage. The trust has consistently outperformed over the last 30 years, delivering more than 2% per annum above its benchmark index since launch. Although future returns cannot be guaranteed, if the region continues to fulfil its economic potential, we believe that the future looks very exciting for active investors in Asia.

ABBAS BARKHORDAR *has been co-manager, with Richard Sennitt, of the Schroder AsiaPacific Fund since March 2021. Previously the trust was managed by Matthew Dobbs.*

Q&A ON US GROWTH TRUST

KIRSTY GIBSON, *co-manager of the Baillie Gifford US Growth (USA), answers our questions about the trust's strategy and portfolio composition.*

Why invest in the US market now?

GIVEN THE CONCENTRATED benchmarks and an uncertain political landscape, being selective about your US exposure is more important than ever. We are more interested in the exciting technological progress that's underway than in the politics. The technological progress is more consequential. AI capabilities continue to accelerate and have exceeded our most optimistic expectations of two years ago. And it is being led by US companies.

It's surprising how little attention this is getting. The passing of the Turing Test earlier in the year generated barely a peep of coverage in the mass media.[1] For decades, this was seen as a critical milestone in the march towards super-intelligence, but that good news doesn't seem to make for good headlines at the moment. AI is starting to change the world, and we're already starting to see this impact our companies.

It's an incredibly exciting time for growth investing, and very few people seem to be paying attention. That's the opportunity. We're living through an extraordinary period of technological advancement. The companies we invest in for you are building better products, serving customers in new ways, and growing more efficiently. Our portfolio companies are demonstrating resilience – they're adapting, scaling, and generating stronger cash flows and improved margins. And that makes us optimistic for a select bunch of exceptional US growth companies.

How big a challenge has the election of Trump proved to be?

President Trump's re-election has introduced heightened uncertainty and market volatility, especially around trade and regulation. That being said, we remain steadfast in pursuing a long-term, conviction-led strategy. We are searching for companies that can adapt and thrive over a decade, not just across political cycles. Given the time period over which we invest (five-to-ten years), it is hard to know which decisions will matter in the long term.

---

1 The Turing Test suggests we will have achieved artificial intelligence when a reasonable person can no longer tell whether an answer comes from a human being or a machine.

In the short run, separating the noise from the signal is hard. We recognise that companies must survive the short run in order to execute on their long-run opportunities. Understanding the resilience and adaptability of the structural growth businesses we look to invest in is where we spend our time, rather than attempting to position our portfolio to the current Administration's decision-making.

Many people say that we have reached an end to US stock market exceptionalism? Do you agree?

No. Despite the political noise, the US remains uniquely positioned to produce transformational companies like Amazon, Tesla, Nvidia, Stripe and SpaceX. These are businesses that simply could not have been built elsewhere, given America's combination of risk-tolerant capital, deep private and public markets, and a culture that attracts the world's brightest talent.

The US is at the epicentre of the AI revolution, with Nvidia powering the infrastructure, OpenAI and Anthropic pushing the frontier models, and Microsoft, Google and others embedding these technologies at scale. History shows that such volatility only serves to highlight which outliers endure, and we believe that America's structural advantages mean it will remain the home of the foundational companies that drive long-term wealth creation.

Why is owning USA superior to investing in a US index fund?

Owning US Growth Trust is not about replicating the index; it's about capturing the outliers that drive it. Academic evidence shows that the vast majority of stock market wealth creation comes from a tiny handful of exceptional companies. An index fund, by definition, is dominated by incumbents and constrained by market weights, whereas our approach is to back the next generation of transformational businesses, from Nvidia and Tesla on the listed side to SpaceX, Stripe and Databricks in private markets. We can hold them with patience, unconstrained by benchmarks, and benefit from the journey long before many are even available in the index. In short, the trust is designed to find tomorrow's winners, not to mirror today's average companies.

So you are maintaining your live-year return targets (2.5x for listed, 5.0x for unlisted companies)?

Yes. Over rolling five-year periods, about 20% of listed companies return at least 2.5x their starting share price. For a trust looking to invest in the most exceptional growth businesses in the US, we must maintain a high bar. The even higher bar for unlisted businesses is a consequence of their less-liquid status, meaning it is not so easy to buy in and sell out of the shares as it is with listed companies.

How does that translate into a target return range for the portfolio?

Using the open-ended Baillie Gifford American Fund as a proxy, our long-run average for the public portfolio is at about 2% p.a. ahead of the S&P 500 over any rolling five-year period since 1997. Given the higher risk/reward profile of the private company exposure, we would expect the US Growth Trust to deliver a higher return than that over any rolling ten-year period. There is no guarantee that this will be achieved over any time period, and actual investment returns may differ from this objective, particularly over shorter time periods.

Five companies have contributed more than 40% of the return since launch. Is that likely to be typical?

Our philosophy is built around the recognition that a small number of stocks drive the majority of stock market returns over the long run. A small number of stocks delivering a large percentage of return is exactly what we would expect given the way we create our portfolios.

What typically have been the reasons for those that have failed?

The reasons a company can fail are numerous. As investors, we operate in the realm of probability. We cannot make any investment with certainty. For the stocks that do not meet our return hurdle, we may have misjudged the opportunity, the culture, or the strength of the competitive advantage. Getting stocks wrong goes hand in hand with our search for outliers. That being said, our sins of omission are far more painful than our sins of commission.

What changes have you made to your strategy in recent years – and why?

Successful high-growth investing requires tolerance for volatility. However, the volatility that we experienced during and after the pandemic exceeded our expectations. We have taken steps to reduce the probability of such extreme outcomes occurring again. For example, we now automatically retest the upside of our listed stocks once they cross our 2.5x return threshold, regardless of the time frame over which this return was generated. We're also more closely monitoring the overall shape of the portfolio to ensure an appropriate balance of growth styles, maturities and structural growth drivers across our listed holdings. Due to the illiquid nature of the private company investments, it is difficult to apply the same guide rails, but when making new investments in private companies, the team has regard to the overall balance in the portfolio.

Were these changes prompted by Saba acquiring its 30% shareholding and campaigning to take on the management of the trust earlier this year?

No. It has been an ongoing process that started back in 2022 after the pandemic. It has not been in response to pressure from any external shareholder. We started to realise that while we invest in exceptional growth businesses, there are different types of exceptional growth businesses. We now differentiate between transformational, dynamic and enduring growth businesses. We probably went a bit too far into early-stage businesses during Covid, so while the philosophy remains the same, we have now adopted a somewhat broader definition of what constitutes an exceptional growth business.

We bought some companies in the run-up to Covid that haven't worked. That is always the case. But we also didn't panic and held on to many companies that took a significant hit during and after Covid, but have since become our strongest performers again, because of the adaptability of their management teams in turning them around. Adaptability is very important. Shopify is a really good example. Shopify was unprofitable during Covid. That was what we would describe as 'discretionary unprofitable'. They were choosing to invest the cash that they were making into growth and it now has a close to 20% free cash flow margin. They've turned it around. That takes time but it's now growing, executing very strongly, and it's embracing AI and doing very well there.

Has the case for private equities been tarnished by recent experience, including the IPO drought and higher interest rates?

While headlines have focused on markdowns and funding slowdowns, we believe the case for private equities remains as compelling as ever. The most transformational businesses, such as Stripe, SpaceX and Databricks, are choosing to stay private for longer, compounding value well before any public listing. Short-term sentiment obscures the reality that private markets continue to be where tomorrow's category leaders are being forged. Our role is to partner patiently with these exceptional companies through periods of volatility, not to be distracted by cyclical noise.

How would you expect the private share in the portfolio to develop over the next few years?

Having a 50% limit on private holdings gives us the flexibility to allocate capital across the public and private markets as we see fit. We don't think about the portfolio in terms of allocations; we are looking to invest in the most exceptional companies in the US, regardless of where they are traded. The 50% limit enables us to think in that manner. Several private holdings in the US Growth Trust could become listed businesses. Every company's decision to IPO is different, but it is clear that becoming a listed business remains a priority for most. The percentage of private companies on 01 October 2025 was 36%.

You have mentioned AI already. What role does AI and AI-related themes now play in the portfolio?

AI is already deeply embedded across the portfolio. Some holdings, such as Nvidia are at the very centre of the infrastructure build-out, powering the compute layer, while others like Databricks, Stripe and Runway are applying AI to unlock new business models and efficiencies. We also see AI as an accelerant for many companies that might not be labelled 'AI stocks', whether it is DoorDash improving its logistics or CoStar enhancing data-driven insights.

At some point, AI will become so ubiquitous that it will resemble the internet. Once considered a discrete theme, today we no longer talk about 'internet companies', because connectivity is assumed. In the same way, we expect AI to become a foundational technology across every sector, woven through almost every business in the portfolio. Our task is not to chase the hype, but to identify which companies are best placed to harness this shift over the long term.

Can you give some examples of how portfolio companies are using AI?

Duolingo, for example, the language tutoring business, is saying that AI is allowing them to do things that they couldn't do before. They thought it was going to take 15 years for them to be on par with a human tutor. They're now saying that's going to be less than five. The speed at which they can develop personalised lessons is much faster than it was before.

Samsara is a technology company for industrial businesses. It provides many pieces of software and hardware which enable these industrial businesses to operate in a more efficient manner. Their first product was a camera that goes in a vehicle and collects data that helps to understand the driving patterns of the lorry driver. Are they braking too hard? Are they speeding? You've got this massive proprietary data set that you can start applying AI to in order to generate insights for your customer base.

I think the really exciting opportunity is going to be those companies embracing AI that we haven't really seen yet. Many of them are building on the infrastructure provided by the Nvidias and the Anthropics and the Metas and the Google Cloud services, all the AI infrastructure people. We own a company called Runway AI, for example, which is creating tools to help people to develop videos. Now, actually, if you want to see this at work, Baillie Gifford did one with me recently. This is all done by building a software layer on top of existing models to generate AI videos.

How are you using AI yourself?

AI at the moment is very useful when I don't know anything about something. So if I'm starting out on a company, or one of my colleagues has written about a company, AI can get it to explain something to me, almost like a five year old, you know: what does this company do? How does it work? That kind of stuff. It's really brilliant for that initial research.

And then it's also really brilliant when you know a lot about something, because you can challenge and correct it. For example, if I'm looking at a business that I know very well, and I'm thinking: how should I think about how this market opportunity evolves over time? I can start to say things like: "what happens if everyone who currently has x disease becomes a patient? How many patients is that?" And then I can say: "what are the reasons why people are not patients?"

You can dig into things a lot more. AI is very powerful for that. At the moment, provided I challenge it, I can use it to bounce thoughts off. It is providing me with a new colleague to bounce ideas off – a very, very super-intelligent colleague that can talk about anything, and has a very broad domain of expertise.

Where it could also be very useful, and where people have already been using algorithms, is for portfolio optimisation. But I think you have to be quite careful what you're optimising for. As a firm, we are optimising for long-termism, supporting companies and navigating the big ups and downs that they have in their share prices, because we believe in the fundamentals. So as long as you can potentially train an AI to understand your philosophy and what you're trying to achieve, that's good.

The biggest risk is that if people don't embrace this, they are probably going to be left behind. Much of our edge as long-term investors is the behavioural side, that willingness to hold on and tolerate uncertainty. Even if you can program an algorithm to do something, ultimately, you're the one that's still giving it those instructions.

Is the investment trust structure an advantage or disadvantage for your way of investing?

I think it is absolutely brilliant for us because it allows shareholders to gain access to companies like SpaceX, Stripe and Epic Games – companies they could not otherwise have invested in – for an extremely reasonable price. It presents more challenges if your shareholders are not aligned with your long-term perspective. If you have a period when performance is not so good, it can make you vulnerable for others to come in and say "we don't like the way you are doing this", and that can be tricky.

One of the challenges for investment trusts is that young people don't necessarily know about them. If you are in your 30s, and you are investing in a pension, why would you not want to invest in all these amazing private companies that will be public companies in future? You are paying 70 basis points for these incredible opportunities when private equity funds in the US are charging two and twenty! We need to get that message out.

Roller Coaster Ride

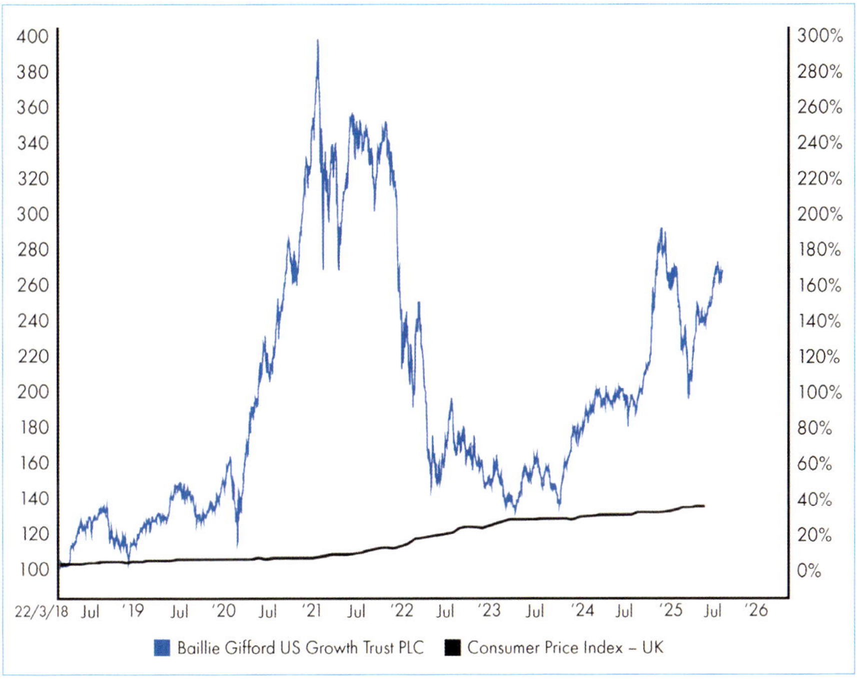

Source: ShareScope. The share price performance of USA (in blue) has been positive (+>160%) but highly volatile since its IPO in 2018, compounded by notable changes in its premium/discount. The NAV has compounded at 15% per annum since launch.

KIRSTY GIBSON *has been co-manager, with Gary Robinson, of Baillie Gifford US Growth since 2020. The trust was one of the targets of Saba Capital's campaign in December 2024, but comfortably survived the ensuing vote and has performed strongly since. It does not pay a dividend. As disclosed in the annual report, the total costs incurred in connection with the general meeting that Saba requisitioned were £319,000.*

2.8%
2.0%
1.8%
2.5%
% change
Total sales
14.5
9.5
8.5
10
7
6.9
5.7
5
3.9
4.2

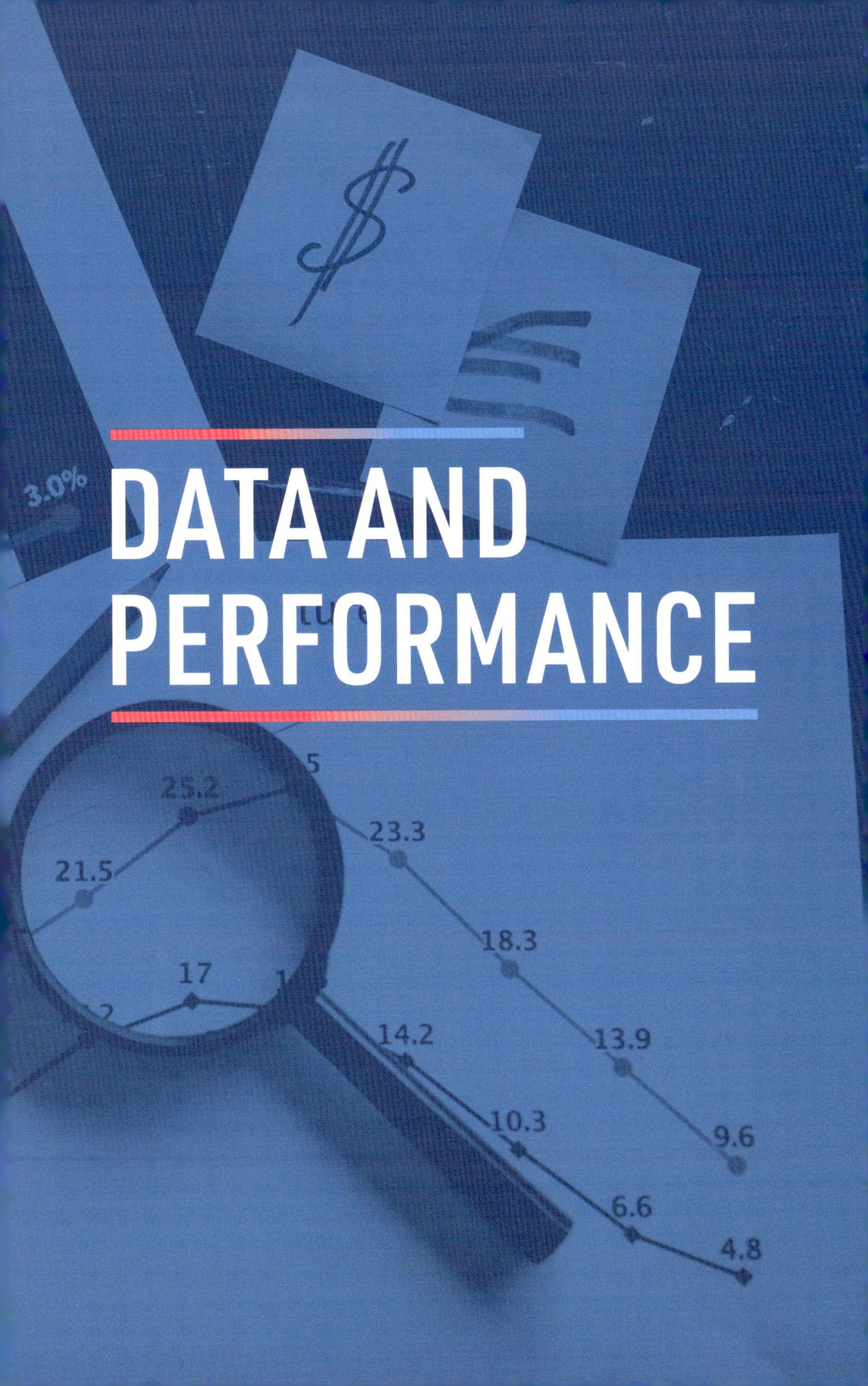

DATA AND PERFORMANCE

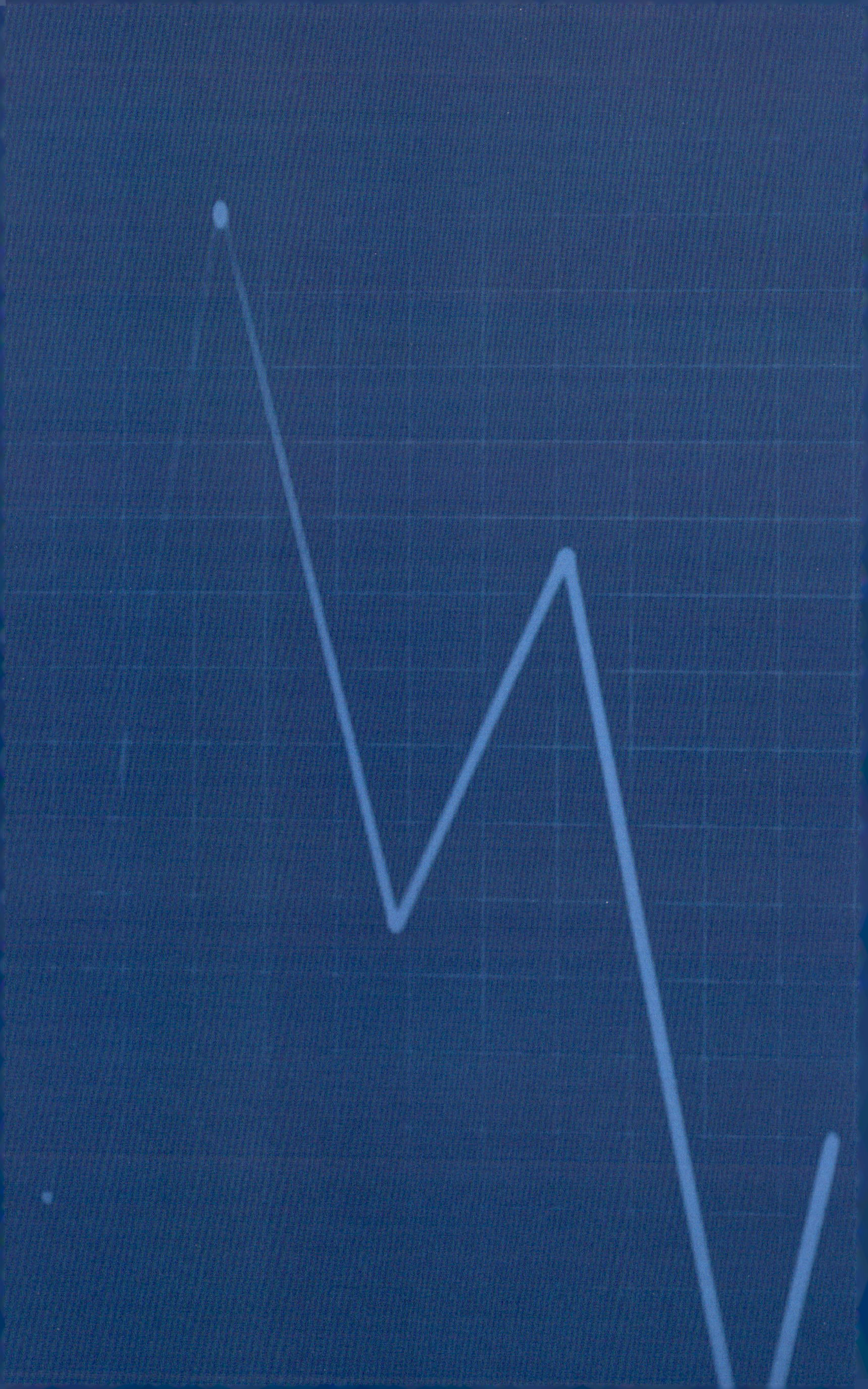

TRUST BASICS

For first-time investors in trusts, here is an overview of investment trusts – what they are and how they invest – from editor JONATHAN DAVIS.

What is an investment trust?

INVESTMENT TRUSTS, ALSO known as investment companies, are a type of collective investment fund. All types of fund pool the money of a large number of different investors and delegate the investment of their pooled assets, typically to a professional fund manager. The idea is that this enables shareholders in the trust to spread their risks and benefit from the professional skills and economies of scale available to an investment management firm. Funds are able to buy and sell investments without paying tax on realised gains.

Collective funds have been a simple and popular way for individual investors to invest their savings for many years, and investment trusts have shared in that success. Today more than £250bn of savers' assets are invested in investment trusts. The first investment trust was launched as long ago as 1868, so they have a long history. Sales of open-ended funds (unit trusts, OEICs and UCITs funds) have grown faster, but investment trust performance has generally been superior.

How do they differ from unit trusts and open-ended funds?

There are several differences. The most important ones are that shares in investment companies are traded on a stock exchange and are overseen by an independent board of directors, like any other listed company. Shareholders have the right to vote at annual general meetings (AGMs) on a range of things, including the election of directors, changes in investment policy and share issuance. Trusts can also, unlike most open-ended funds, borrow money in order to enhance returns. Whereas the number of units in a unit trust rises and falls from day to day in response to supply and demand, an investment trust is able to deploy permanent capital.

What are discounts?

Because shares in investment trusts are traded on a stock exchange, the share price will fluctuate from day to day in response to supply and demand. Sometimes the shares will change hands for less than the net asset value (NAV) per share of the company. At other times they will change hands for more than the NAV per share.

The difference between the share price and the NAV per share is calculated as a percentage of the NAV and is called a discount if the share price is below the equivalent NAV and a premium if it is above the NAV.

What is gearing?

In investment, gearing refers to the ability of an investor to borrow money in an attempt to enhance the returns that flow from his or her investment decisions. If investments rise more rapidly than the cost of the borrowing, this has the effect of producing higher returns. The reverse is also true, meaning that gains and losses are magnified. Investment trusts typically borrow around 5–10% of their assets, although this figure varies widely from one trust to another.

What are the main advantages of investing in an investment trust?

Because the capital is largely fixed, the managers of an investment trust can buy and sell the trust's investments whenever they need, rather than having to buy and sell simply because money is flowing in or out of the fund, as unit trust managers are required to do. The ability to gear, or use borrowed money, can also potentially produce better returns. The fact that the board of an investment trust is directly accountable to the shareholders is important. So too is the ability of boards to smooth the payment of dividend income by putting aside surplus revenue as reserves.

Because their capital base is permanent, investment companies are free to invest in a much wider range of investments than other types of fund. In fact, they can invest in almost anything. Although many of the largest trusts invest in listed stocks and bonds, the biggest growth in recent years has been in a range of more specialist areas, such as renewable energy, infrastructure, debt securities, music royalties and private equity. Investment trusts offer fund investors a broader choice and greater scope for diversification, in other words.

And what are the disadvantages?

The two main disadvantages are share price volatility and potential loss of liquidity. Because investment trusts can trade at a discount to the value of their assets, an investor who sells at the wrong moment may not receive the full asset value for their shares at that point. The day-to-day value of the investment will also fluctuate more than an equivalent open-ended fund. In the case of more specialist trusts, it may not always be possible to buy or sell shares in a trust at a good price because of a lack of liquidity in the market. Investors need to make sure they understand these features before investing.

How many trusts are there?

According to the industry trade body, the Association of Investment Companies, there were just over 380 investment trusts with more than £260bn in assets (as at the end of August 2022). They are split between a number of different sectors, reflecting the regions or type of investments in which they invest. Scottish Mortgage, the largest trust, has approximately £14bn in assets.

What are alternative assets?

While investment trusts have traditionally invested primarily in publicly listed stocks and shares, whose values are known every day, the last decade has seen significant growth in so-called alternative assets. These are trusts which invest in longer term assets which are mostly not traded daily and therefore can be valued only at less frequent intervals. Examples include commercial property, renewable energy, infrastructure and private equity. Many of these alternative trusts are popular because of their ability to pay higher levels of income.

How are they regulated?

All investment companies are regulated by the Financial Conduct Authority. So too are the managers the board appoints to manage the trust's investments. Investment trusts are also subject to the Listing Rules of the stock exchange on which they are listed. The board of directors is accountable to shareholders and regulators for the performance of the trust and the appointment of the manager and are legally bound by the requirements of successive Companies Acts.

How do I invest in an investment trust?

There are a number of different ways. You can buy them directly through a stockbroker or via an online platform. A few larger investment trusts also have monthly savings schemes where you can transfer a fixed sum every month to the company, which then invests it into its shares on your behalf. If you have a financial adviser, or a portfolio manager, they can arrange the investment for you.

What do investment trusts cost?

As with any share, investors in investment trusts will need to pay brokerage commission when buying or selling shares in an investment trust, and also stamp duty on purchases. The managers appointed by the trust's directors to make its investments charge an annual management fee which is paid automatically, together with dealing and administration costs, out of the trust's assets. These management fees typically range from as little as 0.3% to 2.0% or more of the trust's assets.

What are tax wrappers?

Tax wrappers are schemes which allow individual investors, if they comply with the rules set by the government, to avoid tax on part or all of their investments. The two most important tax wrappers are the Individual Savings Account (ISA) and the Self-Invested Personal Pension (SIPP). The majority of investment trusts can be held in an ISA or SIPP. There are annual limits on the amounts that can be invested each year (currently £20,000 for an ISA). Venture capital trusts (VCTs) are a specialist type of investment trust which also have a number of tax advantages, reflecting their higher risk. VCTs invest in start up and early stage businesses.

Who owns investment trusts?

Twenty-five years ago life insurance companies were the biggest investors in investment trusts, which they used to manage their client funds and pensions. These days such institutional investors mostly manage their own investments directly. Other than some specialist types of trust, the largest investors in trusts today are wealth management firms (formerly stockbroking firms), other types of intermediary and, increasingly, private investors. The growing number of individual investors reflects the growing influence of online platforms, which give individual investors the ability to choose their own investments for ISAs, SIPPs and taxable share/fund accounts.

Are they as difficult to understand as some people say?

Investment trusts are a little more complex than a simple open-ended fund, but no more difficult to understand than most types of listed company. It is important to understand the concept of discounts and premiums before you start to invest, but buying, selling and following the fortunes of your investment could not be easier. If you like the idea of making the connoisseur's choice when investing, you will find the effort of understanding investment trusts worthwhile.

Key terms explained

Investment trusts (aka investment companies) pool the money of individual and professional investors and invest it for them in order to generate capital gains, dividend income, or both. These are the most important factors that determine how good an investment they are:

Share price

The price (typically in pence) you will be asked to pay to buy or sell shares in any investment company. Your interest is to see it go up, not down.

Spread

The difference between the price per share to pay if you want to buy and that you will be offered if you wish to sell – can be anything from 0% (good) to 5% or more (bad). The bigger the trust, the tighter the spread should be.

Market capitalisation

The aggregate current value of all the shares a trust has issued – in essence, therefore, what the market in its wisdom thinks the investment company is worth today. (The market is not always wise and would be a duller and less interesting place if it were.)

Net asset value (NAV)

The value of the company's investments less running costs at the most recent valuation point – typically (and ideally) that will be yesterday's quoted market price, but for some types of investment trust, whose assets are not traded on a daily basis, it might be one or more months ago.

Net asset value per share

This is calculated, not surprisingly, by dividing the NAV (see above) by the number of shares in issue. You can compare it directly with the share price to find the discount or premium.

Discount/premium

When the share price is below the investment company's net asset value per share it is said to be trading 'at a discount'; if it trades above the NAV per share, then the trust is selling 'at a premium'.

Dividend yield

How much a trust pays out as income each year to its shareholders, expressed as a percentage of its share price. The usual figure quoted is based on the dividends a company has paid in the previous 12 months. Over time you hope to see the dividend increasing at least in line with inflation.

Dividend hero

A catchy term invented by the industry trade body to describe trusts which have increased their dividend every year for more than 20 consecutive years (see the data section for a full list).

The fund manager

The person (or team) responsible for choosing and managing the investment trust's capital. Will typically be professionally qualified and highly paid. How much value he or she really adds is a lively source of debate.

The board

Investment companies are listed companies, so they must comply with stock exchange rules and appoint a board of independent directors who are legally responsible for overseeing the company and protecting the interests of its shareholders, which ultimately means replacing the manager or closing down the trust if results are not good.

Gearing

A fancy word for borrowing money in order to try and boost the performance of a company's shares – a case of more risk for potentially more reward. A number of different types of borrowing (e.g., with fixed or variable interest rates) can be used.

Fees and charges

What it costs to own shares in an investment trust – a figure that (confusingly) can be calculated in several different ways. More important than it sounds on first hearing.

OCR

Short for Ongoing Charge Ratio, one of the most commonly used formulas used to measure the annual cost of owning a trust. Expressed as a percentage of the NAV.

Sectors

Investment trusts come in many shapes and sizes, so for convenience are categorised into one of a number of different sectors, based on the kind of things that they invest in.

Performance

A popular and over-used term which tells you how much money an investment trust has made for its shareholders over any given period of time – by definition, a backward-looking measurement. It does not guarantee future performance will be as good.

Benchmark

The outcome against which a trust and its shareholders have agreed to measure its performance. This is typically a stock market index relevant to the area or style in which the portfolio is being invested (e.g., the FTSE All-Share index for trusts investing in UK equity markets).

Total return

A way of combining the income a trust pays with the capital gains it also generates (you hope) over time, so as to allow fair comparisons with other trusts and funds. Shown either as a simple percentage gain over the period or as an annualised gain, the compound rate of return per annum.

Risk and return

Riskier investments tend to produce higher returns over time, typically at the cost of doing less well when market conditions are unfavourable and better when they are more helpful. Risk comes in many (dis)guises, however – some more visible than others.

Beta

This is a term used in financial economics to measure the extent to which the shares of a company rise or fall relative to the stock market as a whole. The stock market has a beta of 1.0, so if the market rises 10%, then a trust with a beta of 1.2 is expected to rise by 12% (=10 × 1.2). If it falls by 10%, the shares should fall by 12%.

Alpha

A statistical measure of the additional returns that a trust has made after adjusting for the relative risk of its portfolio. It is often used (not entirely accurately) as shorthand for fund manager skill.

Active management

What is going on when the investment manager of a trust makes a conscious decision not to include in its portfolio all the stocks or shares that make up its benchmark index. The latter can be easily and much more cheaply replicated by a computer – what is known as passive management. All investment trusts are actively managed.

Investment style

An attempt to characterise the way in which the manager of a trust chooses to invest. One common distinction is between value and growth. The former style aims to find companies whose shares are cheap relative to their competitors or historic price. The latter concentrates on finding companies with above average sales and profit growth prospects.

IS THERE ANY DIFFERENCE BETWEEN AN INVESTMENT COMPANY AND INVESTMENT TRUST?

Basically no. Strictly speaking, investment trusts are investment companies but not all investment companies are investment trusts. Feel free to use either term interchangeably, without fear of embarrassment.

CLOSED-END FUNDS

Investment trusts are an example of what is called a 'closed-end fund', meaning that its capital base is intended to be fixed and permanent (unlike unit trusts, OEICs and horribly named UCITs 3 funds, which take in and return money to investors on a daily basis and are therefore called open-ended). The distinction is no longer quite as important as it was, as it has become somewhat easier for successful investment companies to raise new money through regular share issues.

USEFUL SOURCES OF INFORMATION

Industry information

The Association of Investment Companies | www.theaic.co.uk

Data, news and research

Money Makers | www.money-makers.co

Morningstar | www.morningstar.co.uk

Trustnet | www.trustnet.com

Citywire | www.citywire.co.uk

Platforms

Interactive Investor | www.iii.co.uk

Hargreaves Lansdown | www.hl.co.uk

AJ Bell | www.ajbell.co.uk

Fidelity International | www.fidelity.co.uk

News and sponsored research

Edison | www.edisoninvestmentresearch.com

QuotedData | www.quoteddata.com

Trust Intelligence (Kepler Partners) | www.trustintelligence.co.uk

Specialist publications

Investment Trusts Newsletter (McHattie Group) | www.tipsheets.co.uk

Investment Trust Insider (Citywire) | www.citywire.co.uk

Publications that regularly feature investment trusts

Financial Times | www.ft.com

Investors Chronicle | www.investorschronicle.co.uk

Money Makers newsletter | www.money-makers.co

MoneyWeek | www.moneyweek.com

The Telegraph | www.telegraph.co.uk

Investing doesn't have to be stressful, it can feel like a walk in the park.
If you're eager for the kind of returns that active management generates but don't want the nightmare of stomach-churning volatility, Alliance Witan is for you. Our unique investment process is designed to quietly deliver attractive returns on shares from around the world without you needing to leave your comfort zone.
We've increased our dividend every year for an impressive 58 years, making Alliance Witan an ideal centrepiece for your portfolio. Relax. Investing doesn't have to be nerve-wracking, it can feel like a bit of a stroll.
Alliance Witan®
Find your comfort zone
alliancewitan.com

AI AND YOU

DANIEL SUMMERLAND *of Fidelity International discusses how AI is levelling the playing field for retail investors and how board directors can adapt in the new world of AI.*

LET ME START with a confession. When ChatGPT first arrived in November 2022, I was slow off the mark to try it. Another tech fad, I thought. Another distraction from proper research. It wasn't until mid-2024, when I began to dive deep into its practical applications for my work with boards and investors, that I truly grasped its power. The most accurate word I can find to describe its capability is still, simply, transformative.

Now I don't think twice about uploading entire investment trust annual reports into Google's NotebookLM tool and listening to auto-generated podcasts about them, with two AI voices explaining everything I need to know. And I can interrupt them mid-podcast and ask questions. Oh, and did I mention it's free?

The objective of this article is to show you what AI tools can do today to help you be more efficient and make better investment decisions, whether you are managing your ISA from the kitchen table or sitting in a boardroom deciding on buyback strategies. Everything I cover here is practical stuff that really works.

The great information imbalance

The investment trust world has always had an information problem. Not too little information, but too much. Annual reports that run to hundreds of pages. Monthly factsheets. Regulatory News Service (RNS) announcements that drop at 7 am when you are trying to get the kids ready for school or you're still asleep! Broker notes that assume you remember what happened six months ago.

Professional investors have teams to handle this firehose of data. They have analysts who wake up at 6 am to analyse the overnight news and expensive terminals that flag every twitch in the market. The rest of us have evenings and weekends.

The latest generation of large language models (LLMs) such as ChatGPT, Claude and Gemini are like having a tireless research assistant who never needs coffee and doesn't mind working at 11 pm. They can read everything you feed them, remember it all, and answer specific questions about it. They can spot patterns, track changes over time, and explain jargon in plain English.

I think the real revolution here is the democratisation of data. It allows the retail investor to move from simply consuming information to actively interrogating it. Instead of just reading a report, you can now have a conversation with it.

Practical examples you can use at home

So, what does this look like in the real world? For many retail investors, it might start with a simple Google or AI-tool search such as 'What is the best investment trust for exposure to fast-growing smaller companies around the world?' Almost 70% of requests to the Google Assistant are expressed in natural language and search engines are now providing AI-powered responses, with many users not even realising that the change has happened.

For a more sophisticated use case, imagine you have three investment trusts (or even 30! I know some of us do) in your portfolio. Until now, staying on top of them meant hours of reading and note-taking. But what you can do with AI is upload the key documents to your own AI workspace and ask targeted questions, such as:

'Compare the dividend cover across all three trusts for the past three years and present it as a table.'

'What has my largest investment trust said about its unlisted holdings in each report since 2023?'

'Track the trust's buyback volume against its discount over the last 12 months. Has the board's commentary on its discount policy been matched by its actions? Cite all page numbers.'

That final instruction – 'cite all page numbers' – is crucial. These tools occasionally make things up – what the tech world politely calls 'hallucinations' – but they are remarkably accurate when you force them to show their work. This simple discipline of grounding the AI in your own source documents is what separates serious analysis from digital guesswork.

A new research workflow should be built on a simple three-part foundation. First, create a document library for each investment trust you follow. Second, develop your 'permanent questions' – the core things you need to know every time, such as changes to the discount policy or portfolio concentration. Third, maintain a one-page investment thesis for each holding: why you bought it, what would make you sell it, and what you are watching for. Update it quarterly. This disciplined process, powered by AI, transforms a weekend chore into a focused, half-hour review.

A brief case study: from hours to minutes

Rita is a dentist in Leeds with three investment trusts in her ISA. In January, she builds a private library for each, comprising the last few annual reports and relevant RNS announcements. The AI assistant she uses is locked to that folder and must cite page numbers.

She asks one question: 'What has changed in the discount management policy for each investment trust this year?' The answer is a short brief, a small chart of buyback activity, and two lines copied directly from the board statements with links. She (or her AI agent) writes a new line in her one-page summary for one investment trust: 'If the discount drifts beyond 12% without action for more than four weeks, review position.'

Nothing magical happens. What Rita gets is traceability. If her thesis about the investment trust changes, she can show exactly why.

A brief case study: comparing investment trusts

Chloe is a tech professional in London considering an investment in two technology trusts. On the surface, their objectives seem very similar. To understand the real differences, she uploads both trusts' annual reports to her AI assistant and asks it to compare them on portfolio concentration, exposure to mega-cap versus mid-cap tech, and each manager's specific commentaries on artificial intelligence.

The AI generates a side-by-side summary. It highlights that one is more concentrated, with a higher percentage of its assets in its top ten holdings, and has a slightly different take on specific AI sub-sectors. The nuanced comparison helps Chloe decide which trust's strategy better aligns with her own views on the tech market.

Real example output from AI

I prompted a 'thinking' model of ChatGPT to compare three UK-listed income-paying investment trusts as potential investments for a higher-risk, long-horizon ISA investor, using the latest publicly available documents as of October 2025 (the actual prompt was much longer, and AI helped me optimise it).

It took just less than five minutes and came up with a comprehensive analysis. Unfortunately, it got some of the figures wrong when I did some fact checking. I told it so, and asked it to 'do better', which it did, and less than three minutes later I had my answer. I've simplified the figures and anonymised the names but everything else remains the same:

TRUST	MARKET CAP (£M)	YIELD (%)	5-YEAR DIVIDEND GROWTH (%)	DISCOUNT/ PREMIUM	ONGOING CHARGES FIGURE (%)	GEARING (%)
Trust A	3,000	4	>10	Small discount	0.4	0
Trust B	1,000	4	<2	Small premium	0.6	10
Trust C	2,000	5	<2	Small discount	0.5	10

Chat GPT 5's take on these trusts was: 'For a higher-risk ISA with a ten-year view, make Trust A the core: it pairs a low OCF with a proven long-run NAV-compounding record and a quarterly, board-set distribution, currently on a small discount. As a punchier satellite, add Trust B for UK value exposure and solid recent delivery, accepting single-market cyclicality and today's small premium. If you prefer greater natural dividend cover and broader regional exposure, Trust C is a sensible alternative diversifier, albeit with gentler long-term returns.'

To me, it shows we're on the cusp of a radically new way that investors will conduct their research going forward, and highlights the benefit for us all if we adapt quickly to these changes.

A clearer view from the boardroom

This shift is just as profound for directors. One of the challenges in the boardroom is not a lack of information, but a lack of time to process it effectively before making critical decisions. AI can transform that preparation. Imagine it is Tuesday evening and a 200-page board pack has just landed for a Friday meeting. Instead of three late nights of reading, you can now upload the papers to a secure AI workspace (emphasis on secure – never use public tools for confidential materials) and get straight to the point.

'Summarise the key decisions required at this meeting.'

'What has changed in the portfolio's risk profile since the last board pack?'

'Flag any items that contradict previous board decisions.'

Directors can revolutionise their preparation by asking their AI co-thinker to 'play devil's advocate' on each major agenda item. It spots the gaps and raises the awkward questions in advance. The board arrives better prepared, and meetings are shorter and more focused on decision-making. Of course, it wouldn't be right to outsource your own reading and challenge to AI, but these tools are thorough (they definitely read every word) and may well pick up things you would otherwise have missed.

This extends to strategic oversight. Every board wants to know what its peers are doing. Instead of relying on expensive consultant reports, a 'peer tracker' can be built. By feeding it the public documents from a defined peer group, a board can ask: 'Which of our peers have announced a formal discount control target in the last 12 months, and how has their discount behaved since?' It allows boards to act on evidence, not anecdotes.

This can result in better shareholder engagement. For example, by analysing previous years' AGM questions or shareholder letters, boards can anticipate concerns and prepare consistent, accurate responses grounded in their own public statements. This creates a virtuous circle: better-informed investors ask better questions, and better-prepared boards give clearer answers.

This is as much a governance upgrade as it is an efficiency gain. In an environment of increased shareholder activism and intense scrutiny on fees and performance, the ability to act on evidence rather than anecdote is a powerful defensive tool. A board that can demonstrate a data-driven rationale for its decisions – on buybacks, on manager appointments, on fee structures – is a board that is on much firmer ground.

Navigating the risks and looking ahead

As much as I am an evangelist about AI, I also need to acknowledge its current weaknesses. These tools can fail. They can confidently state a trust's discount was 15% when it was actually 5%. They can invent plausible-sounding regulations that do not exist. Never trust them 100% without verifying. Check numbers that matter. And never publish anything generated by AI without thorough human review, especially with the FCA's Consumer Duty in mind, demands communications help retail customers make informed decisions by being understandable and relevant.

There is also the herding risk. If everyone uses the same tools in the same way, we will all reach the same conclusions. The market becomes an echo chamber of AI-generated consensus. The defence against this is to use these tools for what they are good at, which is processing information, while keeping a healthy share of the critical thinking and reasoning to yourself.

We are still in the early days. You might have heard the phrase 'This is the worst that AI will ever be'. The tools will get better, faster, and more reliable. But the fundamental dynamic will not change. They are tools that democratise access to information processing, not judgment, experience, or wisdom. It's unlikely to turn novices into Warren Buffett. But they will help level a playing field that has been tilted toward professional investors for a very long time.

Finally, there is FOMO risk. Competitor companies and providers of investment products are already optimising the way they operate and market what they do, in order to be picked up by AI, much like the search engine optimisation of the past 20 years. Boards have a responsibility to their shareholders to be as visible, transparent and as easy to interpret by the AI tools that they will increasingly be using, or be left behind.

Investment trusts and their directors can thrive in this new world of AI by using these tools to be more transparent, more responsive, and more thoughtful about their shareholders' needs. The investors who succeed will be those who use machines to help them think better, rather than think entirely for them. Revolution? Perhaps. But it's certainly enough of an *evolution* to matter.

DANIEL SUMMERLAND *leads product and business development for Fidelity International's investment companies team and serves as a client director.*

MONEY MAKERS PROFILES

You can read Stuart Watson's in-depth fund profiles and access much more exclusive investment trust analysis and information by becoming a member of the Money Makers Circle. Just go to money-makers.co/membership-join for full details of how to sign up. The aim of the fund profiles is to cover a wide range of trusts that invest both in equities and alternative assets, providing a long-term perspective on what drives their performance and setting out the key points potential investors need to know. More than 200 profiles have been published to date and new ones appear on a weekly basis. The content is independently produced; we don't offer sponsored or broker-led research.

Some of the most recent trusts that have been featured are:

- Henderson Smaller Companies (HSL)
- Mobius Investment Trust (MMIT)
- Renewables Infrastructure Group (TRIG)
- Montanaro UK Smaller Companies (MTU)
- AEW UK REIT (AEWU)
- Herald (HRI)
- Lindsell Train (LTI)
- abrdn New India (ANII)
- Gresham House Energy Storage (GRID)
- Odyssean (OIT)
- Fidelity Special Values (FSV)
- Baillie Gifford European Growth (BGEU)
- HICL Infrastructure (HICL)
- Fidelity Emerging Markets (FEML)
- VietNam Holding (VNH)
- Pershing Square Holdings (PSH)
- Schiehallion (MNTN)
- Tritax Big Box REIT (BBOX)
- European Opportunities (EOT)
- Law Debenture (LWDB)
- HgCapital Trust (HGT)
- RIT Capital Partners (RCP)
- Baillie Gifford US Growth (USA)

The largest equity sectors

AIC SECTOR	# COMPANIES	NET ASSETS (£M)	% INDUSTRY NET ASSETS	MARKET CAP (£M)	% INDUSTRY MARKET CAP	MARKET CAP (£M) 2020	5 YR MARKET CAP % GROWTH	AVERAGE GEARING %
Global	11	31,925	13.6%	29,947	13.7%	30,814	-2.8%	4.0%
North America*	9	16,341	6.9%	12,427	5.7%	3,003	313.9%	7.1%
Flexible Investment	19	14,835	6.3%	10,884	5.0%	8,659	25.7%	16.1%
UK Equity Income	18	11,515	4.9%	11,371	5.2%	8,828	28.8%	7.4%
Global Equity Income	6	6,638	2.8%	6,500	3.0%	2,947	120.6%	12.0%
Global Emerging Markets	10	6,021	2.6%	5,588	2.6%	5,984	-6.6%	5.9%
UK Smaller Companies	21	5,587	2.4%	4,886	2.2%	4,415	10.7%	12.8%
Global Smaller Companies	5	5,499	2.3%	4,823	2.2%	5,201	-7.3%	5.6%
Europe	5	4,123	1.8%	3,963	1.8%	3,495	13.4%	8.2%
UK All Companies	5	4,042	1.7%	3,825	1.8%	3,305	15.7%	9.0%
Japan	5	2,956	1.3%	2,671	1.2%	2,536	5.3%	13.5%
Asia Pacific Equity Income	5	2,802	1.2%	2,655	1.2%	1,782	49.0%	3.7%
Asia Pacific	4	2,620	1.1%	2,400	1.1%	3,203	-25.1%	5.7%
Country Specialist	4	2,403	1.0%	2,010	0.9%	1,955	2.8%	-
China / Greater China	3	2,223	0.9%	2,037	0.9%	2,364	-13.8%	12.5%
European Smaller Companies	4	1,738	0.7%	1,624	0.7%	1,725	-5.8%	6.9%
India / Indian subcontinent	4	1,499	0.6%	1,381	0.6%	858	60.9%	-
Asia Pacific Smaller Companies	3	1,353	0.6%	1,220	0.6%	842	44.9%	12.0%
Japanese Smaller Companies	3	1,047	0.4%	993	0.5%	1,278	-22.4%	10.4%
Financials & Financial Innovation	2	645	0.3%	500	0.2%	201	148.2%	0.7%
North American Smaller Companies	2	408	0.2%	370	0.2%	294	26.1%	7.2%
UK Equity & Bond Income	1	331	0.1%	306	0.1%	200	52.7%	19.2%
Latin America	1	124	0.1%	111	0.1%	148	-24.7%	4.7%
Total	**150**	**126,674**	**53.82%**	**112,491**	**51.60%**	**94,036**	**19.63%**	-
Average							**35.23%**	**8.73%^**

Source: AIC/Morningstar, all figures to 30/09/25 unless otherwise stated.

* Please note Pershing Square holdings which has a current market cap of £7bn, moved from hedge fund to North American sector in January 2022.

^ companies with 0% gearing are ignored.

There are no set rules for what an investment trust can invest in. The trust's strategy does, however, normally have to be outlined in a prospectus and approved by shareholders if, as does happen, the board wishes to change that objective at a later date. For convenience, and to help comparative analysis, trusts are grouped into a number of different sectors, based primarily on their investment focus. These are listed here and on the following three spreads.

The majority of the sector categories are self-explanatory. It is worth noting that individual trusts within each broad sector category will often have somewhat different investment objectives and benchmarks. The 'flexible investment' sector includes a number of trusts which invest across a broad range of asset classes, not just equities. Most of these were previously included in the global sector.

These sectoral classifications are reviewed at regular intervals by a committee of the Association of Investment Companies. These typically result in one or two changes in the classification every year, though these are mostly minor. By tradition the breakdown distinguishes between trusts that invest primarily in large-cap stocks and those that focus on mid-cap and smaller companies.

The table on this page summarises the sectors which, together with healthcare, financials and technology (included on the next spread), are normally described as conventional equity trusts, to distinguish them from so-called 'alternative assets', such as infrastructure, debt and private equity. Counting commercial property as an alternative asset, the split between equity trusts and alternatives remains close to 50 50 today, but the proportion of alternatives trusts, which grew rapidly after the global financial crisis, has been falling slowly over the last three years as interest rates have risen and discounts have widened.

A notable feature of the table is that barely 10% by market capitalisation of these conventional equity trusts have the UK as their primary investment focus. Investment trusts have always had a bias towards investment outside the UK. The aim of the very first trust in 1868, Foreign & Colonial (now F&C), was to enable its shareholders to diversify their portfolios by investing in bonds issued by companies outside the UK.

The significant overseas focus is an important reason why equity investment trusts on average perform quite differently from the FTSE All-Share index. They track world markets more closely than the UK stock market, and for most of the past two decades that has been an advantage, as other markets, the US in particular, have comfortably outperformed the UK.

The average discount across equity trusts comes in this year at 9%, down from around 14% two years ago. The market capitalisation of these trusts has grown by 20% over the past five years, but the number of trusts in this category has shrunk from 169 to 160, with more shrinkage to come as more announced mergers and liquidations come to fruition.

Specialist sectors

AIC SECTOR	# COMPANIES	NET ASSETS (£M)	% INDUSTRY NET ASSETS	MARKET CAP (£M)	% INDUSTRY MARKET CAP	MARKET CAP (£M) 2020	5YR MARKET CAP % GROWTH	AVERAGE GEARING %
Private Equity	15	41,795	17.8%	51,319	23.5%	17,250	197.5%	6.5%
Infrastructure	8	13,380	5.7%	11,154	5.1%	12,242	-8.9%	35.6%
Renewable Energy Infrastructure	18	13,033	5.5%	9,077	4.2%	9,059	0.2%	61.6%
Growth Capital	7	7,667	3.3%	5,926	2.7%	1,230	381.8%	4.0%
Technology & Technology Innovation	4	7,514	3.2%	6,839	3.1%	4,006	70.7%	1.4%
Biotechnology & Healthcare	7	4,111	1.7%	3,368	1.5%	7,948	-57.6%	4.3%
Commodities & Natural Resources	7	2,150	0.9%	2,063	0.9%	1,149	79.5%	8.4%
Hedge Funds*	3	1,565	0.7%	1,390	0.6%	5,928	-76.6%	-
Debt - Structured Finance	5	1,554	0.7%	1,523	0.7%	1,611	-5.4%	-
Debt - Loans & Bonds	6	1,461	0.6%	1,495	0.7%	1,647	-9.2%	8.0%
Debt - Direct Lending	5	1,177	0.5%	1,022	0.5%	3,018	-66.1%	28.2%
Environmental	1	876	0.4%	783	0.4%	995	-21.3%	7.9%
Leasing	4	720	0.3%	559	0.3%	618	-9.6%	230.2%
Infrastructure Securities	2	278	0.1%	247	0.1%	173	42.5%	40.1%
Insurance & Reinsurance Strategies	1	75	0.0%	50	0.0%	198	-74.9%	-
Total	**93**	**97,356**	**41.4%**	**96,815**	**44.4%**	**67,072**	**44.3%**	**-**
Average								**36.9%**

Source: AIC/Morningstar, all figures to 30/09/25 unless otherwise stated.

*Please note Pershing Square holdings which has a current market cap of £7bn, moved from Hedge Fund to North American sector in January 2022.

The specialist sectors are also clearly identified by their name. Unlike conventional equity trusts, which are mainly defined by their regional focus, the specialist sectors are mostly grouped by industry. The specialist sector gives a flavour of the wide range of investment strategies which are available once you look beyond the traditional equity names.

That range has expanded significantly since the global financial crisis with the launch of many new trusts offering access to new asset classes. Last year we were able to see five-year comparisons for some of these newcomers, such as growth capital and debt trusts, although others, such as music royalties and farmland, have already disappeared in the wave of rationalisation that has thinned the ranks of alternatives since 2022.

The market value of private equity, infrastructure, commercial property and renewable energy trusts in combination grew rapidly up until 2021, thanks to a combination of strong performance, the launch of new funds and considerable secondary share issuance. The common feature of these types of trust is that they own physical assets that are not easily traded or listed on exchanges.

The biotechnology and healthcare sector has also seen a significant expansion. Like technology, these qualify as specialist trusts by virtue of their narrow focus on one particular sector of the listed equity market. Unlike alternatives, their appeal lies mainly in the potential for capital growth, not their ability to generate solid and reliable dividend income streams.

Interest rates are a key influence on the performance of most alternatives. Since early 2022 the value of the specialist sectors has fallen sharply as discounts widened and capital values also declined in many cases. They started to recover in Q3 2023, but discounts remain stubbornly wide in many cases. The number of specialist trusts has fallen by more than 10%, from 108 to 93, since the last edition of the *Handbook*.

The universe of listed trusts inevitably changes significantly from decade to decade. That process has intensified recently. Additions include trusts that invest in the space industry, shipping, digital infrastructure, battery storage and energy efficiency, but there has been a steady culling of weaker names. Those that are strong enough to survive the current shakeout will hope to find new buyers as the current cycle unfolds.

The average discount for these specialist sectors has barely changed since the last edition, but on average remains much wider than those of equity trusts, a reversal of the pattern in the low-interest-rate era. The larger, more established alternative asset trusts have meanwhile been prominent in a campaign to change the regulations that require them to report what are often misleadingly high figures about the cost of ownership.

Property sectors

AIC SECTOR	NET ASSETS (£M)	% INDUSTRY NET ASSETS	MARKET CAP (£M)
Property - UK Logistics	5,321	2.3%	4,065
Property - UK Commercial	1,854	0.8%	1,278
Property - UK Residential	1,647	0.7%	1,325
Property Securities	1,115	0.5%	1,017
Property - UK Healthcare	745	0.3%	600
Property - Europe	545	0.2%	371
Property - Debt	404	0.2%	356
Property - Rest of World	118	0.0%	49
Total	**11,748**	**5.0%**	**9,061**
Average			

Top companies

COMPANY NAME	TICKER	AIC SECTOR	MANAGEMENT GROUP
Tritax Big Box REIT	BBOX	Property - UK Logistics	Tritax Management
TR Property	TRY	Property Securities	Columbia Threadneedle
PRS REIT	PRSR	Property - UK Residential	Sigma Capital
Target Healthcare REIT	THRL	Property - UK Healthcare	Target Fund Managers
Warehouse REIT	WHR	Property - UK Logistics	Tilstone Partners
Regional REIT	RGL	Property - UK Commercial	ARA Europe Private Markets
Social Housing REIT	SOHO	Property - UK Residential	Atrato Partners
Custodian Property Income REIT	CREI	Property - UK Commercial	Custodian Capital
Schroder Real Estate	SREI	Property - UK Commercial	Schroder Real Estate Management
Phoenix Spree Deutschland	PSDL	Property - Europe	QSix
Home REIT	HOME	Property - UK Residential	AEW UK Investment Management
Real Estate Credit	RECI	Property - Debt	Cheyne Capital
abrdn European Logistics Income	ASLI	Property - Europe	Aberdeen
Residential Secure Income REIT	RESI	Property - UK Residential	Gresham House
Life Science REIT	LABS	Property - UK Commercial	Ironstone Asset Management
Channel Islands Property	CIP	Property - UK Commercial	Ravenscroft Corporate Finance
AEW UK REIT	AEWU	Property - UK Commercial	AEW UK Investment Management
Schroder European Real Estate	SERE	Property - Europe	Schroder Real Estate Management

	MARKET CAP (£M) 2020	# COMPANIES	5YR MARKET CAP % GROWTH	AVERAGE GEARING %	AVERAGE YIELD %	AVERAGE DISCOUNT %
	264	2	1438.0%	39.4%	5.4%	-18.8%
	7,225	9	-82.3%	80.3%	19.2%	-27.7%
	2,215	5	-40.2%	68.5%	9.1%	-35.3%
	1,095	1	-7.1%	15.5%	5.0%	-8.8%
	795	1	-24.5%	25.4%	6.1%	-19.4%
	1,126	3	-67.1%	76.9%	6.3%	-32.1%
	745	4	-52.2%	29.4%	11.5%	-11.7%
	132	2	-62.9%	31.3%	0.0%	-57.9%
	13,597	**27**				
			-33.4%	**62.7%**	**12.4%**	**-27.5%**

	% YIELD	% 5YR DIVIDEND GROWTH P.A.	GEARING (%)	ONGOING CHARGE %	% 5YR SHARE PRICE TOTAL RETURN	% 5 YEAR NAV TOTAL RETURN	TOTAL ASSETS (£M)	NET ASSETS (£M)	DISCOUNT %
	5.1%	2.3%	33.0%	0.8%	17.4%	48.9%	6,397	4,770	-24.9%
	5.0%	2.6%	15.5%	0.8%	15.5%	7.3%	1,364	1,115	-8.8%
	3.8%	1.5%	44.0%		73.2%	77.0%	1,142	786	-19.6%
	6.1%	-2.5%	25.4%	1.5%	24.9%	47.1%	972	745	-19.4%
	5.7%	0.6%	45.7%	1.4%	34.7%	38.7%	811	551	-12.8%
	7.4%	-25.8%	96.6%	9.3%	-69.2%	-71.1%	722	338	-43.2%
	8.0%	1.4%	54.5%	1.6%	-5.9%	29.9%	690	429	-35.4%
	7.4%	-2.0%	37.4%	1.3%	24.7%	39.6%	648	464	-19.5%
	7.0%	11.2%	49.4%	2.7%	122.1%	43.8%	482	320	-23.1%
	0.0%	-100.0%	91.4%		-48.9%	-43.0%	478	230	-34.4%
	14.5%		104.6%	9.1%			463	217	38.7%
	9.6%	0.0%	27.6%	2.2%	58.2%	44.1%	414	315	-11.8%
	11.2%	-6.3%	110.8%	2.0%	-24.8%	-10.2%	407	183	-26.5%
	7.2%	-3.8%	106.1%	1.4%	-11.6%	3.9%	352	165	-35.4%
	5.5%		43.9%	1.8%			344	235	-45.6%
		0.0%	87.5%			27.4%	247	128	
	7.3%	0.0%	19.8%	1.5%	116.9%	68.4%	229	170	1.7%
	7.7%	-5.2%	28.5%	2.6%	60.9%	-0.3%	192	132	-35.4%

COMPANY NAME	TICKER	AIC SECTOR	MANAGEMENT GROUP
abrdn Property Income	API	Property - UK Commercial	Aberdeen
Value and Indexed Property Income	VIP	Property - UK Commercial	OLIM Property Limited
Alternative Income REIT	AIRE	Property - UK Commercial	M7 Real Estate Financial Services
Ceiba	CBA	Property - Rest of World	Ceiba Investments
Ground Rents Income	GRIO	Property - UK Residential	Schroder Real Estate Management
Starwood European Real Estate Finance	SWEF	Property - Debt	Starwood European Finance Partners
Macau Property Opportunities	MPO	Property - Rest of World	Sniper Capital
Develop North	DVNO	Property - Debt	Tier One Capital
ICG-Longbow Senior Secured UK Property Debt Invest	LBOW	Property - Debt	Longbow Real Estate Capital

Source: AIC/Morningstar, all figures to 30/09/25 unless otherwise stated.

The great majority of commercial property trusts invest directly in physical property, meaning they buy, sell or lease out the bricks and mortar themselves. By their nature they are typically illiquid, since buildings such as offices, shops and factories can take many months to purchase and cannot be sold in a hurry, unlike property company shares which can be bought and sold within minutes.

TR Property (TRY) is differentiated from all these trusts by virtue of being the last remaining example of a trust that invests almost exclusively in the shares of other property companies (in its case drawn from across the whole of Europe). The trust's shares trade like other equities, rising and falling more markedly from day to day than those of trusts which invest directly in property.

Not so long ago most of the biggest trusts in the property sector were generalist trusts, managed by well-established fund management companies. These trusts typically had diversified portfolios of assets across all three of the main categories: shops, offices and industrial buildings. For a while they were supplanted in popularity by trusts specialising in smaller, niche sectors of the market, such as social housing, residential developments, doctors' surgeries, supermarkets and warehouses.

Both these trends have been overwhelmed through rationalisation and consolidation in the last three years. Nearly all the larger diversified trusts have effectively disappeared after a wave of M&A activity involving bids from private

% YIELD	% 5YR DIVIDEND GROWTH P.A.	GEARING (%)	ONGOING CHARGE %	% 5YR SHARE PRICE TOTAL RETURN	% 5 YEAR NAV TOTAL RETURN	TOTAL ASSETS (£M)	NET ASSETS (£M)	DISCOUNT %
103.4%	4.7%	281.6%	2.8%	50.5%	-13.0%	169	35	-36.2%
6.7%	2.7%	50.4%		64.0%	32.6%	147	97	-11.4%
8.7%	4.4%	55.9%	1.5%	110.9%	40.2%	108	67	-15.2%
0.0%	0.0%	0.0%	1.0%	-57.4%	-33.5%	92	92	-58.5%
12.0%	-100.0%	33.2%		-63.5%	-45.8%	71	50	-50.7%
6.3%	-3.3%	0.0%	1.3%	39.2%	25.0%	44	44	-9.6%
0.0%	0.0%	31.3%		-74.4%	-76.5%	35	26	-57.3%
5.2%	-7.8%	31.2%	2.7%	13.3%	21.3%	26	20	-2.8%
25.0%	-100.0%	0.0%		-61.6%	-65.6%	24	24	-22.8%

equity and other property investors, while many of the specialist providers have either suffered the same fate or agreed to wind down their operations.

No fewer than eight of the top 15 commercial property trusts listed in last year's *Handbook* have either disappeared already or are set to do so. Tritax Big Box, which invests in the huge distribution warehouses used by Amazon and others to move products around the country, remains the single largest trust in the sector, despite suffering a significant derating, but now accounts for 40% of the sector's NAV.

Such is the scale of the rationalisation in the industry that the two largest remaining diversified property trusts, Schroder Real Estate and Custodian Property Income, did not even make the top 15 list last year, and two of the trusts that have disappeared, Supermarket Income and Urban Logistics REIT, have been absorbed by LondonMetric, which is not classified as an investment trust but is a listed company in the FTSE 100 index, so still investable by shareholders.

Among the specialist trusts the ranks have been thinned in a variety of ways, the assets typically being acquired by private equity or institutional investors attracted by the exceptionally wide discounts at which their targets were trading. That said, these deals have typically been completed at discounts of between 8% and 10%, giving long-suffering shareholders a useful premium over the prevailing market price, but well down on previous highs. Those that remain offer dividend yields above their historical norm.

VCT sectors

AIC SECTOR	# COMPANIES	NET ASSETS (£M)	% VCT INDUSTRY NET ASSETS
VCT	39	5,795	90.3%
VCT AIM Quoted	7	624	9.7%
Total	**46**	**6,420**	**2.7%**
Average			

Top VCTs

COMPANY NAME	MANAGEMENT GROUP	AIC SECTOR
Octopus Titan	Octopus Investments	VCT
Octopus Apollo	Octopus Investments	VCT
British Smaller Companies	YFM Private Equity	VCT
Albion Enterprise	Albion Capital Group	VCT
Albion Technology & General	Albion Capital Group	VCT
Pembroke B shares	Pembroke Investment Managers	VCT
Baronsmead Second Venture	Gresham House	VCT
Foresight	Foresight Group	VCT
Baronsmead Venture	Gresham House	VCT
Puma 13	Puma Investments	VCT
Unicorn AIM	Unicorn Asset Management	VCT AIM Quoted
British Smaller Companies 2	YFM Private Equity	VCT
ProVen	Beringea	VCT
ProVen Growth and Income	Beringea	VCT
Foresight Enterprise	Foresight Group	VCT
Northern 2	Mercia Asset Management	VCT
Hargreave Hale AIM	Canaccord Genuity	VCT AIM Quoted
Northern 3	Mercia Asset Management	VCT
Northern Venture	Mercia Asset Management	VCT
Albion Crown	Albion Capital Group	VCT
Molten Ventures	Molten Ventures	VCT
Octopus AIM	Octopus Investments	VCT AIM Quoted
Maven Renovar	Maven Capital Partners	VCT AIM Quoted
Foresight Ventures	Foresight Group	VCT
Triple Point Venture shares	Triple Point Investment Management	VCT
Maven Income and Growth 4	Maven Capital Partners	VCT
Octopus AIM 2	Octopus Investments	VCT AIM Quoted
Maven Income and Growth 5	Maven Capital Partners	VCT
Maven Income and Growth	Maven Capital Partners	VCT
Blackfinch Spring	Blackfinch Investments	VCT
Maven Income and Growth 3	Maven Capital Partners	VCT
Octopus Future Generations	Octopus Investments	VCT
Calculus	Calculus Capital	VCT
Puma Alpha	Puma Investments	VCT
Seneca Growth Capital B shares	Seneca Partners Limited	VCT
Guinness	Guinness Global Investors	VCT

	MARKET CAP (£M)	MARKET CAP (£M) 2020	5 YR MARKET CAP % GROWTH	AVERAGE YIELD %
	5,117	3,612	41.7%	6.0%
	575	730	-21.2%	8.2%
	5,692	**4,341**	**31.1%**	
				7.7%

	TOTAL ASSETS (£M)	MARKET CAP (£M)	NET ASSETS (£M)	NET ASSETS 2020 (£M)	LAUNCH DATE	YIELD %	3YR SHARE PRICE TOTAL RETURN %
	803	404	803	910	28/12/2007	12.7%	−67.1%
	528	486	528	139	17/10/2006	5.8%	20.0%
	289	268	289	88	04/04/1996	5.3%	17.8%
	273	256	273	73	05/04/2007	6.0%	16.2%
	272	257	272	85	16/01/2001	5.3%	4.7%
	260	243	260	n/a	01/04/2015	3.2%	−1.5%
	216	207	216	181	30/01/2001	8.9%	−1.4%
	215	199	215	55	02/11/1999	6.3%	31.4%
	213	202	213	164	03/04/1998	7.7%	−0.5%
	203	197	203	20	02/07/2018	5.0%	−7.1%
	193	165	193	245	11/04/2007	8.5%	−11.1%
	177	168	177	61	12/04/2001	5.9%	15.1%
	175	166	175	113	10/04/2000	5.6%	4.1%
	158	151	158	122	31/05/2001	5.9%	−4.9%
	155	155	155	n/a	16/03/1998	6.8%	29.9%
	136	131	136	87	21/04/1999	5.5%	11.3%
	132	127	132	147	29/10/2004	6.5%	−28.2%
	130	124	130	87	17/12/2001	5.4%	10.9%
	130	124	130	95	01/11/1995	5.4%	10.3%
	121	113	121	n/a	08/04/1998	5.5%	6.2%
	119	106	119	n/a	18/05/1998	6.7%	−20.6%
	114	108	114	134	17/03/2004	10.8%	−18.9%
	97	91	97	n/a	22/02/2001	7.9%	−21.2%
	94	97	94	n/a	30/04/1996	4.1%	−25.7%
	92	88	92	n/a	12/04/2019	4.5%	-6.7%
	83	80	83	72	17/02/2005	7.3%	0.2%
	81	77	81	92	25/01/2006	9.9%	−17.5%
	70	67	70	43	04/12/2000	6.4%	4.8%
	67	62	67	39	06/04/2000	7.0%	1.9%
	65	61	65	4	09/04/2020	5.7%	15.7%
	64	61	64	42	12/12/2001	7.2%	−0.6%
	49	47	49	n/a	05/04/2022	0.0%	−14.9%
	48	44	48	19	10/03/2016	5.6%	6.0%
	33	34	33	30	05/06/2020	3.1%	−20.9%
	13	12	13	7	07/09/2018	6.5%	−35.9%
	11	11	11	n/a	11/04/2023	0.0%	

COMPANY NAME	MANAGEMENT GROUP	AIC SECTOR
Fuel Ventures	Sturgeon Ventures	VCT
Gresham House Renewable Energy 2	Gresham House	VCT
Gresham House Renewable Energy 1	Gresham House	VCT
Puma AIM	Puma Investments	VCT AIM Quoted
Praetura Growth	Praetura Ventures	VCT
Oxford Technology 2 – OT4 shares	Oxford Technology 2 Managers	VCT
Oxford Technology 2 – OT1 shares	Oxford Technology 2 Managers	VCT
Oberon AIM	Oberon Investments	VCT AIM Quoted
Oxford Technology 2 – OT3 shares	Oxford Technology 2 Managers	VCT
Oxford Technology 2 – OT2 shares	Oxford Technology 2 Managers	VCT
Seneca Growth Capital	Seneca Partners Limited	VCT

Source: AIC/Morningstar, all figures to 30/09/25 unless otherwise stated.

Venture capital trusts are specialist investment companies that exist to support companies at an early stage of their development, in return for which shareholders in the VCTs are offered potentially attractive tax breaks. Most of these trusts will be investing in unlisted securities, although AIM VCTs, which own mostly shares listed on the Alternative Investment Market, are an exception.

By their nature, most VCTs are designed to remain small and are inherently riskier than conventional equity trusts. Some of the first VCTs to be launched have grown to become mature businesses. Of these, Octopus Titan is probably the best known, having been early investors in at least four big successes, but its performance has since deteriorated badly, underlining that sustained success is far from guaranteed.

Launched in 2007, the trust's market value approached £1bn at its peak, but in common with the majority of VCTs, performance since the first interest rate hikes three years ago has been disappointing. Its shares have fallen by 50% in the last year, surrendering its position as the largest company in the VCT sector by market value and prompting challenges to the board to take action.

For many years the AIC classified VCTs into ten different sub-sectors, reflecting the distinctive kind of business that they were set up to invest in. In 2024, however, it changed its approach, and it now lists just two categories: VCTs and AIM VCTs. The number of VCTs has risen from 46 to 50 since the last edition of the *Handbook*, bucking the trend of the previous year, in part driven by fears of increased taxation under the new Labour government.

The purpose behind giving tax breaks to investors in VCTs is to encourage the financing of early-stage businesses. Many higher-rate taxpayers continue to find the tax-free dividends a particularly strong attraction. The criteria VCTs must meet in order for their shareholders to qualify for the tax benefits have been tightened to make sure VCTs invest in genuine higher-risk, early-stage ventures.

VCT investors are typically reluctant to sell their shares in VCTs, given the tax

TOTAL ASSETS (£M)	MARKET CAP (£M)	NET ASSETS (£M)	NET ASSETS 2020 (£M)	LAUNCH DATE	YIELD %	3YR SHARE PRICE TOTAL RETURN %
11	11	11	n/a	22/03/2024	0.0%	
10	9	10	27	10/01/2011	21.4%	-43.4%
10	8	10	27	10/01/2011	6.1%	-47.5%
6	6	6	n/a	02/04/2025		
6	7	6	n/a	10/04/2024		
2	1	2	n/a	07/09/2004	0.0%	-80.9%
2	1	2	n/a	04/04/1997	0.0%	-47.3%
2	2	2	n/a	03/04/2007	5.6%	-48.4%
1	0	1	n/a	04/04/2002	0.0%	-79.4%
1	0	1	n/a	05/04/2000	0.0%	-77.4%
1	1	1	3	19/04/2002	34.8%	-22.4%

advantages, so liquidity in the secondary market remains poor. In September 2024 the Treasury announced that the tax regime for VCTs would continue until 2035, reflecting their significant contribution to funding technology businesses in particular. Research by the AIC in 2022 found that VCTs had invested £1.7bn into 530 companies in the previous five years.

As the continued strong demand for VCTs shows, the appeal of tax-free dividends remains. Some older vintage trusts have also generated notable tax-exempt capital gains, but that is far from a universal experience. Inevitably, the share prices of many of the larger equity VCTs have suffered from the general weakness of smaller company stocks, while AIM stocks have been particularly badly hit. Labour's first Budget in 2024 cut the inheritance tax relief of AIM-listed stocks by 50%, to the detriment of the seven AIM VCT trusts.

Performance remains mixed, as you might expect. Fewer than half the surviving universe of VCTs have produced positive share price total returns in the last 12 months, but the proportion is slightly better over five and ten years. Given the poor liquidity in VCT shares, the NAVs of these trusts may be lower than the reported numbers suggest. The dividend yields on offer from the most mature VCTs have been maintained even if share prices have declined.

The average dividend yield remains around 6.0% at the time of writing, but note that dividend growth for all but a few has been negative over five years. A number of the more mature VCTs do, however, put money aside every year to help sustain their dividend capacity, since that, along with income tax relief, is the key selling point for investors.

As Alex Davies of The Wealth Club notes in his annual review of the sector, 2024–25 was a record year for inflows to the VCT sector, and with many investors expecting further tax rises in the November 2025 Budget, that pattern could well be maintained in the current financial year.

Largest management groups

MANAGEMENT GROUP	NUMBER OF COMPANIES	TOTAL ASSETS (£M)	NET ASSETS (£M)	MARKET CAP (£M)	AVG MARKET CAP (£M)
3i Group	1	28,297	40,617	27,089	27,089
Baillie Gifford	12	25,257	20,965	22,905	1,909
J.P. Morgan Asset Management	16	14,765	13,105	13,805	863
Pershing Square Capital Management	1	13,373	8,204	11,522	11,522
Columbia Threadneedle	8	10,418	8,777	9,431	1,179
Fidelity	6	7,637	6,186	6,506	1,084
Janus Henderson Investors	8	7,068	6,374	6,522	815
InfraRed Capital Partners	3	7,054	4,310	5,838	1,946
Polar Capital Holdings	3	6,409	5,776	6,294	2,098
Tritax Management	1	6,397	3,585	4,770	4,770
Aberdeen	12	6,360	5,142	5,530	461
Schroders Greencoat	2	6,268	3,148	4,112	2,056
Willis Towers Watson	1	5,542	4,909	5,104	5,104
RIT Capital Partners	1	4,272	2,855	3,898	3,898
BlackRock Investment Management (UK)	9	4,209	3,570	3,783	420
3i Investments	1	4,072	3,334	3,562	3,562
Goldman Sachs Asset Management, L.P.	1	3,926	3,437	3,926	3,926
Allianz Global Investors	3	3,689	3,294	3,546	1,182
Schroder Investment Management	9	3,523	3,088	3,394	377
HarbourVest Advisers L.P.	1	3,325	2,083	3,116	3,116
Amber Infrastructure Group	2	3,127	2,383	2,870	1,435
Frostrow Capital	3	3,064	2,714	2,933	978
Pantheon Ventures	2	3,057	2,033	2,822	1,411
Caledonia	1	3,012	1,988	3,012	3,012
Franklin Templeton	2	2,583	2,303	2,512	1,256
HgCapital	1	2,467	2,284	2,467	2,467
Tetragon Financial Management	1	2,441	1,194	2,441	2,441
Foresight Group	6	2,360	1,348	1,758	293
Gresham House	10	2,275	1,611	1,978	198
Troy Asset Management	2	1,932	1,906	1,917	959
Fundsmith	1	1,841	1,687	1,841	1,841
Invesco Asset Management	3	1,591	1,480	1,540	513
Aberforth Partners	2	1,590	1,334	1,502	751
Asset Value Investors	2	1,587	1,326	1,393	696
Octopus	5	1,574	1,122	1,574	315
Law Debenture	1	1,556	1,430	1,392	1,392
Sequoia	1	1,522	1,198	1,432	1,432
Brevan Howard	1	1,503	1,343	1,503	1,503
Molten Ventures	2	1,493	793	1,313	656
Dragon Capital	1	1,468	1,234	1,468	1,468
RWC Asset Management	3	1,466	1,277	1,366	455
Intermediate Capital Group	1	1,413	905	1,281	1,281
Herald	1	1,322	1,194	1,322	1,322
Patria Capital Partners	1	1,311	825	1,205	1,205

Source: AIC/Morningstar, all figures to 30/09/25 unless otherwise stated.

% TOTAL ASSETS 2025	TOTAL ASSETS 2020 (£M)	% TOTAL ASSETS 2020
10.8%	8,924	4.3%
9.6%	24,157	11.6%
5.6%	11,778	5.6%
5.1%	5,859	2.8%
4.0%	9,840	4.7%
2.9%	4,933	2.4%
2.7%	6,592	3.2%
2.7%	4,809	2.3%
2.4%	3,578	1.7%
2.4%	4,212	2.0%
2.4%	9,856	4.7%
2.4%	3,180	1.5%
2.1%	2,979	1.4%
1.6%	3,352	1.6%
1.6%	3,409	1.6%
1.6%	2,228	1.1%
1.5%	-	-
1.4%	1,976	0.9%
1.3%	3,336	1.6%
1.3%	1,699	0.8%
1.2%	2,350	1.1%
1.2%	7,209	3.5%
1.2%	1,539	0.7%
1.1%	1,935	0.9%
1.0%	2,337	1.1%
0.9%	1,154	0.6%
0.9%	1,661	0.8%
0.9%	758	0.4%
0.9%	-	-
0.7%	1,797	0.9%
0.7%	2,294	1.1%
0.6%	1,832	0.9%
0.6%	1,056	0.5%
0.6%	1,141	0.5%
0.6%	1,613	0.8%
0.6%	784	0.4%
0.6%	1,739	0.8%
0.6%	948	0.5%
0.6%	-	-
0.6%	1,126	0.5%
0.6%	633	0.3%
0.5%	772	0.4%
0.5%	1,296	0.6%
0.5%	-	-

The management groups with the most trust mandates are listed here. The trust sector is a competitive one, in which no management group has a dominant position. There has, however, been some notable consolidation in the last few years. The 20 largest groups manage around 70% of total industry assets, up from less than 50% six years ago, and 60% just 12 months ago.

As well as trusts that have switched from one management firm to another, we have seen an increasing number of mergers between trusts managed by the same management group, with J.P. Morgan, Janus Henderson and Troy Asset Management being prominent examples. Aberdeen (formerly abrdn) has been particularly affected, reducing and reshaping its investment trust portfolio, losing six trusts through mergers and voluntary liquidations.

Management companies themselves have experienced consolidation too, with Columbia Threadneedle acquiring BMO's trusts in 2021, for example, and Schroders taking a 75% stake in Greencoat Capital, the renewable energy specialist. Gresham House has also been sold to a private equity firm.

A number of different factors have driven this changing landscape. Consolidation in the wealth management business and regulatory changes have forced trust boards to decide if they are large enough to continue attracting demand from wealth managers and other traditional buyers of investment trust shares. Shareholders benefit from the lower fees that greater scale allows, but lose the greater choice of investment options that was available before.

In 2018 Baillie Gifford, a private partnership based in Edinburgh, became the largest player in the investment trust sector for the first time, overtaking 3i and J.P. Morgan. It narrowly held onto its lead last year, but this year has been overtaken by 3i Group. Apart from Aberdeen, most of the top ten management companies have increased their share of the market. Departures from the table include Witan, which has been merged into Alliance Trust, Atrato and, announced but not yet completed, Goldman Sachs, manager of Petershill Partners.

Vintage investment trusts

COMPANY NAME	AIC SECTOR	LAUNCH DATE
F&C	Global	19/03/1868
Alliance Witan	Global	21/04/1888
Investment Company	Flexible Investment	01/01/1868
Dunedin Income Growth	UK Equity Income	01/02/1873
Scottish American	Global Equity Income	31/03/1873
JPMorgan American	North America	18/06/1881
Mercantile	UK All Companies	08/12/1884
JPMorgan Global Growth & Income	Global Equity Income	21/04/1887
Henderson Smaller Companies	UK Smaller Companies	16/12/1887
Bankers	Global	13/04/1888
The Global Smaller Companies	Global Smaller Companies	15/02/1889
Merchants	UK Equity Income	16/02/1889
Edinburgh	UK Equity Income	01/03/1889
AVI Global	Global	01/07/1889
Law Debenture	UK Equity Income	12/12/1889
City of London	UK Equity Income	01/01/1891
abrdn Diversified Income and Growth	Flexible Investment	05/01/1898
TR Property	Property Securities	05/05/1905
BlackRock Smaller Companies	UK Smaller Companies	02/05/1906
Baillie Gifford China Growth	China / Greater China	24/01/1907
Murray International	Global Equity Income	18/12/1907
Scottish Mortgage	Global	17/03/1909
Hansa (A share)	Flexible Investment	01/01/1912
Hansa	Flexible Investment	01/01/1912

MARKET CAP (£M)	NET ASSETS (£M)	TICKER	YIELD %	1YR AVG DISCOUNT / PREMIUM %	ONGOING CHARGE %	10YR NAV TOTAL RETURN %	10YR SHARE PRICE TOTAL RETURN %
5,749	6,036	FCIT	1.3%	−8.0%	0.45%	240.7%	245.8%
4,909	5,104	ALW	2.1%	−4.7%	0.56%	208.2%	245.2%
6	7	INV	0.0%	−12.2%	2.00%	33.4%	15.2%
358	387	DIG	6.6%	−9.6%	0.56%	103.6%	109.0%
858	911	SAIN	2.9%	−10.2%	0.58%	225.6%	184.6%
1,906	1,967	JAM	0.7%	−2.2%	0.35%	380.8%	391.4%
1,787	1,905	MRC	3.0%	−10.2%	0.48%	96.6%	104.6%
3,303	3,367	JGGI	4.0%	−0.1%	0.43%	300.2%	331.6%
545	600	HSL	3.2%	−10.8%	0.45%	71.1%	83.3%
1,315	1,391	BNKR	2.1%	−9.9%	0.51%	195.6%	179.5%
739	816	GSCT	1.7%	−10.8%	0.74%	130.6%	106.8%
831	880	MRCH	5.2%	−4.3%	0.52%	136.0%	130.6%
1,124	1,163	EDIN	3.6%	−8.9%	0.51%	86.8%	77.6%
1,083	1,146	AGT	1.3%	−8.5%	0.87%	225.8%	257.1%
1,430	1,392	LWDB	3.1%	1.0%	0.51%	191.5%	218.7%
2,532	2,449	CTY	4.2%	0.1%	0.36%	116.1%	118.7%
139	181	ADIG	12.3%	−33.4%	2.36%	27.0%	9.4%
1,017	1,115	TRY	5.0%	−8.1%	0.78%	59.4%	62.8%
542	591	BRSC	3.3%	−12.2%	0.80%	83.6%	87.2%
185	200	BGCG	0.7%	−10.7%	1.12%	59.0%	77.5%
1,796	1,821	MYI	3.9%	−6.8%	0.52%	199.0%	196.6%
12,806	13,885	SMT	0.4%	−10.5%	0.31%	471.5%	410.3%
205	324	HANA	1.3%	−40.3%	1.10%	108.0%	96.4%
104	162	HAN	1.2%	−38.6%	1.10%	108.6%	89.9%

COMPANY NAME	AIC SECTOR	LAUNCH DATE
Murray Income	UK Equity Income	07/06/1923
Finsbury Growth & Income	UK Equity Income	15/01/1926
Temple Bar	UK Equity Income	24/06/1926
Brunner	Global	01/01/1927
JPMorgan Japanese	Japan	02/08/1927
Monks	Global	06/02/1929
JPMorgan European Growth & Income	Europe	15/03/1929
Shires Income	UK Equity Income	31/03/1929
Canadian General	North America	15/01/1930
Henderson Far East Income	Asia Pacific Equity Income	30/05/1930
3i Group	Private Equity	01/04/1945
Caledonia	Flexible Investment	18/07/1960

Source: AIC/Morningstar, all figures to 30/09/25 unless otherwise stated.

The first investment trust, F&C (FCIT), was formed in 1868 and continues in existence today. It celebrated its 150th anniversary in 2018. A number of other investment companies have also been around for many years. Seventeen can trace their histories back to the 19th century. This is a list of some of the oldest vintage trusts which are still in existence, although their names are not always the same today as they were when launched. It includes every trust created before 1960 and still in existence today.

A number of these trusts were started by wealthy families looking to invest their fortunes in a tax-efficient manner, but have since expanded to include outside investors as well. The first Scottish investment trust, Dunedin Income Growth (DIG), for example, was founded to provide a home for the savings of wealthy textile merchants in Dundee. Caledonia (CLDN) was founded by the Cayzer shipping dynasty and Brunner by one of the families whose chemical businesses combined to form ICI in 1926.

There is no obvious correlation between age and size or quality of trust, although the mere fact of having survived for so long indicates that a trust has successfully established a niche in the market. The wide range of average discounts illustrates the disparity in their liquidity, performance and popularity.

MARKET CAP (£M)	NET ASSETS (£M)	TICKER	YIELD %	1YR AVG DISCOUNT / PREMIUM %	ONGOING CHARGE %	10YR NAV TOTAL RETURN %	10YR SHARE PRICE TOTAL RETURN %
874	928	MUT	4.5%	-9.9%	0.50%	103.1%	111.9%
1,145	1,228	FGT	2.3%	-7.5%	0.61%	103.3%	92.3%
1,016	994	TMPL	4.2%	-4.2%	0.61%	140.3%	160.2%
625	638	BUT	1.7%	-2.8%	0.63%	221.1%	254.5%
1,104	1,220	JFJ	1.0%	-10.4%	0.73%	193.7%	201.5%
2,536	2,648	MNKS	0.0%	-9.9%	0.43%	272.4%	299.0%
542	553	JEGI	3.7%	-7.0%	0.66%	189.0%	210.4%
111	117	SHRS	5.3%	-6.8%	1.00%	113.2%	115.8%
518	896	CGI	2.1%	-43.3%	1.37%	298.9%	250.0%
445	428	HFEL	10.2%	2.9%	1.08%	90.5%	98.8%
40,617	27,089	III	1.8%	54.8%	0.00%	911.5%	1123.5%
1,988	3,012	CLDN	1.9%	-34.5%	0.87%	151.3%	134.2%

Trusts with a founding family often take on third-party investors over time, reducing their shareholdings but retaining a measure of control in return for a broader asset base.

A long history is no guarantee that the trust will survive. Three of the oldest trusts, Witan, founded 1909, Aberdeen Diversified Income and Growth (1898), and Keystone Positive Change (1954) are now out of the sector, through merger, wind-up and rollover respectively. Henderson European Focus Trust (launched 1947) this year merged with its sister trust Henderson Eurotrust (1992) to be renamed Henderson European.

A number of trusts have changed investment manager in recent years. In 2020, four of these trusts: Witan Pacific (now BGCG), Edinburgh Investment Trust (EDIN), Temple Bar (TMPL) and Perpetual Income and Growth (PLI) moved from one management firm to another. Keystone (later KPC) did the same in 2021. Murray Income, which absorbed PLI in 2020 is itself now the subject of a strategic review by its board, which may presage a change of management. After their merger the two European trusts managed by Janus Henderson mentioned above were almost immediately absorbed into the larger Fidelity European.

Long-serving managers

COMPANY NAME	TICKER	AIC SECTOR
Capital Gearing	CGT	Flexible Investment
Lowland	LWI	UK Equity Income
City of London	CTY	UK Equity Income
Herald	HRI	Global Smaller Companies
JPMorgan Emerging Markets	JMG	Global Emerging Markets
CT UK Capital & Income	CTUK	UK Equity Income
JPMorgan UK Small Cap G & I	JUGI	UK Smaller Companies
CT Private Equity	CTPE	Private Equity
BlackRock World Mining	BRWM	Commodities & Natural Resources
European Opportunities	EOT	Europe
Finsbury Growth & Income	FGT	UK Equity Income
HgCapital	HGT	Private Equity
Lindsell Train	LTI	Global
Aberforth Smaller Companies	ASL	UK Smaller Companies
Maven Income and Growth 3	MIG3	VCT Generalist
Impax Environmental Markets	IEM	Environmental
Schroder UK Mid Cap	SCP	UK All Companies
Law Debenture	LWDB	UK Equity Income
Bankers	BNKR	Global
Global Opportunities	GOT	Flexible Investment
Schroder Real Estate	SREI	Property - UK Commercial
TR Property	TRY	Property Securities
Biotech Growth	BIOG	Biotechnology & Healthcare
JPMorgan European G & I	JEGI	Europe
JPMorgan China G & I	JCGI	China / Greater China
Polar Capital Technology	PCT	Technology & Media
Merchants	MRCH	UK Equity Income
Middlefield Canadian Income	MCT	North America
Murray Income	MUT	UK Equity Income
International Biotechnology	IBT	Biotechnology & Healthcare
Volta Finance	VTA	Debt - Structured Finance
Henderson Opportunities	HOT	UK All Companies
UIL	UTL	Flexible Investment
abrdn New India	ANII	India
Foresight	FTV	VCT Generalist
Volta Finance	VTA	Debt - Structured Finance
Partners Group Private Equity	PEY	Private Equity
CQS New City High Yield	NCYF	Debt - Loans & Bonds

MANAGER NAME	START DATE	TENURE	10YR NAV TOTAL RETURN %
Peter Spiller	05/04/1982	43 years 6 months	72.28
James H Henderson	01/01/1990	35 years 9 months	94.50
Job Curtis	01/07/1991	34 years 3 months	116.14
Katie Potts	16/02/1994	31 years 7 months	220.52
Austin Forey	01/06/1994	31 years 4 months	164.49
Julian Cane	01/03/1997	28 years 7 months	103.52
Georgina Brittain	02/01/1998	27 years 9 months	122.89
Hamish Mair	01/02/2000	25 years 8 months	234.58
Evy Hambro	01/09/2000	25 years 1 month	426.65
Alexander Darwall	22/11/2000	24 years 10 months	102.53
Nick Train	11/12/2000	24 years 9 months	103.28
Nic Humphries	01/01/2001	24 years 9 months	404.75
Nick Train	22/01/2001	24 years 8 months	254.26
Euan Robin MacDonald	14/05/2001	24 years 4 months	81.50
Bill Nixon	12/12/2001	23 years 9 months	28.23
Bruce Jenkyn-Jones	22/02/2002	23 years 7 months	197.47
Andy Brough	30/04/2003	22 years 5 months	90.04
James Henderson	01/06/2003	22 years 4 months	191.45
Alex Crooke	01/07/2003	22 years 3 months	195.63
Sandy Nairn	15/12/2003	21 years 9 months	117.01
Nick Montgomery	15/07/2004	21 years 2 months	64.61
Marcus Phayre-Mudge	01/10/2004	21 years 0 months	59.43
Geoffrey C. Hsu	19/05/2005	20 years 4 months	63.97
Alexander Fitzalan Howard	02/08/2005	20 years 2 months	189.04
Shumin Huang	02/01/2006	19 years 9 months	144.57
Ben Rogoff	01/05/2006	19 years 5 months	757.50
Simon Gergel	01/06/2006	19 years 4 months	135.97
Dean Orrico	06/07/2006	19 years 3 months	164.87
Charles Luke	03/10/2006	19 years 0 months	103.10
Ailsa Craig	01/11/2006	18 years 11 months	138.23
Alexandre Martin-Min	15/12/2006	18 years 9 months	128.56
James Henderson	24/01/2007	18 years 8 months	
Charles Jillings/team	20/06/2007	18 years 3 months	102.72
Pruksa Iamthongthong	01/08/2007	18 years 2 months	146.77
James Livingston	01/10/2007	18 years 0 months	85.99
Francois Touati/team	01/10/2007	18 years 0 months	128.56
Rene Biner/team	01/11/2007	17 years 11 months	135.12
Ian Francis	30/11/2007	17 years 10 months	105.42

COMPANY NAME	TICKER	AIC SECTOR
Crystal Amber	CRS	UK Smaller Companies
Crystal Amber	CRS	UK Smaller Companies
Bankers	BNKR	Global
JZ Capital Partners	JZCP	Private Equity
JZ Capital Partners	JZCP	Private Equity
Octopus AIM + 2	OOA	VCT AIM Quoted
Barings Emerging EMEA Opportunities	BEMO	Global Emerging Markets
Personal Assets	PNL	Flexible Investment
NB Private Equity Partners	NBPE	Private Equity
Symphony International Holdings	SIHL	Private Equity
JPMorgan US Smaller Companies	JUSC	North American Smaller Companies
Octopus Titan	OTV2	VCT Generalist
Scottish Mortgage	SMT	Global
ProVen Growth and Income	PGOO	VCT
Mercantile	MRC	UK All Companies
New Star	NSI	Flexible Investment
Baker Steel Resources	BSRT	Commodities & Natural Resources
HarbourVest Global Private Equity	HVPE	Private Equity
Polar Capital Global Healthcare	PCGH	Biotechnology & Healthcare
VinaCapital Vietnam Opportunity	VOF	Country Specialist

Source: AIC/Morningstar, all figures to 30/09/25 unless otherwise stated, excludes companies with <£50m market capitalisation.

Some individual trusts are notable for having long-serving managers who have been running the trust's investments for many years. In many cases the managers also have significant personal shareholdings in the trust. This is typically regarded as auguring well for other shareholders, since it should establish a close alignment of interest between the manager and the shareholders.

Fund management is a well-paid profession, so a manager who stays on after many years in harness can be seen to be demonstrating a real commitment to the business. While some successful fund managers retire early to do other things, those who remain in post for decades are typically enthusiasts who cannot think of anything more interesting or rewarding to do (look at Warren Buffett, who has been running Berkshire Hathaway in his 90s).

In some cases, however, managers or their firms have such a large shareholding in a trust that they effectively control the running of the company. As a result they may not always be as closely aligned with other shareholders as the latter might wish. The managers are effectively being paid to look after their own money, often with a longer-term perspective that makes them worry less about short-term performance or the persistence of a wide discount.

MANAGER NAME	START DATE	TENURE	10YR NAV TOTAL RETURN %
Jonathan Marsh	17/06/2008	17 years 3 months	98.78
Richard Bernstein	17/06/2008	17 years 3 months	98.78
David Smith	01/07/2008	17 years 3 months	195.63
David W. Zalaznick	01/07/2008	17 years 3 months	-50.96
Jay Jordan	01/07/2008	17 years 3 months	-50.96
Kate Tidbury	01/08/2008	17 years 2 months	-5.30
Matthias Siller	01/12/2008	16 years 10 months	130.15
Sebastian Lyon	03/03/2009	16 years 7 months	78.93
Anthony Tutrone/team	13/03/2009	16 years 6 months	198.90
Anil Thadani/team	29/04/2009	16 years 5 months	9.48
Don San Jose	01/05/2009	16 years 5 months	159.07
Jo Oliver	01/05/2009	16 years 5 months	-8.37
Tom Slater	01/08/2009	16 years 2 months	471.54
Stuart Veale	26/10/2009	15 years 11 months	23.63
Anthony Lynch	31/12/2009	15 years 9 months	96.58
Gill Lakin	01/01/2010	15 years 9 months	100.75
Trevor Steel	28/04/2010	15 years 5 months	170.50
John Toomey/team	12/05/2010	15 years 4 months	295.39
Gareth Powell	15/06/2010	15 years 3 months	132.79
Brook Taylor	30/06/2010	15 years 3 months	249.42

Experience is a vital quality when choosing a manager, and many of these long-serving managers have strong performance records. There have been some notable departures in recent years: James Anderson at Scottish Mortgage (SMT), Simon Knott at Rights and Issues (RII: taken over by Jupiter), Max Ward at the Independent Investment Trust (IIT: now absorbed into Monks), Harry Nimmo at abrdn UK Smaller Companies Growth (AUSC: replaced in-house by Abby Glennie); Matthew Dobbs from the Asian team at Schroders; and Simon Edelsten at Mid Wynd International (MWY).

Those joining them in retirement more recently include Bruce Stout at Murray International (MYI), Hugh Young (abrdn Asia Focus) and John Bennett (Henderson European Focus (HEFT). The longest serving manager still managing a trust now remains Peter Spiller at Capital Gearing Trust (CGT), who in 2022 celebrated 40 years of running the portfolio. The table lists all the managers with 15 years or more experience at the same trust.

Investment trust style and size

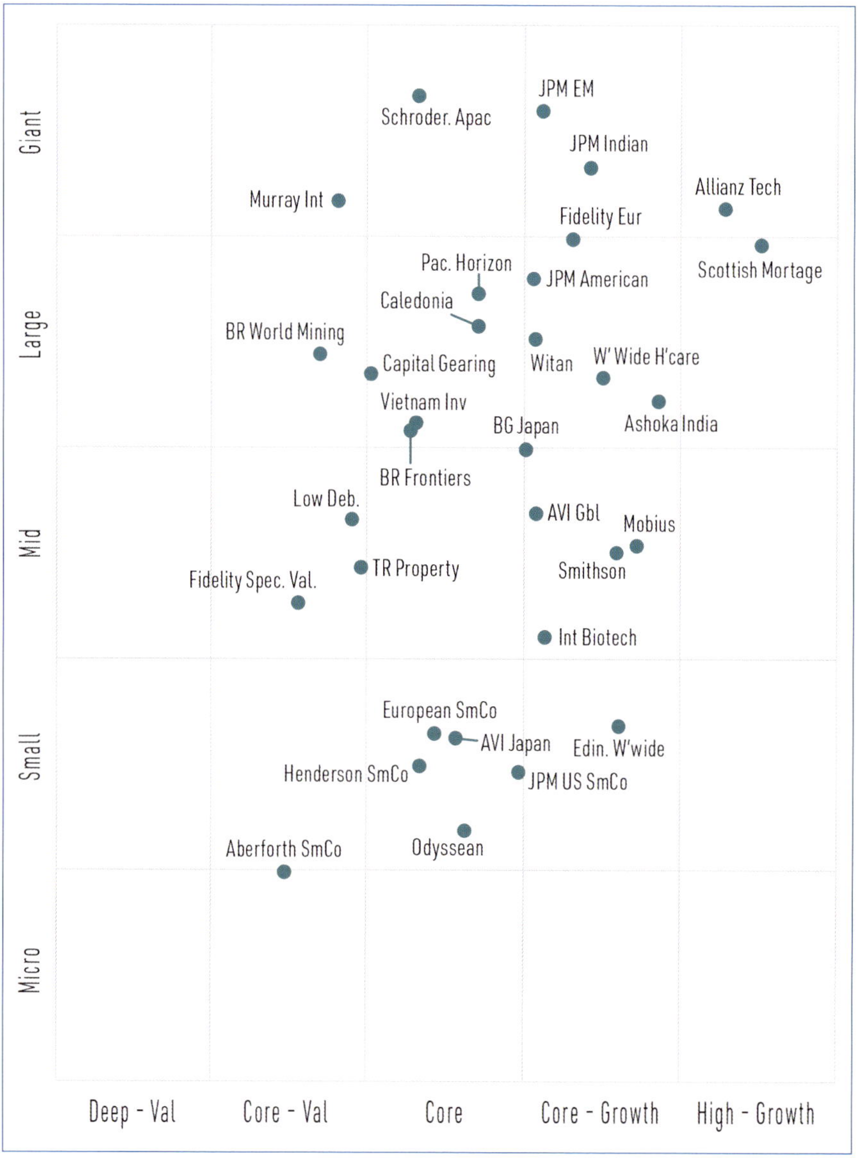

Different trusts in the same broad sector can have different approaches to investing. Analysts like to try and pigeonhole mangers into different categories, in the belief that this can help make investors better informed. The most famous example of this approach is Morningstar's nine-box analysis, which places equity funds of all kinds into a simple square template, essentially based on the kinds of companies whose shares they invest in (small, medium or large cap) and whether they adopt a value, growth or composite style.

If you look at the fact sheets that are provided by Morningstar for individual trusts on the AIC website, this will be part of the analysis you see when comparing one or more trusts. On this page, by way of an illustration, I also show an extract from a broker's report that extends this analysis to a five-by-five grid. It shows a sample of investment trusts and how they compare in these broad style terms.

This can be helpful not only in understanding the style of a trust, but also when working out how they can best be brought together into a portfolio. If you are keen on smaller companies, for example, but are unsure whether market conditions are more conducive to one style or another, there is an argument for diversifying across styles to provide a more balanced overall approach.

A trust such as Aberforth Smaller Companies, the most value-oriented UK-focused smaller companies trust, for example, might be paired with Edinburgh Worldwide, which has a global small-cap mandate but a distinctive growth approach. Murray International and Scottish Mortgage would be another example of polarised approaches that can be held together for diversification reasons.

All that said, not every trust fits easily into a style square framework, and there are other things to look at when comparing individual trust characteristics. The use of gearing is one example, and there are other measures such as volatility and sensitivity to market movements (beta) that are worth considering and are included in the Screener analysis on the AIC website.

Dividend heroes

COMPANY	AIC SECTOR	NUMBER OF CONSECUTIVE YEARS DIVIDEND INCREASED
City of London	UK Equity Income	59
Bankers	Global	58
Alliance Witan	Global	58
Caledonia	Flexible Investment	58
The Global Smaller Companies	Global Smaller Companies	55
F&C	Global	54
Brunner	Global	53
JPMorgan Claverhouse	UK Equity Income	52
Murray Income	UK Equity Income	52
Scottish American	Global Equity Income	51
Merchants	UK Equity Income	43
Scottish Mortgage	Global	43
Value and Indexed Property Income	Property - UK Commercial	38
CT UK Capital & Income	UK Equity Income	31
Schroder Income Growth	UK Equity Income	30
Aberdeen Equity Income	UK Equity Income	24
Athelney	UK Smaller Companies	22
BlackRock Smaller Companies	UK Smaller Companies	22
Henderson Smaller Companies	UK Smaller Companies	22
Murray International	Global Equity Income	20

Source: AIC/Morningstar. Correct as at 30/09/2025.

To qualify as one of the AIC's 'dividend heroes' an investment trust has to have increased its annual dividend payout each and every year for at least 20 years. Given that markets wax and wane, this is only possible because the investment trust structure allows boards to hold back up to 15% of the portfolio income each year as revenue reserves (effectively 'rainy day' money).

This means the trust can call on its reserves during recessions (or indeed pandemics) to continue to pay a dividend. Only during really difficult periods will they be forced to cut it below the previous year's figure. Qualifying as a dividend hero proved particularly popular with shareholders following the global financial crisis and the subsequent decade of very low interest rates and minimal yields from cash and bonds.

Dividend hero status is not a guarantee that the income from a trust will persist indefinitely. Three trusts that featured on the list before the pandemic had to take an axe to their dividends and subsequently lost their place in the rankings, as did the Scottish Investment Trust following its absorption into JPMorgan Global Growth & Income, Witan after the Alliance deal and Artemis Alpha, now merged with another UK equity trust, Aurora.

It is fair to say that some years trusts are only able to preserve their place on the list by making almost insignificant annual increases in the dividend. In some cases the need to preserve dividend hero status can have an inhibiting effect on their ability to maximise returns. Prioritising income obligations is not always optimal from a total return or taxation perspective.

Nevertheless, for many shareholders that does not seem to be much of a concern. Trusts such as the City of London, which heads the list, remain very popular despite not having the best long-term track record on other counts. As the table shows, 20 trusts can claim 20 or more years of consecutive dividend increases and 13 of them have been in that camp for 40 years or more. Murray International joined the list this year.

Coming up behind them are another 31 trusts (see next page) with between ten and 18 years of consecutive dividend increases. One (Lowland) was in the original dividend hero list, but later demoted. Not all of these will move up into the top tier, given the current consolidation trend and the inevitability of another bear market at some point.

At 30 September 2025, the average trailing 12-month yield of the 20 trusts was 3.4%, having grown by an average of 4.5% per annum over the past five years and 5.3% over ten. Yields ranged from 6.7% (Value and Indexed Property Income) to 0.4% (Scottish Mortgage). Dividend hero status is one way investment trusts can differentiate themselves from open-ended funds, which lack the flexibility to ensure a consistently growing dividend policy.

Next generation dividend heroes

COMPANY	AIC SECTOR	NUMBER OF CONSECUTIVE YEARS DIVIDEND INCREASED
Schroder Oriental Income	Asia Pacific Equity Income	18
BlackRock Greater Europe	Europe	18
CQS New City High Yield	Debt - Loans and Bonds	18
Henderson Far East Income	Asia Pacific Equity Income	17
International Public Partnerships	Infrastructure	17
Aberdeen Asian Income	Asia Pacific Equity Income	16
Fidelity Special Values	UK All Companies	15
Lowland	UK Equity Income	15
Law Debenture Corporation	UK Equity Income	15
Invesco Global Equity Income	Global Equity Income	15
TR Property	Property Securities	15
Chelverton UK Dividend	UK Equity Income	14
Aberforth Smaller Companies	UK Smaller Companies	14
Fidelity European	Europe	14
North American Income	North America	14
Dunedin Income Growth	UK Equity Income	14
CT Global Managed Portfolio Income	Flexible Investment	14
Fidelity China Special Situations	China / Greater China	14
CT Private Equity	Private Equity	13
Mid Wynd International	Global	12
Henderson High Income	UK Equity & Bond Income	12
CT UK High Income	UK Equity Income	12
Mercantile	UK All Companies	12
ICG Enterprise	Private Equity	12
Canadian	North America	12
RIT Capital Partners	Flexible Investment	12
Patria Private Equity	Private Equity	10
Foresight Solar	Renewable Energy Infrastructure	10
NextEnergy Solar	Renewable Energy Infrastructure	10
Utilico Emerging Markets	Global Emerging Markets	10
Foresight Environmental Infrastructure	Renewable Energy Infrastructure	10

Source: AIC/Morningstar. Correct as at 30/09/2025.

Largest/most liquid trusts

COMPANY NAME	AIC SECTOR	MANAGEMENT GROUP
3i Group	Private Equity	3i Group
Scottish Mortgage	Global	Baillie Gifford
Pershing Square Holdings	North America	Pershing Square Capital Management
F&C	Global	Columbia Threadneedle
Polar Capital Technology	Technology & Media	Polar Capital Holdings
Alliance Witan	Global	Willis Towers Watson
Tritax Big Box REIT	Property - UK Logistics	Tritax Management
Petershill Partners	Growth Capital	Goldman Sachs Asset Management, L.P.
3i Infrastructure	Infrastructure	3i
JPMorgan Global Growth & Income	Global Equity Income	J.P. Morgan Asset Management
RIT Capital Partners	Flexible	RIT Capital Partners
Monks	Global	Baillie Gifford
City of London	UK Equity Income	Janus Henderson Investors
Greencoat UK Wind	Renewable Energy Infrastructure	Schroders Greencoat
HICL Infrastructure	Infrastructure	InfraRed Capital Partners
International Public Partnerships	Infrastructure	Amber Infrastructure Group
HgCapital	Private Equity	Hg
Templeton Emerging Markets	Global Emerging Markets	Franklin Templeton
Fidelity European	Europe	Fidelity
HarbourVest Global Private Equity	Private Equity	HarbourVest Advisers L.P.
Caledonia	Flexible	Caledonia
JPMorgan American	North America	J.P. Morgan Asset Management
Renewables Infrastructure Group	Renewable Energy Infrastructure	InfraRed Capital Partners
Allianz Technology	Technology & Technology Innovation	Allianz Global Investors
Murray International	Global Equity Income	Aberdeen
Mercantile	UK All Companies	J.P. Morgan Asset Management
Smithson	Global Smaller Companies	Fundsmith
Personal Assets	Flexible	Troy Asset Management
Tetragon Financial Group	Flexible	Tetragon Financial Management
Fidelity China Special Situations	China / Greater China	Fidelity
Pantheon International	Private Equity	Pantheon Ventures
Law Debenture Corporation	UK Equity Income	Law Debenture Corporation
Worldwide Healthcare	Biotechnology & Healthcare	Frostrow Capital
Bankers	Global	Janus Henderson Investors
Fidelity Special Values	UK All Companies	Fidelity
BlackRock World Mining	Commodities & Natural Resources	BlackRock Management (UK)
BH Macro	Hedge Funds	Brevan Howard Capital Management
JPMorgan Emerging Markets	Global Emerging Markets	J.P. Morgan Asset Management
Aberforth Smaller Companies	UK Smaller Companies	Aberforth Partners
Vietnam Enterprise	Country Specialist	Dragon Capital

TICKER	MARKET CAPITALISATION (M)	1MTH DAILY AVG VALUE TRADED (M)	1YR DAILY AVG VALUE TRADED (M)	5YR DAILY AVG VALUE TRADED (M)	% SPREAD
III	39,803	62.35	60.51	41.84	0.2%
SMT	12,812	27.45	22.15	27.92	0.0%
PSH	8,206	6.60	6.29	5.21	0.0%
FCIT	5,749	4.82	4.63	4.21	0.3%
PCT	4,993	13.29	8.97	5.96	0.2%
ALW	4,909	7.22	6.53	3.93	0.2%
BBOX	3,585	8.41	9.19	11.21	0.3%
PHLL	3,437	6.63	1.51		0.3%
3IN	3,334	3.60	3.35	3.21	0.3%
JGGI	3,303	6.17	6.81	3.64	0.3%
RCP	2,855	6.90	4.50	4.14	1.0%
MNKS	2,538	8.38	6.19	5.36	0.3%
CTY	2,532	4.95	3.73	3.52	0.8%
UKW	2,436	5.09	4.72	5.46	0.1%
HICL	2,374	4.31	4.69	5.05	0.8%
INPP	2,294	4.98	4.97	4.82	0.8%
HGT	2,284	4.44	3.42	2.98	0.9%
TEM	2,117	5.27	3.70	2.83	0.2%
FEV	2,088	3.65	2.82	2.01	0.9%
HVPE	2,083	4.76	3.44	3.34	0.5%
CLDN	1,988	1.19	1.43	1.41	0.5%
JAM	1,906	2.91	3.67	2.51	0.4%
TRIG	1,860	3.58	4.21	4.88	0.5%
ATT	1,838	6.03	4.07	3.12	0.4%
MYI	1,796	2.74	2.16	2.08	0.3%
MRC	1,787	4.52	3.74	2.92	0.2%
SSON	1,687	8.37	5.79	6.54	0.1%
PNL	1,624	2.72	2.83	2.93	0.6%
TFG	1,608	0.37	0.26	0.15	2.8%
FCSS	1,598	3.24	2.56	2.68	0.5%
PIN	1,508	4.14	2.83	2.33	0.3%
LWDB	1,430	1.95	1.90	1.50	0.4%
WWH	1,339	5.87	4.95	4.12	0.5%
BNKR	1,316	2.97	2.47	1.93	0.3%
FSV	1,276	2.26	2.00	1.53	0.3%
BRWM	1,274	3.60	2.69	3.10	0.7%
BHMG	1,267	3.55	3.07	2.59	0.6%
JMG	1,265	2.80	2.10	2.27	0.5%
ASL	1,244	2.25	2.28	2.11	0.5%
VEIL	1,236	1.87	1.27	1.24	0.1%

COMPANY NAME	AIC SECTOR	MANAGEMENT GROUP
Sequoia Economic Infrastructure Income	Infrastructure	Sequoia Management
Herald	Global Smaller Companies	Herald Management
Schiehallion	Growth Capital	Baillie Gifford
Finsbury Growth & Income	UK Equity Income	Frostrow Capital
Edinburgh	UK Equity Income	Liontrust Asset Management
JPMorgan Japanese	Japan	J.P. Morgan Asset Management
AVI Global	Global	Asset Value Investors
BioPharma Credit	Debt - Direct Lending	Pharmakon Advisors
TR Property	Property Securities	Columbia Threadneedle
Temple Bar	UK Equity Income	RWC Asset Management (Redwheel)
Canadian General	North America	Morgan Meighen & Associates
Oakley Capital	Private Equity	Oakley Capital
ICG Enterprise	Private Equity	Intermediate Capital Group
TwentyFour Income	Debt - Structured Finance	TwentyFour Asset Management
Murray Income	UK Equity Income	Aberdeen
Ruffer	Flexible	Ruffer
Schroder AsiaPacific	Asia Pacific	Schroder Management
Scottish American	Global Equity Income	Baillie Gifford
Merchants	UK Equity Income	Allianz Global Investors
Invesco Asia Dragon	Asia Pacific Equity Income	Invesco Asset Management
Patria Private Equity	Private Equity	Patria Capital Partners
Greencoat Renewables	Renewable Energy Infrastructure	Schroders Greencoat
Capital Gearing	Flexible	CG Asset Management
Impax Environmental Markets	Environmental	Impax Asset Management
Baillie Gifford US Growth	North America	Baillie Gifford
Cordiant Digital Infrastructure	Infrastructure	Cordiant Capital
The Global Smaller Companies	Global Smaller Companies	Columbia Threadneedle
Schroder Oriental Income	Asia Pacific Equity Income	Schroder Management
Baillie Gifford Japan	Japan	Baillie Gifford Japan
Partners Group Private Equity	Private Equity	Partners Group
Edinburgh Worldwide	Global Smaller Companies	Baillie Gifford
Molten Ventures	Growth Capital	Molten Ventures
NB Private Equity Partners	Private Equity	NB Alternatives Advisers
VinaCapital Vietnam Opportunity	Country Specialist	VinaCapital Management
Pacific Horizon	Asia Pacific	Baillie Gifford
Brunner	Global	Allianz Global Investors
Chrysalis	Growth Capital	G10 Capital Limited
PRS REIT	Property - UK Residential	Sigma Capital
SDCL Efficiency Income	Renewable Energy Infrastructure	Sustainable Development Capital
GCP Infrastructure	Infrastructure	Gravis Capital Management
Fidelity Emerging Markets	Global Emerging Markets	Fidelity
Syncona	Biotechnology & Healthcare	Syncona Management
Target Healthcare REIT	Property - UK Healthcare	Target Fund Managers
BlackRock Greater Europe	Europe	BlackRock Management (UK)
JPMorgan European Discovery	European Smaller Companies	J.P. Morgan Asset Management
Henderson Smaller Companies	UK Smaller Companies	Janus Henderson Investors
JPMorgan European Growth & Income	Europe	J.P. Morgan Asset Management
BlackRock Smaller Companies	UK Smaller Companies	BlackRock Management (UK)
Pantheon Infrastructure	Infrastructure	Pantheon Ventures

TICKER	MARKET CAPITALISATION (M)	1MTH DAILY AVG VALUE TRADED (M)	1YR DAILY AVG VALUE TRADED (M)	5YR DAILY AVG VALUE TRADED (M)	% SPREAD
SEQI	1,198	2.33	1.79	2.12	0.6%
HRI	1,194	4.56	4.02	2.20	0.4%
MNTN	1,168	0.52	0.38	0.18	0.9%
FGT	1,147	5.23	4.88	4.17	0.3%
EDIN	1,124	2.09	1.75	1.83	0.1%
JFJ	1,104	1.88	1.77	1.60	0.4%
AGT	1,083	1.83	1.83	1.47	0.2%
BPCR	1,021	3.17	1.06	1.45	0.2%
TRY	1,017	1.75	2.08	2.12	0.2%
TMPL	1,016	2.88	2.14	1.69	0.3%
CGI	970	0.18	0.24	0.19	3.5%
OCI	952	2.86	1.37	1.16	0.7%
ICGT	905	0.92	0.92	0.94	0.3%
TFIF	883	2.33	1.85	1.36	0.2%
MUT	874	2.68	1.74	1.58	0.4%
RICA	869	1.95	2.52	2.57	0.9%
SDP	862	1.36	1.21	1.20	0.2%
SAIN	858	1.55	1.53	1.16	0.6%
MRCH	831	1.45	1.35	1.20	0.2%
IAD	827	1.19	0.82	0.38	0.7%
PPET	825	1.10	0.52	0.49	0.5%
GRP	816	0.33	0.71	0.54	2.4%
CGT	806	2.10	2.08	2.61	0.2%
IEM	783	3.78	3.00	2.37	0.1%
USA	750	1.53	3.01	2.29	0.4%
CORD	746	0.79	1.10		0.6%
GSCT	740	0.78	0.88	0.84	0.1%
SOI	727	0.91	1.06	1.01	0.3%
BGFD	716	1.35	1.62	1.51	0.4%
PEY	712	2.41	0.72	0.70	0.5%
EWI	708	1.70	2.01	2.19	1.0%
GROW	687	2.60	1.89	2.90	0.5%
NBPE	673	0.91	0.77	0.83	0.4%
VOF	642	0.87	1.12	1.09	0.3%
PHI	626	1.38	1.13	1.46	0.4%
BUT	624	0.69	0.96	0.71	0.8%
CHRY	618	2.03	1.76	1.91	1.0%
PRSR	616	2.18	1.30	0.89	0.4%
SEIT	614	1.29	1.42	1.37	1.1%
GCP	607	1.20	1.06	1.31	1.0%
FEML	607	0.58	0.52	0.64	0.2%
SYNC	601	0.40	0.61	1.14	0.2%
THRL	600	1.09	1.27	1.24	0.3%
BRGE	561	0.99	0.89	0.81	0.2%
JEDT	545	0.79	1.22	1.05	0.7%
HSL	545	1.67	1.42	1.11	0.2%
JEGI	542	1.55	1.36	0.54	0.4%
BRSC	542	2.20	1.82	1.36	0.2%
PINT	525	0.65	0.78		0.9%

COMPANY NAME	AIC SECTOR	MANAGEMENT GROUP
abrdn Asia Focus	Asia Pacific Smaller Companies	Aberdeen
RTW Biotech Opportunities	Biotechnology & Healthcare	RTW
Schroder Asian Total Return	Asia Pacific	Schroder Management
North Atlantic Smaller Companies	Global Smaller Companies	Harwood Capital
Bluefield Solar Income	Renewable Energy Infrastructure	Bluefield Partners
The European Smaller Companies	European Smaller Companies	Janus Henderson Investors
Octopus Apollo	VCT Generalist	Octopus
Warehouse REIT	Property - UK Logistics	Tilstone Partners
Utilico Emerging Markets	Global Emerging Markets	ICM
JPMorgan Indian	India/Indian Subcontinent	J.P. Morgan Asset Management
BlackRock Throgmorton	UK Smaller Companies	BlackRock Management (UK)
JPMorgan Claverhouse	UK Equity Income	J.P. Morgan Asset Management
Henderson Far East Income	Asia Pacific Equity Income	Janus Henderson Investors
Ashoka India Equity	India/Indian Subcontinent	Acorn Asset Management
Foresight Environmental Infrastructure	Renewable Energy Infrastructure	Foresight Group
European Opportunities	Europe	Devon Equity Management
Polar Capital Global Healthcare	Biotechnology & Healthcare	Polar Capital Holdings
Foresight Solar	Renewable Energy Infrastructure	Foresight Group
JPMorgan Global Emerging Markets Income	Global Emerging Markets	J.P. Morgan Asset Management
Nippon Active Value	Japanese Smaller Companies	Rising Sun Management
JPMorgan UK Small Cap Growth & Income	UK Smaller Companies	J.P. Morgan Asset Management
Pacific Assets	Asia Pacific	Stewart Investors
North American Income	North America	Janus Henderson Investors
Octopus Titan	VCT Generalist	Octopus
Invesco Bond Income Plus	Debt - Loans & Bonds	Invesco Asset Management
Gresham House Energy Storage	Renewable Energy Infrastructure	Gresham House
Fidelity Asian Values	Asia Pacific Smaller Companies	Fidelity
Custodian Property Income REIT	Property - UK Commercial	Custodian Capital
Aberdeen Asian Income	Asia Pacific Equity Income	Aberdeen
NextEnergy Solar	Renewable Energy Infrastructure	NextEnergy Capital IM
Dunedin Income Growth	UK Equity Income	Aberdeen
Polar Capital Global Financials	Financials & Financial Innovation	Polar Capital Holdings
abrdn New India	India/Indian Subcontinent	Aberdeen
European Assets	European Smaller Companies	Columbia Threadneedle
Baillie Gifford European Growth	Europe	Baillie Gifford
CT Private Equity	Private Equity	Columbia Threadneedle
Baillie Gifford Shin Nippon	Japanese Smaller Companies	Baillie Gifford
Octopus Renewables Infrastructure	Renewable Energy Infrastructure	Octopus Renewables
CQS New City High Yield	Debt - Loans & Bonds	New City Managers
Lowland	UK Equity Income	Janus Henderson Investors
Schroder Japan	Japan	Schroder Management
Manchester & London	Global	M&L Capital Management
CT UK Capital & Income	UK Equity Income	Columbia Threadneedle
Scottish Oriental Smaller Companies	Asia Pacific Smaller Companies	First Sentier Investors (UK) IM Limited

TICKER	MARKET CAPITALISATION (M)	1MTH DAILY AVG VALUE TRADED (M)	1YR DAILY AVG VALUE TRADED (M)	5YR DAILY AVG VALUE TRADED (M)	% SPREAD
AAS	519	0.86	0.92	0.46	0.8%
RTW	504	2.13	0.61	0.34	0.3%
ATR	501	0.86	0.73	0.71	0.7%
NAS	495	0.37	0.33	0.34	1.3%
BSIF	492	0.93	1.07	1.12	0.1%
ESCT	491	1.79	2.18	0.97	1.8%
OAP3	486	0.00	0.08	0.06	0.0%
WHR	480	2.15	3.63	1.84	0.4%
UEM	461	0.55	0.59	0.62	0.8%
JII	458	0.87	1.00	0.83	0.8%
THRG	453	2.51	2.02	1.62	0.2%
JCH	451	0.49	0.56	0.55	0.2%
HFEL	445	1.51	1.31	1.02	0.2%
AIE	437	1.14	1.28	0.69	0.4%
FGEN	436	1.37	1.23	1.24	0.3%
EOT	436	0.58	1.54	1.57	1.5%
PCGH	431	0.92	0.98	0.68	0.8%
FSFL	422	0.65	0.88	0.94	0.1%
JEMI	420	0.87	0.72	0.66	0.3%
NAVF	416	0.35	0.43	0.31	0.9%
JUGI	414	1.09	0.91	0.58	0.3%
PAC	411	1.86	0.95	0.65	0.3%
NAIT	410	0.50	0.79	0.61	0.7%
OTV2	404	0.01	0.08	0.24	0.0%
BIPS	396	0.80	0.66	0.45	0.6%
GRID	387	0.81	0.56	0.75	0.7%
FAS	381	0.85	0.50	0.46	0.3%
CREI	374	0.44	0.48	0.46	0.1%
AAIF	362	0.92	0.63	0.50	0.4%
NESF	360	1.13	1.32	1.20	0.3%
DIG	358	0.77	0.59	0.49	1.4%
PCFT	353	1.25	2.25	1.20	0.2%
ANII	348	0.53	0.60	0.44	1.0%
EAT	336	1.49	0.73	0.60	0.4%
BGEU	336	0.80	0.59	0.84	0.5%
CTPE	335	0.52	0.42	0.42	1.9%
BGS	334	1.04	1.02	1.14	0.4%
ORIT	332	1.18	0.85	0.95	0.2%
NCYF	332	0.61	0.63	0.49	0.4%
LWI	331	0.43	0.46	0.42	0.3%
SJG	331	0.43	0.45	0.34	0.7%
MNL	326	0.66	0.42	0.30	5.4%
CTUK	323	0.28	0.29	0.24	1.2%
SST	321	0.63	0.41	0.34	0.7%

COMPANY NAME	AIC SECTOR	MANAGEMENT GROUP
BlackRock Frontiers	Global Emerging Markets	BlackRock Management (UK)
Henderson High Income	UK Equity & Bond Income	Janus Henderson Investors
Home REIT	Property - UK Residential	AEW UK Management
Tufton Assets	Leasing	Tufton
JPMorgan Asia Growth & Income	Asia Pacific Equity Income	J.P. Morgan Asset Management
abrdn UK Smaller Companies Growth	UK Smaller Companies	Aberdeen
CC Japan Income & Growth	Japan	Chikara
STS Global Income & Growth	Global Equity Income	Troy Asset Management
Aurora UK Alpha	UK All Companies	Phoenix Asset Management
TwentyFour Select Monthly Income	Debt - Loans & Bonds	TwentyFour Asset Management
Real Estate Credit	Property - Debt	Cheyne Capital
Social Housing REIT	Property - UK Residential	Atrato Partners
VH Global Energy Infrastructure	Renewable Energy Infrastructure	Victory Hill Capital Advisors
Mid Wynd International	Global	Lazard Asset Management
British Smaller Companies	VCT Generalist	YFM Private Equity
Gore Street Energy Storage	Renewable Energy Infrastructure	Gore Street Capital

Source: AIC/Morningstar, data to 30/09/25, all figures in base currency, companies >100m market capitalisation only. Spread = (offer-bid)/offer.

While a small minority of investment trusts are managed directly by the board of directors, the great majority delegate the management of their portfolios to specialist fund managers, employed on annual or multi-year management contracts with a mandate to meet the trust's investment objectives. Those objectives are set by the board of directors and need to be approved by shareholders before any significant changes can be made. (But not always: this year Third Point Offshore Investors (TPOU), the US hedge fund, was able to take advantage of newly introduced rules to convert the trust into an insurance company without offering all shareholders an exit, an unwelcome precedent).

3i, the private equity group, has this year extended its lead over Scottish Mortgage (SMT) as the largest trust by market value. The 3i phenomenon is exceptional; for such a large trust to trade at a huge premium of more than 50% is unprecedented. Its market capitalisation has quadrupled in just three years as its single largest holding, a Dutch retailer called Action, continues to expand and grow in value.

This one trust now accounts for more than 15% of the investment trust sector's total market capitalisation. 3i has benefited from its bold decision not to scale back on its holding in Action to reduce concentration risk in its portfolio (3i is often excluded from aggregate performance figures for investment trusts because its size distorts the results). Although now firmly on a recovery path, Scottish Mortgage meanwhile has seen its market value decline and its shares move from a premium to a discount over the last three years.

TICKER	MARKET CAPITALISATION (M)	1MTH DAILY AVG VALUE TRADED (M)	1YR DAILY AVG VALUE TRADED (M)	5YR DAILY AVG VALUE TRADED (M)	% SPREAD
BRFI	318	0.50	0.45	0.40	0.6%
HHI	306	0.39	0.40	0.31	0.8%
HOME	301	0.00	0.02		0.0%
SHIP	299	0.06	0.16	0.24	2.6%
JAGI	296	0.71	0.74	0.73	0.5%
AUSC	295	1.21	1.01	0.85	0.4%
CCJI	283	0.31	0.38	0.37	6.2%
STS	282	0.38	0.36	0.29	0.8%
ARR	278	0.41	0.41	0.28	1.2%
SMIF	278	1.00	0.75	0.42	0.5%
RECI	278	0.42	0.39	0.40	0.4%
SOHO	277	0.67	0.56	0.58	1.4%
ENRG	274	0.77	0.45		0.9%
MWY	274	1.23	0.95	0.80	0.3%
BSV	268	0.09	0.02	0.01	0.0%
GSF	262	0.57	0.86	0.90	0.2%

The 20 largest individual trusts on this measure accounted for more than 40% of total industry market capitalisation. In contrast, nearly 100 trusts had less than £50m in assets, although this figure includes a large number of venture capital trusts, which are invariably much smaller on average. The largest trusts tend to have the best liquidity, meaning they are easier to buy and sell in size, an increasingly important factor for both institutional and private investors.

The spread between bid and offer prices of the 20 largest trusts averages 0.4%, compared to 1.0% for those with more than £100m market capitalisation. Economies of scale also make it easier for the biggest trusts to accept reduced annual management fees, with Scottish Mortgage, boasting an OCF of just 0.31%, again a prime example. Fees generally have been coming down as boards take advantage of competitive pressures and relatively poor performance to insist on reductions.

A majority of the largest trusts in the sector have been operating for many years, but newcomers can and do break in. Some of the largest newcomers, like Smithson (SSON) and Tritax Big Box REIT (BBOX), raised a lot of money but have dropped down the rankings this year, in part because of extensive share buybacks. Once again the diversity of the investment trust universe is well demonstrated in this table, which lists all the trusts whose market value exceeds £100m.

Saba Capital

Saba holdings 1

FUND	SABA HOLDING (%)	LAST DISCLOSURE	STAKE REVEALED	DISCOUNT (%)
Herald	31.0	08-Oct-25	06-Oct-25	-13.5
Baillie Gifford US Growth	29.3	09-Jan-25	08-Jan-25	-10.1
Edinburgh Worldwide	28.0	29-Sep-25	26-Sep-25	-5.1
River UK Microcap	16.2	01-Oct-25	30-Sep-25	-16.8
Smithson IT	15.0	08-Oct-25	06-Oct-25	-8.9
BlackRock Throgmorton	13.2	18-Sep-25	16-Sep-25	-9.5
Brown Advisory US Smaller	12.2	04-Mar-25	03-Mar-25	-9.6
Impax Environmental	11.1	18-Sep-25	16-Sep-25	-8.8
Utilico Emerging Markets	5.7	23-May-25	22-May-25	-11.4
Fidelity Emerging Markets	5.7	03-Apr-24	02-Apr-24	-8.4
Ecofin Global Utilities	5.1	29-Aug-24	28-Aug-24	-10.0
Henderson Smaller	5.1	24-Feb-25	20-Feb-25	-9.8
abrdn UK Smaller	5.1	21-Oct-24	18-Oct-24	-10.5
Baillie Gifford UK Growth	5.0	25-Mar-25	24-Mar-25	-10.6
BB Biotech	5.0	02-Sep-25	01-Sep-25	-12.6
SDCL Efficiency Income	5.0	03-Sep-25	02-Sep-25	-36.5
JPM UK Small Cap G&I	3.0	19-Mar-24	15-Mar-24	-10.0
Recently disclosed stakes				
Life Science REIT	5.9	18-Sep-25	17-Sep-25	-41.8
Syncona	5.2	18-Sep-25	17-Sep-25	-
Molten Ventures	5.1	25-Sep-25	24-Sep-25	-
Gore St Energy Storage	5.0	08-Oct-25	06-Oct-25	-40.2
Corporate action/in wind down				
Schroder UK Mid Cap	15.0	16-Sep-25	15-Sep-25	-7.0
VPC Specialty Lending	12.1	18-Sep-25	17-Sep-25	-46.6
Aberdeen Diversified I & G	5.1	23-Jun-25	20-Jun-25	-23.0

Saba holdings 2

FUND	SABA HOLDING (%)	LAST DISCLOSURE	STAKE DISCLOSED	DISCOUNT (%)
Reducing stake				
Middlefield Canadian Income	29.2	25-Dec-24	23-Dec-24	-3.1
Crystal Amber	25.4	08-Jul-25	07-Jul-25	-21.3
Blackrock Smaller Companies	10.0	11-Dec-23	10-Dec-23	-12.7
North American IT	5.0	11-Dec-24	10-Dec-24	-4.6
Montanaro European SmlCos	5.0	03-Jun-25	02-Jun-25	-7.9
Worldwide Healthcare	4.9	13-Jun-25	12-Jun-25	-6.6
Baillie Gifford European Growth	4.9	23-Sep-25	23-Sep-25	-7.5
European Opportunities	4.7	16-Feb-24	15-Feb-24	-6.9
JPMorgan European Discovery	4.5	15-May-25	14-May-25	-7.5
Geiger Counter	4.4	18-Jun-25	17-Jun-25	-11.2
Lowland	4.1	30-Jun-25	27-Jun-25	-10.0
Bellevue Healthcare	2.1	22-Jul-25	21-Jul-25	3.4

12-MONTH AVG DISC (%)	MARKET CAP (£M)	NOTES
−8.6	1,184	Continuation vote passed March 2025
−8.0	740	
−5.3	720	Partial returns of capital promised.
−16.3	70	
−10.7	1,654	
−10.9	455	
−10.0	150	Up to 100% tender in 2028 if underperforming.
−10.7	788	Board review ahead of 2025 continuation vote.
−15.9	450	
−10.7	614	
−10.7	237	
−10.7	531	Cont vote passed Oct 2025 after tweaks to strategy.
−9.7	292	
−11.1	241	Buybacks to target single digit discount.
−13.2	1,977	
−40.4	613	
−9.6	410	
−45.1	135	Sept 2025 proposed managed wind down.
–	–	June 2025 proposed orderly realisation.
–	–	
−46.0	303	
−8.6	238	Fee reduction, 3-year cont vote (from 2028), more buybacks.
−67.4	45	In wind down since 2023. £43m distribution of B shares.
−33.2	136	In wind down since 2023. Marketing private assets.

12M AVG DISCOUNT (%)	MARKET CAP (£M)	MAIN ELEMENTS
−6.7	148	Proposed rollover into UCITS ETF or cash exit.
−29.5	93	
−12.2	540	Standstill agreement with Saba until 2027.
−9.2	415	
−9.2	249	Target <10% discount, fee cut, bi-annual tender up to 5% (at 5% disc).
−10.1	1,396	
−11.4	343	
−9.6	438	Tender offer for 25% of share capital at 2% discount in June.
−8.4	545	
−9.4	70	Standstill agreement with Saba until 2026 AGM
−9.0	329	
−4.4	143	Zero DCM replacing annual redemption.

FUND	SABA HOLDING (%)	LAST DISCLOSURE	STAKE DISCLOSED	DISCOUNT (%)
Exit achieved/proposed				
Apax Global Alpha	2.2	–	–	–
European Smaller Companies	0.0	27-May-25	23-May-25	−7.9
Montanaro UK Smaller Cos	0.0	06-Mar-25	05-Mar-25	−10.3
CQS Natural Resources G&I	0.0	01-Oct-25	30-Sep-25	−3.3
Polar Capital Global Financials	0.0	24-Jun-25	23-Jun-25	−4.1
Keystone Positive Change	0.0	–	–	–
Henderson Opportunities	0.0	–	–	–

Source: Broker estimates mid-Oct 2025

If you had any reason to wonder why the name Saba Capital has dominated conversations in the investment trust business for the last year, take a look at the data displayed here, which lists all the trusts in which it has disclosed a shareholding at some point. The first table lists all the trusts in which it currently has disclosed stakes of more than 5%, the threshold for disclosure under current regulation. The second lists the trusts where Saba has either seen boards react with new proposals or has been reducing its holding for whatever reason.

Bear in mind that the holdings listed here are only the ones it has disclosed. There will be others – nobody quite knows how many – in which it has a holding that has not been disclosed because it does not meet the disclosure threshold. In some cases, Saba has built up its voting stake with the use of derivatives and has only chosen to 'materialise' it in preparation for a shareholder vote.

The point that has not been lost on any trust board is that just because there has been no disclosure, it does not mean that their trust is immune from coming under attack at some point. That said, it is clear that the campaign by Saba has been one that has evolved through a number of phases.

Saba mostly started building holdings in UK investment trusts over the course of 2023, when discounts were at their widest. Its first publicly disclosed run-in with a board was with European Opportunities Trust (EOT) in the autumn of 2023, where the trust was facing an impending continuation vote following a run of indifferent performance. That resulted in the trust effectively buying more time by agreeing a capped tender offer and the promise of a further tender offer after three years.

Having steady acquired more shareholdings over the course of 2024, Saba then launched its first co-ordinated public campaign for change in December 2024, by which time it had acquired holdings of 25% to 29% in a number of different trusts, and smaller holdings in several more. It requisitioned shareholder votes at seven trusts seeking to throw out the board, appoint its own directors and take on the running of the trust.

Those seven votes were all defeated as private investors joined wealth managers and others in rebuffing this opportunistic attack. Having garnered massive publicity from its campaign, Saba then followed up by requisitioning four more meetings seeking to pressurise these trusts, which included two of the original seven and two new names, into converting into open-ended funds of some kind. This would have the effect of

12M AVG DISCOUNT (%)	MARKET CAP (£M)	MAIN ELEMENTS
–		Left universe, bought by manager.
–7.2	478	42% shares exit via tender offer; then merger with EAT.
–10.5	125	12% of shares bought back, Saba exits.
–5.3	106	100% tender offer (46% exit); fee cut, enhanced divi 8% pa of NAV).
–4.4	350	44% exit in five-yearly tender in June 2025.
–		Rollover into open-ended BG Positive Change
–		Rollover into JH UK Equity Income

eliminating the discounts and offering shareholders the option to exit at or around net asset value.

The second table lists some of the actions that boards have taken in response to Saba's campaign. They include three trusts, Middlefield Canadian Income, Henderson Opportunities and Keystone Positive Change, which have opted for a rollover into an open-ended vehicle as Saba had been seeking. In five other cases boards have introduced exits or tender offers with a cash option enabling Saba to cash out its shareholding.

Meanwhile, while reducing its shareholdings and taking some profits as discounts have narrowed, Saba remains a prominent shareholder in three of the original seven: Herald, Baillie Gifford US Growth and Edinburgh Worldwide, and retains or has built up disclosable holdings in nearly 20 other trusts. Most of these trusts have discounts of between 8% and 10% and are under pressure to take remedial action of some kind.

It is not easy to calculate how many of these holdings are ones where Saba is sitting on losses, having acquired its shares at an average in cost that is higher than the current share price. The closed-end fund it runs through which it owns many of its shareholdings has not performed particularly well over the past two years, although the UK holdings are only one part of its portfolio. One reason is that Saba has been able to hedge its market exposure with derivatives, so that it is only the discount movements that really matter to it.

However, as one broker which has been involved in negotiating with Saba points out, the hedge fund's campaign is not just about trying to make money in the short term. The real payoff comes from being able to report successes in forcing change upon trusts over here and using the publicity and successful war stories to raise more money for new funds it manages. Some of any new war chest that Saba is able to raise will almost certainly be deployed to follow through and expand its investment trust campaign over here.

That is why boards remain on full alert for signs that Saba has come onto their share register and why other shareholders in the affected trusts may prove to have reason to be thankful to the US raider if its actions help to produce more steps to tackle the discount opportunities which have been allowed to develop over time. In other words, Saba has not gone away, and whatever you might think of its tactics, it has become a potent agent of change.

Best long-term performers

10 years

COMPANY NAME	TICKER	AIC SECTOR
3i Group	III	Private Equity
Allianz Technology	ATT	Technology & Technology Innovation
Polar Capital Technology	PCT	Technology & Technology Innovation
CQS Natural Resources Growth & Income	CYN	Commodities & Natural Resources
HgCapital	HGT	Private Equity
BlackRock World Mining	BRWM	Commodities & Natural Resources
Manchester & London	MNL	Global
Scottish Mortgage	SMT	Global
JPMorgan American	JAM	North America
Pacific Horizon	PHI	Asia Pacific
Rockwood Strategic	RKW	UK Smaller Companies
Oakley Capital	OCI	Private Equity
Geiger Counter	GCL	Commodities & Natural Resources
Golden Prospect Precious Metals	GPM	Commodities & Natural Resources
JPMorgan Global Growth & Income	JGGI	Global Equity Income
Monks	MNKS	Global
BlackRock Energy and Resources Income	BERI	Commodities & Natural Resources
The European Smaller Companies	ESCT	European Smaller Companies
VinaCapital Vietnam Opportunity	VOF	Country Specialist
Baker Steel Resources	BSRT	Commodities & Natural Resources
Schroder Asian Total Return	ATR	Asia Pacific
Patria Private Equity	PPET	Private Equity
Herald	HRI	Global Smaller Companies
Montanaro European Smaller Companies	MTE	European Smaller Companies
Templeton Emerging Markets	TEM	Global Emerging Markets
Canadian General	CGI	North America
AVI Global	AGT	Global
Brunner	BUT	Global
HarbourVest Global Private Equity	HVPE	Private Equity
Invesco Asia Dragon	IAD	Asia Pacific Equity Income
Invesco Global Equity Income	IGET	Global Equity Income
VietNam Holding	VNH	Country Specialist
CT Private Equity	CTPE	Private Equity
F&C	FCIT	Global
Alliance Witan	ALW	Global
Fidelity China Special Situations	FCSS	China / Greater China
Fidelity Asian Values	FAS	Asia Pacific Smaller Companies
North American Income	NAIT	North America
ICG Enterprise	ICGT	Private Equity
JPMorgan Asia Growth & Income	JAGI	Asia Pacific Equity Income
Tetragon Financial Group	TFG	Flexible
Middlefield Canadian Income	MCT	North America
abrdn Asia Focus	AAS	Asia Pacific Smaller Companies
Fidelity European	FEV	Europe
Schroder AsiaPacific	SDP	Asia Pacific

MANAGEMENT GROUP	£100 INITIAL (SHARE PRICE TOTAL RETURN)	ANNUALISED %	£100 INITIAL (NAV TOTAL RETURN)	ANNUALISED %	RANK LAST YEAR
3i Asset Management Ltd	1,218	28.4	1,012	26.0	1
Allianz Global Investors GmbH, UK Branch	1015.00	24.4	937	25.1	2
Polar Capital LLP	821	23.4	856	24.0	4
CQS (UK) LLP	616	19.9	460	16.5	NEW
Hg Pooled Management Ltd	589	19.4	505	17.6	3
BlackRock	580	19.2	526	18.1	NEW
M&L Capital Management	513	17.8	536	18.3	11
Baillie Gifford & Co Limited	500	17.5	573	19.1	7
JP Morgan Asset Management (UK) Ltd	481	17.0	480	17.0	5
Baillie Gifford & Co Limited	469	16.7	464	16.6	20
Rockwood Asset Management	467	16.7	366	13.8	9
Oakley Capital Ltd	463	16.6	457	16.4	8
CQS (UK) LLP	462	16.5	443	16.0	NEW
CQS (UK) LLP	447	16.2	447	16.2	NEW
JP Morgan Asset Management (UK) Ltd	419	15.4	400	14.9	6
Baillie Gifford & Co Limited	395	14.7	372	14.0	24
BlackRock	395	14.7	411	15.2	NEW
Janus Henderson Investors Ltd	393	14.7	354	13.5	16
VinaCapital Management Ltd	388	14.5	346	13.2	18
Baker Steel Capital Managers LLP	371	14.0	271	10.5	NEW
Schroder Management Limited	367	13.9	333	12.8	32
Patria	367	13.9	371	14.0	22
Herald Management Ltd	363	13.7	321	12.4	30
Montanaro Asset Management Limited	355	13.5	347	13.3	21
Franklin Templeton Trust Management Limited	351	13.4	327	12.6	NEW
Morgan Meighen & Associates Limited	350	13.3	399	14.8	42
Asset Value Investors Limited	350	13.3	325	12.5	44
Allianz Global Investors (UK) Ltd	349	13.3	321	12.4	19
HarbourVest Advisers L.P.	345	13.2	395	14.7	27
Invesco Managers Limited	345	13.2	320	12.3	NEW
Invesco Managers Limited	344	13.1	339	13.0	39
Dynam Capital Ltd	341	13.1	319	12.3	12
Columbia Threadneedle Business Limited	340	13.0	335	12.8	17
Columbia Threadneedle Business Limited	339	13.0	341	13.1	29
Towers Watson Management Limited	339	13.0	309	11.9	23
FIL Management (HK) Ltd	337	12.9	305	11.8	NEW
Fidelity Services Ltd	335	12.8	306	11.8	49
Janus Henderson Investors Ltd	334	12.8	315	12.2	48
ICG Plc	325	12.5	348	13.3	47
JP Morgan Asset Management (UK) Ltd	323	12.5	303	11.7	NEW
Tetragon Financial Management LP	323	12.4	282	10.9	NEW
Middlefield Limited	322	12.4	263	10.2	NEW
abrdn Managers Limited	321	12.4	300	11.6	NEW
FIL International	318	12.3	305	11.8	26
Schroder Unit Trusts Limited	314	12.1	298	11.5	NEW

COMPANY NAME	TICKER	AIC SECTOR
Law Debenture Corporation	LWDB	UK Equity Income
BlackRock American Income	BRAI	North America
NB Private Equity Partners	NBPE	Private Equity
JPMorgan European Growth & Income	JEGI	Europe
Impax Environmental Markets	IEM	Environmental
JPMorgan Japanese	JFJ	Japan
JPMorgan European Discovery	JEDT	European Smaller Companies
Murray International	MYI	Global Equity Income
3i Infrastructure	3IN	Infrastructure
BlackRock Greater Europe	BRGE	Europe
Scottish American	SAIN	Global Equity Income
JPMorgan Emerging Markets	JMG	Global Emerging Markets
Schroder Oriental Income	SOI	Asia Pacific Equity Income
Polar Capital Global Financials	PCFT	Financials & Financial Innovation
Bankers	BNKR	Global
JPMorgan Global Emerging Markets Income	JEMI	Global Emerging Markets
Mid Wynd International	MWY	Global
Aberdeen Asian Income	AAIF	Asia Pacific Equity Income
Schroder Japan	SJG	Japan
Pantheon International	PIN	Private Equity
Fidelity Special Values	FSV	UK All Companies

Source: AIC/Morningstar, data to 30/09/25, excludes companies with <10% NAVTR annualised return in the period. UK CPI 10yr annualised figure = 2.52 (Sep 25).

Although there have been a significant number of departures in the last three years, a good number of trusts have survived long enough to have multi-decade track records. The next few pages summarise the best performing trusts over 10, 20 and 30 years. The results are measured as both the value of £100 invested and as a compound annualised rate of return, with dividends reinvested, on both a share price and a NAV basis.

Of around 380 trusts whose data is recorded by the AIC, around a third have been launched in the last ten years. Another third have compiled 20-year records and only a fifth have survived long enough to have a 30-year record. There is a Darwinian process at work in the sector, with the weakest trusts eventually being either liquidated, taken over and renamed, or absorbed into another trust.

The first table is confined to trusts which have delivered an annualised NAV total return of more than 10% per annum. Because of the magical effect of compounding, any trust that can grow at 10% every year will at least double in value every seven years and quadruple every 14. Share price returns can of course be higher or lower than the NAV figure because of discount movements.

It is not wrong to see the table toppers over ten, 20 and 30 years as among the

MANAGEMENT GROUP	£100 INITIAL (SHARE PRICE TOTAL RETURN)	ANNUALISED %	£100 INITIAL (NAV TOTAL RETURN)	ANNUALISED %	RANK LAST YEAR
Janus Henderson Investors Ltd	313	12.1	292	11.3	NEW
BlackRock	312	12.1	286	11.1	46
NB Alternatives Advisers LLC	310	12.0	299	11.6	15
JP Morgan Asset Management (UK) Ltd	305	11.8	289	11.2	NEW
Impax Asset Management Group PLC	301	11.6	298	11.5	34
JP Morgan Asset Management (UK) Ltd	298	11.5	295	11.4	36
JP Morgan Asset Management (UK) Ltd	297	11.5	267	10.3	37
Aberdeen Group PLC	293	11.4	299	11.6	NEW
3i Asset Management Ltd	293	11.3	338	12.9	25
BlackRock Management (UK) Ltd	292	11.3	292	11.3	31
Baillie Gifford & Co Limited	285	11.0	325	12.5	35
JP Morgan Asset Management (UK) Ltd	283	11.0	264	10.2	NEW
Schroder Unit Trusts Limited	283	11.0	284	11.0	NEW
Polar Capital LLP	277	10.7	274	10.6	NEW
Janus Henderson Investors Ltd	275	10.6	295	11.4	50
JP Morgan Asset Management (UK) Ltd	273	10.6	276	10.7	NEW
Lazard Asset Management Ltd	271	10.5	282	10.9	28
abrdn Limited	267	10.3	264	10.2	NEW
Schroder Unit Trusts Limited	266	10.3	271	10.5	NEW
Pantheon Ventures (UK) LLP	264	10.2	314	12.1	43
FIL International	263	10.2	261	10.1	NEW

cream of the crop. It is true that you need to take into account the higher risk of specialist sectors. Technology, smaller companies and single-country funds need higher returns to justify their greater volatility. Despite the recent pickup in inflation, note that inflation over the three periods has averaged 2.5%, 2.6% and 2.3% respectively, so a 10% annualised return is equivalent to a 7.5% real (i.e., inflation-adjusted) return.

The stronger performance of equity markets in the last two years, particularly that of the US market, has brought the ten-year performance figures of many of the table toppers back above the equivalent figures for longer periods. The 30-year period still includes two very bad bear markets (2000–03 and 2007–09), but the 2000–03 bear market has now dropped out of the 20-year figures. An encouraging sign is that the number of trusts with ten-year annualised share price returns of more than 10% has risen from 48 to 66 since last year, reflecting firmer discounts.

The table also shows how the better-performing trusts have changed position in the rankings. While four of the top five remain in that group, newer and improving performers have again joined the top ten. Global and technology trusts continue to dominate this year, but the strongest advances belong to commodity trusts, which have risen strongly on the back of higher prices, for gold and metals in particular.

20 years

COMPANY NAME	TICKER	AIC SECTOR
3i Group	III	Private Equity
Allianz Technology	ATT	Technology & Technology Innovation
Polar Capital Technology	PCT	Technology & Technology Innovation
Scottish Mortgage	SMT	Global
HgCapital	HGT	Private Equity
JPMorgan American	JAM	North America
International Biotechnology	IBT	Biotechnology & Healthcare
abrdn Asia Focus	AAS	Asia Pacific Smaller Companies
Pacific Horizon	PHI	Asia Pacific
abrdn UK Smaller Companies Growth	AUSC	UK Smaller Companies
Lindsell Train	LTI	Global
JPMorgan Global Growth & Income	JGGI	Global Equity Income
Biotech Growth	BIOG	Biotechnology & Healthcare
Invesco Asia Dragon	IAD	Asia Pacific Equity Income
Scottish Oriental Smaller Companies	SST	Asia Pacific Smaller Companies
Fidelity Asian Values	FAS	Asia Pacific Smaller Companies
Schroder Asian Total Return	ATR	Asia Pacific
Schroder AsiaPacific	SDP	Asia Pacific
CT Private Equity	CTPE	Private Equity
Law Debenture Corporation	LWDB	UK Equity Income
The European Smaller Companies	ESCT	European Smaller Companies
Worldwide Healthcare	WWH	Biotechnology & Healthcare
Montanaro European Smaller Companies	MTE	European Smaller Companies
European Opportunities	EOT	Europe
Rockwood Strategic	RKW	UK Smaller Companies
Schroder Oriental Income	SOI	Asia Pacific Equity Income
Herald	HRI	Global Smaller Companies
ICG Enterprise	ICGT	Private Equity
abrdn New India	ANII	India/Indian Subcontinent
VinaCapital Vietnam Opportunity	VOF	Country Specialist
Patria Private Equity	PPET	Private Equity
Pantheon International	PIN	Private Equity
Oryx International Growth	OIG	UK Smaller Companies

Source: AIC/Morningstar, data to 30/09/25, excludes companies with <10% NAVTR annualised return in the period.

UK CPI 10yr annualised figure = 2.6 (Sep 25).

The lists of 20- and 30-year performers show the number of trusts that have delivered double-digit annualised returns over two and three decades. Note for how many of these trusts the share price and NAV total returns are typically not that different. This is evidence of a general truth: over time the discount at which you buy the shares of a top-performing trust matters less than you think.

The return on invested capital of a well-managed trust is far more important than the entry price, which is one reason why a buy-and-hold strategy is often sensible for long-term investors. While discount movements make share prices more volatile, the cyclical swings even out as time goes by. This is true even when the discount movements have been severe: an important message to take away.

MANAGEMENT GROUP	£100 INITIAL INVESTMENT (SHARE PRICE TOTAL RETURN)	ANNUALISED %	£100 INITIAL INVESTMENT (NAV TOTAL RETURN)	ANNUALISED %	RANK LAST YEAR
3i Asset Management Ltd	2,957	18.5	1,570	14.8	1
Allianz Global Investors GmbH, UK Branch – London	2,264	16.9	2,299	17.0	3
Polar Capital LLP	2,108	16.5	2,121	16.5	4
Baillie Gifford & Co Limited.	1,696	15.2	1,499	14.5	5
Hg Pooled Management Ltd	1,354	13.9	1,451	14.3	2
JP Morgan Asset Management (UK) Ltd	1,191	13.2	1,072	12.6	9
Schroder Unit Trusts Limited	1,032	12.4	1,021	12.3	23
abrdn Fund Managers Limited	995	12.2	1,097	12.7	13
Baillie Gifford & Co Limited.	963	12.0	1,031	12.4	16
abrdn Fund Managers Limited	921	11.7	797	10.9	10
Lindsell Train Ltd	921	11.7	1,142	13.0	7
JP Morgan Asset Management (UK) Ltd	916	11.7	859	11.4	12
Frostrow Capital LLP	910	11.7	935	11.8	6
Invesco Fund Managers Limited	904	11.6	849	11.3	17
First Sentier Investors (UK) Funds Ltd	839	11.2	890	11.6	8
Fidelity Investment Services Ltd	835	11.2	673	10.0	20
Schroder Investment Management Limited	825	11.1	736	10.5	28
Schroder Unit Trusts Limited	808	11.0	793	10.9	34
Columbia Threadneedle Investment Business Ltd	798	11.0	902	11.6	18
Janus Henderson Investors Ltd	795	10.9	735	10.5	39
Janus Henderson Investors Ltd	779	10.8	704	10.3	19
Frostrow Capital LLP	762	10.7	818	11.1	32
Montanaro Asset Management Limited	747	10.6	-	-	27
Devon Equity Management Limited	733	10.5	769	10.7	29
Rockwood Asset Management	712	10.3	-	-	54
Schroder Unit Trusts Limited	704	10.3	770	10.7	NEW
Herald Investment Management Ltd	702	10.2	722	10.4	53
ICG Plc	670	10.0	736	10.5	55
abrdn Fund Managers Limited	634	9.7	708	10.3	21
VinaCapital Investment Management Ltd	623	9.6	909	11.7	36
Patria Investments	571	9.1	822	11.1	33
Pantheon Ventures (UK) LLP	507	8.5	713	10.3	57
Harwood Capital Management Ltd	496	8.3	714	10.3	48

Over 20 years the performance story is not that dissimilar to the ten-year data. Six of the top ten this year appear in both lists, although in absolute terms their performance is significantly better over the ten-year period. The tenth-ranked trust now has an almost identical share price rate of return to the equivalent trust this time a year ago but 2.6% below that of the tenth-best performer three years ago.

It is worth noting the number of smaller company trusts that still feature in the 20-year list despite their recent derating. The final column shows how individual trusts have moved up and down the rankings. Notable risers include International Biotech Growth and two Asian trusts, abrdn Asia Focus and Pacific Horizon. Schroder Oriental Income is a newcomer to this particular table.

30 years

COMPANY NAME	TICKER	AIC SECTOR	
3i Group	III	Private Equity	
HgCapital	HGT	Private Equity	
Rights & Issues	RIII	UK Smaller Companies	
Worldwide Healthcare	WWH	Biotechnology & Healthcare	
JPMorgan European Discovery	JEDT	European Smaller Companies	
Scottish Mortgage	SMT	Global	
Fidelity European	FEV	Europe	
Fidelity Special Values	FSV	UK All Companies	
ICG Enterprise	ICGT	Private Equity	
TR Property	TRY	Property Securities	
The European Smaller Companies	ESCT	European Smaller Companies	
Canadian General	CGI	North America	
JPMorgan American	JAM	North America	
AVI Global	AGT	Global	
JPMorgan UK Small Cap Growth & Income	JUGI	UK Smaller Companies	
Herald	HRI	Global Smaller Companies	
Mercantile	MRC	UK All Companies	
Pacific Horizon	PHI	Asia Pacific	
Scottish Oriental Smaller Companies	SST	Asia Pacific Smaller Companies	
Aberforth Smaller Companies	ASL	UK Smaller Companies	
Montanaro European Smaller Companies	MTE	European Smaller Companies	
Pantheon International	PIN	Private Equity	
Law Debenture Corporation	LWDB	UK Equity Income	
JPMorgan Indian	JIGI	India/Indian Subcontinent	
Caledonia	CLDN	Flexible	
North Atlantic Smaller Companies	NAS	Global Smaller Companies	
North American Income	NAIT	North America	
Schroder UK Mid Cap	SCP	UK All Companies	
CQS Natural Resources Growth & Income	CYN	Commodities & Natural Resources	
Aurora UK Alpha	ARR	UK All Companies	

Source: AIC/Morningstar, data to 30/09/25, excludes companies with <10% NAVTR annualised return in the period.
UK CPI 30yr annualised figure = 2.28 (May 25).

Over 30 years the best performers include several by-now-familiar names, such as 3i, HG Capital and Scottish Mortgage, and several European trusts, as well as Rights and Issues. The latter's manager, Simon Knott, handed over to Dan Nickols at Jupiter Asset Management on his retirement two years ago, but the latter has also retired since, so its future performance remains in doubt.

Two trusts which marked the 30th anniversary of their launch this year, Worldwide Healthcare and Fidelity Special Values, join the top ten in the list for the first time and three others come in further down. The number of trusts that have delivered more than 10% annualised share price total return over three decades has risen from the figures a year ago.

The 30-year period includes trusts from nearly a dozen broadly different sectors, suggesting that these trusts do have something special about them, not just the good fortune of operating in the sectors that have performed particularly well. It is also a testament to the breadth and diversity of the investment company sector as a whole.

MANAGEMENT GROUP	£100 INITIAL (SHARE PRICE TOTAL RETURN)	ANNUALISED %	£100 INITIAL (NAV TOTAL RETURN)	ANNUALISED %	RANK LAST YEAR
3i Asset Management Ltd	9,136	16.2	3,599	12.7	1
Hg Pooled Management Ltd	8,907	16.1	6,589	15.0	2
Jupiter Unit Trust Managers Ltd	3,824	12.9	4,934	13.9	3
Frostrow Capital LLP	3,729	12.8	3,850	12.9	NEW
JP Morgan Asset Management (UK) Ltd	3,578	12.7	3,375	12.5	5
Baillie Gifford & Co Limited.	3,542	12.6	3,262	12.3	8
FIL International	3,261	12.3	3,206	12.3	4
FIL International	3,235	12.3	2,984	12.0	NEW
ICG Plc	3,174	12.2	3,462	12.5	6
Columbia Threadneedle Business Limited	2,911	11.9	2,419	11.2	9
Janus Henderson Investors Ltd	2,822	11.8	2,691	11.6	10
Morgan Meighen & Associates Limited	2,518	11.4	2,744	11.7	7
JP Morgan Asset Management (UK) Ltd	2,335	11.1	2,141	10.8	14
Asset Value Investors Limited	2,273	11.0	2,070	10.6	19
JP Morgan Asset Management (UK) Ltd	2,196	10.9	2,030	10.6	11
Herald Management Ltd	2,163	10.8	2,422	11.2	12
JP Morgan Asset Management (UK) Ltd	2,125	10.7	1,773	10.1	18
Baillie Gifford & Co Limited.	2,067	10.6	2,136	10.7	NEW
First Sentier Investors (UK) Funds Ltd	2,065	10.6	2,180	10.8	NEW
Aberforth Partners LLP	1,870	10.3	1,912	10.3	17
Montanaro Asset Management Limited	1,838	10.2	-	-	21
Pantheon Ventures (UK) LLP	1,668	9.8	1,986	10.5	20
Janus Henderson Investors Ltd	1,663	9.8	1,933	10.4	23
JPMorgan Funds Limited	1,496	9.4	1,810	10.1	NEW
Caledonia Plc	1,376	9.1	-	-	-
Harwood Capital LLP	1,261	8.8	1,833	10.2	22
Janus Henderson Investors Ltd	1,214	8.7	-	-	-
Schroder Unit Trusts Limited	978	7.9	-	-	-
CQS (UK) LLP	967	7.9	-	-	-
Phoenix Asset Management Partners	317	3.9	-	-	-

Unsurprisingly, perhaps, the rankings in the list change less markedly than in the ten- and 20-year rankings. Note again how close the NAV and share price total return figures for each trust are to each other, with 3i again being the major exception. Where there are differences, it can be a case of consistently strong performance having produced an improvement in a trust's rating over time.

A year ago the NAV return of several trusts was higher than the share price total return, indicating that there has been a derating over time, but in most cases that has reversed, suggesting that there are fewer outright bargains to be had by purchasing at today's levels.

The best 30-year performers are generally those that operate in growth sectors. Their returns are more volatile from one year to the next, but tend to come out on top in the end. While styles come in and out of fashion, as they have done this year, growth is usually the long-term winner for those who can tolerate the ups and downs along the way. It is another example of the timeless lesson: more volatility, higher returns.

Issuance

Investment Trust Fundraising by Calendar Year

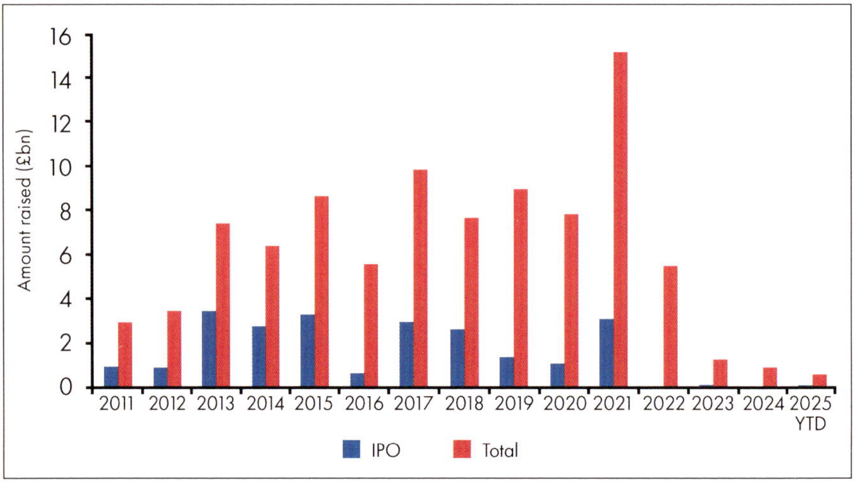

Source: Winterflood Securities/Morningstar. As at 30 September 2025.

COMPANY NAME	SECONDARY FUNDRAISING (£M)
JPMorgan Global Growth & Income	142.1
Henderson Far East Income	42.1
Invesco Bond Income Plus	41.9
M&G Credit Income	41.0
TwentyFour Select Monthly Income	40.3
CQS New City High Yield	36.0
Rockwood Strategic	33.9
TwentyFour Income	28.0
Ashoka India Equity	26.0
Law Debenture Corporation	19.5
Brunner	8.1
Ashoka WhiteOak Emerging Markets	7.5
Onward Opportunities	5.7
EJF	5.3

Source: AIC, excludes VCTs, company data for companies who have raised >£5m in period only.

With the great majority of trusts still trading at a discount, it is no surprise that there has again been very little issuance of shares since last year. There has been no IPO (initial public offering) of significant size for the last four years and a number of planned issues have been scrapped because of poor market conditions. Behind the scenes however it appears that more brokers are now working on potential listing candidates, so the drought may finally be about to end.

The only notable trust to raise money for a new vehicle was Achilles, an activist trust designed to target alternative asset trusts trading on wide discounts. The trust's shareholders include a number who backed the successful attempt to change the board of Hipgnosis Songs and force a more favourable exit.

The IPO process runs to an irregular cycle. Some periods are characterised by a spurt of new issues in a particular segment of the market. Property trusts and hedge funds, for example, were hugely popular in the run up to the financial crisis in 2008. Income-generating trusts operating with alternative assets, notably infrastructure, renewable energy and specialist property, were popular for several years after the global financial crisis.

At any one time, there are always potential IPOs being worked on by brokers, of which only a handful will make it to the starting line. The current drought of IPOs follows a period of several good years in which increasing amounts of new capital were raised for new trusts. Broker Numis Securities noted that 2022 was the worst year for IPOs since they started recording the data in 2000, and this year has been the fourth in succession to be effectively barren.

Secondary issuance is how investment trusts that have already succeeded in obtaining a listing can continue to grow their capital base. By convention investment trusts can only issue new equity if their shares are trading at a premium. The small minority that have breached this convention in the past suffered reputational consequences that can last for years (I can only think of two examples in recent years).

The biggest secondary issuer of shares in the last 12 months has been JPMorgan Global Growth and Income, which completed two mergers and whose enhanced-income policy remains popular with shareholders. No other trust managed to issue more than £50m through secondary issuance. The dozen-or-so-strong list of those finding buyers for new shares mostly included a number of trusts that offer above market dividend yields. Rockwood Strategic, a specialist UK small cap equity trust with a strong track record, was a notable exception.

For the third year running the amount raised overall from share issuance has been well below the amount of capital that has been returned to shareholders via buybacks, tender offers and exits, underlining how the sector has been shrinking in response to unfavourable performance and market conditions. It is also the lowest figure for issuance since 2003.

Return of capital

COMPANY NAME	TICKER	CAPITAL RETURNED 2025 YTD (£M) - TO 30/09/25	SPECIAL DIVIDENDS 2025 YTD (£M) - TO 30/09/25	CAPITAL RETURNED 2025 YTD (£M) INCLUDING SPECIAL DIVIDENDS - TO 30/09/25
The European Smaller Companies	ESCT	355.4	-	355.4
JPMorgan Indian	JII	229.7	-	229.7
European Opportunities	EOT	148.3	-	148.3
Petershill Partners	PHLL	-	121.1	121.1
abrdn European Logistics Income	ASLI	-	119.5	119.5
JPMorgan Global Core Real Assets	JARA	118.7	-	118.7
Starwood European Real Estate Finance	SWEF	111.0	-	111.0
Diverse Income	DIVI	81.2	-	81.2
Weiss Korea Opportunity	WKOF	69.6	-	69.6
VPC Speciality Lending	VSL	-	43.0	43.0
Schroders Capital Global Innovation	INOV	36.6	-	36.6
JZ Capital Partners	JZCP	31.6	-	31.6
Aquila Energy Efficiency	AEET	-	30.0	30.0
Amedeo Air Four Plus	AA4	27.9	-	27.9
Blackrock American Income	BRAI	20.9	-	20.9
Chelverton UK Dividend	SDV	19.3	-	19.3
RM Infrastructure Income	RMII	17.4	-	17.4
EJF	EJFI	15.7	-	15.7
Alternative Liquidity	ALF	14.1	-	14.1
Riverstone Credit Opportunities Income	RCOI	12.3	-	12.3
Unicorn AIM VCT	UAV	-	11.4	11.4
BioPharma Credit	BPCR	-	10.7	10.7
Others (less than £10m returned)				50.4
Total		**1,335**	**360**	**1,696**

There can be a number of reasons why a trust decides to return capital to its shareholders. One can be the decision to liquidate part or all of the trust's capital, typically after poor performance. In some other cases a trust may decide to make a distribution of capital because of the sale of a significant asset that it owns, often via a special dividend. A third factor may be a board trying to limit the discount at which the shares in the trust are trading.

Trusts have returned a record £9.7bn to shareholders through liquidations so far this year (data as at 30th September) as part of the ongoing consolidation in the sector. There will be more to come as other trusts sell, wind up or merge in the coming months. Twenty trusts have returned more than £10m of capital in other ways, including special dividends.

Company liquidations 2025

MONTH	COMPANY	AIC SECTOR	TOTAL ASSETS AT TIME OF LIQUIDATION (£M)
Jul	**Supermarket Income REIT**	Property - UK Commercial	−1,700
Jun	**Urban Logistics REIT**	Property - UK Logistics	−1,077
Jun	**BBGI Global Infrastructure S.A.**	Infrastructure	−1,018
Sep	**Apax Global Alpha**	Private Equity	−962
Feb	**Asia Dragon**	Asia Pacific	−721
May	**Care REIT**	Property - UK Healthcare	−699
Sep	**Henderson European**	Europe	−684
Sep	**Third Point Investors**	Hedge Funds	−568
Feb	**Taylor Maritime**	Leasing	−425
May	**Henderson International Income**	Global Equity Income	−366
Jan	**Blackstone Loan Financing**	Debt - Structured Finance	−320
Jun	**Harmony Energy Income**	Renewable Energy Infrastructure	−275
Jan	**Doric Nimrod Air Two**	Leasing	−185
Mar	**Keystone Positive Change**	UK All Companies	−158
Jan	**Alpha Real**	Property - Debt	−135
Mar	**Menhaden Resource Efficiency**	Environmental	−134
Mar	**Henderson Opportunities**	UK All Companies	−89
Feb	**Triple Point Energy Transition**	Renewable Energy Infrastructure	−82
Mar	**Jupiter Green**	Environmental	−47
Jan	**Dunedin Enterprise**	Private Equity	−35
May	**Miton UK Microcap**	UK Smaller Companies	−22
Mar	**SVM UK Emerging**	Debt - Structured Finance	−6
Feb	**Downing Strategic Micro-Cap**	UK Smaller Companies	−2

Source: AIC.

Share buybacks and tenders

COMPANY NAME	REPURCHASES AND TENDERS (£)	REPURCHASES AS A % OF MARKET CAPITALISATION
Weiss Korea Opportunity	69,999,920	62.8%
Polar Capital Global Financials	296,264,576	67.6%
European Opportunities	458,479,051	59.1%
The European Smaller Companies	363,849,234	61.3%
JPMorgan European Discovery	303,444,581	52.1%
JPMorgan Global Core Real Assets	93,007,065	55.6%
Mid Wynd International	163,882,513	40.8%
JPMorgan India Growth & Income	310,137,093	49.6%
Starwood European Real Estate Finance	141,748,111	45.2%
Biotech Growth	110,033,859	39.5%
Finsbury Growth & Income	616,798,111	35.4%
Riverstone Energy	197,066,388	67.1%
Franklin Global	79,016,621	33.8%
Invesco Select - Managed Liquidity share	460,576	38.9%
RM Infrastructure Income	35,037,671	41.8%
STS Global Income & Growth	67,865,242	33.0%
abrdn UK Smaller Companies Growth	131,092,836	37.4%
Capital Gearing	357,590,531	32.4%
Smithson	750,272,062	35.3%
Fidelity Emerging Markets	196,046,859	36.1%
Impax Environmental Markets	352,024,469	32.7%
Bellevue Healthcare	236,691,535	31.4%
BlackRock American Income	46,270,536	31.5%
Worldwide Healthcare	564,828,231	31.2%
Henderson European Focus	104,655,530	31.3%
Monks	649,689,055	30.5%
Crystal Amber	20,585,443	38.1%
Montanaro European Smaller Companies	65,216,657	28.8%
JPMorgan Asia Growth & Income	83,612,991	26.7%
MIGO Opportunities	18,043,769	23.6%
Scottish Mortgage	2,625,480,172	27.9%
Montanaro UK Smaller Companies	41,531,826	24.8%
Ruffer	236,340,253	22.9%
BlackRock Throgmorton	128,814,695	23.0%
Schroders Capital Global Innovation	48,038,980	35.7%
Geiger Counter	18,058,311	25.8%
Baillie Gifford UK Growth	54,273,995	23.1%
Bankers	264,057,605	21.9%

	SHARE PRICE TOTAL RETURN 01/07/23 TO 30/09/25	DISCOUNT 30/06/23 (%)	DISCOUNT 30/09/25 (%)	CHANGE IN DISCOUNT %
	0.7%	-1.1%	-5.0%	-389.0%
	56.5%	-9.9%	-5.8%	412.0%
	17.4%	-8.3%	-7.6%	69.0%
	57.4%	-15.1%	-5.3%	981.0%
	63.9%	-14.9%	-7.1%	775.0%
	0.4%	-21.5%	-23.5%	-198.0%
	11.3%	-1.5%	-2.0%	-47.0%
	18.3%	-19.3%	-8.8%	1051.0%
	12.6%	-16.0%	-9.6%	635.0%
	29.5%	-5.1%	-9.8%	-468.0%
	5.8%	-4.4%	-6.7%	-232.0%
	39.3%	-49.9%	-18.3%	3166.0%
	16.3%	-1.0%	-2.7%	-170.0%
	n/a	-14.3%	n/a	n/a
	3.0%	-21.3%	-20.5%	84.0%
	17.5%	-0.5%	-0.6%	-6.0%
	31.3%	-13.2%	-9.9%	325.0%
	10.9%	-1.9%	-2.1%	-15.0%
	17.3%	-11.1%	-8.4%	266.0%
	67.0%	-14.3%	-7.6%	671.0%
	9.7%	-7.5%	-10.4%	-293.0%
	-7.7%	-6.8%	-5.1%	167.0%
	27.8%	-7.8%	-3.8%	398.0%
	7.7%	-8.8%	-7.7%	110.0%
	n/a	-11.9%	n/a	n/a
	56.2%	-12.2%	-6.1%	601.0%
	127.7%	-33.3%	-21.2%	1216.0%
	43.4%	-13.8%	-8.0%	577.0%
	39.7%	-9.2%	-8.6%	58.0%
	13.5%	-2.4%	-4.5%	-211.0%
	71.5%	-18.2%	-10.0%	821.0%
	10.3%	-9.5%	-11.2%	-173.0%
	12.8%	-4.4%	-3.6%	88.0%
	10.6%	-5.5%	-10.0%	-453.0%
	-1.7%	-39.3%	-30.9%	840.0%
	15.6%	-19.6%	-10.4%	917.0%
	36.4%	-13.6%	-10.3%	330.0%
	40.7%	-13.0%	-7.8%	525.0%

COMPANY NAME	REPURCHASES AND TENDERS (£)	REPURCHASES AS A % OF MARKET CAPITALISATION
Lowland	66,810,464	21.9%
Aquila Energy Efficiency	17,500,001	30.3%
Personal Assets	306,686,186	17.8%
Invesco Select - Balanced Risk Allocation sh	1,104,172	22.4%
Herald	198,453,721	20.0%
North American Income	74,254,854	19.2%
CVC Income & Growth	15,284,011	18.4%
Invesco Select - UK Equity shares	20,454,114	19.9%
Henderson Smaller Companies	98,526,775	18.4%
Baillie Gifford Shin Nippon	74,965,394	18.7%
Rights & Issues	20,072,558	18.4%
Baillie Gifford Japan	113,788,480	17.7%
abrdn New India	61,793,484	19.7%
International Biotechnology	39,944,564	16.1%
Vietnam Enterprise	227,699,966	18.9%
Dunedin Income Growth	66,789,340	16.8%
The Global Smaller Companies	124,276,193	17.1%
Templeton Emerging Markets	278,376,409	16.7%
BlackRock Energy and Resources Income	24,552,203	15.8%
abrdn Asia Focus	67,931,249	17.0%
BioPharma Credit	155,903,962	17.1%
VinaCapital Vietnam Opportunity	121,515,359	17.3%

Source: theaic.co.uk / Morningstar, Data 01/10/23 to 30/09/25 inclusive. Includes repurchases into treasury.

Investment trusts can reduce their share counts in two main ways: by carrying out share buybacks in the market and by offering shareholders the chance to redeem their shares at or close to net asset value. Trusts have been very busy in both respects over the last few years. This table puts some numbers around this trend, together with the related move in their discounts. Shaded lines show trusts which are effectively disappearing for one reason or another.

The table includes those trusts which have bought back or redeemed the highest proportion of their NAV and market capitalisation over the past 24 months (to 1 October 2025). Last year we only included 12 months' figures. The shaded lines indicate trusts which are in one way or another in the process of putting themselves out of business. The remainder are trusts which are attempting to bring supply and demand for their shares into a better balance, typically with the aim of reducing or eliminating a discount.

The striking headline is that more than 240 trusts have bought back at least some shares in the last two years, with buybacks totalling £9.7bn. While some are

SHARE PRICE TOTAL RETURN 01/07/23 TO 30/09/25	DISCOUNT 30/06/23 (%)	DISCOUNT 30/09/25 (%)	CHANGE IN DISCOUNT %
47.1%	-13.1%	-9.9%	326.0%
52.8%	-39.1%	-30.2%	889.0%
16.6%	-1.1%	-0.6%	51.0%
n/a	-21.3%	n/a	n/a
43.8%	-15.8%	-9.7%	608.0%
38.3%	-12.3%	-8.0%	428.0%
40.3%	-8.9%	-1.1%	776.0%
n/a	-16.3%	n/a	n/a
29.3%	-12.3%	-9.3%	297.0%
5.7%	-13.6%	-9.8%	372.0%
15.4%	-12.3%	-19.4%	-704.0%
37.2%	-10.2%	-10.6%	-48.0%
31.3%	-19.8%	-9.7%	1013.0%
33.0%	-3.8%	-10.8%	-699.0%
25.6%	-18.2%	-15.9%	230.0%
18.6%	-11.1%	-9.1%	198.0%
24.3%	-14.4%	-10.6%	374.0%
57.9%	-13.9%	-8.8%	512.0%
26.0%	-10.7%	-7.4%	334.0%
49.3%	-16.9%	-10.9%	602.0%
25.4%	-17.9%	-8.3%	958.0%
16.7%	-20.1%	-18.8%	124.0%

insignificant amounts. and the disparity between trusts is marked, in other cases they are not. Eighty-seven trusts have bought back more than 10% of their net asset value as it was two years ago, and 95 more than 10% of their market capitalisation at the same date.

In no fewer than 46 cases, the percentage of their market value trusts have bought back is more than 20%. The totals are significantly higher in the last 12 months than in the previous 12 months, indicating how the pressure on boards to take action about discounts has intensified. These figures can be usefully compared to the list of trusts which have adopted discount control policies of one kind or another.

Buybacks have run at an average rate of £1.2bn a year over the past 20 years, but the pick-up in trend is clear. I discuss in the editor's notes how effective all this activity has been in addressing discounts. While the average share price total return of the 240 trusts buying back shares is positive at 25% over two years, the average discount remains higher than it was two years ago, in part because some of the trusts with the widest discounts have disappeared.

Discount movements

AIC SECTOR		TOTAL ASSETS £M	
Global	AIC sector weighted average	35,069.23	
North America	AIC sector weighted average	18,140.83	
Flexible Investment	AIC sector weighted average	15,373.75	
UK Equity Income	AIC sector weighted average	12,488.69	
Global Equity Income	AIC sector weighted average	7,019.26	
Global Emerging Markets	AIC sector weighted average	6,256.32	
UK Smaller Companies	AIC sector weighted average	6,081.55	
Global Smaller Companies	AIC sector weighted average	5,627.60	
UK All Companies	AIC sector weighted average	4,563.98	
Europe	AIC sector weighted average	4,558.82	

Trust discount movement

COMPANY NAME	AIC SECTOR	TICKER	
Scottish Mortgage	Global	SMT	
Pershing Square Holdings	North America	PSH	
F&C	Global	FCIT	
Alliance Witan	Global	ALW	
RIT Capital Partners	Flexible Investment	RCP	
JPMorgan Global Growth & Income	Global Equity Income	JGGI	
Caledonia	Flexible Investment	CLDN	
Monks	Global	MNKS	
City of London	UK Equity Income	CTY	
Fidelity European	Europe	FEV	
Tetragon Financial Group	Flexible Investment	TFG	
Templeton Emerging Markets	Global Emerging Markets	TEM	
Mercantile	UK All Companies	MRC	
JPMorgan American	North America	JAM	
Murray International	Global Equity Income	MYI	
Smithson	Global Smaller Companies	SSON	
Personal Assets	Flexible Investment	PNL	
Law Debenture Corporation	UK Equity Income	LWDB	
Bankers	Global	BNKR	
Fidelity Special Values	UK All Companies	FSV	
Aberforth Smaller Companies	UK Smaller Companies	ASL	
JPMorgan Emerging Markets	Global Emerging Markets	JMG	
Herald	Global Smaller Companies	HRI	
AVI Global	Global	AGT	
Edinburgh	UK Equity Income	EDIN	

	NOW DISCOUNT % 30/09/2025	1YR AGO DISCOUNT % 30/09/2024	3YR AGO DISCOUNT % 30/09/2022	5YR AGO DISCOUNT % 30/09/2020	10YR AGO DISCOUNT % 30/09/2015
	−8.25	−10.02	−7.71	−2.40	−5.08
	−23.00	−24.33	−25.19	−21.49	−9.15
	−22.31	−22.16	−17.32	−14.31	−11.38
	−3.01	−4.97	−3.82	−5.33	−1.56
	−3.13	−3.88	−5.55	−0.31	−0.29
	−4.45	−11.18	−12.05	−11.20	−11.45
	−12.22	−9.96	−13.05	−12.19	−10.75
	−11.40	−12.48	−16.02	−6.03	−9.38
	−6.72	−9.82	−12.96	−12.17	−8.24
	−4.22	−8.28	−11.69	−8.18	−4.05

	TOTAL ASSETS £M	NOW DISCOUNT % 30/09/2025	1YR AGO DISCOUNT % 30/09/2024	3YR AGO DISCOUNT % 30/09/2022	5YR AGO DISCOUNT % 30/09/2020	10YR AGO DISCOUNT % 30/09/2015
	15,473.89	−10.03	−12.09	−10.58	−0.10	3.12
	13,372.83	−28.80	−31.22	−33.81	−30.82	
	6,617.59	−8.03	−9.36	−2.15	−10.68	−6.63
	5,542.29	−5.15	−5.80	−5.11	−5.64	−12.42
	4,272.38	−26.78	−29.90	−15.58	−7.93	−0.79
	3,527.16	−2.39	0.70	−2.17	4.19	−7.06
	3,011.74	−31.95	−35.65	−37.29	−30.25	−20.99
	2,872.85	−6.14	−10.60	−8.23	0.97	−11.62
	2,573.18	2.16	0.44	1.71	−1.50	2.21
	2,443.68	−3.31	−5.71	−10.39	−7.70	−5.27
	2,440.81	−51.08	−69.87	−66.52	−64.50	−44.83
	2,392.42	−8.78	−11.97	−12.65	−12.52	−12.26
	2,232.75	−9.31	−9.89	−16.73	−13.51	−10.07
	2,070.48	−3.39	−3.79	−3.29	−5.68	−3.17
	1,931.18	−2.81	−8.55	−7.30	−4.53	0.26
	1,841.33	−8.40	−11.37	−11.43	2.24	
	1,633.67	−0.61	−0.77	0.14	1.27	−1.07
	1,556.08	2.12	1.09	−3.97	−4.22	−4.02
	1,516.30	−7.75	−11.36	−7.39	0.66	0.13
	1,446.30	−1.36	−8.11	−8.88	−10.74	−1.30
	1,444.59	−11.11	−8.30	−15.13	−12.62	−12.54
	1,409.94	−8.28	−11.97	−11.97	−9.24	−12.95
	1,322.04	−9.68	−11.44	−19.05	−16.45	−20.08
	1,306.98	−6.72	−8.98	−10.39	−9.31	−11.58
	1,282.72	−7.65	−9.68	−10.64	−13.62	1.68

COMPANY NAME	AIC SECTOR	TICKER	
Finsbury Growth & Income	UK Equity Income	FGT	
Temple Bar	UK Equity Income	TMPL	
Canadian General	North America	CGI	
Murray Income	UK Equity Income	MUT	
Scottish American	Global Equity Income	SAIN	
Merchants	UK Equity Income	MRCH	
Ruffer	Flexible Investment	RICA	
The Global Smaller Companies	Global Smaller Companies	GSCT	
Baillie Gifford US Growth	North America	USA	
Capital Gearing	Flexible Investment	CGT	
Edinburgh Worldwide	Global Smaller Companies	EWI	
North Atlantic Smaller Companies	Global Smaller Companies	NAS	
Henderson Smaller Companies	UK Smaller Companies	HSL	
Brunner	Global	BUT	
BlackRock Smaller Companies	UK Smaller Companies	BRSC	
Fidelity Emerging Markets	Global Emerging Markets	FEML	
BlackRock Throgmorton	UK Smaller Companies	THRG	
JPMorgan European Growth & Income	Europe	JEGI	
BlackRock Greater Europe	Europe	BRGE	
Utilico Emerging Markets	Global Emerging Markets	UEM	
European Opportunities	Europe	EOT	
JPMorgan UK Small Cap Growth & Income	UK Smaller Companies	JUGI	
JPMorgan Claverhouse	UK Equity Income	JCH	
JPMorgan Global Emerging Markets Income	Global Emerging Markets	JEMI	
North American Income	North America	NAIT	
Dunedin Income Growth	UK Equity Income	DIG	
Manchester & London	Global	MNL	
BlackRock Frontiers	Global Emerging Markets	BRFI	
Lowland	UK Equity Income	LWI	
Baillie Gifford European Growth	Europe	BGEU	
Castelnau Group	Flexible Investment	CGL	
abrdn UK Smaller Companies Growth	UK Smaller Companies	AUSC	
CT UK Capital & Income	UK Equity Income	CTUK	
Hansa	Flexible Investment	HANA	
Aurora UK Alpha	UK All Companies	ARR	
STS Global Income & Growth	Global Equity Income	STS	
Baillie Gifford UK Growth	UK All Companies	BGUK	
UIL	Flexible Investment	UTL	
Mid Wynd International	Global	MWY	
Schroder UK Mid Cap	UK All Companies	SCP	
Oryx International Growth	UK Smaller Companies	OIG	
Schroder Income Growth	UK Equity Income	SCF	
Invesco Global Equity Income	Global Equity Income	IGET	
Odyssean	UK Smaller Companies	OIT	

TOTAL ASSETS £M	NOW DISCOUNT % 30/09/2025	1YR AGO DISCOUNT % 30/09/2024	3YR AGO DISCOUNT % 30/09/2022	5YR AGO DISCOUNT % 30/09/2020	10YR AGO DISCOUNT % 30/09/2015
1,257.01	−6.72	−8.73	−4.60	−0.72	−0.07
1,069.12	0.86	−6.82	−5.24	−14.01	−3.21
1,046.17	−42.19	−38.87	−34.28	−36.56	−27.09
1,040.21	−6.62	−10.15	−9.85	−7.99	−6.66
1,005.74	−9.26	−8.94	−9.20	5.08	3.39
998.66	−7.38	0.43	0.00	−3.06	−3.64
901.61	−3.56	−4.43	−5.83	−2.32	−0.07
867.40	−10.64	−8.52	−18.12	−9.80	0.77
865.58	−9.44	−10.91	−12.57	6.35	
822.23	−2.07	−1.81	−1.11	2.58	1.90
821.68	−4.92	−9.05	−12.77	2.19	−3.97
775.14	−36.15	−28.81	−31.21	−33.75	−20.36
682.23	−9.29	−10.99	−13.78	−14.52	−11.79
663.20	−3.72	−0.29	−12.71	−16.87	−9.39
661.04	−12.57	−9.68	−14.14	−11.51	−13.53
656.49	−7.61	−11.28	−16.01	−12.09	−11.99
643.57	−10.02	−11.09	−6.20	−3.48	−13.32
596.72	−2.42	−12.15	−15.10	−15.79	−4.33
585.85	−4.23	−5.58	−6.92	−3.54	−3.87
536.59	−10.55	−18.42	−13.27	−13.24	−12.32
527.33	−7.64	−11.09	−14.46	−12.51	0.07
517.83	−9.60	−3.27	−15.62	−15.59	−14.38
495.28	−5.00	−6.39	0.08	−7.46	−7.11
489.85	−8.89	−13.08	−12.50	−8.71	−5.00
480.18	−8.04	−12.81	−4.55	−11.54	−10.64
436.62	−9.09	−11.20	−1.49	−9.79	−7.45
421.35	−22.57	−18.18	−22.88	−1.75	−15.81
413.99	−4.18	−9.35	−10.78	−4.91	−2.35
409.40	−9.88	−12.11	−10.25	−9.14	−2.38
405.23	−8.41	−15.74	−13.49	−2.38	−9.32
386.38	−24.06	−1.52	7.62		
368.69	−9.93	−12.04	−13.73	−7.68	−9.54
351.35	−3.97	−2.86	0.84	−0.26	2.19
324.30	−36.85	−43.11	−41.47	−34.57	−27.77
314.28	−11.39	−10.99	−1.22	−2.33	−0.05
298.47	−0.56	−1.65	1.41	−3.24	−7.47
294.84	−10.30	−13.22	−14.04	−8.04	−10.61
292.73	−32.04	−36.24	−26.65	−44.47	−24.99
279.20	−1.96	−2.55	−0.44	1.08	2.07
275.81	−6.93	−12.33	−11.42	−19.42	−9.28
266.84	−32.32	−19.98	−15.92	−16.73	−10.96
266.14	−7.97	−10.68	−1.03	−5.41	−2.58
252.96	1.93	−9.30	−7.62	−1.66	2.00
224.14	−5.88	0.88	0.13	−6.66	

COMPANY NAME	AIC SECTOR	TICKER
Aberdeen Equity Income	UK Equity Income	AEI
Franklin Global	Global	FRGT
Diverse Income	UK Equity Income	DIVI
Lindsell Train	Global	LTI
abrdn Diversified Income and Growth	Flexible Investment	ADIG
Strategic Equity Capital	UK Smaller Companies	SEC
Middlefield Canadian Income	North America	MCT
Mobius	Global Emerging Markets	MMIT
Hansa	Flexible Investment	HAN
Majedie	Flexible Investment	MAJE
Montanaro UK Smaller Companies	UK Smaller Companies	MTU
Aberforth Geared Value & Income	UK Smaller Companies	AGVI
Marwyn Value Investors	UK Smaller Companies	MVI
Shires Income	UK Equity Income	SHRS
Rockwood Strategic	UK Smaller Companies	RKW
Artemis UK Future Leaders	UK Smaller Companies	AFL
New Star	Flexible Investment	NSI
Rights & Issues	UK Smaller Companies	RIII
BlackRock American Income	North America	BRAI
Crystal Amber	UK Smaller Companies	CRS
Global Opportunities	Flexible Investment	GOT
Barings Emerging EMEA Opportunities	Global Emerging Markets	BEMO
CT UK High Income	UK Equity Income	CHI
CT Global Managed Portfolio Growth	Flexible Investment	CMPG

Source: AIC/Morningstar, all figures to 30/09/25 unless otherwise stated.

This year for the second time we include a table that illustrates how volatile discounts in the investment trust universe can be. The list only covers equity investment trusts with a minimum of £50m in assets. The figures are nevertheless quite striking and underline the essential point that investors who look at investment trusts do have to understand how discounts can and do move from year to year.

What the table shows is the discount of a particular trust at the end of September 2025 with the equivalent figure one, three, five and ten years ago. While some of the names such as Murray International have swung noticeably from premium to discount, others such as Mercantile and Templeton Emerging Markets have maintained a more stable history in terms of rating. The picture would have been more uniformly discouraging if we had included alternative asset trusts, which have derated more, reflecting the move from lower to higher interest rates.

Looking at the main equity sectors, it is also evident that periods when sectors overall trade at a premium are rare to non-existent. One lesson to take away from

TOTAL ASSETS £M	NOW DISCOUNT % 30/09/2025	1YR AGO DISCOUNT % 30/09/2024	3YR AGO DISCOUNT % 30/09/2022	5YR AGO DISCOUNT % 30/09/2020	10YR AGO DISCOUNT % 30/09/2015
206.79	0.01	−3.03	−8.82	−12.51	−0.37
190.66	−2.66	−2.11	−0.28	−0.83	−0.83
187.12	−9.08	−6.92	−5.57	−8.12	−0.18
184.94	−25.38	−19.34	−3.73	3.86	22.16
181.28	−32.84	−32.09	−22.74	−18.33	−0.38
180.87	−13.30	−6.94	−9.04	−19.27	7.18
180.62	−2.14	−14.14	−8.69	−14.61	−14.57
172.87	−3.52	−7.36	−1.13	−11.44	
162.15	−35.86	−41.57	−38.43	−37.26	−24.89
157.10	−11.96	−17.42	−25.76	−26.30	−3.11
155.23	−11.21	−12.82	−9.84	−16.54	−13.27
145.64	−12.27	−17.43			
141.38	−48.34	−51.22	−39.74	−26.13	−17.76
136.29	−5.73	−7.67	−4.53	−6.55	−3.85
134.81	0.75	0.97	−2.10	−18.98	−20.49
132.25	−14.79	−13.87	−16.06	−19.07	−5.03
125.79	−34.22	−36.12	−29.97	−31.48	−33.30
125.70	−19.37	−7.28	−12.29	−5.00	−17.87
124.97	−3.84	−8.51	−4.16	−7.28	−10.12
118.11	−21.16	−33.61	−20.33	−26.53	2.06
116.61	−16.80	−19.45	−17.75	−8.60	−1.76
103.63	−10.07	−21.43	−13.30	−15.43	−8.95
102.10	1.39	−8.84	−6.89	−8.08	−6.06
96.83	−4.99	−1.97	−0.44	−1.62	2.01

that is that years like 2021, when a majority of trusts were trading close to par, are anomalous and investors should become nervous about their sustainability.

A second lesson is that over time discounts do not matter as much as many investors think. For specific trusts, as they go in and out of favour, discount changes can make a huge difference, but the general story is one in which broadly diversified shareholders who can live with the volatility will mostly not come out the worse for the experience.

While bargain hunters prefer times of discount volatility, because of the opportunities they throw up, patient shareholders can mostly afford to remain relatively unruffled. That said, it is also clear that discounts today in many cases are wider than at these earlier historical comparison points, which allows grounds for optimism that they can narrow further in due course, provided boards are on the case.

Discount control policies

COMPANY	AIC SECTOR	DISCOUNT CONTROL MECHANISM	TARGET
BlackRock American Income	North America	DCM	2.0%
BlackRock Energy and Resources Income	Commodities & Natural Resources	DCM	2.0%
AVI Japan Opportunity	Japanese Smaller Companies	DCM	5.0%
BlackRock Latin American	Latin America	DCM	5.0%
VH Global Energy Infrastructure	Renewable Energy Infrastructure	DCM	5.0%
Strategic Equity Capital	UK Smaller Companies	DCM	8.0%
Aurora UK Alpha	UK All Companies	DCM	10.0%
BH Macro	Hedge Funds	DCM	10.0%
CVC Income & Growth	Debt - Loans & Bonds	DCM	10.0%
Greencoat UK Wind	Renewable Energy Infrastructure	DCM	10.0%
JPMorgan Emerging Markets	Global Emerging Markets	DCM	10.0%
NextEnergy Solar	Renewable Energy Infrastructure	DCM	10.0%
Barings Emerging EMEA Opportunities	Global Emerging Markets	DCM	12.0%
Baker Steel Resources	Commodities & Natural Resources	DCM	15.0%

COMPANY	AIC SECTOR	DISCOUNT CONTROL POLICY	TARGET
Bellevue Healthcare	Biotechnology & Healthcare	DCP	0.0%
Capital Gearing	Flexible Investment	DCP	0.0%
M&G Credit Income	Debt - Loans & Bonds	DCP	0.0%
Personal Assets	Flexible Investment	DCP	0.0%
Aberdeen Asian Income	Asia Pacific Equity Income	DCP	5.0%
CT Global Managed Portfolio	Flexible Investment	DCP	5.0%
CT UK High Income	UK Equity Income	DCP	5.0%
Fair Oaks Income 2021	Debt - Structured Finance	DCP	5.0%
Finsbury Growth & Income	UK Equity Income	DCP	5.0%
JPMorgan Claverhouse	UK Equity Income	DCP	5.0%
JPMorgan Global Emerging Markets Income	Global Emerging Markets	DCP	5.0%
JPMorgan Global Growth & Income	Global Equity Income	DCP	5.0%

COMPANY	AIC SECTOR	DISCOUNT CONTROL POLICY	TARGET
NB Distressed Debt Extended Life shares	Debt - Loans & Bonds	DCP	5.0%
NB Distressed Debt New Global shares	Debt - Loans & Bonds	DCP	5.0%
Onward Opportunities	UK Smaller Companies	DCP	5.0%
Ruffer	Flexible Investment	DCP	5.0%
Schroder Asian Total Return	Asia Pacific	DCP	5.0%
Schroder British Opportunities	Growth Capital	DCP	5.0%
Schroder Oriental Income	Asia Pacific Equity Income	DCP	5.0%
Starwood European Real Estate Finance	Property - Debt	DCP	5.0%
Global Smaller Companies	Global Smaller Companies	DCP	5.0%
Tritax Big Box REIT	Property - UK Logistics	DCP	5.0%
TwentyFour Select Monthly Income	Debt - Loans & Bonds	DCP	5.0%
Biotech Growth	Biotechnology & Healthcare	DCP	6.0%
RM Infrastructure Income	Debt - Direct Lending	DCP	6.0%
Worldwide Healthcare	Biotechnology & Healthcare	DCP	6.0%
Allianz Technology	Technology & Technology Innovation	DCP	7.0%
North American Income	North America	DCP	7.0%
Chenavari Toro Income	Debt - Structured Finance	DCP	7.5%
F&C	Global	DCP	7.5%
STS Global Income & Growth	Global Equity Income	DCP	7.5%
abrdn UK Smaller Companies Growth	UK Smaller Companies	DCP	8.0%
International Biotechnology	Biotechnology & Healthcare	DCP	8.0%
JPMorgan Emerging Europe, Middle East & Africa Securities	Global Emerging Markets	DCP	8.0%
European Opportunities	Europe	DCP	9.0%
JPMorgan Asia Growth & Income	Asia Pacific Equity Income	DCP	9.0%
JPMorgan US Smaller Companies	North American Smaller Companies	DCP	9.0%
Pacific Horizon	Asia Pacific	DCP	9.0%
BioPharma Credit	Debt - Direct Lending	DCP	10.0%
Brown Advisory US Smaller Companies	North American Smaller Companies	DCP	10.0%
Ceiba	Property - Rest of World	DCP	10.0%
Fidelity European	Europe	DCP	10.0%

COMPANY	AIC SECTOR	DISCOUNT CONTROL POLICY	TARGET
Fidelity Japan	Japan	DCP	10.0%
Foresight Environmental Infrastructure	Renewable Energy Infrastructure	DCP	10.0%
Foresight Solar Fund	Renewable Energy Infrastructure	DCP	10.0%
Greencoat Renewables	Renewable Energy Infrastructure	DCP	10.0%
Impax Environmental Markets	Environmental	DCP	10.0%
Invesco Asia Dragon	Asia Pacific Equity Income	DCP	10.0%
Invesco Global Equity Income	Global Equity Income	DCP	10.0%
JPMorgan European Growth & Income	Europe	DCP	10.0%
Montanaro European Smaller Companies	European Smaller Companies	DCP	10.0%
Renewables Infrastructure Group	Renewable Energy Infrastructure	DCP	10.0%
Rights & Issues	UK Smaller Companies	DCP	10.0%
Schroder AsiaPacific	Asia Pacific	DCP	10.0%
Value and Indexed Property Income	Property - UK Commercial	DCP	10.0%

Source: AIC, data to 30/09/2025.

Number of investment trusts repurchasing shares

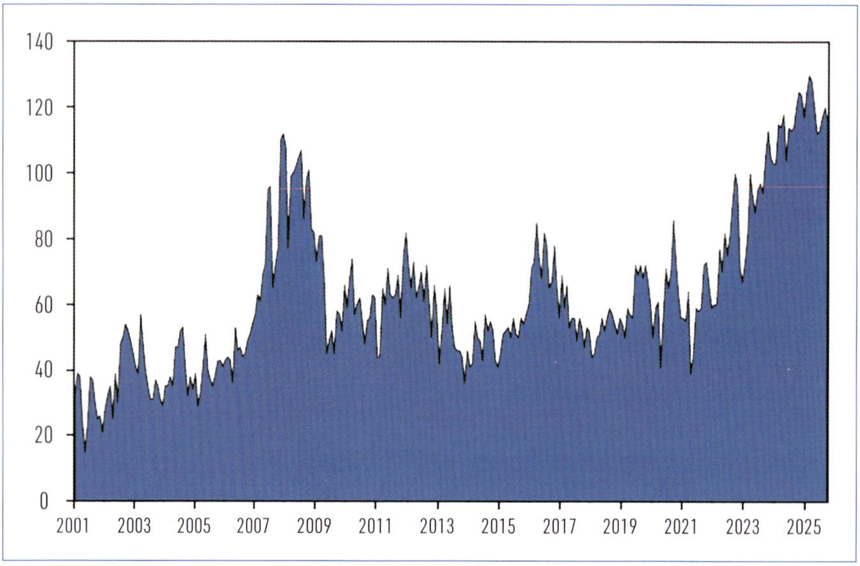

Source: Winterflood Securities/Morningstar as at 30 September 2025.

A significant minority of investment trusts have formally adopted discount control policies designed to reassure shareholders that they will not allow the discount on the trust's shares to widen beyond a certain threshold. The targets vary from zero to 15%; and while some are firm commitments, others are more loosely worded to give boards some discretion to do nothing in 'abnormal' market conditions.

This table lists the most important trusts that according to the Association for Investment Companies have identified a target discount level at which they will take some action. It is important to note that the conditions attached to each commitment vary a lot, so it is always worth checking the specific details by referring to company factsheets, websites and published reports.

The most common commitment is to buy back shares when discounts breach the target. A commitment to make a tender offer allowing shareholders to sell shares close to net asset value at a certain date is another method. Some boards agree to offer shareholders the chance to vote on whether a trust should continue or be wound up if performance falls below a certain target.

For shareholders, the knowledge that discounts will not be allowed to become too wide can be an important positive factor in deciding whether to invest. It is worth looking for details of any such policy when researching a possible investment. The widespread derating of trusts has put the strength of a number of boards' commitments under the spotlight.

More than 50 investment companies now have measures in place with which they attempt to control a specific level of discount and/or reduce discount volatility. The measures include buying back shares in the market, making tender or redemption offers at periodic intervals (enabling those who wish to sell a chance to tender at least a proportion of their shares at a price close to NAV) and agreeing to hold a continuation vote at some date in the future, which if lost can lead to capital being returned or even a winding up.

It is fairly routine for investment companies to adopt the power to buy back their own shares. This requires shareholder approval at a general meeting and more than two-thirds of the companies in the sector have obtained this approval. In 1999 it became possible for investment companies to hold shares they have bought back 'in treasury', meaning they can be retained without being cancelled and so can be reissued later if and when demand for the shares has grown again.

The table shows those trusts which have committed to taking action on discounts of some kind, starting with those with the narrowest targets, trusts that are pursuing a so-called zero discount policy. It is always worth checking out a trust's discount policy and noting how well it is being observed.

Enhanced income trusts

COMPANY NAME	TICKER	CURRENT YIELD (%)	DISCOUNT (%)	MARKET CAP (£M)	TARGET % NAV P.A	PERIOD
Gore Street Energy Storage	GSF	13.5	-50.0	262	7.0%	Q
Volta Finance	VTA	9.0	-7.5	221	8.0%	Q
Partners Group Private Equity	PEY	6.9	-25.9	622	5.0%	S
Montanaro UK Smaller Companies	MTU	6.7	-11.0	125	6.0%	Q
Dunedin Income Growth	DIG	6.6	-9.1	358	6.0%	Q
CT Private Equity	CTPE	6.0	-30.6	335	4.0%	Q
European Assets	EAT	5.9	-6.8	336	6.0%	Q
JPMorgan Asia Growth & Income	JAGI	5.2	-8.8	296	6.0%	Q
BlackRock Latin American	BRLA	5.2	-10.1	111	5.0%	Q
BlackRock American Income	BRAI	4.8	-4.1	120	6.0%	Q
JPMorgan UK Small Cap Growth & Income	JUGI	4.6	-9.4	414	4.0%	Q
Bellevue Healthcare	BBH	4.6	-2.9	140	3.5%	S
JPMorgan India Growth & Income	JII	4.3	-9.0	458	4.0%	Q
Temple Bar	TMPL	4.2	0.8	1,016	5.0%	Q
Artemis UK Future Leaders	AFL	4.0	-14.5	113	4.0%	A
JPMorgan Global Growth & Income	JGGI	4.0	-2.5	3,303	4.0%	Q
Schroder Japan	SJG	4.0	-10.6	331	4.0%	Q
Ecofin Global Utilities and Infrastructure	EGL	3.9	-10.7	228	4.0%	Q
Invesco Asia Dragon	IAD	3.9	-7.8	827	4.0%	Q
JPMorgan European Growth & Income	JEGI	3.7	-2.5	542	4.0%	Q
International Biotechnology	IBT	3.7	-10.8	254	4.0%	S
Invesco Global Equity Income	IGET	3.7	1.5	258	4.0%	Q
JPMorgan China Growth & Income	JCGI	3.6	-9.4	254	4.0%	Q
BlackRock Energy and Resource Income	BERI	3.5	-7.7	152	4.0%	Q
Majedie	MAJE	3.2	-12.0	137	3.0%	Q
JPMorgan Emerging Markets	JMG	1.6	-8.4	1,265	4.0%	Q
JPMorgan Emerging Markets	1.6	−8.4	1,265	Semi-annually		

Source: AIC (as at 30 September 2025). Key: A annual, S semi-annual, Q quarterly.

A small number of investment trusts have adopted a policy known as 'enhanced income' in recent years. In essence this means that they aim to pay out a fixed percentage of their net asset value each year as a dividend, whatever the NAV turns out to be. Typically this figure is around 4%. J.P. Morgan Asset Management is the fund management company most closely associated with this policy. Seven of the 16 trusts it manages have a policy of this kind.

The origins of this practice date back to 2012, when it was decided to give investment trusts the flexibility to pay dividends out of any retained capital profits, not just from current-year income and revenue reserves. To do this, a trust's articles of association need to be amended to give the directors power to make such distributions, with at least 75% approval in a shareholder vote.

Some well-known trusts, including Personal Assets (PNL) and RIT Capital Partners (RCP), have taken this route. However, a number have gone a little further by embracing what is called the enhanced income concept. Rather than just using capital profits to support a progressive dividend policy, they try to appeal to income-seeking investors by saying they will pay a fixed percentage of their NAV each year.

This means shareholders get the reassurance of knowing what the next year's annual payout rate will be, even if the amount of the dividend itself is not known, as that will depend on what the NAV turns out to be. With the rates on savings accounts having been pitiful (until recently), an enhanced income policy can broaden the appeal of a trust to income-focused investors while the extra demand for its shares can help narrow its discount.

The table lists those trusts which have adopted a fixed rate for determining their future dividend payments. These 27 trusts are still a small minority in the investment trust sector, but there are some sizeable trusts in the list. JPMorgan Global Growth & Income (JGGI) is the largest, followed by Bellevue Healthcare (BBH). It is a mixed bag, drawn from a wide range of sectors.

Few of these companies adopted this approach before 2016, so there was no rush towards it when the rules were relaxed in 2012. European Assets has had such a policy since 1999. It used to be a Dutch company, where different rules applied relating to distributions, and only migrated to the UK in 2019. BB Healthcare is the only trust on the list that adopted the enhanced dividend approach when it was first listed.

Almost all these trusts traded at discounts above 10% when they adopted the policy, clearly hoping the approach would allow them to stand out from their peer group. In most cases, the discount has since narrowed, although that could be for several reasons. Some of these trusts still trade on a double-digit discount, so it's certainly not a magic bullet, especially during periods in which gilts and cash offer more attractive yields.

Investment trusts vs open-ended funds

SECTORS	1 YEAR		5 YEARS		10 YEARS	
	INVESTMENT TRUSTS	OEIC/UNIT TRUSTS	INVESTMENT TRUSTS	OEIC/UNIT TRUSTS	INVESTMENT TRUSTS	OEIC/UNIT TRUSTS
Global	113.88	110.61	149.05	158.56	343.73	297.62
Global Equity Income	107.69	110.35	171.74	172.04	275.09	290.49
Flexible Investment	113.13	110.48	143.15	139.55	195.19	202.53
UK Equity Income	115	110.63	197.6	177.56	202.95	190.16
UK All Companies	113.89	109.28	179.57	159.32	205.04	191.79
North America	123.19	113.94	179.74	180.8	365.64	395.24
Europe vs. Europe ex UK	113.16	109.48	155.47	157.11	257.68	248.63
Global Emerging Markets	134.49	116.15	149.58	135.67	248.88	238.29
Asia Pacific vs Asia Pacific ex Japan	114.28	114.46	137.29	135.12	341.82	255.54
Japan	123.95	115.98	134.43	143.75	268.76	250.58
Property - UK Commercial vs. UK Direct Property	105.05	98.38	152.56	101.57	158.72	105.18
UK Smaller Companies	103.86	102.24	159.61	129.01	186.4	176.67
Technology and Technology Innovations	119.59	128.28	164.4	184.23	854.66	661.38
European Smaller Companies	121.52	112.86	155.92	134.6	305.47	235.78
North American Smaller Companies	97.62	105.09	135.22	150.22	235.57	288.35

Source: AIC/Morningstar. Investment trust data is unweighted share price total return. OEIC/unit trust data is unweighted total return.

It is not uncommon for the investment managers of trusts to manage other funds outside the investment trust sector at the same time. In fact, a number of fund managers start their careers managing different kinds of funds (typically unit trusts and OEICs, though also hedge funds) and if successful are encouraged to take over or start an investment trust with a broadly similar investment objective.

Adding an investment trust to their responsibilities gives successful fund managers the opportunity to take advantage of the benefits of the investment trust structure, including the use of gearing and freedom from unhelpful forced selling as a result of fund flows. They can also use derivative securities such as futures and options for investment purposes.

These advantages show up regularly in comparisons between the long-term performance of investment trusts and that of open-ended funds with either the same manager or the same investment objective. Where trusts and similar funds can be directly compared in this way, trusts show up with superior performance records in most periods. Where a trust and an open-ended fund with the same mandate are managed by the same individual, it is rare for the trust not to do better over the longer term.

The degree to which comparable trusts outperform does vary markedly, however, from sector to sector and is not true every year. The table summarises the difference in the performance of directly comparable trust and open-ended equivalent sectors at 30 September 2025. The red-shaded cells show the periods over which trusts in each sector have outperformed, the blue cells when they have underperformed. The majority of sectors are once again outperforming open-ended equivalents now that discounts have begun to stabilise.

It is fair to point out that such simple comparisons can be criticised by statisticians on the grounds that the two samples are very different in size and also may display what is called survivorship bias. In 2018 academics at Cass Business School in London reported that a detailed analysis of investment trust returns between 2000 and 2016 appeared to support their superior performance. However, the study has now been abandoned because of 'data issues', principally the sample size and survivorship bias problems.

Skin in the game

Room for improvement – value of board's aggregate investment expressed as a number of day's fees

COMPANY	AGGREGATE BOARD FEES (£)	AGGREGATE BOARD SHAREHOLDING (£)	AGGREGATE BOARD SHAREHOLDING EXPRESSED AS DAYS FEES (GROSS)	AVERAGE BOARD MEMBER TENURE (YEARS)
JPMorgan Emerging Europe, Middle East & Africa Securities	139,000	6,250	16	2.0
HyrdrogenOne Capital Growth	173,250	12,561	26	2.8
Aquila Energy Efficiency	336,992	24,590	27	3.5
Ecofin US Renewables Infrastructure	165,000	17,029	38	3.7
Fair Oaks Income	138,000	15,708	42	5.3
GCP Asset Backed Income	190,125	27,922	54	5.7
CT UK Capital & Income	173,250	33,513	71	2.0
Schroder European Real Estate	135,000	26,693	72	5.3
Life Science REIT	180,000	43,147	87	3.8
Chelverton UK Dividend	77,000	22,048	105	8.0
Riverstone Energy	465,850	134,695	106	5.4
NB Distressed Debt	146,498	47,724	119	11.5
Premier Miton Global Renewables	84,700	28,470	123	7.3
Social Housing REIT	325,000	119,657	134	5.5
Schroder British Opportunities	155,500	57,592	135	3.0
Foresight Environmental Infrastructure	300,500	117,555	143	3.6
Target Healthcare REIT	227,250	90,204	145	3.4
Harmony Energy Income	244,100	97,274	145	4.0
US Solar	211,365	85,816	148	4.5
Starwood European Real Estate Finance	197,000	81,515	151	6.5
AEW UK REIT	133,000	58,626	161	3.8
RM Infrastructure Income	112,371	50,037	163	9.0
Baillie Gifford European Growth	140,000	64,122	167	3.3
Syncona	561,000	264,664	172	4.6
Crystal Amber	130,000	63,750	179	9.0
NextEnergy Solar	298,000	146,511	179	2.6
JPMorgan US Smaller Companies	149,000	73,313	180	6.0

Source: Companies, Investic Equities analysis.

Chairs with no investment

COMPANY	DIRECTOR	APPOINTMENT	FEE (£)
Oryx International Growth	Nigel Cayzer	1994	32,500
New Star Investment	Geoffrey Howard-Spink	2000	30,000
Chelverton UK Dividend	Howard Myles	2011	30,000
Baker Steel Resources	Fiona Perrott-Humphrey	2020	42,500
Geiger Counter	Professor Ian Reeves CBE	2021	45,000
PRS REIT	Geeta Nanda OBE	2021	52,500
Alternative Income REIT	Simon Bennett	2022	42,000
Fair Oaks Income	Richard Burwood	2023	45,000
Ecofin US Renewables Infrastructure	Brett Miller	2024	55,000
Regional REIT	David Hunter	2025	77,000

Source: Companies, Investic Equities analysis.

Multiple directorships – directors with four investment company directorships

DIRECTORSHIPS (CHAIR)	NAME	DIRECTORSHIPS
4 (3)	David Barron	Baillie Gifford European Growth (BGEU.L), BlackRock American Income (BRAI.L), Dunedin Income Growth (DIG.L), Fidelity Japan (FJV.L)
4 (2)	Andrew Watkins	Ashoka India Equity (AIE.L), Baillie Gifford European Growth (BGEU.L), Chelverton UK Dividend (SDV.L), CT High Income (CHI.L)
4 (1)	June Aitken	BBGI Global Infrastructure (BBGI.L), CC Japan Income & Growth (CCJI.L), JPMorgan Asia Growth & Income (JAGI.L), Schroder Income Growth (SCF.L)
4 (1)	Claire Boyle	Fidelity Special Values (FSV.L), Life Science REIT (LABS.L), Monks (MNKS.L), Nippon Active Value (NAVF.L)
4 (1)	Kate Cornish-Bowden	CC Japan Income & Growth (CCJI.L), European Assets (EAT.L), Finsbury Growth & Income (FGT.L), International Biotechnology (IBT.L)
4 (1)	Sue Inglis	Baillie Gifford US Growth (USA.L), CT Global Managed Portfolio Growth/ Income (CMPG.L/CMPI.L), Invesco Global Equity Income (IGET.L), Seraphim Space (SSIT.L)
4 (1)	Sarah MacAulay	Baillie Gifford China Growth (BGCG.L), Bellevue Healthcare (BBH.L), Fidelity Japan (FJV.L), Schroder Asian Total Return (ATR.L)
4 (1)	Christopher Metcalfe	CT UK Capital & Income Investment (CTUK.L), Franklin Global (FRGT.L), Herald (HRI.L), JPMorgan US Smaller Companies (JUSC.L)
4 (0)	Helena Coles	HgCapital (HGT.L), JPMorgan Emerging Markets (JMG.L), RIT Capital Partners (RCP.L), Schroder Japan (SJG.L)
4 (0)	Stephanie Eastment	Alternative Income REIT (AIRE.L), Herald (HRI.L), Impax Environmental Markets (IEM.L), Murray Income (MUT.L)
4 (0)	Paul Le Page	NextEnergy Solar (NESF.L), RTW Biotech Opportunities (RTW.L), Sequoia Economic Infrastructure Income (SEQI.L), TwentyFour Income (TFIF.L)
4 (0)	Mark Little	abrdn Equity Income (AEI.L), BlackRock Smaller Companies (BRSC.L), Fidelity Emerging Markets (FEML.L), Majedie (MAJE.L)
4 (0)	Abigail Rotheroe	Baillie Gifford Shin Nippon (BGS.L), Greencoat UK Wind (UKW.L), HydrogenOne Capital Growth (HGEN.L), Templeton Emerging Markets (TEM.L)

Source: Companies, Investic Equities analysis.

Earlier this year Alan Brierley, the experienced and widely followed lead investment trust analyst at Investec Securities, published his latest 'Skin in the Game' report, summarising the extent to which directors of trusts have shareholdings in the trusts whose boards they sit on. This year's report is the seventh to have appeared since 2010.

While directors' interests are always publicly available, it is unfortunately less easy to discover how much the managers of a trust's portfolio have invested themselves, unless it exceeds a 3% holding of the issued shares. A number of managers choose to disclose, but the majority do not unless required to do so, a finding that is described in the report as 'frustrating'.

There is no legal requirement for directors to own shares in their trusts, but they are typically encouraged to do so, to help demonstrate that their interests are aligned with the shareholders, if only to a modest extent. In practice, there is considerable divergence across the sector in how far boards and management teams go when it comes to having 'skin in the game'.

Introducing the report in May, Brierley noted that 'with discounts stressed and close to levels last seen during the global financial crisis, this alignment of interest is even more important in helping to underpin investor confidence'. It is therefore encouraging, he says, that having a shareholding has become an accepted norm for directors, in marked contrast to his findings in the first survey back in 2010.

He also concludes that the industry's efforts to achieve greater gender balance on boards has made good progress too, with 44% of all trust directorships now being held by women and 72% of boards meeting the industry target of having at least 40% female representation. Roughly two-thirds of boards also now have at least one person from a minority ethnic background as a director.

Looking more closely at the detail, there are some 25 boards where we do know that the management team collectively has a holding of more than £20m in their trusts. Another 15 have combined holdings of more than £10m. Anecdotally there is some evidence that, if they run both, fund managers given the choice are likely to put more of their own money in the investment trust they run, rather than the open-ended equivalent.

This year I include a table of those trusts where director shareholdings leave 'room for improvement', according to Investec. By this is meant that the aggregate amount owned by the board amounts to less than the value of their annual directors' fees. I have added the ten trusts where the chairs of the trust have no investment at all. The chart shows the number of boards that individual directors sit on; around a quarter sit on either three or four.

Who owns investment trusts?

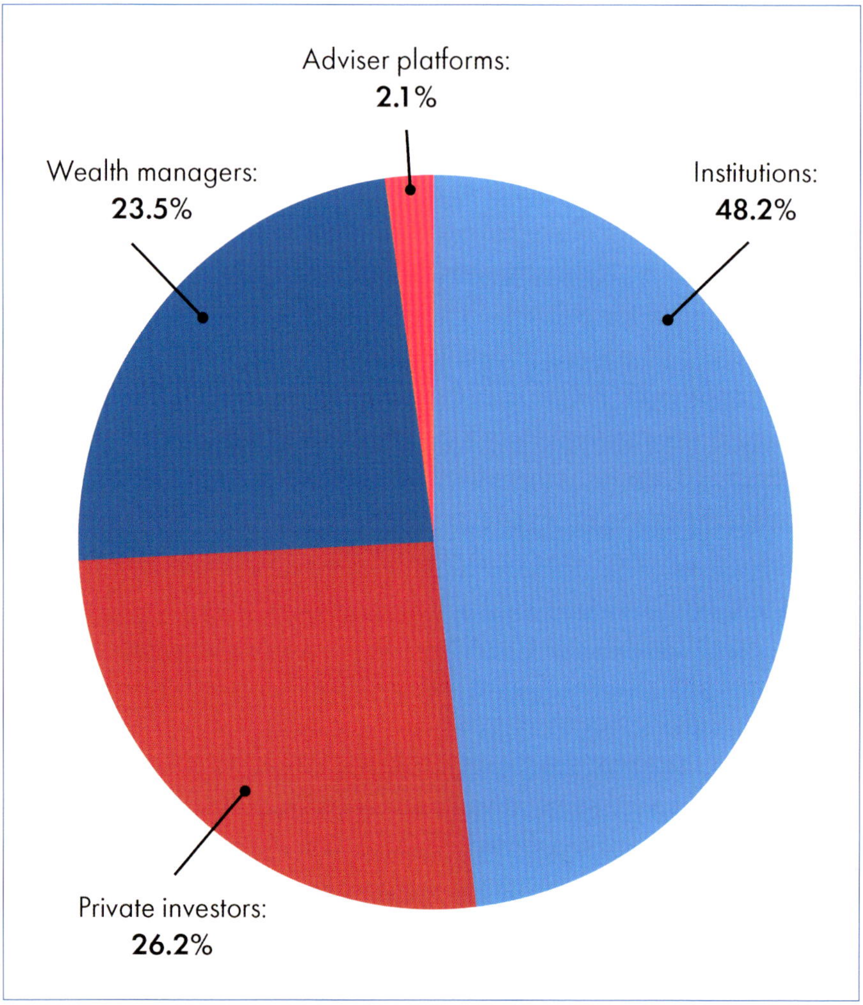

Private investors are becoming an ever more important market for investment trusts. Research by two specialist share register analysis and marketing firms (Richard Davies IR and Warhorse Partners) shows how the proportion of shares in investment trusts held by private investors has been rising over the past decade, thanks in part to the big platforms such as Hargreaves Lansdown, Interactive Investor and AJ Bell. The trend is slow and steady rather than dramatic, but evident nonetheless.

It is strongest in the traditional equity sectors of the universe, where few big institutions such as pension funds and insurance companies remain shareholders. They mostly now manage their investment portfolios directly themselves or by hiring the services of specialist fund managers on bespoke terms. The trend is somewhat less marked in the alternative asset classes.

The wealth management industry, traditionally the biggest buyer of investment trusts since the institutions departed, has meanwhile been consolidating and for a variety of reasons is no longer relying on investment trusts as mainstays of their client portfolios as much as they did.

Another survey by Warhorse and Dianomi in 2022 revealed more about the private investor market for investment trusts. Investment trusts are predominantly owned by older investors; 80% are aged 51 or older. This group has the time to conduct research before investing and typically carefully research and review their investments.

They use a wide range of online and traditional sources of information, tuned to their individual preferences and needs. Half of investors use online platforms, such as Interactive Investor and Hargreaves Lansdown. Around 40% also use third-party websites, such as Trustnet and Morningstar, and read coverage in the national press, for example, the *Telegraph*, the *Times* and the *Mail on Sunday*. Older investors are typically less reliant on social media than younger investors.

Holdings vary significantly among investors. Half of investors have investment holdings valued at less than £250,000. However, over 30% have holdings between £250,000 and £2m. Most investors have multiple holdings of investment trusts. A quarter have 11 or more. Investment diversification is clearly a consideration in decision-making.

Fees

Highest to lowest

COMPANY NAME	AIC SECTOR
Regional REIT	Property - UK Commercial
Alternative Liquidity	Hedge Funds
Life Settlement Assets	Insurance & Reinsurance Strategies
Fuel Ventures	VCT
JPMorgan Emerging Europe, Middle East & Africa	Global Emerging Markets
Aquila Energy Efficiency	Renewable Energy Infrastructure
Puma Alpha	VCT
JPEL Private Equity	Private Equity
Foresight Technology FWT shares	VCT
Sure Ventures	Technology & Technology Innovation
Blackfinch Spring	VCT
Athelney	UK Smaller Companies
Maven Income and Growth 3	VCT
Maven Income and Growth 4	VCT
Octopus Future Generations	VCT
Onward Opportunities	UK Smaller Companies
Triple Point Venture Venture shares	VCT
VietNam Holding	Country Specialist
Oakley Capital	Private Equity
UIL	Flexible Investment
abrdn Property Income	Property - UK Commercial
Chelverton UK Dividend	UK Equity Income
Schroder Real Estate	Property - UK Commercial
Develop North	Property - Debt
Schroder European Real Estate	Property - Europe
Maven Income and Growth	VCT
Hydrogen Capital Growth	Renewable Energy Infrastructure
ProVen Growth and Income	VCT
Riverstone Energy	Commodities & Natural Resources
Molten Ventures	VCT
Puma 13	VCT
Foresight Ventures	VCT
Octopus Titan	VCT
Albion Technology & General	VCT
Albion Enterprise	VCT
Hargreave Hale AIM	VCT AIM Quoted
ProVen	VCT
Octopus Apollo	VCT
Octopus AIM 2	VCT AIM Quoted
JZ Capital Partners	Private Equity
Northern Venture	VCT
abrdn Diversified Income and Growth	Flexible Investment
Riverstone Credit Opportunities Income	Debt - Direct Lending
Maven Income and Growth 5	VCT
Octopus AIM	VCT AIM Quoted
Gresham House Income & Growth	VCT
Ecofin US Renewables Infrastructure	Renewable Energy Infrastructure

TICKER	ONGOING CHARGE %	ONGOING CHARGE DATE	NET ASSETS (£M)
RGL	9.30%	31/12/2024	338
ALF	6.75%	30/06/2024	8
LSAA	5.00%	31/12/2024	75
FVV	4.41%	31/03/2025	11
JEMA	4.17%	31/10/2024	26
AEET	3.80%	31/12/2024	41
PUAL	3.50%	28/02/2025	33
JPEL	3.40%	30/06/2024	23
FWT	3.30%	31/03/2025	41
SURE	3.26%	31/03/2025	13
BFSP	3.19%	31/12/2024	65
ATY	3.13%	31/12/2024	4
MIG3	3.13%	30/11/2024	64
MAV4	3.00%	31/12/2024	83
OFG	3.00%	31/12/2024	49
ONWD	3.00%	31/12/2024	29
TPV	2.98%	28/02/2025	92
VNH	2.97%	30/06/2024	101
OCI	2.87%	31/12/2024	1,268
UTL	2.80%	30/06/2024	199
API	2.80%	31/12/2024	35
SDV	2.79%	30/04/2025	33
SREI	2.70%	31/03/2025	320
DVNO	2.70%	30/11/2024	20
SERE	2.59%	30/09/2024	132
MIG1	2.57%	28/02/2025	67
HGEN	2.53%	31/12/2024	115
PGOO	2.50%	28/02/2025	158
RSE	2.50%	31/12/2024	271
MVCT	2.50%	31/03/2025	119
PU13	2.50%	28/02/2025	203
FVEN	2.50%	31/03/2025	94
OTV2	2.50%	31/12/2024	803
AATG	2.46%	31/12/2024	272
AAEV	2.44%	31/03/2025	273
HHV	2.43%	30/09/2024	132
PVN	2.40%	28/02/2025	175
OAP3	2.40%	31/01/2025	528
OSEC	2.40%	30/11/2024	81
JZCP	2.39%	28/02/2025	180
NVT	2.39%	31/03/2025	130
ADIG	2.36%	30/09/2024	181
RCOI	2.35%	31/12/2024	33
MIG5	2.33%	30/11/2024	70
OOA	2.30%	28/02/2025	114
GHV1	2.30%	30/09/2024	219
RNEW	2.30%	31/12/2024	42

COMPANY NAME	AIC SECTOR
Unicorn AIM	VCT AIM Quoted
Northern 2	VCT
Foresight Enterprise	VCT
Gresham House Income & Growth 2	VCT
NB Distressed Debt New Global shares	Debt - Loans & Bonds
Real Estate Credit	Property - Debt
Albion Crown	VCT
Pershing Square Holdings	North America
Golden Prospect Precious Metals	Commodities & Natural Resources
Oxford Technology 2 - OT2 shares	VCT
Northern 3	VCT
Foresight	VCT
CT Global Managed Portfolio Income	Flexible Investment
Maven Renovar	VCT AIM Quoted
Premier Miton Global Renewables	Infrastructure Securities
Literacy Capital	Private Equity
CT Global Managed Portfolio Growth	Flexible Investment
HarbourVest Global Private Equity	Private Equity
Gabelli Merchant Partners	Hedge Funds
The Investment Company	UK Smaller Companies
Weiss Korea Opportunity	Country Specialist
Augmentum Fintech	Financials & Financial Innovation
abrdn European Logistics Income	Property - Europe

Source: AIC/Morningstar, data to 30/09/25.

The costs that investors have to pay for the privilege of having their investments managed by an investment company is a surprisingly important factor in determining the returns that they obtain. It is standard practice for a fund management firm to charge an annual management fee that is expressed as a percentage, typically somewhere between 0.3% and 2.0% of the amount of the money they look after.

As a result, other things being equal, the larger the trust, the greater a fee the firm will earn, creating an incentive for the management firm to grow the size of the trust. In a rising market, the management firm also benefits from rising fee income even if they fail to outperform the fund's benchmark.

Deceptively modest percentage fees can quickly become big business; a trust with £500m of assets paying a management fee of 0.6% per annum will earn the manager £3m every year for its services, in addition to other administrative expenses, such as accountancy and legal fees. Some fund managers also charge a performance fee, an extra fee that is only paid if the trust beats a given target.

Given that only a minority of fund managers can consistently outperform a benchmark or passive fund equivalent, and the best rarely beat either by 2% per annum over time, the overall annual cost of owning any kind of investment fund can make a huge difference in determining value for money. Regulators have expended a huge amount of time and effort in trying to develop a standardised measure that will allow investors to compare the cost of competing funds.

TICKER	ONGOING CHARGE %	ONGOING CHARGE DATE	NET ASSETS (£M)
UAV	2.30%	30/09/2024	193
NTV	2.30%	31/03/2025	136
FTF	2.30%	31/12/2024	155
GHV2	2.29%	30/09/2024	170
NBDG	2.28%	31/12/2024	11
RECI	2.24%	31/03/2025	315
CRWN	2.24%	30/06/2024	121
PSH	2.22%	31/12/2024	11,522
GPM	2.20%	31/12/2024	98
OXH	2.20%	28/02/2025	1
NTN	2.20%	31/03/2025	130
FTV	2.20%	31/12/2024	215
CMPI	2.17%	31/05/2025	65
MRV	2.10%	31/01/2025	97
PMGR	2.06%	31/12/2024	21
BOOK	2.03%	31/12/2024	312
CMPG	2.02%	31/05/2025	97
HVPE	2.02%	31/01/2025	3,116
GMP	2.01%	30/06/2024	54
INV	2.00%	30/06/2025	7
WKOF	2.00%	31/12/2024	42
AUGM	2.00%	31/03/2025	270
ASLI	2.00%	31/12/2024	183

Many firms these days charge tiered fees, meaning the percentage annual management fee declines once the size of a trust reaches a threshold. The table lists trusts with the highest 'ongoing charge ratios' (a mandatory standard industry measure that has been in place for several years and adds other costs to the management fee) expressed as a percentage. It is unfortunately an imperfect measure.

Note that the table excludes most alternative asset trusts. The issue of how fees should be calculated and reported following the introduction of new regulations by the Financial Conduct Authority has been a contentious issue for several years. Open-ended funds (unit trusts and OEICs) are not subject to the same disclosure requirements, and many in the investment trust business feel that trusts were discriminated against. This has led to some wealth managers refusing to invest in certain trusts and some platforms refusing to list trusts on the grounds that their reported costs were too high.

The Treasury announced in October 2024 that investment companies will no longer have to disclose costs in the previously mandated way. However the final details of what exactly investment companies will be required to disclose about their expenses will not be known until a new fund regulatory regime is introduced. This has been promised by the end of 2025.

Lowest to highest

COMPANY NAME	AIC SECTOR
Scottish Mortgage	Global
JPMorgan American	North America
City of London	UK Equity Income
Monks	Global
JPMorgan Global Growth & Income	Global Equity Income
F&C	Global
Henderson Smaller Companies	UK Smaller Companies
Aurora UK Alpha	UK All Companies
Fair Oaks Income 2021	Debt - Structured Finance
Mercantile	UK All Companies
Ashoka India Equity	India/Indian Subcontinent
Murray Income	UK Equity Income
Bankers	Global
Edinburgh	UK Equity Income
Law Debenture Corporation	UK Equity Income
Merchants	UK Equity Income
Murray International	Global Equity Income
Castelnau Group	Flexible Investment
Dunedin Income Growth	UK Equity Income
Capital Gearing	Flexible Investment
Alliance Witan	Global
BlackRock Throgmorton	UK Smaller Companies
Scottish American	Global Equity Income
Finsbury Growth & Income	UK Equity Income
Temple Bar	UK Equity Income
Brunner	Global
JPMorgan Claverhouse	UK Equity Income
Mid Wynd International	Global
JPMorgan UK Small Cap Growth & Income	UK Smaller Companies
Allianz Technology	Technology & Technology Innovation
Baillie Gifford European Growth	Europe
Franklin Global	Global
JPMorgan European Growth & Income	Europe
Lowland	UK Equity Income
JPMorgan Global Core Real Assets	Flexible Investment
CT UK Capital & Income	UK Equity Income
The European Smaller Companies	European Smaller Companies
Personal Assets	Flexible Investment
Global Opportunities	Flexible Investment
Baillie Gifford Japan	Japan
Fidelity Special Values	UK All Companies
Baillie Gifford UK Growth	UK All Companies
Baillie Gifford US Growth	North America

Source: AIC/Morningstar, data to 30/09/25.

TICKER	ONGOING CHARGE %	ONGOING CHARGE DATE	NET ASSETS (£M)
SMT	0.31%	31/03/2025	13,885
JAM	0.35%	31/12/2024	1,967
CTY	0.36%	30/06/2025	2,449
MNKS	0.43%	30/04/2025	2,648
JGGI	0.43%	30/06/2024	3,367
FCIT	0.45%	31/12/2024	6,036
HSL	0.45%	31/05/2025	600
ARR	0.45%	31/12/2024	314
FAIR	0.46%	31/12/2024	162
MRC	0.48%	31/01/2025	1,905
AIE	0.50%	30/06/2024	456
MUT	0.50%	30/06/2024	928
BNKR	0.51%	31/10/2024	1,391
EDIN	0.51%	31/03/2025	1,163
LWDB	0.51%	31/12/2024	1,392
MRCH	0.52%	31/01/2025	880
MYI	0.52%	31/12/2024	1,821
CGL	0.53%	31/12/2024	338
DIG	0.56%	31/01/2025	387
CGT	0.56%	31/03/2025	822
ALW	0.56%	31/12/2024	5,104
THRG	0.56%	30/11/2024	504
SAIN	0.58%	31/12/2024	911
FGT	0.61%	30/09/2024	1,228
TMPL	0.61%	31/12/2024	994
BUT	0.63%	30/11/2024	638
JCH	0.63%	31/12/2024	465
MWY	0.64%	30/06/2025	279
JUGI	0.64%	31/07/2024	458
ATT	0.64%	31/12/2024	2,027
BGEU	0.65%	30/09/2024	353
FRGT	0.65%	31/01/2025	191
JEGI	0.66%	31/03/2025	553
LWI	0.66%	30/09/2024	361
JARA	0.67%	28/02/2025	71
CTUK	0.67%	30/09/2024	336
ESCT	0.67%	30/06/2024	519
PNL	0.67%	30/04/2025	1,634
GOT	0.68%	31/12/2024	117
BGFD	0.69%	31/08/2024	801
FSV	0.70%	31/08/2024	1,294
BGUK	0.71%	30/04/2025	270
USA	0.72%	31/05/2025	828

Fees charged on market cap

COMPANY NAME	AIC SECTOR	TICKER
abrdn Asia Focus	Asia Pacific Smaller Companies	AAS
Alliance Witan	Global	ALW
Allianz Technology	Technology & Technology Innovation	ATT
AVI Japan Opportunity	Japanese Smaller Companies	AJOT
Baillie Gifford European Growth	Europe	BGEU
Baker Steel Resources	Commodities & Natural Resources	BSRT
Bellevue Healthcare	Biotechnology & Healthcare	BBH
Biotech Growth	Biotechnology & Healthcare	BIOG
BlackRock Income & Growth	UK Equity Income	BRIG
Brown Advisory US Smaller Companies	North American Smaller Companies	BASC
Cordiant Digital Infrastructure	Infrastructure	CORD
Diverse Income	UK Equity Income	DIVI
Ecofin US Renewables Infrastructure	Renewable Energy Infrastructure	RNEW
Edinburgh	UK Equity Income	EDIN
F&C	Global	FCIT
Finsbury Growth & Income	UK Equity Income	FGT
Foresight Environmental Infrastructure	Renewable Energy Infrastructure	FGEN
Foresight Solar	Renewable Energy Infrastructure	FSFL
Greencoat Renewables	Renewable Energy Infrastructure	GRP
Greencoat UK Wind	Renewable Energy Infrastructure	UKW
Gresham House Energy Storage	Renewable Energy Infrastructure	GRID
India Capital Growth	India/Indian Subcontinent	IGC
JPMorgan Asia Growth & Income	Asia Pacific Equity Income	JAGI
JPMorgan Indian	India/Indian Subcontinent	JII
Lindsell Train	Global	LTI
Majedie	Flexible Investment	MAJE
Mercantile	UK All Companies	MRC
MIGO Opportunities	Flexible Investment	MIGO
Mobius	Global Emerging Markets	MMIT
Montanaro European Smaller Companies	European Smaller Companies	MTE
Octopus Renewables Infrastructure	Renewable Energy Infrastructure	ORIT
Odyssean	UK Smaller Companies	OIT
Pacific Assets	Asia Pacific	PAC
Polar Capital Global Healthcare	Biotechnology & Healthcare	PCGH
Renewables Infrastructure Group	Renewable Energy Infrastructure	TRIG
Residential Secure Income REIT	Property - UK Residential	RESI
Schroder UK Mid Cap	UK All Companies	SCP
Schroders Capital Global Innovation	Growth Capital	INOV
Sequoia Economic Infrastructure Income	Infrastructure	SEQI
Social Housing REIT	Property - UK Residential	SOHO
TwentyFour Income	Debt - Structured Finance	TFIF
TwentyFour Select Monthly Income	Debt - Loans & Bonds	SMIF
Warehouse REIT	Property - UK Logistics	WHR

Source: AIC/Morningstar, data to 30/09/25.

A separate issue is how management fees should be calculated. The historical norm has been as a percentage of net asset value. Fund managers argue that their job is to maximise the NAV while it is up to boards to manage the discount, so they think using NAV is reasonable.

The alternative argument is that shareholders and managers should experience the same impact when discounts move, gaining when the shares are at a premium but losing when the discount widens. In theory that should create a greater alignment of interest.

The latter argument is gaining traction. The table opposite lists the growing number of trusts, now more than 10% of the total, whose boards have negotiated fees that are based either on market capitalisation, or whichever is the lower of market capitalisation or net asset value.

Overall the trend in management fees has been down in recent years, and that has continued recently, as the table below shows. Performance fees have become less popular, and a number of trusts have either reduced their base fee or agreed to tier them, so that the percentage fee charged by the management company reduces as the size of the company increases.

Fee changes

FEE AREA	ACTION	2018	2019	2020	2021	2022	2023	2024	2025 YTD
Base fee change	Reduced	41	38	31	23	12	11	19	27
Performance fee change	Reduced	5	1	4	2	2	2	1	0
Performance fee change	Removed	9	4	6	4	3	2	1	3
Tiered fee change	Introduced	16	6	9	10	4	8	5	5
Tiered fee change	Reduced	10	16	11	7	9	10	15	8
	Total changes	43	41	39	31	23	34	39	51

Source: AIC, to 30/09/2025.

Please note: duplication means that the number of occurences in each category will not add up to the 'total changes'.

Platform costs

PLATFORM	£5,000	£15,000
AJ Bell Youinvest	0.65%	0.38%
Aviva Consumer Platform	0.75%	0.48%
Barclays	0.73%	0.41%
Bestinvest	0.80%	0.53%
Charles Stanley Direct	1.20%	0.40%
Fidelity Personal Investing	2.40%	0.80%
Freetrade	1.20%	0.40%
Halifax Share Dealing	1.48%	0.49%
Hargreaves Lansdown	1.41%	0.62%
iDealing	0.88%	0.29%
IG	2.56%	0.85%
interactive investor - Investor Plan	2.88%	0.96%
iWeb	0.40%	0.13%
Trinity Bridge	0.97%	0.49%
Willis Owen	1.00%	0.60%

Source: AIC/the lang cat consultancy, data as at 30/09/2025.

How much does it cost to hold shares in investment trusts on a private investor platform? The table gives an illustrative estimate for most of the largest platforms. The costs are shown as an annual percentage of the value of your portfolio, based on the amount you have invested. The data is collected by the Lang Cat consultancy and published on the AIC website. It is a valuable source of information, albeit with some important caveats.

It is important to note that your investment is assumed to be within an ISA tax wrapper. The figures shown only include ongoing platform fees, additional wrapper charges (if any) and trading charges (where applicable). Other charges, for example the management charges of the investment companies themselves,

	£25,000	£50,000	£100,000	£250,000	£500,000	£1,000,000
	0.25%	0.12%	0.06%	0.02%	0.01%	0.01%
	0.43%	0.39%	0.37%	0.36%	0.35%	0.18%
	0.35%	0.30%	0.27%	0.22%	0.13%	0.09%
	0.48%	0.44%	0.42%	0.41%	0.30%	0.20%
	0.30%	0.30%	0.30%	0.24%	0.12%	0.06%
	0.47%	0.24%	0.12%	0.05%	0.02%	0.01%
	0.24%	0.12%	0.06%	0.02%	0.01%	0.01%
	0.30%	0.15%	0.07%	0.03%	0.01%	0.01%
	0.37%	0.19%	0.09%	0.04%	0.02%	0.01%
	0.18%	0.09%	0.04%	0.02%	0.01%	0.00%
	0.51%	0.26%	0.13%	0.05%	0.03%	0.01%
	0.58%	0.29%	0.14%	0.06%	0.03%	0.01%
	0.08%	0.04%	0.02%	0.01%	0.00%	0.00%
	0.39%	0.32%	0.29%	0.26%	0.26%	0.23%
	0.52%	0.46%	0.38%	0.27%	0.21%	0.18%

are excluded. The data is based on publicly available charging structure information, with some details verified in conversations with platforms.

This table assumes you only hold investment trusts on the platform. A separate table on the website shows how the figure varies if you also hold open-ended funds on the platform. Their platform charges are generally higher, though only for larger portfolios (£50,000 or more). Bear in mind however that charges are not the sole, or even the most important, criterion for choosing a platform. The quality of the service – the range of options, the quality of the research and how smoothly and efficiently the platform works – are every bit as relevant.

AIC website

The AIC has made a number of further improvements to its website, which remains an invaluable resource for private investors looking to research and compare investment trust options. In past editions of the *Handbook* I have highlighted the way that private investors can use the income finder tool to look for yield options and manage dividend payments consistently across the 12 months of the year.

This year I list some of the additional useful information that investors can find when researching investment ideas. The profile page for individual trusts remains the most visited element on the AIC website. As well as a snapshot of the trust chosen, there is an expanded number of tabs that provide more detailed information under a series of headings.

In addition to performance data and the charting function, these include documents (factsheets and the latest half year and annual reports), stock exchange announcements (which you can filter by type) and research from a range of research organisations (but remember that nearly all of this research is funded by the trusts themselves, so treat with care).

Another useful resource is the 'AGM and meetings' function. This allows you to see forthcoming company events, not just the date of the AGM, but also the dates of analyst or shareholder presentations by fund managers, and whether they are online or face to face. Imminent continuation votes, another important element in determining the future of individual trusts, are also listed.

In the example shown, from mid-October this year, you can see just how many events there are, with several scheduled each weekday on average. This illustration includes the European Assets meeting on 16 October 2025, at which shareholders were asked to approve the proposed liquidation and merger into the European Smaller Companies Trust.

Clicking on the little arrow which highlights that this is a liquidation/continuation vote will take you to another page that gives the detail of the meeting and a snapshot of the circular that outlines the main elements of the proposed deal, another helpful innovation. A further click will take you to another page that shows how you can vote if your shares are held on one of the larger platforms, such as Hargreaves Lansdown, AJ Bell or Interactive Investor.

At the moment the problem is that on most platforms, which hold your shares in a nominee account, you won't be automatically notified about forthcoming meetings, unless you opt in. (Interactive Investor is an honourable exception.) You may have to register in order to receive that information and then arrange to register your vote, which is often a quite cumbersome process.

Forthcoming events

Company	AIC sector	Financial year end	Next meeting	Meeting type	Location	Attendance details	Online availability	Continuation / liquidation vote
Investment Company	UK Smaller Companies	June	14/10/2025	AGM	London			
Octopus Titan VCT	VCT	December	14/10/2025	General meeting	London			
Schroder Japan Trust	Japan	July	14/10/2025	Shareholder presentation	Digital only		Online option available	
Target Healthcare REIT	Property - UK Healthcare	June	14/10/2025	Analyst presenation	Digital only		Online option available	
Aurora UK Alpha	UK All Companies	December	15/10/2025	Shareholder presentation	London			
European Assets Trust	European Smaller Companies	December	15/10/2025	General meeting	London			✓
River UK Micro Cap	UK Smaller Companies	September	15/10/2025	Shareholder presentation	Digital only		Online option available	
Crystal Amber Fund	UK Smaller Companies	June	16/10/2025	Shareholder presentation	Digital only		Online option available	
Mid Wynd International	Global	June	16/10/2025	AGM	Edinburgh			
Worldwide Healthcare Trust	Biotechnology & Healthcare	March	16/10/2025	Shareholder presentation	Digital only		Online option available	
Mobius Investment Trust	Global Emerging Markets	November	17/10/2025	Shareholder presentation	Digital only		Online option available	
TwentyFour Income Fund	Debt - Structured Finance	March	17/10/2025	AGM	Guernsey			
TwentyFour Income Fund	Debt - Structured Finance	March	17/10/2025	General meeting	Guernsey			
Seraphim Space Investment Trust	Growth Capital	June	20/10/2025	Analyst presentation	Digital only		Online option available	
Seraphim Space Investment Trust	Growth Capital	June	20/10/2025	Shareholder presentation	Digital only		Online option available	
Barings Emerging EMEA Opportunities	Global Emerging Markets	September	21/10/2025	General meeting	London		Online option available	

Source: AIC.

Following a successful lobbying campaign this year by the AIC and others in the industry, the government has however now pledged to force platforms to keep you informed and make it easier for you to vote your shares. This is one of the positive outcomes that can be attributed to Saba Capital's unwelcome attempt to oust the managers at seven trusts earlier this year. By keeping tabs on the meetings page, however, say once a month, you can quickly see for yourself if a trust you own is giving an update or having a crucial vote.

As mentioned last year, the income finder tool has now been merged with the old watchlist function to create a general portfolio and research management tool which allows you to track and analyse lists of trusts of any kind, not just ones you own for dividend income. Once you have created a watchlist or portfolio, you can view and edit your holdings, and see the value of your portfolios at the last market close.

If you have created a watchlist, you have the option to turn it into a portfolio by adding details of your holdings, entering either the number of shares you own or their value. It is possible to add a cash holding and see how that impacts the total. You can also see charts breaking down your portfolios by company or AIC sector.

This is not a fully-fledged portfolio analysis tool – there are more sophisticated commercial ones for which you have to pay a subscription fee that can run into hundreds of pounds per year – but it is accurate and of course free to use. It will certainly give you a useful broad overview of how your investments are faring.

One function that was on the website before was a screening tool. This was provided by Morningstar, but has now been 'retired'. In its place the AIC has added more details to its 'compare investment companies' function to provide a modified version.

While this allows you to search for and compare trusts that meet certain criteria, some of the more technical data provided by Morningstar in the past (such as alpha, beta and style classifications) are no longer available. For individual trusts they can still be found in a trust's Morningstar factsheet, accessible from the profile page.

Another thing to note is that the charting function does not by default allow you to compare a trust's share price and NAV performance against its chosen benchmark. Instead it offers you comparisons with Morningstar's own proprietary indices of performance. So for example you will be offered Morningstar UK rather than the FTSE All-Share index.

Finally, I feel honour-bound to mention that you can also find links to the Money Makers podcast from the AIC website. Podcasts are a separate category under the 'News & Insights' tab at the top of the 'Home' page. We are exploring ways to include a link to the Money Makers newsletter and indeed to *The Investment Trusts Handbook* itself.

12:35
38 708,27
91 076,16
35 657,69
3 394 701
37 019,36
37 019,36 $
+3,25 %
Line
15m
1h
4h
1d
More
Depth
MA(7):37 595.02

Z-scores

TOP 15 "CHEAP" FUNDS	TICKER	CURRENT DISCOUNT	AVERAGE DISCOUNT (12M)	Z-SCORE (12M)
Strategic Equity Capital	SEC	-13.4	-8.6	-3.1
BlackRock Income & Growth	BRIG	-15.3	-12	-2.1
Odyssean	OIT	-6.2	-1.2	-2
JPMorgan Global Growth & Income	JGGI	-3	-0.2	-1.9
CT Global Managed Portfolio – Income Class	CMPI	-2.3	0.6	-1.8
North Atlantic Smaller Companies	NAS	-36.3	-32.8	-1.7
Onward Opportunities	ONWD	-4.5	3.5	-1.7
RM Infrastructure Income	RMII	-22.1	-15.9	-1.7
Literacy Capital	BOOK	-27.4	-15.6	-1.7
Aquila Euro Renewables (€)	AERI	-36.8	-27.5	-1.6
VietNam Holding	VNH	-10.3	-4.9	-1.5
JPMorgan Global Core Real Assets	JARA	-23.3	-16.6	-1.5
CT Global Managed Portfolio – Growth Class	CMPG	-5.4	-2.2	-1.4
Merchants	MRCH	-7.8	-4.3	-1.4
Ashoka India Equity	AIE	-3	-0.2	-1.4

TOP 15 "DEAR" FUNDS	TICKER	CURRENT DISCOUNT	AVERAGE DISCOUNT (12M)	Z-SCORE (12M)
Fidelity Emerging Markets	FEML	-6	-11	2.8
NB Distressed Debt ($)	NBDD	-0.4	-17.9	2.7
BioPharma Credit ($)	BPCR	-7.7	-12.1	2.6
AVI Global	AGT	-6	-8.5	2.3
Schroder AsiaPacific	SDP	-9.1	-12	2.3
Monks	MNKS	-6.4	-9.9	2.2
Fidelity Special Values	FSV	-0.2	-5.8	2.2
JPMorgan Claverhouse	JCH	-4.1	-5.7	2.1
JPMorgan Global Emerging Markets Income	JEMI	-7.9	-11.5	2.1
NB Distressed Debt – Extended Class ($)	NBDX	-13.6	-28.1	2.1
Oakley Capital	OCI	-22.5	-29.4	2.1
HarbourVest Global Private Equity	HVPE	-32.6	-38.7	2
Ceiba	CBA	-58.5	-67.3	2
Ruffer	RICA	-2.6	-4.4	1.9
European Assets	EAT	-5.7	-10.3	1.9

Source: Winterflood Securities. Data to 02/10/25.

Z-scores measure mathematically how far a trust's current discount or premium has diverged from its volatility-adjusted average over some previous period (days, months or even a year can be used). Brokers and other professional investors calculate the figures regularly in order to look for trading opportunities or good entry/exit points. A minus figure for a z-score suggests that a trust looks 'cheap' relative to its past discount history; and a positive figure the reverse.

There may, however, be a good reason for the change in sentiment towards a particular trust, so they are a blunt instrument without specialist knowledge and should never be relied on by inexperienced investors. If you already have a specific investment trust on your watchlist and are looking for a good moment to buy, then checking the z-scores can be useful in timing your purchase.

Bear in mind however that discounts widen for a reason; if the z-score is looking attractive, it is often because there is some negative story or headline out there. By the same token, if you are thinking of selling part or all of a holding, it can make sense to do so when the trust's shares are showing up as 'dear' in the z-score rankings. Since most investors tend to hold the trusts they own for a number of years, these opportunities do not arise very often in practice.

The table of one-year z-scores shown opposite is for illustration only. The data was current at 1 October 2025, but remember that z-scores can be volatile and change quickly. Trusts in the upper part of the table, which look 'cheap' at that point, can easily appear in the 'dear' section of the table a few weeks later, having gained in price and seen the discount narrow in the interim.

Investment trusts are best held for the longer term. A consistent 15% return over 20 years, if you are smart enough to find such a thing, will be worth far more at the end of the period (nearly 19 times your original investment) than anything bought in the hope of gaining from a short-term z-score movement. Nevertheless, they are useful at the margin, both in identifying possible opportunities and in determining good buying/selling points.

SPONSORS

We are grateful to our sponsors for helping to distribute copies of *The Investment Trusts Handbook* to the widest possible audience. They are required to remind you that the value of investments and the income from them can go down as well as up, and investors may not get back the amounts originally invested. Please remember also that past performance is not a reliable guide to future performance.

Aberdeen investment trusts

If you are keen to capture the potential offered by global investment markets, turn to Aberdeen investment trusts. Managed by teams of experts, each trust is designed to bring together the most compelling opportunities we can find to target the investment growth or income you're looking for.

Aberdeen is a global investment company that helps clients and customers plan, save, and invest for the future. Our purpose is to enable our clients to be better investors.

We manage and administer £518bn AUMA (as at 30 June 2025) and our strategy is to deliver client-led growth. We are structured around three businesses – Investments, Adviser and interactive investor – focused on the changing needs of our clients.

The capabilities in our Investments business are built on the strength of our insight – generated from wide-ranging research, worldwide investment expertise and local market knowledge.

Our Adviser business provides financial planning solutions and technology for UK financial advisers, enabling them to create value for their businesses and their clients.

Interactive investor, the UK's second largest direct-to-consumer investment platform, enables individuals in the UK to plan, save and invest in the way that works for them.

Allianz

Global Investors

About Allianz Global Investors

Allianz Global Investors is a leading active asset manager, managing €562bn in assets for individuals, families and institutions worldwide. Our goal is to actively shape the future of investing for all our clients, wherever their location and whatever their objectives.

Allianz Global Investors and its predecessors have been managing investment trusts since 1889, providing investors with access to investment opportunities around the world. Each trust is a company listed and traded on the London Stock Exchange that has its own independent board of directors whose duty it is to look after your interests as an investor.

Established in 1889, The Merchants Trust PLC has, throughout its history, provided shareholders with an opportunity to benefit from investment in a diversified portfolio of leading companies with strong balance sheets and the potential to pay attractive dividends. Merchants aims to provide its investors with an efficient, competitive and cost-effective way to achieve an above average level of income and income growth together with long-term capital growth through a policy of investing mainly in higher-yielding large UK companies.

The Brunner Investment Trust PLC aims to provide growth in capital and dividends over the long term by seeking out the world's most exciting growth opportunities. We believe that it's the quality of the company that matters, not its location – so through Brunner, investors can access a spread of high-quality growth companies operating in different sectors and countries in a single portfolio. The Trust favours large, well-financed businesses with global reach, pricing power and brand strength.

Allianz Technology Trust invests in a diversified but focused portfolio of companies that use technology in an innovative way to gain a competitive advantage. Particular emphasis is placed on companies that are addressing major growth trends with innovation that replaces existing technology or radically changes products and services and the way in which they are supplied to customers. The manager aims to invest in the most attractive technology shares globally, seeking to identify the leading companies in emerging technology growth sub-sectors.

AGT – over four decades of fundamental investing

AVI Global Trust (AGT) provides expertly managed exposure to the opportunities presented in various parts of the world.

The investment objective is to achieve capital growth through a focused portfolio of global equities.

The investment strategy identifies valuation anomalies to create a concentrated, unique, and diversified portfolio of stocks. The investment manager then engages with these companies to improve shareholder value.

How we achieve our investment objective

- We invest into a concentrated portfolio of stocks.
- We follow our distinctive fundamental value investment style.
- We seek out good quality, neglected securities trading at a discount to their net asset value (NAV).
- We improve shareholder value through active engagement.
- We build a contrarian benchmark-agnostic unconstrained portfolio.
- We provide diversification due to the nature of our holdings.

Our robust investment philosophy guides investment decisions

Emphasis is placed on three factors:

1. companies with attractive assets, where there is potential for growth in value;
2. a significant discount to a fair net asset value; and
3. identifiable catalysts for value realisation.

A concentrated, high-conviction core portfolio of c. 30± investments allows for detailed research which forms the cornerstone of our approach.

AVI took over the investment management of AGT in 1985. The experience gained from over four decades of following our unique investment style is key to our in-depth understanding of our universe of opportunities in a constantly changing environment.

AGT's long-term track record bears witness to the success of this approach, with a NAV total return well in excess of its benchmark. We believe this strategy remains as appealing as ever and we continue to find plenty of exciting opportunities.

Columbia Threadneedle Investments

Columbia Threadneedle Investments is one of the leading investment trust managers, tracing its heritage back to 1868 when F&C Investment Trust, the world's oldest collective investment scheme, was launched.

Today, Columbia Threadneedle manages seven investment trusts with over £10bn in assets, providing clients with a range of investment opportunities across equities, property and private equity. Each trust is tailored to offer clients different aims and objectives with the option of capital growth, income or a combination of both, offered through portfolios with specific regional focuses or global remits. Clients can invest directly into Columbia Threadneedle's suite of investment trusts via its own Savings Plan, where you can invest in a range of ISAs or a general investment account. You can sign up and manage investments online, on the phone or by post. You can also invest through a third-party investment platform.

Columbia Threadneedle's investment trust business is part of its global asset management business, which is entrusted with £503bn on behalf of individual, institutional and corporate clients around the world.[1]

The business employs more than 2,300 people, including approximately 550 investment professionals based in North America, Europe and Asia.[2] As well as investment trusts, Columbia Threadneedle offers clients a wide range of strategies across equities, fixed income and alternatives, as well as specialist responsible investment capabilities and a comprehensive suite of solutions.

Columbia Threadneedle Investments is the global asset management group of Ameriprise Financial, a leading US-based financial services provider. As part of Ameriprise, it is supported by a large and well-capitalised diversified financial services firm. Your capital is at risk.

1 As at 23 October 2025, Columbia Threadneedle Investments.

2 Source: Ameriprise Financial Q2 2025 earnings release – assets under management and advisement.

INVESTMENT TRUST	WEBSITE	OBJECTIVE	SECTOR
F&C Investment Trust	www.fandc.com	Our flagship trust, established in 1868. The objective of F&C Investment Trust is to deliver long-term growth in capital and income. F&C has provided 54 years of annual dividend increases, classifying the company as an AIC Dividend Hero and is a FTSE 100 listed company*. F&C Investment Trust looks to add value through stock selection from a range of diversified, but focused investment strategies. Fund Manager Paul Niven's Investment process starts with strategic asset allocation, considering where to invest for the long term whilst also considering the tactical investment environment, seeking to take advantage of shorter-term market opportunities. F&C focuses on global growth assets, investing predominantly in listed equity and taking advantage of the investment trust structure to make selected investments into Private Equity.	Global
The Global Smaller Companies Trust	www.globalsmallercompanies.co.uk	The Global Smaller Companies Trust seeks to provide investors with exposure to the long-term growth potential within the thousands of smaller sized companies listed on global stock-markets. The trust focuses investment efforts on high quality, well managed, financially robust and profitable companies. In addition to a good track record, the trust wants their holdings to be moving with the times and making the necessary investment in their businesses to take account of the changing world in which we live. The team-based investment approach allows broad coverage and in-depth analysis of the companies in which they invest. The portfolio is intentionally diversified to give investors genuine global exposure across the spectrum of sectors, seeking out the best opportunities wherever they may be.	Global Smaller Companies
CT UK Capital & Income Trust	www.ctcapitalandincome.co.uk	CT UK Capital and Income Investment Trust aims to offer a reliable income while at the same time seeking to grow the size of your investment. The trust carefully identifies companies that are growing and profitable today and have the strong, sustainable foundations to be able to continue that profitable growth into the future. Whether you are looking for regular income now, or to reinvest your dividends for long term growth, CT UK Capital and Income Investment Trust can play an important part in your investments.	UK Equity Income
CT Private Equity Trust	www.ctprivateequitytrust.com	CT Private Equity Trust offers access to the potential benefits of investment in unlisted companies – an opportunity that typically lies beyond the reach of individual investors. The Company's portfolio is comprised of private equity funds and stakes in individual private businesses, which have been carefully selected with a view to generating capital growth over the medium to long term.	Private Equity

INVESTMENT TRUST	WEBSITE	OBJECTIVE	SECTOR
CT Global Managed Portfolio Trust	www.ctglobalmanagedportfolio.co.uk	CT Global Managed Portfolio Trust is a 'multi-manager' investment trust, investing in a range of investment companies to provide investors with exposure to different investment managers and markets within a single investment trust. There are two portfolio's to choose from Growth Portfolio: Aims to provide Growth shareholders with capital growth from a diversified portfolio of investment companies. The Portfolio invests in a diversified portfolio of at least 25 investment companies that have underlying investment exposures across a range of geographic regions and sectors. Income Portfolio: Aims to provide Income shareholders with an attractive level of income, with the potential for income and capital growth from a diversified portfolio of at least 25 investment companies that have underlying investment exposures across a range of geographic regions and sectors.	Flexible Investment
CT UK High Income Trust	www.ctukhighincome.co.uk	The Trust aims to provide an attractive return in the form of dividends and/or capital repayments, together with prospects for capital growth. CT UK High Income Trust invests predominantly in UK equities and equity-related securities of companies across the market capitalisation spectrum.	UK Equity Income
TR Property Trust	www.trproperty.com	TR Property's investment objective is to maximise total returns by investing in the shares and securities of property companies and property related businesses internationally and also in investment property located in the UK. It has focused on property investing for over 40 years, a record of steady, benchmark-beating returns. The Company makes it easy to gain broad and diverse exposure to the UK and European commercial property sector.	Property Securities

About Fidelity International

Fidelity International provides world-class investment solutions and retirement expertise to institutions, individuals, and their advisers – to help our clients build better futures for themselves and generations to come.

As a private company, we think generationally and invest for the long term. Helping clients to save for retirement and other long-term investing objectives has been at the core of our business for over 50 years.

We are responsible for total client assets of £672.6bn from over 2.9 million clients across the UK, Continental Europe and Asia Pacific.[1]

Our UK investment trust business

Fidelity has over 30 years' experience managing investment companies and manages over £5bn in assets across five investment trusts. These are all focused on equity growth strategies.

As a major platform distributor, Fidelity is able to offer its own investment trusts and those managed by third parties to professional investors and retail investors alike through a range of different product wrappers. Fidelity also promotes its range of trusts directly to institutions and wealth managers through its highly experienced in-house sales teams.

We offer our own investment solutions and access to those of others and deliver services relating to investing; for individual investors and their advisers we provide guidance to help them invest in a simple and cost-effective way.

For institutions including pension funds, banks and insurance companies we offer tailored investment solutions and full-service asset management outsourcing. And for employers we provide workplace pension administration services on top, or independently, of investment management.

---

1 Source for all data: FIL International, 30 June 2025.

About India Capital Growth Fund

PANTHEON
INTERNATIONAL

About Pantheon

Pantheon has been at the forefront of private markets investing for more than 40 years, earning a reputation for providing innovative solutions covering the full lifecycle of investments, from primary fund commitments to co-investments and secondary purchases, across private equity, infrastructure, private credit and real estate.

We partner with more than 700 clients, including institutional investors of all sizes as well as a growing number of private wealth advisers and investors, with approximately $76bn in discretionary assets under management (as at 31 March 2025).

Using creative approaches informed by our specialised experience and delivered by a global team of professionals based in offices across Europe, the Americas and Asia, we invest with purpose and lead with expertise to help build secure financial futures.

Key facts:

- More than **40 years** of investing experience in private markets
- **US$76bn+** in discretionary assets under management
- Serving **700+ clients**, including both institutional investors and private wealth clients
- 13 global offices across **three** continents
- Global workforce includes more than **130 investment professionals**

Pantheon's investment prowess is underpinned by deep relationships with hundreds of high-quality fund managers across all of our asset classes, having invested in over 3,100 funds and with more than 660 advisory board seats held, confirming our status as a reference investor globally. Across our platform, we leverage our network to provide access to differentiated and often-proprietary investment opportunities, with a focus on partnering with best-in-breed specialist managers in segments benefitting from strong, structural tailwinds.

Pantheon has actively managed two London Stock Exchange-listed investment companies, Pantheon International Plc (PIN) and FTSE-250 listed Pantheon Infrastructure Plc (PINT), since they were launched in 1987 and 2021 respectively.

About Pantheon International Plc (PIN)

PIN is a FTSE 250 private equity investment trust, overseen by an experienced, independent board of directors and managed by Pantheon, one of the leading private equity investment managers worldwide. PIN provides investors with liquid access to a global portfolio of fast-growing private companies that are managed by many of the best private equity managers in the world.

Through its flexible investment approach, PIN focuses on high quality, profitable businesses in resilient sectors that can weather a range of macroeconomic environments. PIN has a track record of NAV outperformance over the long term and manages risk strategically through diversification and rigorous investment selection, based on Pantheon's extensive experience, international platform and robust investment due diligence processes.

ACKNOWLEDGEMENTS

Producing *The Investment Trusts Handbook 2026* is, as it has been for the last nine years, an intensive and collective effort. Thanks to all of those who have helped to bring it to fruition, whether as contributors or handmaidens to the production process.

At Harriman House: Myles Hunt, Sally Tickner, Nick Fletcher, Tracy Bundey, Victoria Lawson-McKittrick and Charlotte Smith. Thank you also to Chris Wild.

From our sponsors: Louise Bouverat (abrdn), Oliver Lago (Allianz Global investors), Lucy Draper (AssetCo), Kimmberly Lau (Asset Value Investors), Vicky Toshney (Baillie Gifford), Manish Chavda (Columbia Threadneedle), John Ennis, Dominic Newman and Olivia Wray (Fidelity), Will Gold (Goodhart), Kerry Haxby-Dean and Kelly Stracey (JP Morgan), Vicki Bradley (Pantheon), Sunil Kler and (Schroders), Candace Beesley and Alisha Desai (WTW).

Contributors and interviewees: Mark Atkinson, Mike Balfour, Abbas Barkhodar, John Baron, Alan Bartlett, Rachel Beagles, Alan Brierley, James Carthew, Ben Conway, Arthur Copple, Richard Curling, Alex Davies, Simon Elliott, George Ensor, Simon Gergel, Kirsty Gibson, Hugh Gimber, Nick Greenwood, Peter Hewitt, Alastair Laing, Anthony Leatham, Andrew McHattie, Thomas Moore, Charlotte Morris, David Moss, Gaurav Narain, Paul Niven, Neil Rogan, Daniel Summerland, Tom Treanor, Stuart Watson, Ben Williams, Joe Winkley, Andrew Worne and Alex Wright.

Research: Ewan Lovett-Turner (Deutsche Numis), Christopher Brown (J.P. Morgan Pavry (Devon Equity Management), William Heathcoat Amory (Kepler Intelligence), Ed Marten and James Carthew (QuotedData), Emma Bird and Joe Winkley (Winterflood Securities).

Statistics: big thanks again this year to David Michael and Sophie Driscoll at the AIC for all their help in providing the performance statistics and a lot of other data.

Important information

Please note that everything you read in these pages is independently edited and provided for information and research purposes. Without knowledge of your individual circumstances and tolerance for risk, it is impossible – and prohibited by the Financial Conduct Authority – to give individual investment advice. However, all the opinions expressed here are honestly held and believed to be accurate at the time of writing. Please remember also that past performance, while helpful, is not a reliable guide to future performance. The value of investments and the income from them can go down as well as up.